William Leybourn

The Ready Reckoner

Trader's Sure Guide

William Leybourn

The Ready Reckoner
Trader's Sure Guide

ISBN/EAN: 9783744734752

Printed in Europe, USA, Canada, Australia, Japan

Cover: Foto ©Andreas Hilbeck / pixelio.de

More available books at **www.hansebooks.com**

THE TWENTY-FIRST EDITION OF
THE

READY RECKONER;
OR,

Trader's Sure Guide.

CONTAINING

TABLES READY CAST UP,

Adapted to the Ufe of all who deal by Wholefale or Retail;

EXHIBITING, AT ONE VIEW,

The AMOUNT or VALUE of any Number or Quantity of Goods or Merchandize, from *One* up to *Ten Thoufand,* At the various Prices, from *One Farthing* to *One Pound.*

TO WHICH ARE PREFIXED,

I. A TABLE, directing how to buy and fell by the Hundred; and,

II. TABLES of the AMOUNT of EXPENCES, &c. by the Day, Week, Month, and Year.

AND AT THE END ARE ADDED,

I. TABLES of INTEREST, at *Five per Cent. per Annum,* from *One Pound* to *Five Hundred Pounds,* and from *One* to *Three Hundred and Sixty-five Days.*

II. TABLES of COMMISSION, or BROKERAGE, from *One Eighth* to *One Pound per Cent.* on any Sum, from *One Shilling* to *Ten Thoufand Pounds.*

III. A TABLE, fhewing the Number of Days, from any Day in one Month to the fame Day in any other.

BY WILLIAM LEYBOURNE.

London:

Printed for B. LAW and Son; C. DILLY; F. and C. RIVINGTON; W. LOWNDES; G. WILKIE; T. N. LONGMAN; J. SCATCHERD; J. WALKER; H. D. SYMONDS; VERNOR and HOOD; and LEE and HURST.

DUTIES on BILLS, PROMISSORY NOTES, RECEIPTS, &c.

BILLS or NOTES after Sight or Date.

For	2l. and not exceeding	30l.		Eight Pence.
Above	30	ditto	- 50	One Shilling.
Above	50	ditto	100	One Shil. & 4d.
Above	100	ditto	200	Two Shillings.
Above	200	- - - -		Two Shil. & 8d.

NOTES to Bearer on Demand.
Re-iffuable (after payment) where firft iffued.

For	5l. and not exceeding	5l. 5s.		Four Pence.
Above	5l. 5s.	ditto	30l.	Six Pence.

Above 30l. &c. the fame duties as to the foregoing Notes after date.

NOTES to Bearer on Demand.
Re-iffuable (after payment) at any place.

For	5l. and not exceeding	5l. 5s.		Eight Pence.
Above	5l. 5s.	ditto	30l.	One Shil. & 4d.

FOREIGN BILLS of EXCHANGE.
Viz. Bills drawn in Great Britain upon Foreign Countries.

For 100l.	- - - -	Eight Pence.
Above 100l. and not exceeding 200l.		One Shilling.
Above 200l. - - - - -		One Shil. & 4d.

RECEIPTS.

For	2l.	and under	20l.	Two Pence.
	20l.	———	50l.	Four Pence.
	50l.	———	100l.	Six Pence.
	100l.	———	500l.	One Shilling.
	500l.	and upwards	-	Two Shillings.
For every Receipt in FULL		-		Two Shillings.

LEGACIES.

Every Bequeft of 20l.—5s. If the Property of the Teftator amount to 100l. each Legacy to a Brother or Sifter, 2l. per cent. To an Uncle, or Aunt, or Firft Coufin, 3l. per cent. To a Second Coufin, 4l. per cent. Further of Kin, or Stranger, 6l. per cent. Wife, Children, or Grand-children, for all under 20l.—2s. 6d. 20l. to 100l.—5s. 100l. and upwards, 20s. on the amount of the fum bequeathed.

BONDS not exceeding 100l.		Ten Shillings.
Above 100l. and not -	500l.	Twenty Shillings.
500l. and upwards,	-	Thirty Shillings.

All other Bonds, Agreements, and Indentures, 10s.

ADVERTISEMENT

TO THE

TWENTY-FIRST EDITION.

AS the Ufefulnefs of this Book hath occafioned Two fpurious Editions, under fpecious Titles; it may be proper to obferve, that, one of them is printed in a fmaller and lefs diftinguifhable Type; and that the Face of the other, compared with this Edition, befpeaks it an inferior Imitation.

The Tables in the following Work rife in Order, from *One Farthing* to *Two Shillings*, by the Addition of *One Farthing* each Rife; from *Two Shillings* to *Three*, by the Addition of *One Halfpenny*; from *Three Shillings* to *Ten*, by *One Penny*; and from *Ten Shillings* to *One Pound*, by *Six-pence*. At the Bottom of each Table is fet down the *Great* or *Long Hundred*, viz. 112 *lbs.* by which moft heavy Goods are bought and fold; the *Grofs*, viz. *Twelve Dozen*, by which Gloves, Buttons, &c. are bought and fold; the *Wey of Cheefe*, *Salt*, &c. which is 256 *lbs.*; the Number of *Days in a Year*, by which the Amount of Daily Expences, or Wages, may be known; and likewife the Number of Feet in a *folid Rod* of Brick Wall, which are 272.

(JANUARY, 1798)

A TABLE *directing how to* Buy, *and* Sell, *by the* Hundred.

d.	q.	l.	s.	d.	d.	q.	l.	s.	d.	d.	q.	l.	s.	d.
0	1	0	2	4	8	1	3	17	0	16	1	7	11	8
0	2	0	4	8	8	2	3	19	4	16	2	7	14	0
0	3	0	7	0	8	3	4	1	8	16	3	7	16	4
1	0	0	9	4	9	0	4	4	0	17	0	7	18	8
1	1	0	11	8	9	1	4	6	4	17	1	8	1	0
1	2	0	14	0	9	2	4	8	8	17	2	8	3	4
1	3	0	16	4	9	3	4	11	0	17	3	8	5	8
2	0	0	18	8	10	0	4	13	4	18	0	8	8	0
2	1	1	1	0	10	1	4	15	8	18	1	8	10	4
2	2	1	3	4	10	2	4	18	0	18	2	8	12	8
2	3	1	5	8	10	3	5	0	4	18	3	8	15	0
3	0	1	8	0	11	0	5	2	8	19	0	8	17	4
3	1	1	10	4	11	1	5	5	0	19	1	8	19	8
3	2	1	12	8	11	2	5	7	4	19	2	9	2	0
3	3	1	15	0	11	3	5	9	8	19	3	9	4	4
4	0	1	17	4	12	0	5	12	0	20	0	9	6	8
4	1	1	19	8	12	1	5	14	4	20	1	9	9	0
4	2	2	2	0	12	2	5	16	8	20	2	9	11	4
4	3	2	4	4	12	3	5	19	0	20	3	9	13	8
5	0	2	6	8	13	0	6	1	4	21	0	9	16	0
5	1	2	9	0	13	1	6	3	8	21	1	9	18	4
5	2	2	11	4	13	2	6	6	0	21	2	10	0	8
5	3	2	13	8	13	3	6	8	4	21	3	10	3	0
6	0	2	16	0	14	0	6	10	8	22	0	10	5	4
6	1	2	18	4	14	1	6	13	0	22	1	10	7	8
6	2	3	0	8	14	2	6	15	4	22	2	10	10	0
6	3	3	3	0	14	3	6	17	8	22	3	10	12	4
7	0	3	5	4	15	0	7	0	0	23	0	10	14	8
7	1	3	7	8	15	1	7	2	4	23	1	10	17	0
7	2	3	10	0	15	2	7	4	8	23	2	10	19	4
7	3	3	12	4	15	3	7	7	0	23	3	11	1	8
8	0	3	14	8	16	0	7	9	4	24	0	11	4	0

The,

The USE of the TABLE directing how to Buy, and Sell, by the Hundred.

IF you buy any Thing by the *Great*, or *Long Hundred*, [reckoning 112 Pounds to the Hundred,] and would know, by the *Pound*, what the *Hundred* is valued at, obferve the following DIRECTIONS.

EXAMPLE I.

IF You Buy Goods at [4 Pence, 3 Farthings,] the *Pound*; Look in the *Table* for 4*d*. 3*q*. in the Firft Column, and againft it in the Second Column, you will find 2*l*. 4*s*. 4*d*. And *fo much*, at that *Rate*, 112 *Pounds* come to.

EXAMPLE II.

IF 1 C Weight, or 112 Pounds, [coft 4 Pounds, 1 Shilling, 8 Pence;] To know how much it is by the *Pound*, Look 4*l*. 1*s*. 8*d*. in the Fourth Column of the *Table*, and right againft it, in the Column next the Left-Hand, you will find 8*d*. 3*q*. And *fo much*, at that *Rate*, it comes to by the *Pound*.

Again; If You Buy One Hundred Weight of Goods, [for 4 Pounds, 1 Shilling, 8 Pence,] and *retail* it at 10 Pence the *Pound*, it comes at that *Rate*, to 4*l*. 13*s*. 4*d*. Then take 4*l*. 1*s*. 8*d*. from it, you will find yourfelf, by the *Remainder*, 11*s*. 8*d*. a Gainer, &c.

AND, in this Manner, you may, with much Eafe, calculate any *Quantity*, according to the *True Value*, in the TABLE of how to To *Buy*, and *Sell*, by the *Hundred*.

A TABLE *of the* Amount *of* Expences, &c.

N. B. *In the Two following* Tables, *the* Month *is only* 28 Days.

By Day.		By Week.			By Month.			By Year.		
s.	d.	l.	s.	d.	l	s.	d.	l.	s.	d.
0	1	0	0	7	0	2	4	1	10	5
0	2	0	1	2	0	4	8	3	0	10
0	3	0	1	9	0	7	0	4	11	3
0	4	0	2	4	0	9	4	6	1	8
0	5	0	2	11	0	11	8	7	12	1
0	6	0	3	6	0	14	0	9	2	6
0	7	0	4	1	0	16	4	10	12	11
0	8	0	4	8	0	18	8	12	3	4
0	9	0	5	3	1	1	0	13	13	9
0	10	0	5	10	1	3	4	15	4	2
0	11	0	6	5	1	5	8	16	14	7
1	0	0	7	0	1	8	0	18	5	0
2	0	0	14	0	2	16	0	36	10	0
3	0	1	1	0	4	4	0	54	15	0
4	0	1	8	0	5	12	0	73	0	0
5	0	1	15	0	7	0	0	91	5	0
6	0	2	2	0	8	8	0	109	10	0
7	0	2	9	0	9	16	0	127	15	0
8	0	2	16	0	11	4	0	146	0	0
9	0	3	3	0	12	12	0	164	5	0
10	0	3	10	0	14	0	0	182	10	0
11	0	3	17	0	15	8	0	200	15	0
12	0	4	4	0	16	16	0	219	0	0
13	0	4	11	0	18	4	0	237	5	0
14	0	4	18	0	19	12	0	255	10	0
15	0	5	5	0	21	0	0	273	15	0
16	0	5	12	0	22	8	0	292	0	0
17	0	5	19	0	23	16	0	310	5	0
18	0	6	6	0	25	4	0	328	10	0
19	0	6	13	0	26	12	0	346	15	0
20	0	7	0	0	28	0	0	365	0	0

A TABLE of the Amount of Expences, &c.

By Year.	By Month.				By Week.				By Day.			
l.	l.	s.	d.	f.	l.	s.	d.	f.	l.	s.	d.	f.
1	0	1	6	2	0	0	4	2	0	0	0	3
2	0	3	0	3	0	0	9	1	0	0	1	1
3	0	4	7	1	0	1	1	3	0	0	2	0
4	0	6	1	3	0	1	6	2	0	0	2	3
5	0	7	8	0	0	1	11	0	0	0	3	1
6	0	9	2	2	0	2	3	2	0	0	4	0
7	0	10	9	0	0	2	8	1	0	0	4	2
8	0	12	3	1	0	3	0	3	0	0	5	1
9	0	13	9	3	0	3	5	2	0	0	6	0
10	0	15	4	0	0	3	10	0	0	0	6	2
11	0	16	10	2	0	4	2	3	0	0	7	1
12	0	18	5	0	0	4	7	1	0	0	8	0
13	0	19	11	1	0	4	11	3	0	0	8	2
14	1	1	5	3	0	5	4	2	0	0	9	1
15	1	3	0	1	0	5	9	0	0	0	9	3
16	1	4	6	2	0	6	1	3	0	0	10	2
17	1	6	1	0	0	6	6	1	0	0	11	1
18	1	7	7	2	0	6	10	3	0	0	11	3
19	1	9	1	3	0	7	3	2	0	1	0	2
20	1	10	8	1	0	7	8	0	0	1	1	1
30	2	6	0	1	0	11	6	0	0	1	7	3
40	3	1	4	2	0	15	4	0	0	2	2	1
50	3	16	8	2	0	19	2	1	0	2	9	0
60	4	12	0	3	1	3	0	1	0	3	3	2
70	5	7	4	3	1	6	10	1	0	3	10	0
80	6	2	9	0	1	10	8	1	0	4	4	2
90	6	18	1	0	1	14	6	1	0	4	11	1
100	7	13	5	0	1	18	4	1	0	5	5	3
200	15	6	10	1	3	16	8	2	0	10	11	2
300	23	0	3	1	5	15	0	3	0	16	5	1
400	30	13	8	2	7	13	5	0	1	1	11	0
500	38	7	1	2	9	11	9	1	1	7	4	3
1000	76	14	3	0	19	3	6	3	2	14	9	2

Use *of the following* Tables.

EXAMPLE I. If 1 Yard of *Tape* coſt 5 Farthings, or, 1 Penny 1 Farthing; What will 46 coſt? Turn to the *Table* of 5 Farthings, and on the Top of the Column, under *N.* you will find 46, againſt which you will find 4*s.* 9*d.* 2*q.* Or, If you would know what 46 Ells come to, *or,* 46 Yards of any Thing, *or,* 46 Pints, *or,* 46 Ounces; *So likewiſe* 46 Pounds, at 5 Farthings the Pound, come to the ſame Sum, *viz.* 4*s.* 9*d.* 2*q.* Or, 46 Grofs, at 5 Farthings the Grofs, come to the ſame Sum of 4*s.* 9*d.* 2*q.* *Likewiſe,* 46 Days in the Year, at 5 Farthings the Day, come to 4*s.* 9*d.* 2*q.*

EXAMPLE II. I would know, What [112 *lbs.*] of Tobacco-duſt will come to at 6*d.* a Pound.

	l.	*s.*	*d.*
Look on the Top for 6*d.* you will find			
The *Great Hundred* at the Bottom [112 *lbs.*]	2	16	0
The *Grofs*, which is [144] - - - - -	3	12	0
The *Wey*, which is [256 *lbs.*] - - - - -	6	8	0
The *Days* in a *Year*, which are [365] - -	9	2	6
The *Feet* in a *Rod*, which are [272] - - -	6	16	0

And ſo much Each comes to.

A General Rule *to know if the* Numbers *in this* Book *are* Truly *Printed.*

EXAMPLE. Suppoſe this Queſtion. *At* 7 *Farthings the* Pound, *What will* 97 Pounds *Coſt?*

The *Anfwer*, by the *Table*, will be 14 Shillings, 1 Penny, 3 Farthings; and, that *This* is the *True Refolve*, is proved thus:

		l.	*s.*	*d.*	*q.*
40 }	At that *Rate*, comes to	0	5	10	0
57 }		0	8	3	3
97		0	14	1	3

N.	l.	s.	d.	q.
1	0	0	0	1
2	0	0	0	2
3	0	0	0	3
4	0	0	1	0
5	0	0	1	1
6	0	0	1	2
7	0	0	1	3
8	0	0	2	0
9	0	0	2	1
10	0	0	2	2
11	0	0	2	3
12	0	0	3	0
13	0	0	3	1
14	0	0	3	2
15	0	0	3	3
16	0	0	4	0
17	0	0	4	1
18	0	0	4	2
19	0	0	4	3
20	0	0	5	0
21	0	0	5	1
22	0	0	5	2
23	0	0	5	3
24	0	0	6	0
25	0	0	6	1
26	0	0	6	2
27	0	0	6	3
[28]	0	0	7	0
29	0	0	7	1
30	0	0	7	2
31	0	0	7	3
32	0	0	8	0
33	0	0	8	1
34	0	0	8	2
35	0	0	8	3
36	0	0	9	0
37	0	0	9	1
38	0	0	9	2
39	0	0	9	3
40	0	0	10	0
41	0	0	10	1
42	0	0	10	2
43	0	0	10	3
44	0	0	11	0

N.	l.	s.	d.	q.
45	0	0	11	1
46	0	0	11	2
47	0	0	11	3
48	0	1	0	0
49	0	1	0	1
50	0	1	0	2
51	0	1	0	3
52	0	1	1	0
53	0	1	1	1
54	0	1	1	2
55	0	1	1	3
[56]	0	1	2	0
57	0	1	2	1
58	0	1	2	2
59	0	1	2	3
60	0	1	3	0
61	0	1	3	1
62	0	1	3	2
63	0	1	3	3
64	0	1	4	0
65	0	1	4	1
66	0	1	4	2
67	0	1	4	3
68	0	1	5	0
69	0	1	5	1
70	0	1	5	2
71	0	1	5	3
72	0	1	6	0
73	0	1	6	1
74	0	1	6	2
75	0	1	6	3
76	0	1	7	0
77	0	1	7	1
78	0	1	7	2
79	0	1	7	3
80	0	1	8	0
81	0	1	8	1
82	0	1	8	2
83	0	1	8	3
[84]	0	1	9	0
85	0	1	9	1
86	0	1	9	2
87	0	1	9	3
88	0	1	10	0

N.	l.	s.	d.	q.
89	0	1	10	1
90	0	1	10	2
91	0	1	10	3
92	0	1	11	0
93	0	1	11	1
94	0	1	11	2
95	0	1	11	3
96	0	2	0	0
97	0	2	0	1
98	0	2	0	2
99	0	2	0	3
100	0	2	1	0
200	0	4	2	0
300	0	6	3	0
400	0	8	4	0
500	0	10	5	0
600	0	12	6	0
700	0	14	7	0
800	0	16	8	0
900	0	18	9	0
1000	1	0	10	0
2000	2	1	8	0
3000	3	2	6	0
4000	4	3	4	0
5000	5	4	2	0
6000	6	5	0	0
7000	7	5	10	0
8000	8	6	8	0
9000	9	7	6	0
10000	10	8	4	0

Great Hundred
112 | 0 2 4 0

Grofs
144 | 0 3 0 0

Wey
256 | 0 5 4 0

Days in a Year
365 | 0 7 7 1

Feet in a Rod
272 | 0 5 8 0

B

N.	l.	s.	d.	q.	N.	l.	s.	d.	q.	N	l.	s.	d.	q.
1	0	0	0	2	45	0	1	10	2	89	0	3	8	2
2	0	0	1	0	46	0	1	11	0	90	0	3	9	0
3	0	0	1	2	47	0	1	11	2	91	0	3	9	2
4	0	0	2	0	48	0	2	0	0	92	0	3	10	0
5	0	0	2	2	49	0	2	0	2	93	0	3	10	2
6	0	0	3	0	50	0	2	1	0	94	0	3	10	0
7	0	0	3	2	51	0	2	1	2	95	0	3	11	2
8	0	0	4	0	52	0	2	2	0	96	0	4	0	0
9	0	0	4	2	53	0	2	2	2	97	0	4	0	2
10	0	0	5	0	54	0	2	3	0	98	0	4	1	0
11	0	0	5	2	55	0	2	3	2	99	0	4	1	2
12	0	0	6	0	[56]	0	2	4	0	100	0	4	2	0
13	0	0	6	2	57	0	2	4	2	200	0	8	4	0
14	0	0	7	0	58	0	2	5	0	300	0	12	6	0
15	0	0	7	2	59	0	2	5	2	400	0	16	8	0
16	0	0	8	0	60	0	2	6	0	500	1	0	10	0
17	0	0	8	2	61	0	2	6	2	600	1	5	0	0
18	0	0	9	0	62	0	2	7	0	700	1	9	2	0
19	0	0	9	2	63	0	2	7	2	800	1	13	4	0
20	0	0	10	0	64	0	2	8	0	900	1	17	6	0
21	0	0	10	2	65	0	2	8	2	1000	2	1	8	0
22	0	0	11	0	66	0	2	9	0	2000	4	3	4	0
23	0	0	11	2	67	0	2	9	2	3000	6	5	0	0
24	0	1	0	0	68	0	2	10	0	4000	8	6	8	0
25	0	1	0	2	69	0	2	10	2	5000	10	8	4	0
26	0	1	1	0	70	0	2	11	0	6000	12	10	0	0
27	0	1	1	2	71	0	2	11	2	7000	14	11	8	0
[28]	0	1	2	0	72	0	3	0	0	8000	16	13	4	0
29	0	1	2	2	73	0	3	0	2	9000	18	15	0	0
30	0	1	3	0	74	0	3	1	0	10000	20	16	8	0
31	0	1	3	2	75	0	3	1	2					
32	0	1	4	0	76	0	3	2	0					
33	0	1	4	2	77	0	3	2	2					
34	0	1	5	0	78	0	3	3	0					
35	0	1	5	2	79	0	3	3	2					
36	0	1	6	0	80	0	3	4	0					
37	0	1	6	2	81	0	3	4	2					
38	0	1	7	0	82	0	3	5	0					
39	0	1	7	2	83	0	3	5	2					
40	0	1	8	0	[84]	0	3	6	0					
41	0	1	8	2	85	0	3	6	2					
42	0	1	9	0	86	0	3	7	0					
43	0	1	9	2	87	0	3	7	2					
44	0	1	10	0	88	0	3	8	0					

Great Hundred

112 | 0   4   8   0

Grofs

144 | 0   6   0   0

Wey

256 | 0   10   8   0

Days in a Year

365 | 0   15   2   2

Feet in a Rod

272 | 0   11   4   0

N.	l.	s.	d.	q.
1	0	0	0	3
2	0	0	1	2
3	0	0	2	1
4	0	0	3	0
5	0	0	3	3
6	0	0	4	2
7	0	0	5	1
8	0	0	6	0
9	0	0	6	3
10	0	0	7	2
11	0	0	8	1
12	0	0	9	0
13	0	0	9	3
14	0	0	10	2
15	0	0	11	1
16	0	1	0	0
17	0	1	0	3
18	0	1	1	2
19	0	1	2	1
20	0	1	3	0
21	0	1	3	3
22	0	1	4	2
23	0	1	5	1
24	0	1	6	0
25	0	1	6	3
26	0	1	7	2
27	0	1	8	1
[28]	0	1	9	0
29	0	1	9	3
30	0	1	10	2
31	0	1	11	1
32	0	2	0	0
33	0	2	0	3
34	0	2	1	2
35	0	2	2	1
36	0	2	3	0
37	0	2	3	3
38	0	2	4	2
39	0	2	5	1
40	0	2	6	0
41	0	2	6	3
42	0	2	7	2
43	0	2	8	1
44	0	2	9	0

N.	l.	s.	d.	q.
45	0	2	9	3
46	0	2	10	2
47	0	2	11	1
48	0	3	0	0
49	0	3	0	3
50	0	3	1	2
51	0	3	2	1
52	0	3	3	0
53	0	3	3	3
54	0	3	4	2
55	0	3	5	1
[56]	0	3	6	0
57	0	3	6	3
58	0	3	7	2
59	0	3	8	1
60	0	3	9	0
61	0	3	9	3
62	0	3	10	2
63	0	3	11	1
64	0	4	0	0
65	0	4	0	3
66	0	4	1	2
67	0	4	2	1
68	0	4	3	0
69	0	4	3	3
70	0	4	4	2
71	0	4	5	1
72	0	4	6	0
73	0	4	6	3
74	0	4	7	2
75	0	4	8	1
76	0	4	9	0
77	0	4	9	3
78	0	4	10	2
79	0	4	11	1
80	0	5	0	0
81	0	5	0	3
82	0	5	1	2
83	0	5	2	1
[84]	0	5	3	0
85	0	5	3	3
86	0	5	4	2
87	0	5	5	1
88	0	5	6	0

N.	l.	s.	d.	q.
89	0	5	6	3
90	0	5	7	2
91	0	5	8	1
92	0	5	9	0
93	0	5	9	3
94	0	5	10	2
95	0	5	11	1
96	0	6	0	0
97	0	6	0	3
98	0	6	1	2
99	0	6	2	1
100	0	6	3	0
200	0	12	6	0
300	0	18	9	0
400	1	5	0	0
500	1	11	3	0
600	1	17	6	0
700	2	3	9	0
800	2	10	0	0
900	2	16	3	0
1000	3	2	6	0
2000	6	5	0	0
3000	9	7	6	0
4000	12	10	0	0
5000	15	12	6	0
6000	18	15	0	0
7000	21	17	6	0
8000	25	0	0	0
9000	28	2	6	0
10000	31	5	0	0

Great Hundred

112 | 0 7 0 0

Grofs

144 | 0 9 0 0

Wey

256 | 0 16 0 0

Days in a Year

365 | 1 2 9 3

Feet in a Rod

272 | 0 17 0 0

N.	l.	s.	d.
1	0	0	1
2	0	0	2
3	0	0	3
4	0	0	4
5	0	0	5
6	0	0	6
7	0	0	7
8	0	0	8
9	0	0	9
10	0	0	10
11	0	0	11
12	0	1	0
13	0	1	1
14	0	1	2
15	0	1	3
16	0	1	4
17	0	1	5
18	0	1	6
19	0	1	7
20	0	1	8
21	0	1	9
22	0	1	10
23	0	1	11
24	0	2	0
25	0	2	1
26	0	2	2
27	0	2	3
[28]	0	2	4
29	0	2	5
30	0	2	6
31	0	2	7
32	0	2	8
33	0	2	9
34	0	2	10
35	0	2	11
36	0	3	0
37	0	3	1
38	0	3	2
39	0	3	3
40	0	3	4
41	0	3	5
42	0	3	6
43	0	3	7
44	0	3	8

N.	l.	s.	d.
45	0	3	9
46	0	3	10
47	0	3	11
48	0	4	0
49	0	4	1
50	0	4	2
51	0	4	3
52	0	4	4
53	0	4	5
54	0	4	6
55	0	4	7
[56]	0	4	8
57	0	4	9
58	0	4	10
59	0	4	11
60	0	5	0
61	0	5	1
62	0	5	2
63	0	5	3
64	0	5	4
65	0	5	5
66	0	5	6
67	0	5	7
68	0	5	8
69	0	5	9
70	0	5	10
71	0	5	11
72	0	6	0
73	0	6	1
74	0	6	2
75	0	6	3
76	0	6	4
77	0	6	5
78	0	6	6
79	0	6	7
80	0	6	8
81	0	6	9
82	0	6	10
83	0	6	11
[84]	0	7	0
85	0	7	1
86	0	7	2
87	0	7	3
88	0	7	4

N.	l.	s.	d.
89	0	7	5
90	0	7	6
91	0	7	7
92	0	7	8
93	0	7	9
94	0	7	10
95	0	7	11
96	0	8	0
97	0	8	1
98	0	8	2
99	0	8	3
100	0	8	4
200	0	16	8
300	1	5	0
400	1	13	4
500	2	1	8
600	2	10	0
700	2	18	4
800	3	6	8
900	3	15	0
1000	4	3	4
2000	8	6	8
3000	12	10	0
4000	16	13	4
5000	20	16	8
6000	25	0	0
7000	29	3	4
8000	33	6	8
9000	37	10	0
10000	41	13	4

Great Hundred

112	0	9	4

Grofs

144	0	12	0

Wey

256	1	1	4

Days in a Year

365	1	10	5

Feet in a Rod

272	1	2	8

N.	l.	s.	d.	q.
1	0	0	1	1
2	0	0	2	2
3	0	0	3	3
4	0	0	5	0
5	0	0	6	1
6	0	0	7	2
7	0	0	8	3
8	0	0	10	0
9	0	0	11	1
10	0	1	0	2
11	0	1	1	3
12	0	1	3	0
13	0	1	4	1
14	0	1	5	2
15	0	1	6	3
16	0	1	8	0
17	0	1	9	1
18	0	1	10	2
19	0	1	11	3
20	0	2	1	0
21	0	2	2	1
22	0	2	3	2
23	0	2	4	3
24	0	2	6	0
25	0	2	7	1
26	0	2	8	2
27	0	2	9	3
[28]	0	2	11	0
29	0	3	0	1
30	0	3	1	2
31	0	3	2	3
32	0	3	4	0
33	0	3	5	1
34	0	3	6	2
35	0	3	7	3
36	0	3	9	0
37	0	3	10	1
38	0	3	11	2
39	0	4	0	3
40	0	4	2	0
41	0	4	3	1
42	0	4	4	2
43	0	4	5	3
44	0	4	7	0

N.	l.	s.	d.	q.
45	0	4	8	1
46	0	4	9	2
47	0	4	10	3
48	0	5	0	0
49	0	5	1	1
50	0	5	2	2
51	0	5	3	3
52	0	5	5	0
53	0	5	6	1
54	0	5	7	2
55	0	5	8	3
[56]	0	5	10	0
57	0	5	11	1
58	0	6	0	2
59	0	6	1	3
60	0	6	3	0
61	0	6	4	1
62	0	6	5	2
63	0	6	6	3
64	0	6	8	0
65	0	6	9	1
66	0	6	10	2
67	0	6	11	3
68	0	7	1	0
69	0	7	2	1
70	0	7	3	2
71	0	7	4	3
72	0	7	6	0
73	0	7	7	1
74	0	7	8	2
75	0	7	9	3
76	0	7	11	0
77	0	8	0	1
78	0	8	1	2
79	0	8	2	3
80	0	8	4	0
81	0	8	5	1
82	0	8	6	2
83	0	8	7	3
[84]	0	8	9	0
85	0	8	10	1
86	0	8	11	2
87	0	9	0	3
88	0	9	2	0

N.	l.	s.	d.	q.
89	0	9	3	1
90	0	9	4	2
91	0	9	5	3
92	0	9	7	0
93	0	9	8	1
94	0	9	9	2
95	0	9	10	3
96	0	10	0	0
97	0	10	1	1
98	0	10	2	2
99	0	10	3	3
100	0	10	5	0
200	1	0	10	0
300	1	11	3	0
400	2	1	8	0
500	2	12	1	0
600	3	2	6	0
700	3	12	11	0
800	4	3	4	0
900	4	13	9	0
1000	5	4	2	0
2000	10	8	4	0
3000	15	12	6	0
4000	20	16	8	0
5000	26	0	10	0
6000	31	5	0	0
7000	36	9	2	0
8000	41	13	4	0
9000	46	17	6	0
10000	52	1	8	0

Great Hundred
112 | 0 11 8 0

Grofs
144 | 0 15 0 0

Wey
256 | 1 6 8 0

Days in a Year
365 | 1 18 0 1

Feet in a Rod
272 | 1 8 4 0

N.	l.	s.	d.	d.	N.	l.	s.	d.	q.	N.	l.	s.	d.	q.
1	0	0	1	2	45	0	5	7	2	89	0	11	1	2
2	0	0	3	0	46	0	5	9	0	90	0	11	3	0
3	0	0	4	2	47	0	5	10	2	91	0	11	4	2
4	0	0	6	0	48	0	6	0	0	92	0	11	6	0
5	0	0	7	2	49	0	6	1	2	93	0	11	7	2
6	0	0	9	0	50	0	6	3	0	94	0	11	9	0
7	0	0	10	2	51	0	6	4	2	95	0	11	10	2
8	0	1	0	0	52	0	6	6	0	96	0	12	0	0
9	0	1	1	2	53	0	6	7	2	97	0	12	1	2
10	0	1	3	0	54	0	6	9	0	98	0	12	3	0
11	0	1	4	2	55	0	6	10	2	99	0	12	4	2
12	0	1	6	0	[56]	0	7	0	0	100	0	12	6	0
13	0	1	7	2	57	0	7	1	2	200	1	5	0	0
14	0	1	9	0	58	0	7	3	0	300	1	17	6	0
15	0	1	10	2	59	0	7	4	2	400	2	10	0	0
16	0	2	0	0	60	0	7	6	0	500	3	2	6	0
17	0	2	1	2	61	0	7	7	2	600	3	15	0	0
18	0	2	3	0	62	0	7	9	0	700	4	7	6	0
19	0	2	4	2	63	0	7	10	2	800	5	0	0	0
20	0	2	6	0	64	0	8	0	0	900	5	12	6	0
21	0	2	7	2	65	0	8	1	2	1000	6	5	0	0
22	0	2	9	0	66	0	8	3	0	2000	12	10	0	0
23	0	2	10	2	67	0	8	4	2	3000	18	15	0	0
24	0	3	0	0	68	0	8	6	0	4000	25	0	0	0
25	0	3	1	2	69	0	8	7	2	5000	31	5	0	0
26	0	3	3	0	70	0	8	9	0	6000	37	10	0	0
27	0	3	4	2	71	0	8	10	2	7000	43	15	0	0
[28]	0	3	6	0	72	0	9	0	0	8000	50	0	0	0
29	0	3	7	2	73	0	9	1	2	9000	56	5	0	0
30	0	3	9	0	74	0	9	3	0	10000	62	10	0	0
31	0	3	10	2	75	0	9	4	2					
32	0	4	0	0	76	0	9	6	0					
33	0	4	1	2	77	0	9	7	2					
34	0	4	3	0	78	0	9	9	0					
35	0	4	4	2	79	0	9	10	2					
36	0	4	6	0	80	0	10	0	0					
37	0	4	7	2	81	0	10	1	2					
38	0	4	9	0	82	0	10	3	0					
39	0	4	10	2	83	0	10	4	2					
40	0	5	0	0	[84]	0	10	6	0					
41	0	5	1	2	85	0	10	7	2					
42	0	5	3	0	86	0	10	9	0					
43	0	5	4	2	87	0	10	10	2					
44	0	5	6	0	88	0	11	0	0					

Great Hundred
112 | 0 14 0 0

Gross
144 | 0 18 0 0

Wey
256 | 1 12 0 0

Days in a Year
365 | 2 5 7 2

Feet in a Rod
272 | 1 14 0 0

N.	l.	s.	d.	q.	N.	l.	s.	d.	q.	N.	l.	s.	d.	q.
1	0	0	1	3	45	0	6	6	3	89	0	12	11	3
2	0	0	3	2	46	0	6	8	2	90	0	13	1	2
3	0	0	5	1	47	0	6	10	1	91	0	13	3	1
4	0	0	7	0	48	0	7	0	0	92	0	13	5	0
5	0	0	8	3	49	0	7	1	3	93	0	13	6	3
6	0	0	10	2	50	0	7	3	2	94	0	13	8	2
7	0	1	0	1	51	0	7	5	1	95	0	13	10	1
8	0	1	2	0	52	0	7	7	0	96	0	14	0	0
9	0	1	3	3	53	0	7	8	3	97	0	14	1	3
10	0	1	5	2	54	0	7	10	2	98	0	14	3	2
11	0	1	7	1	55	0	8	0	1	99	0	14	5	1
12	0	1	9	0	[56]	0	8	2	0	100	0	14	7	0
13	0	1	10	3	57	0	8	3	3	200	1	9	2	0
14	0	2	0	2	58	0	8	5	2	300	2	3	9	0
15	0	2	2	1	59	0	8	7	1	400	2	18	4	0
16	0	2	4	0	60	0	8	9	0	500	3	12	11	0
17	0	2	5	3	61	0	8	10	3	600	4	7	6	0
18	0	2	7	2	62	0	9	0	2	700	5	2	1	0
19	0	2	9	1	63	0	9	2	1	800	5	16	8	0
20	0	2	11	0	64	0	9	4	0	900	6	11	3	0
21	0	3	0	3	65	0	9	5	3	1000	7	5	10	0
22	0	3	2	2	66	0	9	7	2	2000	14	11	8	0
23	0	3	4	1	67	0	9	9	1	3000	21	17	6	0
24	0	3	6	0	68	0	9	11	0	4000	29	3	4	0
25	0	3	7	3	69	0	10	0	3	5000	36	9	2	0
26	0	3	9	2	70	0	10	2	2	6000	43	15	0	0
27	0	3	11	1	71	0	10	4	1	7000	51	0	10	0
[28]	0	4	1	0	72	0	10	6	0	8000	58	6	8	0
29	0	4	2	3	73	0	10	7	3	9000	65	12	6	0
30	0	4	4	2	74	0	10	9	2	10000	72	18	4	0
31	0	4	6	1	75	0	10	11	1					
32	0	4	8	0	76	0	11	1	0					
33	0	4	9	3	77	0	11	2	3	Great Hundred				
34	0	4	11	2	78	0	11	4	2	112	0	16	4	0
35	0	5	1	1	79	0	11	6	1	Grofs				
36	0	5	3	0	80	0	11	8	0	114	1	1	0	0
37	0	5	4	3	81	0	11	9	3	Wey				
38	0	5	6	2	82	0	11	11	2	256	1	17	4	0
39	0	5	8	1	83	0	12	1	1	Days in a Year				
40	0	5	10	0	[84]	0	12	3	0	365	2	13	2	3
41	0	5	11	3	85	0	12	4	3	Feet in a Rod				
42	0	6	1	2	86	0	12	6	2	272	1	19	8	0
43	0	6	3	1	87	0	12	8	1					
44	0	6	5	0	88	0	12	10	0					

N.	l.	s.	d.
1	0	0	2
2	0	0	4
3	0	0	6
4	0	0	8
5	0	0	10
6	0	1	0
7	0	1	2
8	0	1	4
9	0	1	6
10	0	1	8
11	0	1	10
12	0	2	0
13	0	2	2
14	0	2	4
15	0	2	6
16	0	2	8
17	0	2	10
18	0	3	0
19	0	3	2
20	0	3	4
21	0	3	6
22	0	3	8
23	0	3	10
24	0	4	0
25	0	4	2
26	0	4	4
27	0	4	6
[28]	0	4	8
29	0	4	10
30	0	5	0
31	0	5	2
32	0	5	4
33	0	5	6
34	0	5	8
35	0	5	10
36	0	6	0
37	0	6	2
38	0	6	4
39	0	6	6
40	0	6	8
41	0	6	10
42	0	7	0
43	0	7	2
44	0	7	4

N.	l.	s.	d.
45	0	7	6
46	0	7	8
47	0	7	10
48	0	8	0
49	0	8	2
50	0	8	4
51	0	8	6
52	0	8	8
53	0	8	10
54	0	9	0
55	0	9	2
[56]	0	9	4
57	0	9	6
58	0	9	8
59	0	9	10
60	0	10	0
61	0	10	2
62	0	10	4
63	0	10	6
64	0	10	8
65	0	10	10
66	0	11	0
67	0	11	2
68	0	11	4
69	0	11	6
70	0	11	8
71	0	11	10
72	0	12	0
73	0	12	2
74	0	12	4
75	0	12	6
76	0	12	8
77	0	12	10
78	0	13	0
79	0	13	2
80	0	13	4
81	0	13	6
82	0	13	8
83	0	13	10
[84]	0	14	0
85	0	14	2
86	0	14	4
87	0	14	6
88	0	14	8

N.	l.	s.	d.
89	0	14	10
90	0	15	0
91	0	15	2
92	0	15	4
93	0	15	6
94	0	15	8
95	0	15	10
96	0	16	0
97	0	16	2
98	0	16	4
99	0	16	6
100	0	16	8
200	1	13	4
300	2	10	0
400	3	6	8
500	4	3	4
600	5	0	0
700	5	16	8
800	6	13	4
900	7	10	0
1000	8	6	8
2000	16	13	4
3000	25	0	0
4000	33	6	8
5000	41	13	4
6000	50	0	0
7000	58	6	8
8000	66	13	4
9000	75	0	0
10000	83	6	8

Great Hundred

112 | 0 18 8

Grofs

144 | 1 4 0

Wey

256 | 2 2 8

Days in a Year

365 | 3 0 10

Feet in a Rod

272 | 2 5 4

N.	l.	s.	d.	q.	N.	l.	s.	d.	q.	N.	l.	s.	d.	q.
1	0	0	2	1	45	0	8	5	1	89	0	16	8	1
2	0	0	4	2	46	0	8	7	2	90	0	16	10	2
3	0	0	6	3	47	0	8	9	3	91	0	17	0	3
4	0	0	9	0	48	0	9	0	0	92	0	17	3	0
5	0	0	11	1	49	0	9	2	1	93	0	17	5	1
6	0	1	1	2	50	0	9	4	2	94	0	17	7	2
7	0	1	3	3	51	0	9-	6	3	95	0	17	9	3
8	0	1	6	0	52	0	9	9	0	96	0	18	0	0
9	0	1	8	1	53	0	9	11	1	97	0	18	2	1
10	0	1	10	2	54	0	10	1	2	98	0	18	4	2
11	0	2	0	3	55	0	10	3	3	99	0	18	6	3
12	0	2	3	0	[56]	0	10	6	0	100	0	18	9	0
13	0	2	5	1	57	0	10	8	1	200	1	17	6	0
14	0	2	7	2	58	0	10	10	2	300	2	16	3	0
15	0	2	9	3	59	0	11	0	3	400	3	15	0	0
16	0	3	0	0	60	0	11	3	0	500	4	13	9	0
17	0	3	2	1	61	0	11	5	1	600	5	12	6	0
18	0	3	4	2	62	0	11	7	2	700	6	11	3	0
19	0	3	6	3	63	0	11	9	3	800	7	10	0	0
20	0	3	9	0	64	0	12	0	0	900	8	8	9	0
21	0	3	11	1	65	0	12	2	1	1000	9	7	6	0
22	0	4	1	2	66	0	12	4	2	2000	18	15	0	0
23	0	4	3	3	67	0	12	6	3	3000	28	2	6	0
24	0	4	6	0	68	0	12	9	0	4000	37	10	0	0
25	0	4	8	1	69	0	12	11	1	5000	46	17	6	0
26	0	4	10	2	70	0	13	1	2	6000	56	5	0	0
27	0	5	0	3	71	0	13	3	3	7000	65	12	6	0
[28]	0	5	3	0	72	0	13	6	0	8000	75	0	0	0
29	0	5	5	1	73	0	13	8	1	9000	84	7	6	0
30	0	5	7	2	74	0	13	10	2	10000	93	15	0	0
31	0	5	9	3	75	0	14	0	3					
32	0	6	0	0	76	0	14	3	0					
33	0	6	2	1	77	0	14	5	1	Great Hundred				
34	0	6	4	2	78	0	14	7	2	112	1	1	0	0
35	0	6	6	3	79	0	14	9	3	Grofs				
36	0	6	9	0	80	0	15	0	0	144	1	7	0	0
37	0	6	11	1	81	0	15	2	1	Wey				
38	0	7	1	2	82	0	15	4	2	256	2	8	0	0
39	0	7	3	3	83	0	15	6	3	Days in a Year				
40	0	7	6	0	[84]	0	15	9	0	365	3	8	5	1
41	0	7	8	1	85	0	15	11	1	Feet in a Rod				
42	0	7	10	2	86	0	16	1	2	272	2	11	0	0
43	0	8	0	3	87	0	16	3	3					
44	0	8	3	0	88	0	16	6	0					

N.	l.	s.	d.	q.	N.	l.	s.	d.	q.	N.	l.	s.	d.	q.
1	0	0	2	2	45	0	9	4	2	89	0	18	6	2
2	0	0	5	0	46	0	9	7	0	90	0	18	9	0
3	0	0	7	2	47	0	9	9	2	91	0	18	11	2
4	0	0	10	0	48	0	10	0	0	92	0	19	2	0
5	0	1	0	2	49	0	10	2	2	93	0	19	4	2
6	0	1	3	0	50	0	10	5	0	94	0	19	7	0
7	0	1	5	2	51	0	10	7	2	95	0	19	9	2
8	0	1	8	0	52	0	10	10	0	96	1	0	0	0
9	0	1	10	2	53	0	11	0	2	97	1	0	2	2
10	0	2	1	0	54	0	11	3	0	98	1	0	5	0
11	0	2	3	2	55	0	11	5	2	99	1	0	7	2
12	0	2	6	0	[56]	0	11	8	0	100	1	0	10	0
13	0	2	8	2	57	0	11	10	2	200	2	1	8	0
14	0	2	11	0	58	0	12	1	0	300	3	2	6	0
15	0	3	1	2	59	0	12	3	2	400	4	3	4	0
16	0	3	4	0	60	0	12	6	0	500	5	4	2	0
17	0	3	6	2	61	0	12	8	2	600	6	5	0	0
18	0	3	9	0	62	0	12	11	0	700	7	5	10	0
19	0	3	11	2	63	0	13	1	2	800	8	6	8	0
20	0	4	2	0	64	0	13	4	0	900	9	7	6	0
21	0	4	4	2	65	0	13	6	2	1000	10	8	4	0
22	0	4	7	0	66	0	13	9	0	2000	20	16	8	0
23	0	4	9	2	67	0	13	11	2	3000	31	5	0	0
24	0	5	0	0	68	0	14	2	0	4000	41	13	4	0
25	0	5	2	2	69	0	14	4	2	5000	52	1	8	0
26	0	5	5	0	70	0	14	7	0	6000	62	10	0	0
27	0	5	7	2	71	0	14	9	2	7000	72	18	4	0
[28]	0	5	10	0	72	0	15	0	0	8000	83	6	8	0
29	0	6	0	2	73	0	15	2	2	9000	93	15	0	0
30	0	6	3	0	74	0	15	5	0	10000	104	3	4	0
31	0	6	5	2	75	0	15	7	2					
32	0	6	8	0	76	0	15	10	0					
33	0	6	10	2	77	0	16	0	2					
34	0	7	1	0	78	0	16	3	0					
35	0	7	3	2	79	0	16	5	2					
36	0	7	6	0	80	0	16	8	0					
37	0	7	8	2	81	0	16	10	2					
38	0	7	11	0	82	0	17	1	0					
39	0	8	1	2	83	0	17	3	2					
40	0	8	4	0	[84]	0	17	6	0					
41	0	8	6	2	85	0	17	8	2					
42	0	8	9	0	86	0	17	11	0					
43	0	8	11	2	87	0	18	1	2					
44	0	9	2	0	88	0	18	4	0					

Great Hundred

112 | 1 3 4 0

Grofs

144 | 1 10 0 0

Wey

256 | 2 13 4 0

Days in a Year

365 | 3 16 0 2

Feet in a Rod

272 | 2 16 8 0

N.	l.	s.	d.	q.
1	0	0	2	3
2	0	0	5	2
3	0	0	8	1
4	0	0	11	0
5	0	1	1	3
6	0	1	4	2
7	0	1	7	1
8	0	1	10	0
9	0	2	0	3
10	0	2	3	2
11	0	2	6	1
12	0	2	9	0
13	0	2	11	3
14	0	3	2	2
15	0	3	5	1
16	0	3	8	0
17	0	3	10	3
18	0	4	1	2
19	0	4	4	1
20	0	4	7	0
21	0	4	9	3
22	0	5	0	2
23	0	5	3	1
24	0	5	6	0
25	0	5	8	3
26	0	5	11	2
27	0	6	2	1
[28]	0	6	5	0
29	0	6	7	3
30	0	6	10	2
31	0	7	1	1
32	0	7	4	0
33	0	7	6	3
34	0	7	9	2
35	0	8	0	1
36	0	8	3	0
37	0	8	5	3
38	0	8	8	2
39	0	8	11	1
40	0	9	2	0
41	0	9	4	3
42	0	9	7	2
43	0	9	10	1
44	0	10	1	0

N.	l.	s.	d.	q.
45	0	10	3	3
46	0	10	6	2
47	0	10	9	1
48	0	11	0	0
49	0	11	2	3
50	0	11	5	2
51	0	11	8	1
52	0	11	11	0
53	0	12	1	3
54	0	12	4	2
55	0	12	7	1
[56]	0	12	10	0
57	0	13	0	3
58	0	13	3	2
59	0	13	6	1
60	0	13	9	0
61	0	13	11	3
62	0	14	2	2
63	0	14	5	1
64	0	14	8	0
65	0	14	10	3
66	0	15	1	2
67	0	15	4	1
68	0	15	7	0
69	0	15	9	3
70	0	16	0	2
71	0	16	3	1
72	0	16	6	0
73	0	16	8	3
74	0	16	11	2
75	0	17	2	1
76	0	17	5	0
77	0	17	7	3
78	0	17	10	2
79	0	18	1	1
80	0	18	4	0
81	0	18	6	3
82	0	18	9	2
83	0	19	0	1
[84]	0	19	3	0
85	0	19	5	3
86	0	19	8	2
87	0	19	11	1
88	1	0	2	0

N.	l.	s.	d.	d.
89	1	0	4	3
90	1	0	7	2
91	1	0	10	1
92	1	1	1	0
93	1	1	3	3
94	1	1	6	2
95	1	1	9	1
96	1	2	0	0
97	1	2	2	3
98	1	2	5	2
99	1	2	8	1
100	1	2	11	0
200	2	5	10	0
300	3	8	9	0
400	4	11	8	0
500	5	14	7	0
600	6	17	6	0
700	8	0	5	0
800	9	3	4	0
900	10	6	3	0
1000	11	9	2	0
2000	22	18	4	0
3000	34	7	6	0
4000	45	16	8	0
5000	57	5	10	0
6000	68	15	0	0
7000	80	4	2	0
8000	91	13	4	0
9000	103	2	6	0
10000	114	11	8	0

Great Hundred

112 | 1   5   8   0

Grofs

114 | 1   13   0   0

Wey

256 | 2   18   8   0

Days in a Year

365 | 4   3   7   3

Feet in a Rod

272 | 3   2   4   0

N.	l.	s.	d.
1	0	0	3
2	0	0	6
3	0	0	9
4	0	1	0
5	0	1	3
6	0	1	6
7	0	1	9
8	0	2	0
9	0	2	3
10	0	2	6
11	0	2	9
12	0	3	0
13	0	3	3
14	0	3	6
15	0	3	9
16	0	4	0
17	0	4	3
18	0	4	6
19	0	4	9
20	0	5	0
21	0	5	3
22	0	5	6
23	0	5	9
24	0	6	0
25	0	6	3
26	0	6	6
27	0	6	9
28	0	7	0
29	0	7	3
30	0	7	6
31	0	7	9
32	0	8	0
33	0	8	3
34	0	8	6
35	0	8	9
36	0	9	0
37	0	9	3
38	0	9	6
39	0	9	9
40	0	10	0
41	0	10	3
42	0	10	6
43	0	10	9
44	0	11	0

N.	l.	s.	d.
45	0	11	3
46	0	11	6
47	0	11	9
48	0	12	0
49	0	12	3
50	0	12	6
51	0	12	9
52	0	13	0
53	0	13	3
54	0	13	6
55	0	13	9
[56]	0	14	0
57	0	14	3
58	0	14	6
59	0	14	9
60	0	15	0
61	0	15	3
62	0	15	6
63	0	15	9
64	0	16	0
65	0	16	3
66	0	16	6
67	0	16	9
68	0	17	0
69	0	17	3
70	0	17	6
71	0	17	9
72	0	18	0
73	0	18	3
74	0	18	6
75	0	18	9
76	0	19	0
77	0	19	3
78	0	19	6
79	0	19	9
80	1	0	0
81	1	0	3
82	1	0	6
83	1	0	9
[84]	1	1	0
85	1	1	3
86	1	1	6
87	1	1	9
88	1	2	0

N.	l.	s.	d.
89	1	2	3
90	1	2	6
91	1	2	9
92	1	3	0
93	1	3	3
94	1	3	6
95	1	3	9
96	1	4	0
97	1	4	3
98	1	4	6
99	1	4	9
100	1	5	0
200	2	10	0
300	3	15	0
400	5	0	0
500	6	5	0
600	7	10	0
700	8	15	0
800	10	0	0
900	11	5	0
1000	12	10	0
2000	25	0	0
3000	37	10	0
4000	50	0	0
5000	62	10	0
6000	75	0	0
7000	87	10	0
8000	100	0	0
9000	112	10	0
10000	125	0	0

Great Hundred

112 | 1 8 0

Grofs

144 | 1 16 0

Wey

256 | 3 4 0

Days in a Year

365 | 4 11 3

Feet in a Rod

272 | 3 8 0

N.	l.	s.	d.	q.	N.	l.	s.	d.	q.	N.	l.	s.	d.	q.
1	0	0	3	1	45	0	12	2	1	89	1	4	1	1
2	0	0	6	2	46	0	12	5	2	90	1	4	4	2
3	0	0	9	3	47	0	12	8	3	91	1	4	7	3
4	0	1	1	0	48	0	13	0	0	92	1	4	11	0
5	0	1	4	1	49	0	13	3	1	93	1	5	2	1
6	0	1	7	2	50	0	13	6	2	94	1	5	5	2
7	0	1	10	3	51	0	13	9	3	95	1	5	8	3
8	0	2	2	0	52	0	14	1	0	96	1	6	0	0
9	0	2	5	1	53	0	14	4	1	97	1	6	3	1
10	0	2	8	2	54	0	14	7	2	98	1	6	6	2
11	0	2	11	3	55	0	14	10	3	99	1	6	9	3
12	0	3	3	0	[56]	0	15	2	0	100	1	7	1	0
13	0	3	6	1	57	0	15	5	1	200	2	14	2	0
14	0	3	9	2	58	0	15	8	2	300	4	1	3	0
15	0	4	0	3	59	0	15	11	3	400	5	8	4	0
16	0	4	4	0	60	0	16	3	0	500	6	15	5	0
17	0	4	7	1	61	0	16	6	1	600	8	2	6	0
18	0	4	10	2	62	0	16	9	2	700	9	9	7	0
19	0	5	1	3	63	0	17	0	3	800	10	16	8	0
20	0	5	5	0	64	0	17	4	0	900	12	3	9	0
21	0	5	8	1	65	0	17	7	1	1000	13	10	10	0
22	0	5	11	2	66	0	17	10	2	2000	27	1	8	0
23	0	6	2	3	67	0	18	1	3	3000	40	12	6	0
24	0	6	6	0	68	0	18	5	0	4000	54	3	4	0
25	0	6	9	1	69	0	18	8	1	5000	67	14	2	0
26	0	7	0	2	70	0	18	11	2	6000	81	5	0	0
27	0	7	3	3	71	0	19	2	3	7000	94	15	10	0
[28]	0	7	7	0	72	0	19	6	0	8000	108	6	8	0
29	0	7	10	1	73	0	19	9	1	9000	121	17	6	0
30	0	8	1	2	74	1	0	0	2	10000	135	8	4	0
31	0	8	4	3	75	1	0	3	3					
32	0	8	8	0	76	1	0	7	0					
33	0	8	11	1	77	1	0	10	1					
34	0	9	2	2	78	1	1	1	2					
35	0	9	5	3	79	1	1	4	3					
36	0	9	9	0	80	1	1	8	0					
37	0	10	0	1	81	1	1	11	1					
38	0	10	3	2	82	1	2	2	2					
39	0	10	6	3	83	1	2	5	3					
40	0	10	10	0	[84]	1	2	9	0					
41	0	11	1	1	85	1	3	0	1					
42	0	11	4	2	86	1	3	3	2					
43	0	11	7	3	87	1	3	6	3					
44	0	11	11	0	88	1	3	10	0					

Great Hundred
112 | 1 10 4 0

Gross
114 | 1 19 0 0

Wey
256 | 3 9 4 0

Days in a Year
365 | 4 18 10 1

Feet in a Rod
272 | 3 13 8 0

C

N.	l.	s.	d.	q.	N.	l.	s.	d.	q.	N.	l.	s.	d.	q.
1	0	0	3	2	45	0	13	1	2	89	1	5	11	2
2	0	0	7	0	46	0	13	5	0	90	1	6	3	0
3	0	0	10	2	47	0	13	8	2	91	1	6	6	2
4	0	1	2	0	48	0	14	0	0	92	1	6	10	0
5	0	1	5	2	49	0	14	3	2	93	1	7	1	2
6	0	1	9	0	50	0	14	7	0	94	1	7	5	0
7	0	2	0	2	51	0	14	10	2	95	1	7	8	2
8	0	2	4	0	52	0	15	2	0	96	1	8	0	0
9	0	2	7	2	53	0	15	5	2	97	1	8	3	2
10	0	2	11	0	54	0	15	9	0	98	1	8	7	0
11	0	3	2	2	55	0	16	0	2	99	1	8	10	2
12	0	3	6	0	[56]	0	16	4	0	100	1	9	2	0
13	0	3	9	2	57	0	16	7	2	200	2	18	4	0
14	0	4	1	0	58	0	16	11	0	300	4	7	6	0
15	0	4	4	2	59	0	17	2	2	400	5	16	8	0
16	0	4	8	0	60	0	17	6	0	500	7	5	10	0
17	0	4	11	2	61	0	17	9	2	600	8	15	0	0
18	0	5	3	0	62	0	18	1	0	700	10	4	2	0
19	0	5	6	2	63	0	18	4	2	800	11	13	4	0
20	0	5	10	0	64	0	18	8	0	900	13	2	6	0
21	0	6	1	2	65	0	18	11	2	1000	14	11	8	0
22	0	6	5	0	66	0	19	3	0	2000	29	3	4	0
23	0	6	8	2	67	0	19	6	2	3000	43	15	0	0
24	0	7	0	0	68	0	19	10	0	4000	58	6	8	0
25	0	7	3	2	69	1	0	1	2	5000	72	18	4	0
26	0	7	7	0	70	1	0	5	0	6000	87	10	0	0
27	0	7	10	2	71	1	0	8	2	7000	102	1	8	0
[28]	0	8	2	0	72	1	1	0	0	8000	116	13	4	0
29	0	8	5	2	73	1	1	3	2	9000	131	5	0	0
30	0	8	9	0	74	1	1	7	0	10000	145	16	8	0
31	0	9	0	2	75	1	1	10	2					
32	0	9	4	0	76	1	2	2	0					
33	0	9	7	2	77	1	2	5	2					
34	0	9	11	0	78	1	2	9	0					
35	0	10	2	2	79	1	3	0	2					
36	0	10	6	0	80	1	3	4	0					
37	0	10	9	2	81	1	3	7	2					
38	0	11	1	0	82	1	3	11	0					
39	0	11	4	2	83	1	4	2	2					
40	0	11	8	0	[84]	1	4	6	0					
41	0	11	11	2	85	1	4	9	2					
42	0	12	3	0	86	1	5	1	0					
43	0	12	6	2	87	1	5	4	2					
44	0	12	10	0	88	1	5	8	0					

Great Hundred

112 | 1 12 8 0

Grofs

144 | 2 2 0 0

Wey

256 | 3 14 8 0

Days in a Year

365 | 5 6 5 2

Feet in a Rod

272 | 3 19 4 0

N.	l.	s.	d.	q.	N.	l.	s.	d.	q.	N.	l.	s.	d.	q.
1	0	0	3	3	45	0	14	0	3	89	1	7	9	3
2	0	0	7	2	46	0	14	4	2	90	1	8	1	2
3	0	0	11	1	47	0	14	8	1	91	1	8	5	1
4	0	1	3	0	48	0	15	0	0	92	1	8	9	0
5	0	1	6	3	49	0	15	3	3	93	1	9	0	3
6	0	1	10	2	50	0	15	7	2	94	1	9	4	2
7	0	2	2	1	51	0	15	11	1	95	1	9	8	1
8	0	2	6	0	52	0	16	3	0	96	1	10	0	0
9	0	2	9	3	53	0	16	6	3	97	1	10	3	3
10	0	3	1	2	54	0	16	10	2	98	1	10	7	2
11	0	3	5	1	55	0	17	2	1	99	1	10	11	1
12	0	3	9	0	[56]	0	17	6	0	100	1	11	3	0
13	0	4	0	3	57	0	17	9	3	200	3	2	6	0
14	0	4	4	2	58	0	18	1	2	300	4	13	9	0
15	0	4	8	1	59	0	18	5	1	400	6	5	0	0
16	0	5	0	0	60	0	18	9	0	500	7	16	3	0
17	0	5	3	3	61	0	19	0	3	600	9	7	6	0
18	0	5	7	2	62	0	19	4	2	700	10	18	9	0
19	0	5	11	1	63	0	19	8	1	800	12	10	0	0
20	0	6	3	0	64	1	0	0	0	900	14	1	3	0
21	0	6	6	3	65	1	0	3	3	1000	15	12	6	0
22	0	6	10	2	66	1	0	7	2	2000	31	5	0	0
23	0	7	2	1	67	1	0	11	1	3000	46	17	6	0
24	0	7	6	0	68	1	1	3	0	4000	62	10	0	0
25	0	7	9	3	69	1	1	6	3	5000	78	2	6	0
26	0	8	1	2	70	1	1	10	2	6000	93	15	0	0
27	0	8	5	1	71	1	2	2	1	7000	109	7	6	0
[28]	0	8	9	0	72	1	2	6	0	8000	125	0	0	0
29	0	9	0	3	73	1	2	9	3	9000	140	12	6	0
30	0	9	4	2	74	1	3	1	2	10000	156	5	0	0
31	0	9	8	1	75	1	3	5	1					
32	0	10	0	0	76	1	3	9	0					
33	0	10	3	3	77	1	4	0	3					
34	0	10	7	2	78	1	4	4	2					
35	0	10	11	1	79	1	4	8	1					
36	0	11	3	0	80	1	5	0	0					
37	0	11	6	3	81	1	5	3	3					
38	0	11	10	2	82	1	5	7	2					
39	0	12	2	1	83	1	5	11	1					
40	0	12	6	0	[84]	1	6	3	0					
41	0	12	9	3	85	1	6	6	3					
42	0	13	1	2	86	1	6	10	2					
43	0	13	5	1	87	1	7	2	1					
44	0	13	9	0	88	1	7	6	0					

Great Hundred
112 | 1 15 0 0

Grefs
144 | 2 5 0 0

Wey
256 | 4 0 0 0

Days in a Year
365 | 5 14 0 3

Feet in a Rod
272 | 4 5 0 0

N.	l.	s.	d.	N.	l.	s.	d.	N.	l.	s.	d.
1	0	0	4	45	0	15	0	89	1	9	8
2	0	0	8	46	0	15	4	90	1	10	0
3	0	1	0	47	0	15	8	91	1	10	4
4	0	1	4	48	0	16	0	92	1	10	8
5	0	1	8	49	0	16	4	93	1	11	0
6	0	2	0	50	0	16	8	94	1	11	4
7	0	2	4	51	0	17	0	95	1	11	8
8	0	2	8	52	0	17	4	96	1	12	0
9	0	3	0	53	0	17	8	97	1	12	4
10	0	3	4	54	0	18	0	98	1	12	8
11	0	3	8	55	0	18	4	99	1	13	0
12	0	4	0	[56]	0	18	8	100	1	13	4
13	0	4	4	57	0	19	0	200	3	6	8
14	0	4	8	58	0	19	4	300	5	0	0
15	0	5	0	59	0	19	8	400	6	13	4
16	0	5	4	60	1	0	0	500	8	6	8
17	0	5	8	61	1	0	4	600	10	0	0
18	0	6	0	62	1	0	8	700	11	13	4
19	0	6	4	63	1	1	0	800	13	6	8
20	0	6	8	64	1	1	4	900	15	0	0
21	0	7	0	65	1	1	8	1000	16	13	4
22	0	7	4	66	1	2	0	2000	33	6	8
23	0	7	8	67	1	2	4	3000	50	0	0
24	0	8	0	68	1	2	8	4000	66	13	4
25	0	8	4	69	1	3	0	5000	83	6	8
26	0	8	8	70	1	3	4	6000	100	0	0
27	0	9	0	71	1	3	8	7000	116	13	4
[28]	0	9	4	72	1	4	0	8000	133	6	8
29	0	9	8	73	1	4	4	9000	150	0	0
30	0	10	0	74	1	4	8	10000	166	13	4
31	0	10	4	75	1	5	0				
32	0	10	8	76	1	5	4				
33	0	11	0	77	1	5	8	*Great Hundred*			
34	0	11	4	78	1	6	0	112 |	1	17	4
35	0	11	8	79	1	6	4	*Grofs*			
36	0	12	0	80	1	6	8	144 |	2	8	0
37	0	12	4	81	1	7	0	*Wey*			
38	0	12	8	82	1	7	4	256 |	4	5	4
39	0	13	0	83	1	7	8	*Days in a Year*			
40	0	13	4	[84]	1	8	0	365 |	6	1	8
41	0	13	8	85	1	8	4	*Feet in a Rod*			
42	0	14	0	86	1	8	8	272 |	4	10	8
43	0	14	4	87	1	9	0				
44	0	14	8	88	1	9	4				

N.	l.	s.	d.	q.	N.	l.	s.	d.	q.	N.	l.	s.	d.	q.
1	0	0	4	1	45	0	15	11	1	89	1	11	6	1
2	0	0	8	2	46	0	16	3	2	90	1	11	10	2
3	0	1	0	3	47	0	16	7	3	91	1	12	2	3
4	0	1	5	0	48	0	17	0	0	92	1	12	7	0
5	0	1	9	1	49	0	17	4	1	93	1	12	11	1
6	0	2	1	2	50	0	17	8	2	94	1	13	3	2
7	0	2	5	3	51	0	18	0	3	95	1	13	7	3
8	0	2	10	0	52	0	18	5	0	96	1	14	0	0
9	0	3	2	1	53	0	18	9	1	97	1	14	4	1
10	0	3	6	2	54	0	19	1	2	98	1	14	8	2
11	0	3	10	3	55	0	19	5	3	99	1	15	0	3
12	0	4	3	0	[56]	0	19	10	0	100	1	15	5	0
13	0	4	7	1	57	1	0	2	1	200	3	10	10	0
14	0	4	11	2	58	1	0	6	2	300	5	6	3	0
15	0	5	3	3	59	1	0	10	3	400	7	1	8	0
16	0	5	8	0	60	1	1	3	0	500	8	17	1	0
17	0	6	0	1	61	1	1	7	1	600	10	12	6	0
18	0	6	4	2	62	1	1	11	2	700	12	7	11	0
19	0	6	8	3	63	1	2	3	3	800	14	3	4	0
20	0	7	1	0	64	1	2	8	0	900	15	18	9	0
21	0	7	5	1	65	1	3	0	1	1000	17	14	2	0
22	0	7	9	2	66	1	3	4	2	2000	35	8	4	0
23	0	8	1	3	67	1	3	8	3	3000	53	2	6	0
24	0	8	6	0	68	1	4	1	0	4000	70	16	8	0
25	0	8	10	1	69	1	4	5	1	5000	88	10	10	0
26	0	9	2	2	70	1	4	9	2	6000	106	5	0	0
27	0	9	6	3	71	1	5	1	3	7000	123	19	2	0
[28]	0	9	11	0	72	1	5	6	0	8000	141	13	4	0
29	0	10	3	1	73	1	5	10	1	9000	159	7	6	0
30	0	10	7	2	74	1	6	2	2	10000	177	1	8	0
31	0	10	11	3	75	1	6	6	3					
32	0	11	4	0	76	1	6	11	0					
33	0	11	8	1	77	1	7	3	1	Great Hundred				
34	0	12	0	2	78	1	7	7	2	112	1	19	8	0
35	0	12	4	3	79	1	7	11	3	Grofs				
36	0	12	9	0	80	1	8	4	0	144	2	11	0	0
37	0	13	1	1	81	1	8	8	1	Wey				
38	0	13	5	2	82	1	9	0	2	256	4	10	8	0
39	0	13	9	3	83	1	9	4	3	Days in a Year				
40	0	14	2	0	[84]	1	9	9	0	365	6	9	3	1
41	0	14	6	1	85	1	10	1	1	Feet in a Rod				
42	0	14	10	2	86	1	10	5	2	272	4	16	4	0
43	0	15	2	3	87	1	10	9	3					
44	0	15	7	0	88	1	11	2	0					

C 3

N.	l.	s.	d.	q.	N.	l.	s.	d.	q.	N.	l.	s.	d.	q.
1	0	0	4	2	45	0	16	10	2	89	1	13	4	2
2	0	0	9	0	46	0	17	3	0	90	1	13	9	0
3	0	1	1	2	47	0	17	7	2	91	1	14	1	2
4	0	1	6	0	48	0	18	0	0	92	1	14	6	0
5	0	1	10	2	49	0	18	4	2	93	1	14	10	2
6	0	2	3	0	50	0	18	9	0	94	1	15	3	0
7	0	2	7	2	51	0	19	1	2	95	1	15	7	2
8	0	3	0	0	52	0	19	6	0	96	1	16	0	0
9	0	3	4	2	53	0	19	10	2	97	1	16	4	2
10	0	3	9	0	54	1	0	3	0	98	1	16	9	0
11	0	4	1	2	55	1	0	7	2	99	1	17	1	2
12	0	4	6	0	[56]	1	1	0	0	100	1	17	6	0
13	0	4	10	2	57	1	1	4	2	200	3	15	0	0
14	0	5	3	0	58	1	1	9	0	300	5	12	6	0
15	0	5	7	2	59	1	2	1	2	400	7	10	0	0
16	0	6	0	0	60	1	2	6	0	500	9	7	6	0
17	0	6	4	2	61	1	2	10	2	600	11	5	0	0
18	0	6	9	0	62	1	3	3	0	700	13	2	6	0
19	0	7	1	2	63	1	3	7	2	800	15	0	0	0
20	0	7	6	0	64	1	4	0	0	900	16	17	6	0
21	0	7	10	2	65	1	4	4	2	1000	18	15	0	0
22	0	8	3	0	66	1	4	9	0	2000	37	10	0	0
23	0	8	7	2	67	1	5	1	2	3000	56	5	0	0
24	0	9	0	0	68	1	5	6	0	4000	75	0	0	0
25	0	9	4	2	69	1	5	10	2	5000	93	15	0	0
26	0	9	9	0	70	1	6	3	0	6000	112	10	0	0
27	0	10	1	2	71	1	6	7	2	7000	131	5	0	0
[28]	0	10	6	0	72	1	7	0	0	8000	150	0	0	0
29	0	10	10	2	73	1	7	4	2	9000	168	15	0	0
30	0	11	3	0	74	1	7	9	0	10000	187	10	0	0
31	0	11	7	2	75	1	8	1	2					
32	0	12	0	0	76	1	8	6	0					
33	0	12	4	2	77	1	8	10	2					
34	0	12	9	0	78	1	9	3	0		Great Hundred			
35	0	13	1	2	79	1	9	7	2	112	2	2	0	0
36	0	13	6	0	80	1	10	0	0		Grofs			
37	0	13	10	2	81	1	10	4	2	144	2	14	0	0
38	0	14	3	0	82	1	10	9	0		Wey			
39	0	14	7	2	83	1	11	1	2	256	4	16	0	0
40	0	15	0	0	[84]	1	11	6	0		Days in a Year			
41	0	15	4	2	85	1	11	10	2	365	6	16	10	2
42	0	15	9	0	86	1	12	3	0		Feet in a Rod			
43	0	16	1	2	87	1	12	7	2	272	5	2	0	0
44	0	16	6	0	88	1	13	0	0					

N.	l.	s.	d.	q.	N.	l.	s.	d.	q.	N.	l.	s.	d.	q.
1	0	0	4	3	45	0	17	9	3	89	1	15	2	3
2	0	0	9	2	46	0	18	2	2	90	1	15	7	2
3	0	1	2	1	47	0	18	7	1	91	1	16	0	1
4	0	1	7	0	48	0	19	0	0	92	1	16	5	0
5	0	1	11	3	49	0	19	4	3	93	1	16	9	3
6	0	2	4	2	50	0	19	9	2	94	1	17	2	2
7	0	2	9	1	51	1	0	2	1	95	1	17	7	1
8	0	3	2	0	52	1	0	7	0	96	1	18	0	0
9	0	3	6	3	53	1	0	11	3	97	1	18	4	3
10	0	3	11	2	54	1	1	4	2	98	1	18	9	2
11	0	4	4	1	55	1	1	9	1	99	1	19	2	1
12	0	4	9	0	[56]	1	2	2	0	100	1	19	7	0
13	0	5	1	3	57	1	2	6	3	200	3	19	2	0
14	0	5	6	2	58	1	2	11	2	300	5	18	9	0
15	0	5	11	1	59	1	3	4	1	400	7	18	4	0
16	0	6	4	0	60	1	3	9	0	500	9	7	11	0
17	0	6	8	3	61	1	4	1	3	600	11	17	6	0
18	0	7	1	2	62	1	4	6	2	700	13	17	1	0
19	0	7	6	1	63	1	4	11	1	800	15	16	8	0
20	0	7	11	0	64	1	5	4	0	900	17	16	3	0
21	0	8	3	3	65	1	5	8	3	1000	19	15	10	0
22	0	8	8	2	66	1	6	1	2	2000	39	11	8	0
23	0	9	1	1	67	1	6	6	1	3000	59	7	6	0
24	0	9	6	0	68	1	6	11	0	4000	79	3	4	0
25	0	9	10	3	69	1	7	3	3	5000	98	19	2	0
26	0	10	3	2	70	1	7	8	2	6000	118	15	0	0
27	0	10	8	1	71	1	8	1	1	7000	138	10	10	0
[28]	0	11	1	0	72	1	8	6	0	8000	158	6	8	0
29	0	11	5	3	73	1	8	10	3	9000	178	2	6	0
30	0	11	10	2	74	1	9	3	2	10000	197	18	4	0
31	0	12	3	1	75	1	9	8	1					
32	0	12	8	0	76	1	10	1	0					
33	0	13	0	3	77	1	10	5	3	Great Hundred				
34	0	13	5	2	78	1	10	10	2	112	2	4	4	0
35	0	13	10	1	79	1	11	3	1	Grofs				
36	0	14	3	0	80	1	11	8	0	144	2	17	0	0
37	0	14	7	3	81	1	12	0	3	Wey				
38	0	15	0	2	82	1	12	5	2	256	5	1	4	0
39	0	15	5	1	83	1	12	10	1	Days in a Year				
40	0	15	10	0	[84]	1	13	3	0	305	7	4	5	3
41	0	16	2	3	85	1	13	7	3	Feet in a Rod				
42	0	16	7	2	86	1	14	0	2	272	5	7	8	0
43	0	17	0	1	87	1	14	5	1					
44	0	17	5	0	88	1	14	10	0					

N.	l.	s.	d.	N.	l.	s.	d.	N.	l.	s.	d.
1	0	0	5	45	0	18	9	89	1	17	1
2	0	0	10	46	0	19	2	90	1	17	6
3	0	1	3	47	0	19	7	91	1	17	11
4	0	1	8	48	1	0	0	92	1	18	4
5	0	2	1	49	1	0	5	93	1	18	9
6	0	2	6	50	1	0	10	94	1	19	2
7	0	2	11	51	1	1	3	95	1	19	7
8	0	3	4	52	1	1	8	96	2	0	0
9	0	3	9	53	1	2	1	97	2	0	5
10	0	4	2	54	1	2	6	98	2	0	10
11	0	4	7	55	1	2	11	99	2	1	3
12	0	5	0	[56]	1	3	4	100	2	1	8
13	0	5	5	57	1	3	9	200	4	3	4
14	0	5	10	58	1	4	2	300	6	5	0
15	0	6	3	59	1	4	7	400	8	6	8
16	0	6	8	60	1	5	0	500	10	8	4
17	0	7	1	61	1	5	5	600	12	10	0
18	0	7	6	62	1	5	10	700	14	11	8
19	0	7	11	63	1	6	3	800	16	13	4
20	0	8	4	64	1	6	8	900	18	15	0
21	0	8	9	65	1	7	1	1000	20	16	8
22	0	9	2	66	1	7	6	2000	41	13	4
23	0	9	7	67	1	7	11	3000	62	10	0
24	0	10	0	68	1	8	4	4000	83	6	8
25	0	10	5	69	1	8	9	5000	104	3	4
26	0	10	10	70	1	9	2	6000	125	0	0
27	0	11	3	71	1	9	7	7000	145	16	8
[28]	0	11	8	72	1	10	0	8000	166	13	4
29	0	12	1	73	1	10	5	9000	187	10	0
30	0	12	6	74	1	10	10	10000	208	6	8
31	0	12	11	75	1	11	3				
32	0	13	4	76	1	11	8				
33	0	13	9	77	1	12	1	Great Hundred			
34	0	14	2	78	1	12	6	112	2	6	8
35	0	14	7	79	1	12	11	Gross			
36	0	15	0	80	1	13	4	144	3	0	0
37	0	15	5	81	1	13	9	Wey			
38	0	15	10	82	1	14	2	256	5	6	8
39	0	16	3	83	1	14	7	Days in a Year			
40	0	16	8	[84]	1	15	0	365	7	12	1
41	0	17	1	85	1	15	5	Feet in a Rod			
42	0	17	6	86	1	15	10	272	5	13	4
43	0	17	11	87	1	16	3				
44	0	18	4	88	1	16	8				

N.	l.	s.	d.	q.
1	0	0	5	1
2	0	0	10	2
3	0	1	3	3
4	0	1	9	0
5	0	2	2	1
6	0	2	7	2
7	0	3	0	3
8	0	3	6	0
9	0	3	11	1
10	0	4	4	2
11	0	4	9	3
12	0	5	3	0
13	0	5	8	1
14	0	6	1	2
15	0	6	6	3
16	0	7	0	0
17	0	7	5	1
18	0	7	10	2
19	0	8	3	3
20	0	8	9	0
21	0	9	2	1
22	0	9	7	2
23	0	10	0	3
24	0	10	6	0
25	0	10	11	1
26	0	11	4	2
27	0	11	9	3
[28]	0	12	3	0
29	0	12	8	1
30	0	13	1	2
31	0	13	6	3
32	0	14	0	0
33	0	14	5	1
34	0	14	10	2
35	0	15	3	3
36	0	15	9	0
37	0	16	2	1
38	0	16	7	2
39	0	17	0	3
40	0	17	6	0
41	0	17	11	1
42	0	18	4	2
43	0	18	9	3
44	0	19	3	0

N.	l.	s.	d.	q.
45	0	19	8	1
46	1	0	1	2
47	1	0	6	3
48	1	1	0	0
49	1	1	5	1
50	1	1	10	2
51	1	2	3	3
52	1	2	9	0
53	1	3	2	1
54	1	3	7	2
55	1	4	0	3
[56]	1	4	6	0
57	1	4	11	1
58	1	5	4	2
59	1	5	9	3
60	1	6	3	0
61	1	6	8	1
62	1	7	1	2
63	1	7	6	3
64	1	8	0	0
65	1	8	5	1
66	1	8	10	2
67	1	9	3	3
68	1	9	9	0
69	1	10	2	1
70	1	10	7	2
71	1	11	0	3
72	1	11	6	0
73	1	11	11	1
74	1	12	4	2
75	1	12	9	3
76	1	13	3	0
77	1	13	8	1
78	1	14	1	2
79	1	14	6	3
80	1	15	0	0
81	1	15	5	1
82	1	15	10	2
83	1	16	3	3
[84]	1	16	9	0
85	1	17	2	1
86	1	17	7	2
87	1	18	0	3
88	1	18	6	0

N.	l.	s.	d.	q.
89	1	18	11	1
90	1	19	4	2
91	1	19	9	3
92	2	0	3	0
93	2	0	8	1
94	2	1	1	2
95	2	1	6	3
96	2	2	0	0
97	2	2	5	1
98	2	2	10	2
99	2	3	3	3
100	2	3	9	0
200	4	7	6	0
300	6	11	3	0
400	8	15	0	0
500	10	18	9	0
600	13	2	6	0
700	15	6	3	0
800	17	10	0	0
900	19	13	9	0
1000	21	17	6	0
2000	43	15	0	0
3000	65	12	6	0
4000	87	10	0	0
5000	109	7	6	0
6000	131	5	0	0
7000	153	2	6	0
8000	175	0	0	0
9000	196	17	6	0
10000	218	15	0	0

Great Hundred

112	2	9	0	0

Grofs

144	3	3	0	0

Wey

256	5	12	0	0

Days in a Year

365	7	19	8	1

Feet in a Rod

272	5	19	0	0

N.	l.	s.	d.	q.	N.	l.	s.	d.	q.	N	l	s.	d.	q.
1	0	0	5	2	45	1	0	7	2	89	.	0	9	2
2	0	0	11	0	46	1	1	1	0	90	2	1	3	0
3	0	1	4	2	47	1	1	6	2	91	2	1	8	2
4	0	1	10	0	48	1	2	0	0	92	2	2	2	0
5	0	2	3	2	49	1	2	5	2	93	2	2	7	2
6	0	2	9	0	50	1	2	11	0	94	2	3	1	0
7	0	3	2	2	51	1	3	4	2	95	2	3	6	2
8	0	3	8	0	52	1	3	10	0	96	2	4	0	0
9	0	4	1	2	53	1	4	3	2	97	2	4	5	2
10	0	4	7	0	54	1	4	9	0	98	2	4	11	0
11	0	5	0	2	55	1	5	2	2	99	2	5	4	2
12	0	5	6	0	[56]	1	5	8	0	100	2	5	10	0
13	0	5	11	2	57	1	6	1	2	200	4	11	8	0
14	0	6	5	0	58	1	6	7	0	300	6	17	6	0
15	0	6	10	2	59	1	7	0	2	400	9	3	4	0
16	0	7	4	0	60	1	7	6	0	500	11	9	2	0
17	0	7	9	2	61	1	7	11	2	600	13	15	0	0
18	0	8	3	0	62	1	8	5	0	700	16	0	10	0
19	0	8	8	2	63	1	8	10	2	800	18	6	8	0
20	0	9	2	0	64	1	9	4	0	900	20	12	6	0
21	0	9	7	2	65	1	9	9	2	1000	22	18	4	0
22	0	10	1	0	66	1	10	3	0	2000	45	16	8	0
23	0	10	6	2	67	1	10	8	2	3000	68	15	0	0
24	0	11	0	0	68	1	11	2	0	4000	91	13	4	0
25	0	11	5	2	69	1	11	7	2	5000	114	11	8	0
26	0	11	11	0	70	1	12	1	0	6000	137	10	0	0
27	0	12	4	2	71	1	12	6	2	7000	160	8	4	0
[28]	0	12	10	0	72	1	13	0	0	8000	183	6	8	0
29	0	13	3	2	73	1	13	5	2	9000	206	5	0	0
30	0	13	9	0	74	1	13	11	0	10000	229	3	4	0
31	0	14	2	2	75	1	14	4	2					
32	0	14	8	0	76	1	14	10	0					
33	0	15	1	2	77	1	15	3	2					
34	0	15	7	0	78	1	15	9	0		Great Hundred			
35	0	16	0	2	79	1	16	2	2	112	2	11	4	0
36	0	16	6	0	80	1	16	8	0		Grofs			
37	0	16	11	2	81	1	17	1	2	144	3	6	0	0
38	0	17	5	0	82	1	17	7	0		Wey			
39	0	17	10	2	83	1	18	0	2	256	5	17	4	0
40	0	18	4	0	[84]	1	18	6	0		Days in a Year			
41	0	18	9	2	85	1	18	11	2	365	8	7	3	2
42	0	19	3	0	86	1	19	5	0		Feet in a Rod			
43	0	19	8	2	87	1	19	10	2	272	6	4	8	0
44	1	0	2	0	88	2	0	4	0					

N.	l.	s.	d.	q	N.	l.	s.	d.	q.	N.	l.	s.	d.	q.
1	0	0	5	3	45	1	1	6	3	89	2	2	7	3
2	0	0	11	2	46	1	2	0	2	90	2	3	1	2
3	0	1	5	1	47	1	2	6	1	91	2	3	7	1
4	0	1	11	0	48	1	3	0	0	92	2	4	1	0
5	0	2	4	3	49	1	3	5	3	93	2	4	6	3
6	0	2	10	2	50	1	3	11	2	94	2	5	0	2
7	0	3	4	1	51	1	4	5	1	95	2	5	6	1
8	0	3	10	0	52	1	4	11	0	96	2	6	0	0
9	0	4	3	3	53	1	5	4	3	97	2	6	5	3
10	0	4	9	2	54	1	5	10	2	98	2	6	11	2
11	0	5	3	1	55	1	6	4	1	99	2	7	5	1
12	0	5	9	0	[56]	1	6	10	0	100	2	7	11	0
13	0	6	2	3	57	1	7	3	3	200	4	15	10	0
14	0	6	8	2	58	1	7	9	2	300	7	3	9	0
15	0	7	2	1	59	1	8	3	1	400	9	11	8	0
16	0	7	8	0	60	1	8	9	0	500	11	19	7	0
17	0	8	1	3	61	1	9	2	3	600	14	7	6	0
18	0	8	7	2	62	1	9	8	2	700	16	15	5	0
19	0	9	1	1	63	1	10	2	1	800	19	3	4	0
20	0	9	7	0	64	1	10	8	0	900	21	11	3	0
21	0	10	0	3	65	1	11	1	3	1000	23	19	2	0
22	0	10	6	2	66	1	11	7	2	2000	47	18	4	0
23	0	11	0	1	67	1	12	1	1	3000	71	17	6	0
24	0	11	6	0	68	1	12	7	0	4000	95	16	8	0
25	0	11	11	3	69	1	13	0	3	5000	119	15	10	0
26	0	12	5	2	70	1	13	6	2	6000	143	15	0	0
27	0	12	11	1	71	1	14	0	1	7000	166	14	2	0
[28]	0	13	5	0	72	1	14	6	0	8000	191	13	4	0
29	0	13	10	3	73	1	14	11	3	9000	215	12	6	0
30	0	14	4	2	74	1	15	5	2	10000	239	11	8	0
31	0	14	10	1	75	1	15	11	1					
32	0	15	4	0	76	1	16	5	0					
33	0	15	9	3	77	1	16	10	3					
34	0	16	3	2	78	1	17	4	2					
35	0	16	9	1	79	1	17	10	1					
36	0	17	3	0	80	1	18	4	0					
37	0	17	8	3	81	1	18	9	3					
38	0	18	2	2	82	1	19	3	2					
39	0	18	8	1	83	1	19	9	1					
40	0	19	2	0	[84]	2	0	3	0					
41	0	19	7	3	85	2	0	8	3					
42	1	0	1	2	86	2	1	2	2					
43	1	0	7	1	87	2	1	8	1					
44	1	1	1	0	88	2	2	2	0					

Great Hundred

112 | 2 13 8 0

Grofs

144 | 3 9 0 0

Wey

256 | 6 2 8 0

Days in a Year

365 | 8 14 10 3

Feet in a Rod

272 | 6 10 4 0

N.	l.	s.	d.	N.	l.	s.	d.	N.	l.	s.	d.
1	0	0	6	45	1	2	6	89	2	4	6
2	0	1	0	46	1	3	0	90	2	5	0
3	0	1	6	47	1	3	6	91	2	5	6
4	0	2	0	48	1	4	0	92	2	6	0
5	0	2	6	49	1	4	6	93	2	6	6
6	0	3	0	50	1	5	0	94	2	7	0
7	0	3	6	51	1	5	6	95	2	7	6
8	0	4	0	52	1	6	0	96	2	8	0
9	0	4	6	53	1	6	6	97	2	8	6
10	0	5	0	54	1	7	0	98	2	9	0
11	0	5	6	55	1	7	6	99	2	9	6
12	0	6	0	[56]	1	8	0	100	2	10	0
13	0	6	6	57	1	8	6	200	5	0	0
14	0	7	0	58	1	9	0	300	7	10	0
15	0	7	6	59	1	9	6	400	10	0	0
16	0	8	0	60	1	10	0	500	12	10	0
17	0	8	6	61	1	10	6	600	15	0	0
18	0	9	0	62	1	11	0	700	17	10	0
19	0	9	6	63	1	11	6	800	20	0	0
20	0	10	0	64	1	12	0	900	22	10	0
21	0	10	6	65	1	12	6	1000	25	0	0
22	0	11	0	66	1	13	0	2000	50	0	0
23	0	11	6	67	1	13	6	3000	75	0	0
24	0	12	0	68	1	14	0	4000	100	0	0
25	0	12	6	69	1	14	6	5000	125	0	0
26	0	13	0	70	1	15	0	6000	150	0	0
27	0	13	6	71	1	15	6	7000	175	0	0
[28]	0	14	0	72	1	16	0	8000	200	0	0
29	0	14	6	73	1	16	6	9000	225	0	0
30	0	15	0	74	1	17	0	10000	250	0	0
31	0	15	6	75	1	17	6				
32	0	16	0	76	1	18	0				
33	0	16	6	77	1	18	6				
34	0	17	0	78	1	19	0				
35	0	17	6	79	1	19	6				
36	0	18	0	80	2	0	0				
37	0	18	6	81	2	0	6				
38	0	19	0	82	2	1	0				
39	0	19	6	83	2	1	6				
40	1	0	0	[84]	2	2	0				
41	1	0	6	85	2	2	6				
42	1	1	0	86	2	3	0				
43	1	1	6	87	2	3	6				
44	1	2	0	88	2	4	0				

Great Hundred

112 | 2 16 0

Grofs

114 | 3 12 0

Wey

256 | 6 8 0

Days in a Year

365 | 9 2 6

Feet in a Rod

272 | 6 16 0

N.	l.	s.	d.	q.	N.	l.	s.	d.	q.	N.	l.	s.	d.	q.
1	0	0	6	1	45	1	3	5	1	89	2	6	4	1
2	0	1	0	2	46	1	3	11	2	90	2	6	10	2
3	0	1	6	3	47	1	4	5	3	91	2	7	4	3
4	0	2	1	0	48	1	5	0	0	92	2	7	11	0
5	0	2	7	1	49	1	5	6	1	93	2	8	5	1
6	0	3	1	2	50	1	6	0	2	94	2	8	11	2
7	0	3	7	3	51	1	6	6	3	95	2	9	5	3
8	0	4	2	0	52	1	7	1	0	96	2	10	0	0
9	0	4	8	1	53	1	7	7	1	97	2	10	6	1
10	0	5	2	2	54	1	8	1	2	98	2	11	0	2
11	0	5	8	3	55	1	8	7	3	99	2	11	6	3
12	0	6	3	0	[56]	1	9	2	0	100	2	12	1	0
13	0	6	9	1	57	1	9	8	1	200	5	4	2	0
14	0	7	3	2	58	1	10	2	2	300	7	16	3	0
15	0	7	9	3	59	1	10	8	3	400	10	8	4	0
16	0	8	4	0	60	1	11	3	0	500	13	0	5	0
17	0	8	10	1	61	1	11	9	1	600	15	12	6	0
18	0	9	4	2	62	1	12	3	2	700	18	4	7	0
19	0	9	10	3	63	1	12	9	3	800	20	16	8	0
20	0	10	5	0	64	1	13	4	0	900	23	8	9	0
21	0	10	11	1	65	1	13	10	1	1000	26	0	10	0
22	0	11	5	2	66	1	14	4	2	2000	52	1	8	0
23	0	11	11	3	67	1	14	10	3	3000	78	2	6	0
24	0	12	6	0	68	1	15	5	0	4000	104	3	4	0
25	0	13	0	1	69	1	15	11	1	5000	130	4	2	0
26	0	13	6	2	70	1	16	5	2	6000	156	5	0	0
27	0	14	0	3	71	1	16	11	3	7000	182	5	10	0
[28]	0	14	7	0	72	1	17	6	0	8000	208	6	8	0
29	0	15	1	1	73	1	18	0	1	9000	234	7	6	0
30	0	15	7	2	74	1	18	6	2	10000	260	8	4	0
31	0	16	1	3	75	1	19	0	3					
32	0	16	8	0	76	1	19	7	0					
33	0	17	2	1	77	2	0	1	1	Great Hundred				
34	0	17	8	2	78	2	0	7	2	112	2	18	4	0.
35	0	18	2	3	79	2	1	1	3	Grofs				
36	0	18	9	0	80	2	1	8	0	114	3	15	0	0
37	0	19	3	1	81	2	2	2	1	Wey				
38	0	19	9	2	82	2	2	8	2	256	6	13	4	0
39	1	0	3	3	83	2	3	2	3	Days in a Year				
40	1	0	10	0	[84]	2	3	9	0	365	9	10	1	1
41	1	1	4	1	85	2	4	3	1	Feet in a Rod				
42	1	1	10	2	86	2	4	9	2	272	7	1	8	0
43	1	2	4	3	87	2	5	3	3					
44	1	2	11	0	88	2	5	10	0					

D

N.	l.	s.	d.	q.	N.	l.	s.	d.	q.	N.	l.	s.	d.	q.
1	0	0	6	2	45	1	4	4	2	89	2	8	2	2
2	0	1	1	0	46	1	4	11	0	90	2	8	9	0
3	0	1	7	2	47	1	5	5	2	91	2	9	3	2
4	0	2	2	0	48	1	6	0	0	92	2	9	10	0
5	0	2	8	2	49	1	6	6	2	93	2	10	4	2
6	0	3	3	0	50	1	7	1	0	94	2	10	11	0
7	0	3	9	2	51	1	7	7	2	95	2	11	5	2
8	0	4	4	0	52	1	8	2	0	96	2	12	0	0
9	0	4	10	2	53	1	8	8	2	97	2	12	6	2
10	0	5	5	0	54	1	9	3	0	98	2	13	1	0
11	0	5	11	2	55	1	9	9	2	99	2	13	7	2
12	0	6	6	0	[56]	1	10	4	0	100	2	14	2	0
13	0	7	0	2	57	1	10	10	2	200	5	8	4	0
14	0	7	7	0	58	1	11	5	0	300	8	2	6	0
15	0	8	1	2	59	1	11	11	2	400	10	16	8	0
16	0	8	8	0	60	1	12	6	0	500	13	10	10	0
17	0	9	2	2	61	1	13	0	2	600	16	5	0	0
18	0	9	9	0	62	1	13	7	0	700	18	19	2	0
19	0	10	3	2	63	1	14	1	2	800	21	13	4	0
20	0	10	10	0	64	1	14	8	0	900	24	7	6	0
21	0	11	4	2	65	1	15	2	2	1000	27	1	8	0
22	0	11	11	0	66	1	15	9	0	2000	54	3	4	0
23	0	12	5	2	67	1	16	3.2		3000	81	5	0	0
24	0	13	0	0	68	1	16	10	0	4000	108	6	8	0
25	0	13	6	2	69	1	17	4	2	5000	135	8	4	0
26	0	14	1	0	70	1	17	11	0	6000	162	10	0	0
27	0	14	7	2	71	1	18	5	2	7000	189	11	8	0
[28]	0	15	2	0	72	1	19	0	0	8000	216	13	4	0
29	0	15	8	2	73	1	19	6	2	9000	243	15	0	0
30	0	16	3	0	74	2	0	1	0	10000	270	16	8	0
31	0	16	9	2	75	2	0	7	2					
32	0	17	4	0	76	2	1	2	0					
33	0	17	10	2	77	2	1	8	2					
34	0	18	5	0	78	2	2	3	0					
35	0	18	11	2	79	2	2	9	2					
36	0	19	6	0	80	2	3	4	0					
37	1	0	0	2	81	2	3	10	2					
38	1	0	7	0	82	2	4	5	0					
39	1	1	1	2	83	2	4	11	2					
40	1	1	8	0	[84]	2	5	6	0					
41	1	2	2	2	85	2	6	0	2					
42	1	2	9	0	86	2	6	7	0					
43	1	3	3	2	87	2	7	1	2					
44	1	3	10	0	88	2	7	8	0					

Great Hundred

112 | 3 0 8 0

Grofs

144 | 3 18 0 0

Wey

256 | 6 18 8 0

Days in a Year

365 | 9 17 8 2

Feet in a Rod

272 | 7 7.4 0

N.	l.	s.	d.	q.	N.	l.	s.	d.	q.	N.	l.	s.	d.	q.
1	0	0	6	3	45	1	5	3	3	89	2	10	0	3
2	0	1	1	2	46	1	5	10	2	90	2	10	7	2
3	0	1	8	1	47	1	6	5	1	91	2	11	2	1
4	0	2	3	0	48	1	7	0	0	92	2	11	9	0
5	0	2	9	3	49	1	7	6	3	93	2	12	3	3
6	0	3	4	2	50	1	8	1	2	94	2	12	10	2
7	0	3	11	1	51	1	8	8	1	95	2	13	5	1
8	0	4	6	0	52	1	9	3	0	96	2	14	0	0
9	0	5	0	3	53	1	9	9	3	97	2	14	6	3
10	0	5	7	2	54	1	10	4	2	98	2	15	1	2
11	0	6	2	1	55	1	10	11	1	99	2	15	8	1
12	0	6	9	0	[56]	1	11	6	0	100	2	16	3	0
13	0	7	3	3	57	1	12	0	3	200	5	12	6	0
14	0	7	10	2	58	1	12	7	2	300	8	8	9	0
15	0	8	5	1	59	1	13	2	1	400	11	5	0	0
16	0	9	0	0	60	1	13	9	0	500	14	1	3	0
17	0	9	6	3	61	1	14	3	3	600	16	17	6	0
18	0	10	1	2	62	1	14	10	2	700	19	13	9	0
19	0	10	8	1	63	1	15	5	1	800	22	10	0	0
20	0	11	3	0	64	1	16	0	0	900	25	6	3	0
21	0	11	9	3	65	1	16	6	3	1000	28	2	6	0
22	0	12	4	2	66	1	17	1	2	2000	56	5	0	0
23	0	12	11	1	67	1	17	8	1	3000	84	7	6	0
24	0	13	6	0	68	1	18	3	0	4000	112	10	0	0
25	0	14	0	3	69	1	18	9	3	5000	140	12	6	0
26	0	14	7	2	70	1	19	4	2	6000	168	15	0	0
27	0	15	2	1	71	1	19	11	1	7000	196	17	6	0
[28]	0	15	9	0	72	2	0	6	0	8000	225	0	0	0
29	0	16	3	3	73	2	1	0	3	9000	253	2	6	0
30	0	16	10	2	74	2	1	7	2	10000	281	5	0	0
31	0	17	5	1	75	2	2	2	1					
32	0	18	0	0	76	2	2	9	0					
33	0	18	6	3	77	2	3	3	3		*Great Hundred*			
34	0	19	1	2	78	2	3	10	2	112	3	3	0	0
35	0	19	8	1	79	2	4	5	1		*Grofs*			
36	1	0	3	0	80	2	5	0	0	144	4	1	0	0
37	1	0	9	3	81	2	5	6	3		*Wey*			
38	1	1	4	2	82	2	6	1	2	256	7	4	0	0
39	1	1	11	1	83	2	6	8	1		*Days in a Year*			
40	1	2	6	0	[84]	2	7	3	0	365	10	5	3	3
41	1	3	0	3	85	2	7	9	3		*Feet in a Rod*			
42	1	3	7	2	86	2	8	4	2	272	7	13	0	0
43	1	4	2	1	87	2	8	11	1					
44	1	4	9	0	88	2	9	6	0					

N.	l.	s.	d.	N.	l.	s.	d.	N.	l.	s.	d.
1	0	0	7	45	1	6	3	89	2	11	11
2	0	1	2	46	1	6	10	90	2	12	6
3	0	1	9	47	1	7	5	91	2	13	1
4	0	2	4	48	1	8	0	92	2	13	8
5	0	2	11	49	1	8	7	93	2	14	3
6	0	3	6	50	1	9	2	94	2	14	10
7	0	4	1	51	1	9	9	95	2	15	5
8	0	4	8	52	1	10	4	96	2	16	0
9	0	5	3	53	1	10	11	97	2	16	7
10	0	5	10	54	1	11	6	98	2	17	2
11	0	6	5	55	1	12	1	99	2	17	9
12	0	7	0	[56]	1	12	8	100	2	18	4
13	0	7	7	57	1	13	3	200	5	16	8
14	0	8	2	58	1	13	10	300	8	15	0
15	0	8	9	59	1	14	5	400	11	13	4
16	0	9	4	60	1	15	0	500	14	11	8
17	0	9	11	61	1	15	7	600	17	10	0
18	0	10	6	62	1	16	2	700	20	8	4
19	0	11	1	63	1	16	9	800	23	6	8
20	0	11	8	64	1	17	4	900	26	5	0
21	0	12	3	65	1	17	11	1000	29	3	4
22	0	12	10	66	1	18	6	2000	58	6	8
23	0	13	5	67	1	19	1	3000	87	10	0
24	0	14	0	68	1	19	8	4000	116	13	4
25	0	14	7	69	2	0	3	5000	145	16	8
26	0	15	2	70	2	0	10	6000	175	0	0
27	0	15	9	71	2	1	5	7000	204	3	4
[28]	0	16	4	72	2	2	0	8000	233	6	8
29	0	16	11	73	2	2	7	9000	262	10	0
30	0	17	6	74	2	3	2	10000	291	13	4
31	0	18	1	75	2	3	9				
32	0	18	8	76	2	4	4				
33	0	19	3	77	2	4	11		Great Hundred		
34	0	19	10	78	2	5	6	112	3	5	4
35	1	0	5	79	2	6	1		Grofs		
36	1	1	0	80	2	6	8	144	4	4	0
37	1	1	7	81	2	7	3		Wey		
38	1	2	2	82	2	7	10	256	7	9	4
39	1	2	9	83	2	8	5		Days in a Year		
40	1	3	4	[84]	2	9	0	365	10	12	11
41	1	3	11	85	2	9	7		Feet in a Rod		
42	1	4	6	86	2	10	2	272	7	18	8
43	1	5	1	87	2	10	9				
44	1	5	8	88	2	11	4				

N.	l.	s.	d.	q.	N.	l.	s.	d.	q.	N.	l.	s.	d.	q.
1	0	0	7	1	45	1	7	2	1	89	2	13	9	1
2	0	1	2	2	46	1	7	9	2	90	2	14	4	2
3	0	1	9	3	47	1	8	4	3	91	2	14	11	3
4	0	2	5	0	48	1	9	0	0	92	2	15	7	0
5	0	3	0	1	49	1	9	7	1	93	2	16	2	1
6	0	3	7	2	50	1	10	2	2	94	2	16	9	2
7	0	4	2	3	51	1	10	9	3	95	2	17	4	3
8	0	4	10	0	52	1	11	5	0	96	2	18	0	0
9	0	5	5	1	53	1	12	0	1	97	2	18	7	1
10	0	6	0	2	54	1	12	7	2	98	2	19	2	2
11	0	6	7	3	55	1	13	2	3	99	2	19	9	3
12	0	7	3	0	[56]	1	13	10	0	100	3	0	5	0
13	0	7	10	1	57	1	14	5	1	200	6	0	10	0
14	0	8	5	2	58	1	15	0	2	300	9	1	3	0
15	0	9	0	3	59	1	15	7	3	400	12	1	8	0
16	0	9	8	0	60	1	16	3	0	500	15	2	1	0
17	0	10	3	1	61	1	16	10	1	600	18	2	6	0
18	0	10	10	2	62	1	17	5	2	700	21	2	11	0
19	0	11	5	3	63	1	18	0	3	800	24	3	4	0
20	0	12	1	0	64	1	18	8	0	900	27	3	9	0
21	0	12	8	1	65	1	19	3	1	1000	30	4	2	0
22	0	13	3	2	66	1	19	10	2	2000	60	8	4	0
23	0	13	10	3	67	2	0	5	3	3000	90	12	6	0
24	0	14	6	0	68	2	1	1	0	4000	120	16	8	0
25	0	15	1	1	69	2	1	8	1	5000	151	0	10	0
26	0	15	8	2	70	2	2	3	2	6000	181	5	0	0
27	0	16	3	3	71	2	2	10	3	7000	211	9	2	0
[28]	0	16	11	0	72	2	3	6	0	8000	241	13	4	0
29	0	17	6	1	73	2	4	1	1	9000	271	17	6	0
30	0	18	1	2	74	2	4	8	2	10000	302	1	8	0
31	0	18	8	3	75	2	5	3	3					
32	0	19	4	0	76	2	5	11	0					
33	0	19	11	1	77	2	6	6	1		Great Hundred			
34	1	0	6	2	78	2	7	1	2	112	3	7	8	0
35	1	1	1	3	79	2	7	8	3		Grofs			
36	1	1	9	0	80	2	8	4	0	144	4	7	0	0
37	1	2	4	1	81	2	8	11	1		Wey			
38	1	2	11	2	82	2	9	6	2	256	7	14	8	0
39	1	3	6	3	83	2	10	1	3		Days in a Year			
40	1	4	2	0	[84]	2	10	9	0	365	11	0	6	1
41	1	4	9	1	85	2	11	4	1		Feet in a Rod			
42	1	5	4	2	86	2	11	11	2	272	8	4	4	0
43	1	5	11	3	87	2	12	6	3					
44	1	6	7	0	88	2	13	2	0					

N.	l.	s.	d.	q.	N.	l.	s.	d.	q.	N.	l.	s.	d.	q.
1	0	0	7	2	45	1	8	1	2	89	2	15	7	2
2	0	1	3	0	46	1	8	9	0	90	2	16	3	0
3	0	1	10	2	47	1	9	4	2	91	2	16	10	2
4	0	2	6	0	48	1	10	0	0	92	2	17	6	0
5	0	3	1	2	49	1	10	7	2	93	2	18	1	2
6	0	3	9	0	50	1	11	3	0	94	2	18	9	0
7	0	4	4	2	51	1	11	10	2	95	2	19	4	2
8	0	5	0	0	52	1	12	6	0	96	3	0	0	0
9	0	5	7	2	53	1	13	1	2	97	3	0	7	2
10	0	6	3	0	54	1	13	9	0	98	3	1	3	0
11	0	6	10	2	55	1	14	4	2	99	3	1	10	2
12	0	7	6	0	[56]	1	15	0	0	100	3	2	6	0
13	0	8	1	2	57	1	15	7	2	200	6	5	0	0
14	0	8	9	0	58	1	16	3	0	300	9	7	6	0
15	0	9	4	2	59	1	16	10	2	400	12	10	0	0
16	0	10	0	0	60	1	17	6	0	500	15	12	6	0
17	0	10	7	2	61	1	18	1	2	600	18	15	0	0
18	0	11	3	0	62	1	18	9	0	700	21	17	6	0
19	0	11	10	2	63	1	19	4	2	800	25	0	0	0
20	0	12	6	0	64	2	0	0	0	900	28	2	6	0
21	0	13	1	2	65	2	0	7	2	1000	31	5	0	0
22	0	13	9	0	66	2	1	3	0	2000	62	10	0	0
23	0	14	4	2	67	2	1	10	2	3000	93	15	0	0
24	0	15	0	0	68	2	2	6	0	4000	125	0	0	0
25	0	15	7	2	69	2	3	1	2	5000	156	5	0	0
26	0	16	3	0	70	2	3	9	0	6000	187	10	0	0
27	0	16	10	2	71	2	4	4	2	7000	218	15	0	0
[28]	0	17	6	0	72	2	5	0	0	8000	250	0	0	0
29	0	18	1	2	73	2	5	7	2	9000	281	5	0	0
30	0	18	9	0	74	2	6	3	0	10000	312	10	0	0
31	0	19	4	2	75	2	6	10	2					
32	1	0	0	0	76	2	7	6	0					
33	1	0	7	2	77	2	8	1	2					
34	1	1	3	0	78	2	8	9	0					
35	1	1	10	2	79	2	9	4	2					
36	1	2	6	0	80	2	10	0	0					
37	1	3	1	2	81	2	10	7	2					
38	1	3	9	0	82	2	11	3	0					
39	1	4	4	2	83	2	11	10	2					
40	1	5	0	0	[84]	2	12	6	0					
41	1	5	7	2	85	2	13	1	2					
42	1	6	3	0	86	2	13	9	0					
43	1	6	10	2	87	2	14	4	2					
44	1	7	6	0	88	2	15	0	0					

Great Hundred

112 | 3   10   0   0

Grofs

144 | 4   10   0   0

Wey

256 | 8   0   0   0

Days in a Year

365 | 11   8   1   2

Feet in a Rod

272 | 8   10   0   0

N.	l.	s.	d.	q.	N.	l.	s.	d.	q.	N.	l.	s.	d.	q.
1	0	0	7	3	45	1	9	0	3	89	2	17	5	3
2	0	1	3	2	46	1	9	8	2	90	2	18	1	2
3	0	1	11	1	47	1	10	4	1	91	2	18	9	1
4	0	2	7	0	48	1	11	0	0	92	2	19	5	0
5	0	3	2	3	49	1	11	7	3	93	3	0	0	3
6	0	3	10	2	50	1	12	3	2	94	3	0	8	2
7	0	4	6	1	51	1	12	11	1	95	3	1	4	1
8	0	5	2	0	52	1	13	7	0	96	3	2	0	0
9	0	5	9	3	53	1	14	2	3	97	3	2	7	3
10	0	6	5	2	54	1	14	10	2	98	3	3	3	2
11	0	7	1	1	55	1	15	6	1	99	3	3	11	1
12	0	7	9	0	[56]	1	16	2	0	100	3	4	7	0
13	0	8	4	3	57	1	16	9	3	200	6	9	2	0
14	0	9	0	2	58	1	17	5	2	300	9	13	9	0
15	0	9	8	1	59	1	18	1	1	400	12	18	4	0
16	0	10	4	0	60	1	18	9	0	500	16	2	11	0
17	0	10	11	3	61	1	19	4	3	600	19	7	6	0
18	0	11	7	2	62	2	0	0	2	700	22	12	1	0
19	0	12	3	1	63	2	0	8	1	800	25	16	8	0
20	0	12	11	0	64	2	1	4	0	900	29	1	3	0
21	0	13	6	3	65	2	1	11	3	1000	32	5	10	0
22	0	14	2	2	66	2	2	7	2	2000	64	11	8	0
23	0	14	10	1	67	2	3	3	1	3000	96	17	6	0
24	0	15	6	0	68	2	3	11	0	4000	129	3	4	0
25	0	16	1	3	69	2	4	6	3	5000	161	9	2	0
26	0	16	9	2	70	2	5	2	2	6000	193	15	0	0
27	0	17	5	1	71	2	5	10	1	7000	226	0	10	0
[28]	0	18	1	0	72	2	6	6	0	8000	258	6	8	0
29	0	18	8	3	73	2	7	1	3	9000	290	12	6	0
30	0	19	4	2	74	2	7	9	2	10000	322	18	4	0
31	1	0	0	1	75	2	8	5	1					
32	1	0	8	0	76	2	9	1	0					
33	1	1	3	3	77	2	9	8	3					
34	1	1	11	2	78	2	10	4	2					
35	1	2	7	1	79	2	11	0	1					
36	1	3	3	0	80	2	11	8	0					
37	1	3	10	3	81	2	12	3	3					
38	1	4	6	2	82	2	12	11	2					
39	1	5	2	1	83	2	13	7	1					
40	1	5	10	0	[84]	2	14	3	0					
41	1	6	5	3	85	2	14	10	3					
42	1	7	1	2	86	2	15	6	2					
43	1	7	9	1	87	2	16	2	1					
44	1	8	5	0	88	2	16	10	0					

Great Hundred

112		3	12	4	0

Grofs

144		4	13	0	0

Wey

256		8	5	4	0

Days in a Year

365		11	15	8	3

Feet in a Rod

272		8	15	8	0

N.	l.	s.	d.	N.	l.	s.	d.	N.	l.	s.	d.
1	0	0	8	45	1	10	0	89	2	19	4
2	0	1	4	46	1	10	8	90	3	0	0
3	0	2	0	47	1	11	4	91	3	0	8
4	0	2	8	48	1	12	0	92	3	1	4
5	0	3	4	49	1	12	8	93	3	2	0
6	0	4	0	50	1	13	4	94	3	2	8
7	0	4	8	51	1	14	0	95	3	3	4
8	0	5	4	52	1	14	8	96	3	4	0
9	0	6	0	53	1	15	4	97	3	4	8
10	0	6	8	54	1	16	0	98	3	5	4
11	0	7	4	55	1	16	8	99	3	6	0
12	0	8	0	[56]	1	17	4	100	3	6	8
13	0	8	8	57	1	18	0	200	6	13	4
14	0	9	4	58	1	18	8	300	10	0	0
15	0	10	0	59	1	19	4	400	13	6	8
16	0	10	8	60	2	0	0	500	16	13	4
17	0	11	4	61	2	0	8	600	20	0	0
18	0	12	0	62	2	1	4	700	23	6	8
19	0	12	8	63	2	2	0	800	26	13	4
20	0	13	4	64	2	2	8	900	30	0	0
21	0	14	0	65	2	3	4	1000	33	6	8
22	0	14	8	66	2	4	0	2000	66	13	4
23	0	15	4	67	2	4	8	3000	100	0	0
24	0	16	0	68	2	5	4	4000	133	6	8
25	0	16	8	69	2	6	0	5000	166	13	4
26	0	17	4	70	2	6	8	6000	200	0	0
27	0	18	0	71	2	7	4	7000	233	6	8
[28]	0	18	8	72	2	8	0	8000	266	13	4
29	0	19	4	73	2	8	8	9000	300	0	0
30	1	0	0	74	2	9	4	10000	333	6	8
31	1	0	8	75	2	10	0				
32	1	1	4	76	2	10	8				
33	1	2	0	77	2	11	4				
34	1	2	8	78	2	12	0				
35	1	3	4	79	2	12	8				

Great Hundred

112	3	14	8

36	1	4	0	80	2	13	4
37	1	4	8	81	2	14	0
38	1	5	4	82	2	14	8
39	1	6	0	83	2	15	4
40	1	6	8	[84]	2	16	0

Grofs

144	4	16	0

Wey

256	8	10	8

41	1	7	4	85	2	16	8
42	1	8	0	86	2	17	4
43	1	8	8	87	2	18	0
44	1	9	4	88	2	18	8

Days in a Year

365	12	3	4

Feet in a Rod

272	9	1	4

N.	l.	s.	d.	q.
1	0	0	8	1
2	0	1	4	2
3	0	2	0	3
4	0	2	9	0
5	0	3	5	1
6	0	4	1	2
7	0	4	9	3
8	0	5	6	0
9	0	6	2	1
10	0	6	10	2
11	0	7	6	3
12	0	8	3	0
13	0	8	11	1
14	0	9	7	2
15	0	10	3	3
16	0	11	0	0
17	0	11	8	1
18	0	12	4	2
19	0	13	0	3
20	0	13	9	0
21	0	14	5	1
22	0	15	1	2
23	0	15	9	3
24	0	16	6	0
25	0	17	2	1
26	0	17	10	2
27	0	18	6	3
[28]	0	19	3	0
29	0	19	11	1
30	1	0	7	2
31	1	1	3	3
32	1	2	0	0
33	1	2	8	1
34	1	3	4	2
35	1	4	0	3
36	1	4	9	0
37	1	5	5	1
38	1	6	1	2
39	1	6	9	3
40	1	7	6	0
41	1	8	2	1
42	1	8	10	2
43	1	9	6	3
44	1	10	3	0
45	1	10	11	1
46	1	11	7	2
47	1	12	3	3
48	1	13	0	0
49	1	13	8	1
50	1	14	4	2
51	1	15	0	3
52	1	15	9	0
53	1	16	5	1
54	1	17	1	2
55	1	17	9	3
[56]	1	18	6	0
57	1	19	2	1
58	1	19	10	2
59	2	0	6	3
60	2	1	3	0
61	2	1	11	1
62	2	2	7	2
63	2	3	3	3
64	2	4	0	0
65	2	4	8	1
66	2	5	4	2
67	2	6	0	3
68	2	6	9	0
69	2	7	5	1
70	2	8	1	2
71	2	8	9	3
72	2	9	6	0
73	2	10	2	1
74	2	10	10	2
75	2	11	6	3
76	2	12	3	0
77	2	12	11	1
78	2	13	7	2
79	2	14	3	3
80	2	15	0	0
81	2	15	8	1
82	2	16	4	2
83	2	17	0	3
[84]	2	17	9	0
85	2	18	5	1
86	2	19	1	2
87	2	19	9	3
88	3	0	6	0
89	3	1	2	1
90	3	1	10	2
91	3	2	6	3
92	3	3	3	0
93	3	3	11	1
94	3	4	7	2
95	3	5	3	3
96	3	6	0	0
97	3	6	8	1
98	3	7	4	2
99	3	8	0	3
100	3	8	9	0
200	6	17	6	0
300	10	6	3	0
400	13	15	0	0
500	17	3	9	0
600	20	12	6	0
700	24	1	3	0
800	27	10	0	0
900	30	18	9	0
1000	34	7	6	0
2000	68	15	0	0
3000	103	2	6	0
4000	137	10	0	0
5000	171	17	6	0
6000	206	5	0	0
7000	240	12	6	0
8000	275	0	0	0
9000	309	7	6	0
10000	343	15	0	0

Great Hundred

112	3	17	0	0
		Grofs		
144	4	19	0	0
		Wey		
256	8	16	0	0
	Days in a Year			
365	12	10	11	1
	Feet in a Rod			
272	9	7	0	0

N.	l.	s.	d.	q.	N.	l.	s.	d.	q.	N.	l.	s.	d.	q.
1	0	0	8	2	45	1	11	10	2	89	3	3	0	2
2	0	1	5	0	46	1	12	7	0	90	3	3	9	0
3	0	2	1	2	47	1	13	3	2	91	3	4	5	2
4	0	2	10	-	48	1	14	0	0	92	3	5	2	0
5	0	3	6	2	49	1	14	8	2	93	3	5	10	2
6	0	4	3	0	50	1	15	5	0	94	3	6	7	0
7	0	4	11	2	51	1	16	1	2	95	3	7	3	2
8	0	5	8	0	52	1	16	10	0	96	3	8	0	0
9	0	6	4	2	53	1	17	6	2	97	3	8	8	2
10	0	7	1	0	54	1	18	3	0	98	3	9	5	0
11	0	7	9	2	55	1	18	11	2	99	3	10	1	2
12	0	8	6	0	[56]	1	19	8	0	100	3	10	10	0
13	0	9	2	2	57	2	0	4	2	200	7	1	8	0
14	0	9	11	0	58	2	1	1	0	300	10	12	6	0
15	0	10	7	2	59	2	1	9	2	400	14	3	4	0
16	0	11	4	0	60	2	2	6	0	500	17	14	2	0
17	0	12	0	2	61	2	3	2	2	600	21	5	0	0
18	0	12	9	0	62	2	3	11	0	700	24	15	10	0
19	0	13	5	2	63	2	4	7	2	800	28	6	8	0
20	0	14	2	0	64	2	5	4	0	900	31	17	6	0
21	0	14	10	2	65	2	6	0	2	1000	35	8	4	0
22	0	15	7	0	66	2	6	9	0	2000	70	16	8	0
23	0	16	3	2	67	2	7	5	2	3000	106	5	0	0
24	0	17	0	0	68	2	8	2	0	4000	141	13	4	0
25	0	17	8	2	69	2	8	10	2	5000	177	1	8	0
26	0	18	5	0	70	2	9	7	0	6000	212	10	0	0
27	0	19	1	2	71	2	10	3	2	7000	247	18	4	0
[28]	0	19	10	0	72	2	11	0	0	8000	283	6	8	0
29	1	0	6	2	73	2	11	8	2	9000	318	15	0	0
30	1	1	3	0	74	2	12	5	0	10000	354	3	4	0
31	1	1	11	2	75	2	13	1	2					
32	1	2	8	0	76	2	13	10	0					
33	1	3	4	2	77	2	14	6	2	*Great Hundred*				
34	1	4	1	0	78	2	15	3	0	112	3	19	4	0
35	1	4	9	2	79	2	15	11	2	*Gross*				
36	1	5	6	0	80	2	16	8	0	144	5	2	0	0
37	1	6	2	2	81	2	17	4	2	*Wey*				
38	1	6	11	0	82	2	18	1	0	256	9	1	4	0
39	1	7	7	2	83	2	18	9	2	*Days in a Year*				
40	1	8	4	0	[84]	2	19	6	0	365	12	18	6	2
41	1	9	0	2	85	3	0	2	2	*Feet in a Rod*				
42	1	9	9	0	86	3	0	11	0	272	9	12	8	0
43	1	10	5	2	87	3	1	7	2					
44	1	11	2	0	88	3	2	4	0					

N.	l.	s.	d.	q.
1	0	0	8	3
2	0	1	5	2
3	0	2	2	1
4	0	2	11	0
5	0	3	7	3
6	0	4	4	2
7	0	5	1	1
8	0	5	10	0
9	0	6	6	3
10	0	7	3	2
11	0	8	0	1
12	0	8	9	0
13	0	9	5	3
14	0	10	2	2
15	0	10	11	1
16	0	11	8	0
17	0	12	4	3
18	0	13	1	2
19	0	13	10	1
20	0	14	7	0
21	0	15	3	3
22	0	16	0	2
23	0	16	9	1
24	0	17	6	0
25	0	18	2	3
26	0	18	11	2
27	0	19	8	1
[28]	1	0	5	0
29	1	1	1	3
30	1	1	10	2
31	1	2	7	1
32	1	3	4	0
33	1	4	0	3
34	1	4	9	2
35	1	5	6	1
36	1	6	3	0
37	1	6	11	3
38	1	7	8	2
39	1	8	5	1
40	1	9	2	0
41	1	9	10	3
42	1	10	7	2
43	1	11	4	1
44	1	12	1	0

N.	l.	s.	d.	q.
45	1	12	9	3
46	1	13	6	2
47	1	14	3	1
48	1	15	0	0
49	1	15	8	3
50	1	16	5	2
51	1	17	2	1
52	1	17	11	0
53	1	18	7	3
54	1	19	4	2
55	2	0	1	1
[56]	2	0	10	0
57	2	1	6	3
58	2	2	3	2
59	2	3	0	1
60	2	3	9	0
61	2	4	5	3
62	2	5	2	2
63	2	5	11	1
64	2	6	8	0
65	2	7	4	3
66	2	8	1	2
67	2	8	10	1
68	2	9	7	0
69	2	10	3	3
70	2	11	0	2
71	2	11	9	1
72	2	12	6	0
73	2	13	2	3
74	2	13	11	2
75	2	14	8	1
76	2	15	5	0
77	2	16	1	3
78	2	16	10	2
79	2	17	7	1
80	2	18	4	0
81	2	19	0	3
82	2	19	9	2
83	3	0	6	1
[84]	3	1	3	0
85	3	1	11	3
86	3	2	8	2
87	3	3	5	1
88	3	4	2	0

N.	l.	s.	d.	q.
89	3	4	10	3
90	3	5	7	2
91	3	6	4	1
92	3	7	1	0
93	3	7	9	3
94	3	8	6	2
95	3	9	3	1
96	3	10	0	0
97	3	10	8	3
98	3	11	5	2
99	3	12	2	1
100	3	12	11	0
200	7	5	10	0
300	10	18	9	0
400	14	11	8	0
500	18	4	7	0
600	21	17	6	0
700	25	10	5	0
800	29	3	4	0
900	32	16	3	0
1000	36	9	2	0
2000	72	18	4	0
3000	109	7	6	0
4000	145	16	6	0
5000	182	5	10	0
6000	218	15	0	0
7000	255	4	2	0
8000	291	13	4	0
9000	328	2	6	0
10000	364	11	8	0

Great Hundred

112	4	1	8	0

Grofs

144	5	5	0	0

Wey

256	9	6	8	0

Days in a Year

365	13	6	1	3

Feet in a Rod

272	9	18	4	0

N.	l.	s.	d.
1	0	0	9
2	0	1	6
3	0	2	3
4	0	3	0
5	0	3	9
6	0	4	6
7	0	5	3
8	0	6	0
9	0	6	9
10	0	7	6
11	0	8	3
12	0	9	0
13	0	9	9
14	0	10	6
15	0	11	3
16	0	12	0
17	0	12	9
18	0	13	6
19	0	14	3
20	0	15	0
21	0	15	9
22	0	16	6
23	0	17	3
24	0	18	0
25	0	18	9
26	0	19	6
27	1	0	3
[28]	1	1	0
29	1	1	9
30	1	2	6
31	1	3	3
32	1	4	0
33	1	4	9
34	1	5	6
35	1	6	3
36	1	7	0
37	1	7	9
38	1	8	6
39	1	9	3
40	1	10	0
41	1	10	9
42	1	11	6
43	1	12	3
44	1	13	0

N.	l.	s.	d.
45	1	13	9
46	1	14	6
47	1	15	3
48	1	16	0
49	1	16	9
50	1	17	6
51	1	18	3
52	1	19	0
53	1	19	9
54	2	0	6
55	2	1	3
[56]	2	2	0
57	2	2	9
58	2	3	6
59	2	4	3
60	2	5	0
61	2	5	9
62	2	6	6
63	2	7	3
64	2	8	0
65	2	8	9
66	2	9	6
67	2	10	3
68	2	11	0
69	2	11	9
70	2	12	6
71	2	13	3
72	2	14	0
73	2	14	9
74	2	15	6
75	2	16	3
76	2	17	0
77	2	17	9
78	2	18	6
79	2	19	3
80	3	0	0
81	3	0	9
82	3	1	6
83	3	2	3
[84]	3	3	0
85	3	3	9
86	3	4	6
87	3	5	3
88	3	6	0

N.	l.	s.	d.
89	3	6	9
90	3	7	6
91	3	8	3
92	3	9	0
93	3	9	9
94	3	10	6
95	3	11	3
96	3	12	0
97	3	12	9
98	3	13	6
99	3	14	3
100	3	15	0
200	7	10	0
300	11	5	0
400	15	0	0
500	18	15	0
600	22	10	0
700	26	5	0
800	30	0	0
900	33	15	0
1000	37	10	0
2000	75	0	0
3000	112	10	0
4000	150	0	0
5000	187	10	0
6000	225	0	0
7000	262	10	0
8000	300	0	0
9000	337	10	0
10000	375	0	0

Great Hundred

112	4	4	0

Grofs

114	5	8	0

Wey

256	9	12	0

Days in a Year

365	13	13	9

Feet in a Rod

272	10	4	0

N.	l.	s.	d.	q.
1	0	0	9	1
2	0	1	6	2
3	0	2	3	3
4	0	3	1	0
5	0	3	10	1
6	0	4	7	2
7	0	5	4	3
8	0	6	2	0
9	0	6	11	1
10	0	7	8	2
11	0	8	5	3
12	0	9	3	0
13	0	10	0	1
14	0	10	9	2
15	0	11	6	3
16	0	12	4	0
17	0	13	1	1
18	0	13	10	2
19	0	14	7	3
20	0	15	5	0
21	0	16	2	1
22	0	16	11	2
23	0	17	8	3
24	0	18	6	0
25	0	19	3	1
26	1	0	0	2
27	1	0	9	3
[28]	1	1	7	0
29	1	2	4	1
30	1	3	1	2
31	1	3	10	3
32	1	4	8	0
33	1	5	5	1
34	1	6	2	2
35	1	6	11	3
36	1	7	9	0
37	1	8	6	1
38	1	9	3	2
39	1	10	0	3
40	1	10	10	0
41	1	11	7	1
42	1	12	4	2
43	1	13	1	3
44	1	13	11	0

N.	l.	s.	d.	q.
45	1	14	8	1
46	1	15	5	2
47	1	16	2	3
48	1	17	0	0
49	1	17	9	1
50	1	18	6	2
51	1	19	3	3
52	2	0	1	0
53	2	0	10	1
54	2	1	7	2
55	2	2	4	3
[56]	2	3	2	0
57	2	3	11	1
58	2	4	8	2
59	2	5	5	3
60	2	6	3	0
61	2	7	0	1
62	2	7	9	2
63	2	8	6	3
64	2	9	4	0
65	2	10	1	1
66	2	10	10	2
67	2	11	7	3
68	2	12	5	0
69	2	13	2	1
70	2	13	11	2
71	2	14	8	3
72	2	15	6	0
73	2	16	3	1
74	2	17	0	2
75	2	17	9	3
76	2	18	7	0
77	2	19	4	1
78	3	0	1	2
79	3	0	10	3
80	3	1	8	0
81	3	2	5	1
82	3	3	2	2
83	3	3	11	3
[84]	3	4	9	0
85	3	5	6	1
86	3	6	3	2
87	3	7	0	3
88	3	7	10	0

N.	l.	s.	d.	q.
89	3	8	7	1
90	3	9	4	2
91	3	10	1	3
92	3	10	11	0
93	3	11	8	1
94	3	12	5	2
95	3	13	2	3
96	3	14	0	0
97	3	14	9	1
98	3	15	6	2
99	3	16	3	3
100	3	17	1	0
200	7	14	2	0
300	11	11	3	0
400	15	8	4	0
500	19	5	5	0
600	23	2	6	0
700	26	19	7	0
800	30	16	8	0
900	34	13	9	0
1000	38	10	10	0
2000	77	1	8	0
3000	115	12	6	0
4000	154	3	4	0
5000	192	14	2	0
6000	231	5	0	0
7000	269	15	10	0
8000	308	6	8	0
9000	346	17	6	0
10000	385	8	4	0

Great Hundred

112	4	6	4	0

Grofs

144	5	11	0	0

Wey

256	9	17	4	0

Days in a Year

365	14	1	4	1

Feet in a Rod

272	10	9	8	0

E

N.	l.	s.	d.	q.
1	0	0	9	2
2	0	1	7	0
3	0	2	4	2
4	0	3	2	0
5	0	3	11	2
6	0	4	9	0
7	0	5	6	2
8	0	6	4	0
9	0	7	1	2
10	0	7	11	0
11	0	8	8	2
12	0	9	6	0
13	0	10	3	2
14	0	11	1	0
15	0	11	10	2
16	0	12	8	0
17	0	13	5	2
18	0	14	3	0
19	0	15	0	2
20	0	15	10	0
21	0	16	7	2
22	0	17	5	0
23	0	18	2	2
24	0	19	0	0
25	0	19	9	2
26	1	0	7	0
27	1	1	4	2
[28]	1	2	2	0
29	1	2	11	2
30	1	3	9	0
31	1	4	6	2
32	1	5	4	0
33	1	6	1	2
34	1	6	11	0
35	1	7	8	2
36	1	8	6	0
37	1	9	3	2
38	1	10	1	0
39	1	10	10	2
40	1	11	8	0
41	1	12	5	2
42	1	13	3	0
43	1	14	0	2
44	1	14	10	0
45	1	15	7	2
46	1	16	5	0
47	1	17	2	2
48	1	18	0	0
49	1	18	9	2
50	1	19	7	0
51	2	0	4	2
52	2	1	2	0
53	2	1	11	2
54	2	2	9	0
55	2	3	6	2
[56]	2	4	4	0
57	2	5	1	2
58	2	5	11	0
59	2	6	8	2
60	2	7	6	0
61	2	8	3	2
62	2	9	1	0
63	2	9	10	2
64	2	10	8	0
65	2	11	5	2
66	2	12	3	0
67	2	13	0	2
68	2	13	10	0
69	2	14	7	2
70	2	15	5	0
71	2	16	2	2
72	2	17	0	0
73	2	17	9	2
74	2	18	7	0
75	2	19	4	2
76	3	0	2	0
77	3	0	11	2
78	3	1	9	0
79	3	2	6	2
80	3	3	4	0
81	3	4	1	2
82	3	4	11	0
83	3	5	8	2
[84]	3	6	6	0
85	3	7	3	2
86	3	8	1	0
87	3	8	10	2
88	3	9	8	0
89	3	10	5	2
90	3	11	3	0
91	3	12	0	2
92	3	12	10	0
93	3	13	7	2
94	3	14	5	0
95	3	15	2	2
96	3	16	0	0
97	3	16	9	2
98	3	17	7	0
99	3	18	4	2
100	3	19	2	0
200	7	18	4	0
300	11	17	6	0
400	15	16	8	0
500	19	15	10	0
600	23	15	0	0
700	27	14	2	0
800	31	13	4	0
900	35	12	6	0
1000	39	11	8	0
2000	79	3	4	0
3000	118	15	0	0
4000	158	6	8	0
5000	197	18	4	0
6000	237	10	0	0
7000	277	1	8	0
8000	316	13	4	0
9000	356	5	0	0
10000	395	16	8	0

Great Hundred

112	4	8	8	0

Grofs

144	5	14	0	0

Wey

256	10	2	8	0

Days in a Year

365	14	8	11	2

Feet in a Rod

272	10	15	4	0

N.	l.	s.	d.	q.	N.	l.	s.	d.	q.	N.	l.	s.	d.	q.
1	0	0	9	3	45	1	16	6	3	89	3	12	3	3
2	0	1	7	2	46	1	17	4	2	90	3	13	1	2
3	0	2	5	1	47	1	18	2	1	91	3	13	11	1
4	0	3	3	0	48	1	19	0	0	92	3	14	9	0
5	0	4	0	3	49	1	19	9	3	93	3	15	6	3
6	0	4	10	2	50	2	0	7	2	94	3	16	4	2
7	0	5	8	1	51	2	1	5	1	95	3	17	2	1
8	0	6	6	0	52	2	2	3	0	96	3	18	0	0
9	0	7	3	3	53	2	3	0	3	97	3	18	9	3
10	0	8	1	2	54	2	3	10	2	98	3	19	7	2
11	0	8	11	1	55	2	4	8	1	99	4	0	5	1
12	0	9	9	0	[56]	2	5	6	0	100	4	1	3	0
13	0	10	6	3	57	2	6	3	3	200	8	2	6	0
14	0	11	4	2	58	2	7	1	2	300	12	3	9	0
15	0	12	2	1	59	2	7	11	1	400	16	5	0	0
16	0	13	0	0	60	2	8	9	0	500	20	6	3	0
17	0	13	9	3	61	2	9	6	3	600	24	7	6	0
18	0	14	7	2	62	2	10	4	2	700	28	8	9	0
19	0	15	5	1	63	2	11	2	1	800	32	10	0	0
20	0	16	3	0	64	2	12	0	0	900	36	11	3	0
21	0	17	0	3	65	2	12	9	3	1000	40	12	6	0
22	0	17	10	2	66	2	13	7	2	2000	81	5	0	0
23	0	18	8	1	67	2	14	5	1	3000	121	17	6	0
24	0	19	6	0	68	2	15	3	0	4000	162	10	0	0
25	1	0	3	3	69	2	16	0	3	5000	203	2	6	0
26	1	1	1	2	70	2	16	10	2	6000	243	15	0	0
27	1	1	11	1	71	2	17	8	1	7000	284	7	6	0
[28]	1	2	9	0	72	2	18	6	0	8000	325	0	0	0
29	1	3	6	3	73	2	19	3	3	9000	365	12	6	0
30	1	4	4	2	74	3	0	1	2	10000	406	5	0	0
31	1	5	2	1	75	3	0	11	1					
32	1	6	0	0	76	3	1	9	0					
33	1	6	9	3	77	3	2	6	3					
34	1	7	7	2	78	3	3	4	2					
35	1	8	5	1	79	3	4	2	1					
36	1	9	3	0	80	3	5	0	0					
37	1	10	0	3	81	3	5	9	3					
38	1	10	10	2	82	3	6	7	2					
39	1	11	8	1	83	3	7	5	1					
40	1	12	6	0	[84]	3	8	3	0					
41	1	13	3	3	85	3	9	0	3					
42	1	14	1	2	86	3	9	10	2					
43	1	14	11	1	87	3	10	8	1					
44	1	15	9	0	88	3	11	6	0					

Great Hundred

112	4	11	0	0

Gross

144	5	17	0	0

Wey

256	10	8	0	0

Days in a Year

365	14	16	6	3

Feet in a Rod

272	11	1	0	0

N.	l.	s.	d.	N.	l.	s.	d.	N.	l.	s.	d.
1	0	0	10	45	1	17	6	89	3	14	2
2	0	1	8	46	1	18	4	90	3	15	0
3	0	2	6	47	1	19	2	91	3	15	10
4	0	3	4	48	2	0	0	92	3	16	8
5	0	4	2	49	2	0	10	93	3	17	6
6	0	5	0	50	2	1	8	94	3	18	4
7	0	5	10	51	2	2	6	95	3	19	2
8	0	6	8	52	2	3	4	96	4	0	0
9	0	7	6	53	2	4	2	97	4	0	10
10	0	8	4	54	2	5	0	98	4	1	8
11	0	9	2	55	2	5	10	99	4	2	6
12	0	10	0	[56]	2	6	8	100	4	3	4
13	0	10	10	57	2	7	6	200	8	6	8
14	0	11	8	58	2	8	4	300	12	10	0
15	0	12	6	59	2	9	2	400	16	13	4
16	0	13	4	60	2	10	0	500	20	16	8
17	0	14	2	61	2	10	10	600	25	0	0
18	0	15	0	62	2	11	8	700	29	3	4
19	0	15	10	63	2	12	6	800	33	6	8
20	0	16	8	64	2	13	4	900	37	10	0
21	0	17	6	65	2	14	2	1000	41	13	4
22	0	18	4	66	2	15	0	2000	83	6	8
23	0	19	2	67	2	15	10	3000	125	0	0
24	1	0	0	68	2	16	8	4000	166	13	4
25	1	0	10	69	2	17	6	5000	208	6	8
26	1	1	8	70	2	18	4	6000	250	0	0
27	1	2	6	71	2	19	2	7000	291	13	4
[28]	1	3	4	72	3	0	0	8000	333	6	8
29	1	4	2	73	3	0	10	9000	375	0	0
30	1	5	0	74	3	1	8	10000	416	13	4
31	1	5	10	75	3	2	6				
32	1	6	8	76	3	3	4				
33	1	7	6	77	3	4	2	Great Hundred			
34	1	8	4	78	3	5	0	112	4	13	4
35	1	9	2	79	3	5	10	Grefs			
36	1	10	0	80	3	6	8	144	6	0	0
37	1	10	10	81	3	7	6	Wey			
38	1	11	8	82	3	8	4	256	10	13	4
39	1	12	6	83	3	9	2	Days in a Year			
40	1	13	4	[84]	3	10	0	365	15	4	2
41	1	14	2	85	3	10	10	Feet in a Rod			
42	1	15	0	86	3	11	8	272	11	6	8
43	1	15	10	87	3	12	6				
44	1	16	8	88	3	13	4				

N.	l.	s.	d.	q.
1	0	0	10	1
2	0	1	8	2
3	0	2	6	3
4	0	3	5.	0
5	0	4	3	1
6	0	5	1	2
7	0	5	11	3
8	0	6	10	0
9	0	7	8	1
10	0	8	6	2
11	0	9	4	3
12	0	10	3	0
13	0	11	1	1
14	0	11	11	2
15	0	12	9	3
16	0	13	8	0
17	0	14	6	1
18	0	15	4	2
19	0	16	2	3
20	0	17	1	0
21	0	17	11	1
22	0	18	9	2
23	0	19	7	3
24	1	0	6	0
25	1	1	4	1
26	1	2	2	2
27	1	3	0	3
[28]	1	3	11	0
29	1	4	9	1
30	1	5	7	2
31	1	6	5	3
32	1	7	4	0
33	1	8	2	1
34	1	9	0	2
35	1	9	10	3
36	1	10	9	0
37	1	11	7	1
38	1	12	5	2
39	1	13	3	3
40	1	14	2	0
41	1	15	0	1
42	1	15	10	2
43	1	16	8	3
44	1	17	7	0

N.	l.	s.	d.	q.
45	1	18	5	1
46	1	19	3	2
47	2	0	1	3
48	2	1	0	0
49	2	1	10	1
50	2	2	8	2
51	2	3	6	3
52	2	4	5	0
53	2	5	3	1
54	2	6	1	2
55	2	6	11	3
[56]	2	7	10	0
57	2	8	8	1
58	2	9	6	2
59	2	10	4	3
60	2	11	3	0
61	2	12	1	1
62	2	12	11	2
63	2	13	9	3
64	2	14	8	0
65	2	15	6	1
66	2	16	4	2
67	2	17	2	3
68	2	18	1	0
69	2	18	11	1
70	2	19	9	2
71	3	0	7	3
72	3	1	6	0
73	3	2	4	1
74	3	3	2	2
75	3	4	0	3
76	3	4	11	0
77	3	5	9	1
78	3	6	7	2
79	3	7	5	3
80	3	8	4	0
81	3	9	2	1
82	3	10	0	2
83	3	10	10	3
[84]	3	11	9	0
85	3	12	7	1
86	3	13	5	2
87	3	14	3	3
88	3	15	2	0

N.	l.	s.	d.	q.
89	3	16	0	1
90	3	16	10	2
91	3	17	8	3
92	3	18	7	0
93	3	19	5	1
94	4	0	3	2
95	4	1	1	3
96	4	2	0	0
97	4	2	10	1
98	4	3	8	2
99	4	4	6	3
100	4	5	5	0
200	8	10	10	0
300	12	16	3	0
400	17	1	8	0
500	21	7	1	0
600	25	12	6	0
700	29	17	11	0
800	34	3	4	0
900	38	8	9	0
1000	42	14	2	0
2000	85	8	4	0
3000	128	2	6	0
4000	170	16	8	0
5000	213	10	10	0
6000	256	5	0	0
7000	298	19	2	0
8000	341	13	4	0
9000	384	7	6	0
10000	427	1	8	0

Great Hundred

112	4	15	8	0

Grefs

144	6	3	0	0

Wey

256	10	18	8	0

Days in a Year

365	15	11	9	1

Feet in a Rod

272	11	12	4	0

E 3

N.	l.	s.	d.	q.	N.	l.	s.	d.	q.	N	l.	s.	d.	q.
1	0	0	10	2	45	1	19	4	2	89	3	17	10	2
2	0	1	9	0	46	2	0	3	0	90	3	18	9	0
3	0	2	7	2	47	2	1	1	2	91	3	19	7	2
4	0	3	6	0	48	2	2	0	0	92	4	0	6	0
5	0	4	4	2	49	2	2	10	2	93	4	1	4	2
6	0	5	3	0	50	2	3	9	0	94	4	2	3	0
7	0	6	1	2	51	2	4	7	2	95	4	3	1	2
8	0	7	0	0	52	2	5	6	0	96	4	4	0	0
9	0	7	10	2	53	2	6	4	2	97	4	4	10	2
10	0	8	9	0	54	2	7	3	0	98	4	5	9	0
11	0	9	7	2	55	2	8	1	2	99	4	6	7	2
12	0	10	6	0	[56]	2	9	0	0	100	4	7	6	0
13	0	11	4	2	57	2	9	10	2	200	8	15	0	0
14	0	12	3	0	58	2	10	9	0	300	13	2	6	0
15	0	13	1	2	59	2	11	7	2	400	17	10	0	0
16	0	14	0	0	60	2	12	6	0	500	21	17	6	0
17	0	14	10	2	61	2	13	4	2	600	26	5	0	0
18	0	15	9	0	62	2	14	3	0	700	30	12	6	0
19	0	16	7	2	63	2	15	1	2	800	35	0	0	0
20	0	17	6	0	64	2	16	0	0	900	39	7	6	0
21	0	18	4	2	65	2	16	10	2	1000	43	15	0	0
22	0	19	3	0	66	2	17	9	0	2000	87	10	0	0
23	1	0	1	2	67	2	18	7	2	3000	131	5	0	0
24	1	1	0	0	68	2	19	6	0	4000	175	0	0	0
25	1	1	10	2	69	3	0	4	2	5000	218	15	0	0
26	1	2	9	0	70	3	1	3	0	6000	262	10	0	0
27	1	3	7	2	71	3	2	1	2	7000	306	5	0	0
[28]	1	4	6	0	72	3	3	0	0	8000	350	0	0	0
29	1	5	4	2	73	3	3	10	2	9000	393	15	0	0
30	1	6	3	0	74	3	4	9	0	10000	437	10	0	0
31	1	7	1	2	75	3	5	7	2					
32	1	8	0	0	76	3	6	6	0					
33	1	8	10	2	77	3	7	4	2	*Great Hundred*				
34	1	9	9	0	78	3	8	3	0	112	4	18	0	0
35	1	10	7	2	79	3	9	1	2	*Grofs*				
36	1	11	6	0	80	3	10	0	0	144	6	6	0	0
37	1	12	4	2	81	3	10	10	2	*Wey*				
38	1	13	3	0	82	3	11	9	0	256	11	4	0	0
39	1	14	1	2	83	3	12	7	2	*Days in a Year*				
40	1	15	0	0	[84]	3	13	6	0	365	15	19	4	2
41	1	15	10	2	85	3	14	4	2	*Feet in a Rod*				
42	1	16	9	0	86	3	15	3	0	272	11	18	0	0
43	1	17	7	2	87	3	16	1	2					
44	1	18	6	0	88	3	17	0	0					

N.	l.	s.	d.	q.
1	0	0	10	3
2	0	1	9	2
3	0	2	8	1
4	0	3	7	0
5	0	4	5	3
6	0	5	4	2
7	0	6	3	1
8	0	7	2	0
9	0	8	0	3
10	0	8	11	2
11	0	9	10	1
12	0	10	9	0
13	0	11	7	3
14	0	12	6	2
15	0	13	5	1
16	0	14	4	0
17	0	15	2	3
18	0	16	1	2
19	0	17	0	1
20	0	17	11	0
21	0	18	9	3
22	0	19	8	2
23	1	0	7	1
24	1	1	6	0
25	1	2	4	3
26	1	3	3	2
27	1	4	2	1
[28]	1	5	1	0
29	1	5	11	3
30	1	6	10	2
31	1	7	9	1
32	1	8	8	0
33	1	9	6	3
34	1	10	5	2
35	1	11	4	1
36	1	12	3	0
37	1	13	1	3
38	1	14	0	2
39	1	14	11	1
40	1	15	10	0
41	1	16	8	3
42	1	17	7	2
43	1	18	6	1
44	1	19	5	0

N.	l.	s.	d.	q.
45	2	0	3	3
46	2	1	2	2
47	2	2	1	1
48	2	3	0	0
49	2	3	10	3
50	2	4	9	2
51	2	5	8	1
52	2	6	7	0
53	2	7	5	3
54	2	8	4	2
55	2	9	3	1
[56]	2	10	2	0
57	2	11	0	3
58	2	11	11	2
59	2	12	10	1
60	2	13	9	0
61	2	14	7	3
62	2	15	6	2
63	2	16	5	1
64	2	17	4	0
65	2	18	2	3
66	2	19	1	2
67	3	0	0	1
68	3	0	11	0
69	3	1	9	3
70	3	2	8	2
71	3	3	7	1
72	3	4	6	0
73	3	5	4	3
74	3	6	3	2
75	3	7	2	1
76	3	8	1	0
77	3	8	11	3
78	3	9	10	2
79	3	10	9	1
80	3	11	8	0
81	3	12	6	3
82	3	13	5	2
83	3	14	4	1
[84]	3	15	3	0
85	3	16	1	3
86	3	17	0	2
87	3	17	11	1
88	3	18	10	0

N.	l.	s.	d.	q.
89	3	19	8	3
90	4	0	7	2
91	4	1	6	1
92	4	2	5	0
93	4	3	3	3
94	4	4	2	2
95	4	5	1	1
96	4	6	0	0
97	4	6	10	3
98	4	7	9	2
99	4	8	8	1
100	4	9	7	0
200	8	19	2	0
300	13	8	9	0
400	17	18	4	0
500	22	7	11	0
600	26	17	6	0
700	31	7	1	0
800	35	16	8	0
900	40	6	3	0
1000	44	15	10	0
2000	89	11	8	0
3000	134	7	6	0
4000	179	3	4	0
5000	223	19	2	0
6000	268	15	0	0
7000	313	10	10	0
8000	358	6	8	0
9000	403	2	6	0
10000	447	18	4	0

Great Hundred

112 | 5 0 4 0

Grofs

144 | 6 9 0 0

Wey

256 | 11 9 4 0

Days in a Year

365 | 16 6 11 3

Feet in a Rod

272 | 12 3 8 0

N.	l.	s.	d.
1	0	0	11
2	0	1	10
3	0	2	9
4	0	3	8
5	0	4	7
6	0	5	6
7	0	6	5
8	0	7	4
9	0	8	3
10	0	9	2
11	0	10	1
12	0	11	0
13	0	11	11
14	0	12	10
15	0	13	9
16	0	14	8
17	0	15	7
18	0	16	6
19	0	17	5
20	0	18	4
21	0	19	3
22	1	0	2
23	1	1	1
24	1	2	0
25	1	2	11
26	1	3	10
27	1	4	9
[28]	1	5	8
29	1	6	7
30	1	7	6
31	1	8	5
32	1	9	4
33	1	10	3
34	1	11	2
35	1	12	1
36	1	13	0
37	1	13	11
38	1	14	10
39	1	15	9
40	1	16	8
41	1	17	7
42	1	18	6
43	1	19	5
44	2	0	4

N.	l.	s.	d.
45	2	1	3
46	2	2	2
47	2	3	1
48	2	4	0
49	2	4	11
50	2	5	10
51	2	6	9
52	2	7	8
53	2	8	7
54	2	9	6
55	2	10	5
[56]	2	11	4
57	2	12	3
58	2	13	2
59	2	14	1
60	2	15	0
61	2	15	11
62	2	16	10
63	2	17	9
64	2	18	8
65	2	19	7
66	3	0	6
67	3	1	5
68	3	2	4
69	3	3	3
70	3	4	2
71	3	5	1
72	3	6	0
73	3	6	11
74	3	7	10
75	3	8	9
76	3	9	8
77	3	10	7
78	3	11	6
79	3	12	5
80	3	13	4
81	3	14	3
82	3	15	2
83	3	16	1
[84]	3	17	0
85	3	17	11
86	3	18	10
87	3	19	9
88	4	0	8

N.	l.	s.	d.
89	4	1	7
90	4	2	6
91	4	3	5
92	4	4	4
93	4	5	3
94	4	6	2
95	4	7	1
96	4	8	0
97	4	8	11
98	4	9	10
99	4	10	9
100	4	11	8
200	9	3	4
300	13	15	0
400	18	6	8
500	22	18	4
600	27	10	0
700	32	1	8
800	36	13	4
900	41	5	0
1000	45	16	8
2000	91	13	4
3000	137	10	0
4000	183	6	8
5000	229	3	4
6000	275	0	0
7000	320	16	8
8000	366	13	4
9000	412	10	0
10000	458	6	8

Great Hundred

112	5	2	8

Gross

144	6	12	0

Wey

256	11	14	8

Days in a Year

365	16	14	7

Feet in a Rod

272	12	9	4

N.	l.	s.	d.	q.
1	0	0	11	1
2	0	1	10	2
3	0	2	9	3
4	0	3	9	0
5	0	4	8	1
6	0	5	7	2
7	0	6	6	3
8	0	7	6	0
9	0	8	5	1
10	0	9	4	2
11	0	10	3	3
12	0	11	3	0
13	0	12	2	1
14	0	13	1	2
15	0	14	0	3
16	0	15	0	0
17	0	15	11	1
18	0	16	10	2
19	0	17	9	3
20	0	18	9	0
21	0	19	8	1
22	1	0	7	2
23	1	1	6	3
24	1	2	6	0
25	1	3	5	1
26	1	4	4	2
27	1	5	3	3
[28]	1	6	3	0
29	1	7	2	1
30	1	8	1	2
31	1	9	0	3
32	1	10	0	0
33	1	10	11	1
34	1	11	10	2
35	1	12	9	3
36	1	13	9	0
37	1	14	8	1
38	1	15	7	2
39	1	16	6	3
40	1	17	6	0
41	1	18	5	1
42	1	19	4	2
43	2	0	3	3
44	2	1	3	0
45	2	2	2	1
46	2	3	1	2
47	2	4	0	3
48	2	5	0	0
49	2	5	11	1
50	2	6	10	2
51	2	7	9	3
52	2	8	9	0
53	2	9	8	1
54	2	10	7	2
55	2	11	6	3
[56]	2	12	6	0
57	2	13	5	1
58	2	14	4	2
59	2	15	3	3
60	2	16	3	0
61	2	17	2	1
62	2	18	1	2
63	2	19	0	3
64	3	0	0	0
65	3	0	11	1
66	3	1	10	2
67	3	2	9	3
68	3	3	9	0
69	3	4	8	1
70	3	5	7	2
71	3	6	6	3
72	3	7	6	0
73	3	8	5	1
74	3	9	4	2
75	3	10	3	3
76	3	11	3	0
77	3	12	2	1
78	3	13	1	2
79	3	14	0	3
80	3	15	0	0
81	3	15	11	1
82	3	16	10	2
83	3	17	9	3
[84]	3	18	9	0
85	3	19	8	1
86	4	0	7	2
87	4	1	6	3
88	4	2	6	0
89	4	3	5	1
90	4	4	4	2
91	4	5	3	3
92	4	6	3	0
93	4	7	2	1
94	4	8	1	2
95	4	9	0	3
96	4	10	0	0
97	4	10	11	1
98	4	11	10	2
99	4	12	9	3
100	4	13	9	0
200	9	7	6	0
300	14	1	3	0
400	18	15	0	0
500	23	8	9	0
600	28	2	6	0
700	32	16	3	9
800	37	10	0	0
900	42	3	9	0
1000	46	17	6	0
2000	93	15	0	0
3000	140	12	6	0
4000	187	10	0	0
5000	234	7	6	0
6000	281	5	0	0
7000	328	2	6	0
8000	375	0	0	0
9000	421	17	6	0
10000	468	15	0	0

Great Hundred
112	5	5	0	0

Grofs
144	6	15	0	0

Wey
256	12	0	0	0

Days in a Year
365	17	2	2	1

Feet in a Rod
272	12	15	0	0

N.	l.	s.	d.	q.
1	0	0	11	2
2	0	1	11	0
3	0	2	10	2
4	0	3	10	0
5	0	4	9	2
6	0	5	9	0
7	0	6	8	2
8	0	7	8	0
9	0	8	7	2
10	0	9	7	0
11	0	10	6	2
12	0	11	6	0
13	0	12	5	2
14	0	13	5	0
15	0	14	4	2
16	0	15	4	0
17	0	16	3	2
18	0	17	3	0
19	0	18	2	2
20	0	19	2	0
21	1	0	1	2
22	1	1	1	0
23	1	2	0	2
24	1	3	0	0
25	1	3	11	2
26	1	4	11	0
27	1	5	10	2
[28]	1	6	10	0
29	1	7	9	2
30	1	8	9	0
31	1	9	8	2
32	1	10	8	0
33	1	11	7	2
34	1	12	7	0
35	1	13	6	2
36	1	14	6	0
37	1	15	5	2
38	1	16	5	0
39	1	17	4	2
40	1	18	4	0
41	1	19	3	2
42	2	0	3	0
43	2	1	2	2
44	2	2	2	0

N.	l.	s.	d.	q.
45	2	3	1	2
46	2	4	1	0
47	2	5	0	2
48	2	6	0	0
49	2	6	11	2
50	2	7	11	0
51	2	8	10	2
52	2	9	10	0
53	2	10	9	2
54	2	11	9	0
55	2	12	8	2
[56]	2	13	8	0
57	2	14	7	2
58	2	15	7	0
59	2	16	6	2
60	2	17	6	0
61	2	18	5	2
62	2	19	5	0
63	3	0	4	2
64	3	1	4	0
65	3	2	3	2
66	3	3	3	0
67	3	4	2	2
68	3	5	2	0
69	3	6	1	2
70	3	7	1	0
71	3	8	0	2
72	3	9	0	0
73	3	9	11	2
74	3	10	11	0
75	3	11	10	2
76	3	12	10	0
77	3	13	9	2
78	3	14	9	0
79	3	15	8	2
80	3	16	8	0
81	3	17	7	2
82	3	18	7	0
83	3	19	6	2
[84]	4	0	6	0
85	4	1	5	2
86	4	2	5	0
87	4	3	4	2
88	4	4	4	0

N.	l.	s.	d.	q.
89	4	5	5	2
90	4	6	3	0
91	4	7	2	2
92	4	8	2	0
93	4	9	1	2
94	4	10	1	0
95	4	11	0	2
96	4	12	0	0
97	4	12	11	2
98	4	13	11	0
99	4	14	10	2
100	4	15	10	0
200	9	11	8	0
300	14	7	6	0
400	19	3	4	0
500	23	19	2	0
600	28	15	0	0
700	33	10	10	0
800	38	6	8	0
900	43	2	6	0
1000	47	18	4	0
2000	95	16	8	0
3000	143	15	0	0
4000	191	13	4	0
5000	239	11	8	0
6000	287	10	0	0
7000	335	8	4	0
8000	383	6	8	0
9000	431	5	0	0
10000	479	3	4	0

Great Hundred

112 | 5 7 4 0

Gross

144 | 6 18 0 0

Wey

256 | 12 5 4 0

Days in a Year

365 | 17 9 9 2

Feet in a Rod

272 | 13 0 8 0

N.	l.	s.	d.	q.	N.	l.	s.	d.	q.	N.	l.	s.	d.	q.
1	0	0	11	3	45	2	4	0	3	89	4	7	1	3
2	0	1	11	2	46	2	5	0	2	90	4	8	1	2
3	0	2	11	1	47	2	6	0	1	91	4	9	1	1
4	0	3	11	0	48	2	7	0	0	92	4	10	1	0
5	0	4	10	3	49	2	7	11	3	93	4	11	0	3
6	0	5	10	2	50	2	8	11	2	94	4	12	0	2
7	0	6	10	1	51	2	9	11	1	95	4	13	0	1
8	0	7	10	0	52	2	10	11	0	96	4	14	0	0
9	0	8	9	3	53	2	11	10	3	97	4	14	11	3
10	0	9	9	2	54	2	12	10	2	98	4	15	11	2
11	0	10	9	1	55	2	13	10	1	99	4	16	11	1
12	0	11	9	0	[56]	2	14	10	0	100	4	17	11	0
13	0	12	8	3	57	2	15	9	3	200	9	15	10	0
14	0	13	8	2	58	2	16	9	2	300	14	13	9	0
15	0	14	8	1	59	2	17	9	1	400	19	11	8	0
16	0	15	8	0	60	2	18	9	0	500	24	9	7	0
17	0	16	7	3	61	2	19	8	3	600	29	7	6	0
18	0	17	7	2	62	3	0	8	2	700	34	5	5	0
19	0	18	7	1	63	3	1	8	1	800	39	3	4	0
20	0	19	7	0	64	3	2	8	0	900	44	1	3	0
21	1	0	6	3	65	3	3	7	3	1000	48	19	2	0
22	1	1	6	2	66	3	4	7	2	2000	97	18	4	0
23	1	2	6	1	67	3	5	7	1	3000	146	17	6	0
24	1	3	6	0	68	3	6	7	0	4000	195	16	8	0
25	1	4	5	3	69	3	7	6	3	5000	244	15	10	0
26	1	5	5	2	70	3	8	6	2	6000	293	15	0	0
27	1	6	5	1	71	3	9	6	1	7000	342	14	2	0
[28]	1	7	5	0	72	3	10	6	0	8000	391	13	4	0
29	1	8	4	3	73	3	11	5	3	9000	440	12	6	0
30	1	9	4	2	74	3	12	5	2	10000	489	11	8	0
31	1	10	4	1	75	3	13	5	1					
32	1	11	4	0	76	3	14	5	0					
33	1	12	3	3	77	3	15	4	3	*Great Hundred*				
34	1	13	3	2	78	3	16	4	2	112	5	9	8	0
35	1	14	3	1	79	3	17	4	1	*Grofs*				
36	1	15	3	0	80	3	18	4	0	144	7	1	0	0
37	1	16	2	3	81	3	19	3	3	*Wey*				
38	1	17	2	2	82	4	0	3	2	256	12	10	8	0
39	1	18	2	1	83	4	1	3	1	*Days in a Year*				
40	1	19	2	0	[84]	4	2	3	0	365	17	17	4	3
41	2	0	1	3	85	4	3	2	3	*Feet in a Rod*				
42	2	1	1	2	86	4	4	2	2	272	13	6	4	0
43	2	2	1	1	87	4	5	2	1					
44	2	3	1	0	88	4	6	2	0					

N.	l.	s.	d.	N.	l.	s.	d.	N.	l.	s.	d.
1	0	1	0	45	2	5	0	89	4	9	0
2	0	2	0	46	2	6	0	90	4	10	0
3	0	3	0	47	2	7	0	91	4	11	0
4	0	4	0	48	2	8	0	92	4	12	0
5	0	5	0	49	2	9	0	93	4	13	0
6	0	6	0	50	2	10	0	94	4	14	0
7	0	7	0	51	2	11	0	95	4	15	0
8	0	8	0	52	2	12	0	96	4	16	0
9	0	9	0	53	2	13	0	97	4	17	0
10	0	10	0	54	2	14	0	98	4	18	0
11	0	11	0	55	2	15	0	99	4	19	0
12	0	12	0	[56]	2	16	0	100	5	0	0
13	0	13	0	57	2	17	0	200	10	0	0
14	0	14	0	58	2	18	0	300	15	0	0
15	0	15	0	59	2	19	0	400	20	0	0
16	0	16	0	60	3	0	0	500	25	0	0
17	0	17	0	61	3	1	0	600	30	0	0
18	0	18	0	62	3	2	0	700	35	0	0
19	0	19	0	63	3	3	0	800	40	0	0
20	1	0	0	64	3	4	0	900	45	0	0
21	1	1	0	65	3	5	0	1000	50	0	0
22	1	2	0	66	3	6	0	2000	100	0	0
23	1	3	0	67	3	7	0	3000	150	0	0
24	1	4	0	68	3	8	0	4000	200	0	0
25	1	5	0	69	3	9	0	5000	250	0	0
26	1	6	0	70	3	10	0	6000	300	0	0
27	1	7	0	71	3	11	0	7000	350	0	0
[28]	1	8	0	72	3	12	0	8000	400	0	0
29	1	9	0	73	3	13	0	9000	450	0	0
30	1	10	0	74	3	14	0	10000	500	0	0
31	1	11	0	75	3	15	0				
32	1	12	0	76	3	16	0				
33	1	13	0	77	3	17	0				
34	1	14	0	78	3	18	0				
35	1	15	0	79	3	19	0				
36	1	16	0	80	4	0	0				
37	1	17	0	81	4	1	0				
38	1	18	0	82	4	2	0				
39	1	19	0	83	4	3	0				
40	2	0	0	[84]	4	4	0				
41	2	1	0	85	4	5	0				
42	2	2	0	86	4	6	0				
43	2	3	0	87	4	7	0				
44	2	4	0	88	4	8	0				

Great Hundred

112	5	12	0

Grofs

144	7	4	0

Wey

256	12	16	0

Days in a Year

365	18	5	0

Feet in a Rod

272	13	12	0

N.	l.	s.	d.	q.
1	0	1	0	1
2	0	2	0	2
3	0	3	0	3
4	0	4	1	0
5	0	5	1	1
6	0	6	1	2
7	0	7	1	3
8	0	8	2	0
9	0	9	2	1
10	0	10	2	2
11	0	11	2	3
12	0	12	3	0
13	0	13	3	1
14	0	14	3	2
15	0	15	3	3
16	0	16	4	0
17	0	17	4	1
18	0	18	4	2
19	0	19	4	3
20	1	0	5	0
21	1	1	5	1
22	1	2	5	2
23	1	3	5	3
24	1	4	6	0
25	1	5	6	1
26	1	6	6	2
27	1	7	6	3
[28]	1	8	7	0
29	1	9	7	1
30	1	10	7	2
31	1	11	7	3
32	1	12	8	0
33	1	13	8	1
34	1	14	8	2
35	1	15	8	3
36	1	16	9	0
37	1	17	9	1
38	1	18	9	2
39	1	19	9	3
40	2	0	10	0
41	2	1	10	1
42	2	2	10	2
43	2	3	10	3
44	2	4	11	0

N.	l.	s.	d.	q.
45	2	5	11	1
46	2	6	11	2
47	2	7	11	3
48	2	9	0	0
49	2	10	0	1
50	2	11	0	2
51	2	12	0	3
52	2	13	1	0
53	2	14	1	1
54	2	15	1	2
55	2	16	1	3
[56]	2	17	2	0
57	2	18	2	1
58	2	19	2	2
59	3	0	2	3
60	3	1	3	0
61	3	2	3	1
62	3	3	3	2
63	3	4	3	3
64	3	5	4	0
65	3	6	4	1
66	3	7	4	2
67	3	8	4	3
68	3	9	5	0
69	3	10	5	1
70	3	11	5	2
71	3	12	5	3
72	3	13	6	0
73	3	14	6	1
74	3	15	6	2
75	3	16	6	3
76	3	17	7	0
77	3	18	7	1
78	3	19	7	2
79	4	0	7	3
80	4	1	8	0
81	4	2	8	1
82	4	3	8	2
83	4	4	8	3
[84]	4	5	9	0
85	4	6	9	1
86	4	7	9	2
87	4	8	9	3
88	4	9	10	0

N.	l.	s.	d.	q.
89	4	10	10	1
90	4	11	10	2
91	4	12	10	3
92	4	13	11	0
93	4	14	11	1
94	4	15	11	2
95	4	16	11	3
96	4	18	0	0
97	4	19	0	1
98	5	0	0	2
99	5	1	0	3
100	5	2	1	0
200	10	4	2	0
300	15	6	3	0
400	20	8	4	0
500	25	10	5	0
600	30	12	6	0
700	35	14	7	0
800	40	16	8	0
900	45	18	9	0
1000	51	0	10	0
2000	102	1	8	0
3000	153	2	6	0
4000	204	3	4	0
5000	255	4	2	0
6000	306	5	0	0
7000	357	5	10	0
8000	408	6	8	0
9000	459	7	6	0
10000	510	8	4	0

Great Hundred

112 | 5 14 4 0

Grofs

144 | 7 7 0 0

Wey

256 | 13 1 4 0

Days in a Year

365 | 18 12 7 1

Feet in a Rod

272 | 13 17 8 0

F

N.	l.	s.	d.	q.	N.	l.	s.	d.	q.	N.	l.	s.	d.	q.
1	0	1	0	2	45	2	6	10	2	89	4	12	8	2
2	0	2	1	0	46	2	7	11	0	90	4	13	9	0
3	0	3	1	2	47	2	8	11	2	91	4	14	9	2
4	0	4	2	0	48	2	10	0	0	92	4	15	10	0
5	0	5	2	2	49	2	11	0	2	93	4	16	10	2
6	0	6	3	0	50	2	12	1	0	94	4	17	11	0
7	0	7	3	2	51	2	13	1	2	95	4	18	11	2
8	0	8	4	0	52	2	14	2	0	96	5	0	0	0
9	0	9	4	2	53	2	15	2	2	97	5	1	0	2
10	0	10	5	0	54	2	16	3	0	98	5	2	1	0
11	0	11	5	2	55	2	17	3	2	99	5	3	1	2
12	0	12	6	0	[56]	2	18	4	0	100	5	4	2	0
13	0	13	6	2	57	2	19	4	2	200	10	8	4	0
14	0	14	7	0	58	3	0	5	0	300	15	12	6	0
15	0	15	7	2	59	3	1	5	2	400	20	16	8	0
16	0	16	8	0	60	3	2	6	0	500	26	0	10	0
17	0	17	8	2	61	3	3	6	2	600	31	5	0	0
18	0	18	9	0	62	3	4	7	0	700	36	9	2	0
19	0	19	9	2	63	3	5	7	2	800	41	13	4	0
20	1	0	10	0	64	3	6	8	0	900	46	17	6	0
21	1	1	10	2	65	3	7	8	2	1000	52	1	8	0
22	1	2	11	0	66	3	8	9	0	2000	104	3	4	0
23	1	3	11	2	67	3	9	9	2	3000	156	5	0	0
24	1	5	0	0	68	3	10	10	0	4000	208	6	8	0
25	1	6	0	2	69	3	11	10	2	5000	260	8	4	0
26	1	7	1	0	70	3	12	11	0	6000	312	10	0	0
27	1	8	1	2	71	3	13	11	2	7000	364	11	8	0
[28]	1	9	2	0	72	3	15	0	0	8000	416	13	4	0
29	1	10	2	2	73	3	16	0	2	9000	468	15	0	0
30	1	11	3	0	74	3	17	1	0	10000	520	16	8	0
31	1	12	3	2	75	3	18	1	2					
32	1	13	4	0	76	3	19	2	0					
33	1	14	4	2	77	4	0	2	2		*Great Hundred*			
34	1	15	5	0	78	4	1	3	0	112	5	16	8	0
35	1	16	5	2	79	4	2	3	2		*Grofs*			
36	1	17	6	0	80	4	3	4	0	144	7	10	0	0
37	1	18	6	2	81	4	4	4	2		*Wey*			
38	1	19	7	0	82	4	5	5	0	256	13	6	8	0
39	2	0	7	2	83	4	6	5	2		*Days in a Year*			
40	2	1	8	0	[84]	4	7	6	0	365	19	0	2	2
41	2	2	8	2	85	4	8	6	2		*Feet in a Rod*			
42	2	3	9	0	86	4	9	7	0	272	14	3	4	0
43	2	4	9	2	87	4	10	7	2					
44	2	5	10	0	88	4	11	8	0					

N.	l.	s.	d.	q.	N.	l.	s.	d.	q.	N.	l.	s.	d.	q.
1	0	1	0	3	45	2	7	9	3	89	4	14	6	3
2	0	2	1	2	46	2	8	10	2	90	4	15	7	2
3	0	3	2	1	47	2	9	11	1	91	4	16	8	1
4	0	4	3	0	48	2	11	0	0	92	4	17	9	0
5	0	5	3	3	49	2	12	0	3	93	4	18	9	3
6	0	6	4	2	50	2	13	1	2	94	4	19	10	2
7	0	7	5	1	51	2	14	2	1	95	5	0	11	1
8	0	8	6	0	52	2	15	3	0	96	5	2	0	0
9	0	9	6	3	53	2	16	3	3	97	5	3	0	3
10	0	10	7	2	54	2	17	4	2	98	5	4	1	2
11	0	11	8	1	55	2	18	5	1	99	5	5	2	1
12	0	12	9	0	[56]	2	19	6	0	100	5	6	3	0
13	0	13	9	3	57	3	0	6	3	200	10	12	6	0
14	0	14	10	2	58	3	1	7	2	300	15	18	9	0
15	0	15	11	1	59	3	2	8	1	400	21	5	0	0
16	0	17	0	0	60	3	3	9	0	500	26	11	3	0
17	0	18	0	3	61	3	4	9	3	600	31	17	6	0
18	0	19	1	2	62	3	5	10	2	700	37	3	9	0
19	1	0	2	1	63	3	6	11	1	800	42	10	0	0
20	1	1	3	0	64	3	8	0	0	900	47	16	3	0
21	1	2	3	3	65	3	9	0	3	1000	53	2	6	0
22	1	3	4	2	66	3	10	1	2	2000	106	5	0	0
23	1	4	5	1	67	3	11	2	1	3000	159	7	6	0
24	1	5	6	0	68	3	12	3	0	4000	212	10	0	0
25	1	6	6	3	69	3	13	3	3	5000	265	12	6	0
26	1	7	7	2	70	3	14	4	2	6000	318	15	0	0
27	1	8	8	1	71	3	15	5	1	7000	371	17	6	0
[28]	1	9	9	0	72	3	16	6	0	8000	425	0	0	0
29	1	10	9	3	73	3	17	6	3	9000	478	2	6	0
30	1	11	10	2	74	3	18	7	2	10000	531	5	0	0
31	1	12	11	1	75	3	19	8	1					
32	1	14	0	0	76	4	0	9	0					
33	1	15	0	3	77	4	1	9	3					
34	1	16	1	2	78	4	2	10	2					
35	1	17	2	1	79	4	3	11	1					
36	1	18	3	0	80	4	5	0	0					
37	1	19	3	3	81	4	6	0	3					
38	2	0	4	2	82	4	7	1	2					
39	2	1	5	1	83	4	8	2	1					
40	2	2	6	0	[84]	4	9	3	0					
41	2	3	6	3	85	4	10	3	3					
42	2	4	7	2	86	4	11	4	2					
43	2	5	8	1	87	4	12	5	1					
44	2	6	9	0	88	4	13	6	0					

Great Hundred

112 | 5 19 0 0

Grofs

144 | 7 13 0 0

Wey

256 | 13 12 0 0

Days in a Year

365 | 19 7 9 3

Feet in a Rod

272 | 14 9 0 0

N.	l.	s.	d.	N.	l.	s.	d.	N.	l.	s.	d.
1	0	1	1	45	2	8	9	89	4	16	5
2	0	2	3	46	2	9	10	90	4	17	6
3	0	3	3	47	2	10	11	91	4	18	7
4	0	4	4	48	2	12	0	92	4	19	8
5	0	5	5	49	2	13	1	93	5	0	9
6	0	6	6	50	2	14	2	94	5	1	10
7	0	7	7	51	2	15	3	95	5	2	11
8	0	8	8	52	2	16	4	96	5	4	0
9	0	9	9	53	2	17	5	97	5	5	1
10	0	10	10	54	2	18	6	98	5	6	2
11	0	11	11	55	2	19	7	99	5	7	3
12	0	13	0	[56]	3	0	8	100	5	8	4
13	0	14	1	57	3	1	9	200	10	16	8
14	0	15	2	58	3	2	10	300	16	5	0
15	0	16	3	59	3	3	11	400	21	13	4
16	0	17	4	60	3	5	0	500	27	1	8
17	0	18	5	61	3	6	1	600	32	10	0
18	0	19	6	62	3	7	2	700	37	18	4
19	1	0	7	63	3	8	3	800	43	6	8
20	1	1	8	64	3	9	4	900	48	15	0
21	1	2	9	65	3	10	5	1000	54	3	4
22	1	3	10	66	3	11	6	2000	108	6	8
23	1	4	11	67	3	12	7	3000	162	10	0
24	1	6	0	68	3	13	8	4000	216	13	4
25	1	7	1	69	3	14	9	5000	270	16	8
26	1	8	2	70	3	15	10	6000	325	0	0
27	1	9	3	71	3	16	11	7000	379	3	4
[28]	1	10	4	72	3	18	0	8000	433	6	8
29	1	11	5	73	3	19	1	9000	487	10	0
30	1	12	6	74	4	0	2	10000	541	13	4
31	1	13	7	75	4	1	3				
32	1	14	8	76	4	2	4				
33	1	15	9	77	4	3	5				
34	1	16	10	78	4	4	6				
35	1	17	11	79	4	5	7				
36	1	19	0	80	4	6	8				
37	2	0	1	81	4	7	9				
38	2	1	2	82	4	8	10				
39	2	2	3	83	4	9	11				
40	2	3	4	[84]	4	11	0				
41	2	4	5	85	4	12	1				
42	2	5	6	86	4	13	2				
43	2	6	7	87	4	14	3				
44	2	7	8	88	4	15	4				

Great Hundred
112 | 6 1 4

Grofs
144 | 7 16 0

Wey
256 | 13 17 4

Days in a Year
365 | 19 15 5

Feet in a Rod
272 | 14 14 8

N.	l.	s.	d.	q.
1	0	1	1	1
2	0	2	2	2
3	0	3	3	3
4	0	4	5	0
5	0	5	6	1
6	0	6	7	2
7	0	7	8	3
8	0	8	10	0
9	0	9	11	1
10	0	11	0	2
11	0	12	1	3
12	0 13	3	0	
13	0	14	4	1
14	0	15	5	2
15	0	16	6	3
16	0	17	8	0
17	0	18	9	1
18	0	19	10	2
19	1	0	11	3
20	1	2	1	0
21	1	3	2	1
22	1	4	3	2
23	1	5	4	3
24	1	6	6	0
25	1	7	7	1
26	1	8	8	2
27	1	9	9	3
[28]	1	10	11	0
29	1	12	0	1
30	1	13	1	2
31	1	14	2	3
32	1	15	4	0
33	1	16	5	1
34	1	17	6	2
35	1	18	7	3
36	1	19	9	0
37	2	0	10	1
38	2	1	11	2
39	2	3	0	3
40	2	4	2	0
41	2	5	3	1
42	2	6	4	2
43	2	7	5	3
44	2	8	7	0

N.	l.	s.	d.	q.
45	2	9	8	1
46	2	10	9	2
47	2	11	10	3
48	2	13	0	0
49	2	14	1	1
50	2	15	2	2
51	2	16	3	3
52	2	17	5	0
53	2	18	6	1
54	2	19	7	2
55	3	0	8	3
[56]	3	1	10	0
57	3	2	11	1
58	3	4	0	2
59	3	5	1	3
60	3	6	3	0
61	3	7	4	1
62	3	8	5	2
63	3	9	6	3
64	3	10	8	0
65	3	11	9	1
66	3	12	10	2
67	3	13	11	3
68	3	15	1	0
69	3	16	2	1
70	3	17	3	2
71	3	18	4	3
72	3	19	6	0
73	4	0	7	1
74	4	1	8	2
75	4	2	9	3
76	4	3	11	0
77	4	5	0	1
78	4	6	1	2
79	4	7	2	3
80	4	8	4	0
81	4	9	5	1
82	4	10	6	2
83	4	11	7	3
[84]	4	12	9	0
85	4	13	10	1
86	4	14	11	2
87	4	16	0	3
88	4	17	2	0

N.	l.	s.	d.	q.
89	4	18	3	1
90	4	19	4	2
91	5	0	5	3
92	5	1	7	0
93	5	2	8	1
94	5	3	9	2
95	5	4	10	3
96	5	6	0	0
97	5	7	1	1
98	5	8	2	2
99	5	9	3	3
100	5	10	5	0
200	11	0	10	0
300	16	11	3	0
400	22	1	8	0
500	27	12	1	0
600	33	2	6	0
700	38	12	11	0
800	44	3	4	0
900	49	13	9	0
1000	55	4	2	0
2000	110	8	4	0
3000	165	12	6	0
4000	220	16	8	0
5000	276	0	10	0
6000	331	5	0	0
7000	386	9	2	0
8000	441	13	4	0
9000	496	17	6	0
10000	552	1	8	0

Great Hundred

112	6	3	8	0

Grofs

144	7	19	0	0

Wey

256	14	2	8	0

Days in a Year

365	20	3	0	1

Feet in a Rod

272	15	0	4	0

N.	l.	s.	d.	q.	N.	l.	s.	d.	q.	N.	l.	s.	d.	q.
1	0	1	1	2	45	2	10	7	2	89	5	0	1	2
2	0	2	3	0	46	2	11	9	0	90	5	1	3	0
3	0	3	4	2	47	2	12	10	2	91	5	2	4	2
4	0	4	6	0	48	2	14	0	0	92	5	3	6	0
5	0	5	7	2	49	2	15	1	2	93	5	4	7	2
6	0	6	9	0	50	2	16	3	0	94	5	5	9	0
7	0	7	10	2	51	2	17	4	2	95	5	6	10	2
8	0	9	0	0	52	2	18	6	0	96	5	8	0	0
9	0	10	1	2	53	2	19	7	2	97	5	9	1	2
10	0	11	3	0	54	3	0	9	0	98	5	10	3	0
11	0	12	4	2	55	3	1	10	2	99	5	11	4	2
12	0	13	6	0	[56]	3	3	0	0	100	5	12	6	0
13	0	14	7	2	57	3	4	1	2	200	11	5	0	0
14	0	15	9	0	58	3	5	3	0	300	16	17	6	0
15	0	16	10	2	59	3	6	4	2	400	22	10	0	0
16	0	18	0	0	60	3	7	6	0	500	28	2	6	0
17	0	19	1	2	61	3	8	7	2	600	33	15	0	0
18	1	0	3	0	62	3	9	9	0	700	39	7	0	0
19	1	1	4	2	63	3	10	10	2	800	45	0	0	0
20	1	2	6	0	64	3	12	0	0	900	50	12	6	0
21	1	3	7	2	65	3	13	1	2	1000	56	5	0	0
22	1	4	9	0	66	3	14	3	0	2000	112	10	0	0
23	1	5	10	2	67	3	15	4	2	3000	168	15	0	0
24	1	7	0	0	68	3	16	6	0	4000	225	0	0	0
25	1	8	1	2	69	3	17	7	2	5000	281	5	0	0
26	1	9	3	0	70	3	18	9	0	6000	337	10	0	0
27	1	10	4	2	71	3	19	10	2	7000	393	15	0	0
[28]	1	11	6	0	72	4	1	0	0	8000	450	0	0	0
29	1	12	7	2	73	4	2	1	2	9000	506	5	0	0
30	1	13	9	0	74	4	3	3	0	10000	562	10	0	0
31	1	14	10	2	75	4	4	4	2					
32	1	16	0	0	76	4	5	6	0					
33	1	17	1	2	77	4	6	7	2					
34	1	18	3	0	78	4	7	9	0					
35	1	19	4	2	79	4	8	10	2					
36	2	0	6	0	80	4	10	0	0					
37	2	1	7	2	81	4	11	1	2					
38	2	2	9	0	82	4	12	3	0					
39	2	3	10	2	83	4	13	4	2					
40	2	5	0	0	[84]	4	14	6	0					
41	2	6	1	2	85	4	15	7	2					
42	2	7	3	0	86	4	16	9	0					
43	2	8	4	2	87	4	17	10	2					
44	2	9	6	0	88	4	19	0	0					

Great Hundred

112. | 6 6 0 0

Grofs

144 | 8 2 0 0

Wey

256 | 14 8 0 0

Days in a Year

365 | 20 10 7 2

Feet in a Rod

272 | 15 6 0 0

N.	l.	s.	d.	q.
1	0	1	1	3
2	0	2	3	2
3	0	3	5	1
4	0	4	7	0
5	0	5	8	3
6	0	6	10	2
7	0	8	0	1
8	0	9	2	0
9	0	10	3	3
10	0	11	5	2
11	0	12	7	1
12	0	13	9	0
13	0	14	10	3
14	0	16	0	2
15	0	17	2	1
16	0	18	4	0
17	0	19	5	3
18	1	0	7	2
19	1	1	9	1
20	1	2	11	0
21	1	4	0	3
22	1	5	2	2
23	1	6	4	1
24	1	7	6	0
25	1	8	7	3
26	1	9	9	2
27	1	10	11	1
[28]	1	12	1	0
29	1	13	2	3
30	1	14	4	2
31	1	15	6	1
32	1	16	8	0
33	1	17	9	3
34	1	18	11	2
35	2	0	1	1
36	2	1	3	0
37	2	2	4	3
38	2	3	6	2
39	2	4	8	1
40	2	5	10	0
41	2	6	11	3
42	2	8	1	2
43	2	9	3	1
44	2	10	5	0

N.	l.	s.	d.	q.
45	2	11	6	3
46	2	12	8	2
47	2	13	10	1
48	2	15	0	0
49	2	16	1	3
50	2	17	3	2
51	2	18	5	1
52	2	19	7	0
53	3	0	8	3
54	3	1	10	2
55	3	3	0	1
56	3	4	2	0
57	3	5	3	3
58	3	6	5	2
59	3	7	7	1
60	3	8	9	0
61	3	9	10	3
62	3	11	0	2
63	3	12	2	1
64	3	13	4	0
65	3	14	5	3
66	3	15	7	2
67	3	16	9	1
68	3	17	11	0
69	3	19	0	3
70	4	0	2	2
71	4	1	4	1
72	4	2	6	0
73	4	3	7	3
74	4	4	9	2
75	4	5	11	1
76	4	7	1	0
77	4	8	2	3
78	4	9	4	2
79	4	10	6	1
80	4	11	8	0
81	4	12	9	3
82	4	13	11	2
83	4	15	1	1
[84]	4	16	3	0
85	4	17	4	3
86	4	18	6	2
87	4	19	8	1
88	5	0	10	0

N.	l.	s.	d.	q.
89	5	1	11	3
90	5	3	1	2
91	5	4	3	1
92	5	5	5	0
93	5	6	6	3
94	5	7	8	2
95	5	8	10	1
96	5	10	0	0
97	5	11	1	3
98	5	12	3	2
99	5	13	5	1
100	5	14	7	0
200	11	9	2	0
300	17	3	9	0
400	22	18	4	0
500	28	12	11	0
600	34	7	6	0
700	40	2	1	0
800	45	16	8	0
900	51	11	3	0
1000	57	5	10	0
2000	114	11	8	0
3000	171	17	6	0
4000	229	3	4	0
5000	286	9	2	0
6000	343	15	0	0
7000	401	0	10	0
8000	458	6	8	0
9000	515	12	6	0
10000	572	18	4	0

Great Hundred

	l.	s.	d.	q.
112	6	8	4	0

Gross

	l.	s.	d.	q.
144	8	5	0	0

Wey

	l.	s.	d.	q.
256	14	13	4	0

Days in a Year

	l.	s.	d.	q.
365	20	18	2	3

Feet in a Rod

	l.	s.	d.	q.
272	15	11	8	0

N.	l.	s.	d.	N.	l.	s.	d.	N.	l.	s.	d.
1	0	1	2	45	2	12	6	89	5	3	10
2	0	2	4	46	2	13	8	90	5	5	0
3	0	3	6	47	2	14	10	91	5	6	2
4	0	4	8	48	2	16	0	92	5	7	4
5	0	5	10	49	2	17	2	93	5	8	6
6	0	7	0	50	2	18	4	94	5	9	8
7	0	8	2	51	2	19	6	95	5	10	10
8	0	9	4	52	3	0	8	96	5	12	0
9	0	10	6	53	3	1	10	97	5	13	2
10	0	11	8	54	3	3	0	98	5	14	4
11	0	12	10	55	3	4	2	99	5	15	6
12	0	14	0	[56]	3	5	4	100	5	16	8
13	0	15	2	57	3	6	6	200	11	13	4
14	0	16	4	58	3	7	8	300	17	10	0
15	0	17	6	59	3	8	10	400	23	6	8
16	0	18	8	60	3	10	0	500	29	3	4
17	0	19	10	61	3	11	2	600	35	0	8
18	1	1	0	62	3	12	4	700	40	16	0
19	1	2	2	63	3	13	6	800	46	13	4
20	1	3	4	64	3	14	8	900	52	10	8
21	1	4	6	65	3	15	10	1000	58	6	8
22	1	5	8	66	3	17	0	2000	116	13	4
23	1	6	10	67	3	18	2	3000	175	0	0
24	1	8	0	68	3	19	4	4000	233	6	8
25	1	9	2	69	4	0	6	5000	291	13	4
26	1	10	4	70	4	1	8	6000	350	0	0
27	1	11	6	71	4	2	10	7000	408	6	8
[28]	1	12	8	72	4	4	0	8000	466	13	4
29	1	13	10	73	4	5	2	9000	525	0	0
30	1	15	0	74	4	6	4	10000	583	6	8
31	1	16	2	75	4	7	6				
32	1	17	4	76	4	8	8				
33	1	18	6	77	4	9	10	*Great Hundred*			
34	1	19	8	78	4	11	0	112	6	10	8
35	2	0	10	79	4	12	2	*Grofs*			
36	2	2	0	80	4	13	4	144	8	8	0
37	2	3	2	81	4	14	6	*Wey*			
38	2	4	4	82	4	15	8	256	14	18	8
39	2	5	6	83	4	16	10	*Days in a Year*			
40	2	6	8	[84]	4	18	0	365	21	5	10
41	2	7	10	85	4	19	2	*Feet in a Rod*			
42	2	9	0	86	5	0	4	272	15	17	4
43	2	10	2	87	5	1	6				
44	2	11	4	88	5	2	8				

N.	l.	s.	d.	q.
1	0	1	2	1
2	0	2	4	2
3	0	3	6	3
4	0	4	9	0
5	0	5	11	1
6	0	7	1	2
7	0	8	3	3
8	0	9	6	0
9	0	10	8	1
10	0	11	10	2
11	0	13	0	3
12	0	14	3	0
13	0	15	5	1
14	0	16	7	2
15	0	17	9	3
16	0	19	0	0
17	1	0	2	1
18	1	1	4	2
19	1	2	6	3
20	1	3	9	0
21	1	4	11	1
22	1	6	1	2
23	1	7	3	3
24	1	8	6	0
25	1	9	8	1
26	1	10	10	2
27	1	12	0	3
[28]	1	13	3	0
29	1	14	5	1
30	1	15	7	2
31	1	16	9	3
32	1	18	0	0
33	1	19	2	1
34	2	0	4	2
35	2	1	6	3
36	2	2	9	0
37	2	3	11	1
38	2	5	1	2
39	2	6	3	3
40	2	7	6	0
41	2	8	8	1
42	2	9	10	2
43	2	11	0	3
44	2	12	3	0

N.	l.	s.	d.	q.
45	2	13	5	1
46	2	14	7	2
47	2	15	9	3
48	2	17	0	0
49	2	18	2	1
50	2	19	4	2
51	3	0	6	3
52	3	1	9	0
53	3	2	11	1
54	3	4	1	2
55	3	5	3	3
[56]	3	6	6	0
57	3	7	8	1
58	3	8	10	2
59	3	10	0	3
60	3	11	3	0
61	3	12	5	1
62	3	13	7	2
63	3	14	9	3
64	3	16	0	0
65	3	17	2	1
66	3	18	4	2
67	3	19	6	3
68	4	0	9	0
69	4	1	11	1
70	4	3	1	2
71	4	4	3	3
72	4	5	6	0
73	4	6	8	1
74	4	7	10	2
75	4	9	0	3
76	4	10	3	0
77	4	11	5	1
78	4	12	7	2
79	4	13	9	3
80	4	15	0	0
81	4	16	2	1
82	4	17	4	2
83	4	18	6	3
[84]	4	19	9	0
85	5	0	11	1
86	5	2	1	2
87	5	3	3	3
88	5	4	6	0

N.	l.	s.	d.	q.
89	5	5	8	1
90	5	6	10	2
91	5	8	0	3
92	5	9	3	0
93	5	10	5	1
94	5	11	7	2
95	5	12	9	3
96	5	14	0	0
97	5	15	2	1
98	5	16	4	2
99	5	17	6	3
100	5	18	9	0
200	11	17	6	0
300	17	16	3	0
400	23	15	0	0
500	29	13	9	0
600	35	12	6	0
700	41	11	3	0
800	47	10	0	0
900	53	8	9	0
1000	59	7	6	0
2000	118	15	0	0
3000	178	2	6	0
4000	237	10	0	0
5000	296	17	6	0
6000	356	5	0	0
7000	415	12	6	0
8000	475	0	0	0
9000	534	7	6	0
10000	593	15	0	0

Great Hundred

112	6	13	0	0

Grofs

144	8	11	0	0

Wey

256	15	4	0	0

Days in a Year

365	21	13	5	1

Feet in a Rod

272	16	3	0	0

N.	l.	s.	d.	q.
1	0	1	2	2
2	0	2	5	0
3	0	3	7	●
4	0	4	10	0
5	0	6	0	2
6	0	7	3	0
7	0	8	5	2
8	0	9	8	0
9	0	10	10	2
10	0	12	1	0
11	0	13	3	2
12	0	14	6	0
13	0	15	8	2
14	0	16	11	0
15	0	18	1	2
16	0	19	4	0
17	1	0	6	2
18	1	1	9	0
19	1	2	11	2
20	1	4	2	0
21	1	5	4	2
22	1	6	7	0
23	1	7	9	2
24	1	9	0	0
25	1	10	2	2
26	1	11	5	0
27	1	12	7	2
[28]	1	13	10	0
29	1	15	0	2
30	1	16	3	0
31	1	17	5	2
32	1	18	8	0
33	1	19	10	2
34	2	1	1	0
35	2	2	3	2
36	2	3	6	0
37	2	4	8	2
38	2	5	11	0
39	2	7	1	2
40	2	8	4	0
41	2	9	6	2
42	2	10	9	0
43	2	11	11	2
44	2	13	2	0

N.	l.	s.	d.	q.
45	2	14	4	2
46	2	15	7	0
47	2	16	9	2
48	2	18	0	0
49	2	19	2	2
50	3	0	5	0
51	3	1	7	2
52	3	2	10	0
53	3	4	0	2
54	3	5	3	0
55	3	6	5	2
[56]	3	7	8	0
57	3	8	10	2
58	3	10	1	0
59	3	11	3	2
60	3	12	6	0
61	3	13	8	2
62	3	14	11	0
63	3	16	1	2
64	3	17	4	0
65	3	18	6	2
66	3	19	9	0
67	4	0	11	2
68	4	2	2	0
69	4	3	4	2
70	4	4	7	0
71	4	5	9	2
72	4	7	0	0
73	4	8	2	2
74	4	9	5	0
75	4	10	7	2
76	4	11	10	0
77	4	13	0	2
78	4	14	3	0
79	4	15	5	2
80	4	16	8	0
81	4	17	10	2
82	4	19	1	0
83	5	0	3	2
[84]	5	1	6	0
85	5	2	8	2
86	5	3	11	0
87	5	5	1	2
88	5	6	4	0

N.	l.	s.	d.	q.
89	5	7	6	2
90	5	8	9	0
91	5	9	11	2
92	5	11	2	0
93	5	12	4	2
94	5	13	7	0
95	5	14	9	2
96	5	16	0	0
97	5	17	2	2
98	5	18	5	0
99	5	19	7	2
100	6	0	10	0
200	12	1	8	0
300	18	2	6	0
400	24	3	4	0
500	30	4	2	0
600	36	5	0	0
700	42	5	10	0
800	48	6	8	0
900	54	7	6	0
1000	60	8	4	0
2000	120	16	8	0
3000	181	5	0	0
4000	241	13	4	0
5000	302	1	8	0
6000	362	10	0	0
7000	422	18	4	0
8000	483	6	8	0
9000	543	15	0	0
10000	604	3	4	0

Great Hundred

112 | 6 15 4 0

Grofs

144 | 8 14 0 0

Wey

256 | 15 9 4 0

Days in a Year

365 | 22 1 0 2

Feet in a Rod

272 | 16 8 8 0

N.	l.	s.	d.	q.	N.	l.	s.	d.	q.	N.	l.	s.	d.	q.
1	0	1	2	3	45	2	15	3	3	89	5	9	4	3
2	0	2	5	2	46	2	16	6	2	90	5	10	7	2
3	0	3	8	1	47	2	17	9	1	91	5	11	10	1
4	0	4	11	0	48	2	19	0	0	92	5	13	1	0
5	0	6	1	3	49	3	0	2	3	93	5	14	3	3
6	0	7	4	2	50	3	1	5	2	94	5	15	6	2
7	0	8	7	1	51	3	2	8	1	95	5	16	9	1
8	0	9	10	0	52	3	3	11	0	96	5	18	0	0
9	0	11	0	3	53	3	5	1	3	97	5	19	2	3
10	0	12	3	2	54	3	6	4	2	98	6	0	5	2
11	0	13	6	1	55	3	7	7	1	99	6	1	8	1
12	0	14	9	0	[56]	3	8	10	0	100	6	2	11	0
13	0	15	11	3	57	3	10	0	3	200	12	5	10	0
14	0	17	2	2	58	3	11	3	2	300	18	8	9	0
15	0	18	5	1	59	3	12	6	1	400	24	11	8	0
16	0	19	8	0	60	3	13	9	0	500	30	14	7	0
17	1	0	10	3	61	3	14	11	3	600	36	17	6	0
18	1	2	1	2	62	3	16	2	2	700	43	0	5	0
19	1	3	4	1	63	3	17	5	1	800	49	3	4	0
20	1	4	7	0	64	3	18	8	0	900	55	6	3	0
21	1	5	9	3	65	3	19	10	3	1000	61	9	2	0
22	1	7	0	2	66	4	1	1	2	2000	122	18	4	0
23	1	8	3	1	67	4	2	4	1	3000	184	7	6	0
24	1	9	6	0	68	4	3	7	0	4000	245	16	8	0
25	1	10	8	3	69	4	4	9	3	5000	307	5	10	0
26	1	11	11	2	70	4	6	0	2	6000	368	15	0	0
27	1	13	2	1	71	4	7	3	1	7000	430	4	2	0
[28]	1	14	5	0	72	4	8	6	0	8000	491	13	4	0
29	1	15	7	3	73	4	9	8	3	9000	553	2	6	0
30	1	16	10	2	74	4	10	11	2	10000	614	16	8	0
31	1	18	1	1	75	4	12	2	1					
32	1	19	4	0	76	4	13	5	0					
33	2	0	6	3	77	4	14	7	3	*Great Hundred*				
34	2	1	9	2	78	4	15	10	2	112	6	17	8	0
35	2	3	0	1	79	4	17	1	1	*Grofs*				
36	2	4	3	0	80	4	18	4	0	144	8	17	0	0
37	2	5	5	3	81	4	19	6	3	*Wey*				
38	2	6	8	2	82	5	0	9	2	256	15	14	8	0
39	2	7	11	1	83	5	2	0	1	*Days in a Year*				
40	2	9	2	0	[84]	5	3	3	0	365	22	8	7	3
41	2	10	4	3	85	5	4	5	3	*Feet in a Rod*				
42	2	11	7	2	86	5	5	8	2	272	16	14	4	0
43	2	12	10	1	87	5	6	11	1					
44	2	14	1	0	88	5	8	2	0					

N.	l.	s.	d.	N.	l.	s.	d.	N.	l.	s.	d.
1	0	1	3	45	2	16	3	89	5	11	3
2	0	2	6	46	2	17	6	90	5	12	6
3	0	3	9	47	2	18	9	91	5	13	9
4	0	5	0	48	3	0	0	92	5	15	0
5	0	6	3	49	3	1	3	93	5	16	3
6	0	7	6	50	3	2	6	94	5	17	6
7	0	8	9	51	3	3	9	95	5	18	9
8	0	10	0	52	3	5	0	96	6	0	0
9	0	11	3	53	3	6	3	97	6	1	3
10	0	12	6	54	3	7	6	98	6	2	6
11	0	13	9	55	3	8	9	99	6	3	9
12	0	15	0	[56]	3	10	0	100	6	5	0
13	0	16	3	57	3	11	3	200	12	10	0
14	0	17	6	58	3	12	6	300	18	15	0
15	0	18	9	59	3	13	9	400	25	0	0
16	1	0	0	60	3	15	0	500	31	5	0
17	1	1	3	61	3	16	3	600	37	10	0
18	1	2	6	62	3	17	6	700	43	15	0
19	1	3	9	63	3	18	9	800	50	0	0
20	1	5	0	64	4	0	0	900	56	5	0
21	1	6	3	65	4	1	3	1000	62	10	0
22	1	7	6	66	4	2	6	2000	125	0	0
23	1	8	9	67	4	3	9	3000	187	10	0
24	1	10	0	68	4	5	0	4000	250	0	0
25	1	11	3	69	4	6	3	5000	312	10	0
26	1	12	6	70	4	7	6	6000	375	0	0
27	1	13	9	71	4	8	9	7000	437	10	0
[28]	1	15	0	72	4	10	0	8000	500	0	0
29	1	16	3	73	4	11	3	9000	562	10	0
30	1	17	6	74	4	12	6	10000	625	0	0
31	1	18	9	75	4	13	9				
32	2	0	0	76	4	15	0				
33	2	1	3	77	4	16	3	*Great Hundred*			
34	2	2	6	78	4	17	6	112	7	0	0
35	2	3	9	79	4	18	9	*Groſs*			
36	2	5	0	80	5	0	0	144	9	0	0
37	2	6	3	81	5	1	3	*Wey*			
38	2	7	6	82	5	2	6	256	16	0	0
39	2	8	9	83	5	3	9	*Days in a Year*			
40	2	10	0	[84]	5	5	0	365	22	16	3
41	2	11	3	85	5	6	3	*Feet in a Rod*			
42	2	12	6	86	5	7	6	272	17	0	0
43	2	13	9	87	5	8	9				
44	2	15	0	88	5	10	0				

N.	l.	s.	d.	q.
1	0	1	3	1
2	0	2	6	2
3	0	3	9	3
4	0	5	1	0
5	0	6	4	1
6	0	7	7	2
7	0	8	10	3
8	0	10	2	0
9	0	11	5	1
10	0	12	8	2
11	0	13	11	3
12	0	15	3	0
13	0	16	6	1
14	0	17	9	2
15	0	19	0	3
16	1	0	4	0
17	1	1	7	1
18	1	2	10	2
19	1	4	1	3
20	1	5	5	0
21	1	6	8	1
22	1	7	11	2
23	1	9	2	3
24	1	10	6	0
25	1	11	9	1
26	1	13	0	2
27	1	14	3	3
[28]	1	15	7	0
29	1	16	10	1
30	1	18	1	2
31	1	19	4	3
32	2	0	8	0
33	2	1	11	1
34	2	3	2	2
35	2	4	5	3
36	2	5	9	0
37	2	7	0	1
38	2	8	3	2
39	2	9	6	3
40	2	10	10	0
41	2	12	1	1
42	2	13	4	2
43	2	14	7	3
44	2	15	11	0

N.	l.	s.	d.	q.
45	2	17	2	1
46	2	18	5	2
47	2	19	8	3
48	3	1	0	0
49	3	2	3	1
50	3	3	6	2
51	3	4	9	3
52	3	6	1	0
53	3	7	4	1
54	3	8	7	2
55	3	9	10	3
[56]	3	11	2	0
57	3	12	5	1
58	3	13	8	2
59	3	14	11	3
60	3	16	3	0
61	3	17	6	1
62	3	18	9	2
63	4	0	0	3
64	4	1	4	0
65	4	2	7	1
66	4	3	10	2
67	4	5	1	3
68	4	6	5	0
69	4	7	8	1
70	4	8	11	2
71	4	10	2	3
72	4	11	6	0
73	4	12	9	1
74	4	14	0	2
75	4	15	3	3
76	4	16	7	0
77	4	17	10	1
78	4	19	1	2
79	5	0	4	3
80	5	1	8	0
81	5	2	11	1
82	5	4	2	2
83	5	5	5	3
[84]	5	6	9	0
85	5	8	0	1
86	5	9	3	2
87	5	10	6	3
88	5	11	10	0

N.	l.	s.	d.	q.
89	5	13	1	1
90	5	14	4	2
91	5	15	7	3
92	5	16	11	0
93	5	18	2	1
94	5	19	5	2
95	6	0	8	3
96	6	2	0	0
97	6	3	3	1
98	6	4	6	2
99	6	5	9	3
100	6	7	1	0
200	12	14	2	0
300	19	1	3	0
400	25	8	4	0
500	31	15	5	0
600	38	2	6	0
700	44	9	7	0
800	50	16	8	0
900	57	3	9	0
1000	63	10	10	0
2000	127	1	8	0
3000	190	12	6	0
4000	254	3	4	0
5000	317	14	2	0
6000	381	5	0	0
7000	444	15	10	0
8000	508	6	8	0
9000	571	17	6	0
10000	635	8	4	0

Great Hundred

112 | 7 2 4 0

Grofs

144 | 9 3 0 0

Wey

256 | 16 5 4 0

Days in a Year

365 | 23 3 10 1

Feet in a Rod

272 | 17 5 8 0

N.	l.	s.	d.	q	N.	l.	s.	d.	q	N.	l.	s.	d.	q
1	0	1	3	2	45	2	18	1	2	89	5	14	11	2
2	0	2	7	0	46	2	19	5	0	90	5	16	3	0
3	0	3	10	2	47	3	0	8	2	91	5	17	6	2
4	0	5	2	0	48	3	2	0	0	92	5	18	10	0
5	0	6	5	2	49	3	3	3	2	93	6	0	1	2
6	0	7	9	0	50	3	4	7	0	94	6	1	5	0
7	0	9	0	2	51	3	5	10	2	95	6	2	8	2
8	0	10	4	0	52	3	7	2	0	96	6	4	0	0
9	0	11	7	2	53	3	8	5	2	97	6	5	3	2
10	0	12	11	0	54	3	9	9	0	98	6	6	7	0
11	0	14	2	2	55	3	11	0	2	99	6	7	10	2
12	0	15	6	0	[56]	3	12	4	0	100	6	9	2	0
13	0	16	9	2	57	3	13	7	2	200	12	18	4	0
14	0	18	1	0	58	3	14	11	0	300	19	7	6	0
15	0	19	4	2	59	3	16	2	2	400	25	16	8	0
16	1	0	8	0	60	3	17	6	0	500	32	5	10	0
17	1	1	11	2	61	3	18	9	2	600	38	15	0	0
18	1	3	3	0	62	4	0	1	0	700	45	4	2	0
19	1	4	6	2	63	4	1	4	2	800	51	13	4	0
20	1	5	10	0	64	4	2	8	0	900	58	2	6	0
21	1	7	1	2	65	4	3	11	2	1000	64	11	8	0
22	1	8	5	0	66	4	5	3	0	2000	129	3	4	0
23	1	9	8	2	67	4	6	6	2	3000	193	15	0	0
24	1	11	0	0	68	4	7	10	0	4000	258	6	8	0
25	1	12	3	2	69	4	9	1	2	5000	322	18	4	0
26	1	13	7	0	70	4	10	5	0	6000	387	10	0	0
27	1	14	10	2	71	4	11	8	2	7000	452	1	8	0
[28]	1	16	2	0	72	4	13	0	0	8000	516	13	4	0
29	1	17	5	2	73	4	14	3	2	9000	581	5	0	0
30	1	18	9	0	74	4	15	7	0	10000	645	16	8	0
31	2	0	0	2	75	4	16	10	2					
32	2	1	4	0	76	4	18	2	0					
33	2	2	7	2	77	4	19	5	2			*Great Hundred*		
34	2	3	11	0	78	5	0	9	0	112	7	4	8	0
35	2	5	2	2	79	5	2	0	2			*Grofs*		
36	2	6	6	0	80	5	3	4	0	144	9	6	0	0
37	2	7	9	2	81	5	4	7	2			*Wey*		
38	2	9	1	0	82	5	5	11	0	256	16	10	8	0
39	2	10	4	2	83	5	7	2	2			*Days in a Year*		
40	2	11	8	0	[84]	5	8	6	0	365	23	11	5	2
41	2	12	11	2	85	5	9	9	2			*Feet in a Rod*		
42	2	14	3	0	86	5	11	1	0	272	17	11	4	0
43	2	15	6	2	87	5	12	4	2					
44	2	16	10	0	88	5	13	8	0					

N.	l.	s.	d.	q.	N.	l.	s.	d.	q.	N.	l.	s.	d.	q.
1	0	1	3	3	45	2	19	0	3	89	5	16	9	3
2	0	2	7	2	46	3	0	4	2	90	5	18	1	2
3	0	3	11	1	47	3	1	8	1	91	5	19	5	1
4	0	5	3	0	48	3	3	0	0	92	6	0	9	0
5	0	6	6	3	49	3	4	3	3	93	6	2	0	3
6	0	7	10	2	50	3	5	7	2	94	6	3	4	2
7	0	9	2	1	51	3	6	11	1	95	6	4	8	1
8	0	10	6	0	52	3	8	3	0	96	6	6	0	0
9	0	11	9	3	53	3	9	6	3	97	6	7	3	3
10	0	13	1	2	54	3	10	10	2	98	6	8	7	2
11	0	14	5	1	55	3	12	2	1	99	6	9	11	1
12	0	15	9	0	[56]	3	13	6	0	100	6	11	3	0
13	0	17	0	3	57	3	14	9	3	200	13	2	6	0
14	0	18	4	2	58	3	16	1	2	300	19	13	9	0
15	0	19	8	1	59	3	17	5	1	400	26	5	0	0
16	1	1	0	0	60	3	18	9	0	500	32	10	3	0
17	1	2	3	3	61	4	0	0	3	600	39	7	6	0
18	1	3	7	2	62	4	1	4	2	700	45	18	9	0
19	1	4	11	1	63	4	2	8	1	800	52	10	0	0
20	1	6	3	0	64	4	4	0	0	900	59	1	3	0
21	1	7	6	3	65	4	5	3	3	1000	65	12	6	0
22	1	8	10	2	66	4	6	7	2	2000	131	5	0	0
23	1	10	2	1	67	4	7	11	1	3000	196	17	6	0
24	1	11	6	0	68	4	9	3	0	4000	262	10	0	0
25	1	12	9	3	69	4	10	6	3	5000	328	2	6	0
26	1	14	1	2	70	4	11	10	2	6000	393	15	0	0
27	1	15	5	1	71	4	13	2	1	7000	459	7	6	0
[28]	1	16	9	0	72	4	14	6	0	8000	525	0	0	0
29	1	18	0	3	73	4	15	9	3	9000	590	12	6	0
30	1	19	4	2	74	4	17	1	2	10000	656	5	0	0
31	2	0	8	1	75	4	18	5	1					
32	2	2	0	0	76	4	19	9	0					
33	2	3	3	3	77	5	1	0	3		*Great Hundred*			
34	2	4	7	2	78	5	2	4	2	112	7	7	0	0
35	2	5	11	1	79	5	3	8	1		*Grofs*			
36	2	7	3	0	80	5	5	0	0	144	9	9	0	0
37	2	8	6	3	81	5	6	3	3		*Wey*			
38	2	9	10	2	82	5	7	7	2	256	16	16	0	0
39	2	11	2	1	83	5	8	11	1		*Days in a Year*			
40	2	12	6	0	[84]	5	10	3	0	365	23	19	0	3
41	2	13	9	3	85	5	11	6	3		*Feet in a Rod*			
42	2	15	1	2	86	5	12	10	2	272	17	17	0	0
43	2	16	5	1	87	5	14	2	1					
44	2	17	9	0	88	5	15	6	0					

N.	l.	s.	d.	N.	l.	s.	d.	N.	l.	s.	d.
1	0	1	4	45	3	0	0	89	5	18	8
2	0	2	8	46	3	1	4	90	6	0	0
3	0	4	0	47	3	2	8	91	6	1	4
4	0	5	4	48	3	4	0	92	6	2	8
5	0	6	8	49	3	5	4	93	6	4	0
6	0	8	0	50	3	6	8	94	6	5	4
7	0	9	4	51	3	8	0	95	6	6	8
8	0	10	8	52	3	9	4	96	6	8	0
9	0	12	0	53	3	10	8	97	6	9	4
10	0	13	4	54	3	12	0	98	6	10	8
11	0	14	8	55	3	13	4	99	6	12	0
12	0	16	0	[56]	3	14	8	100	6	13	4
13	0	17	4	57	3	16	0	200	13	6	8
14	0	18	8	58	3	17	4	300	20	0	0
15	1	0	0	59	3	18	8	400	26	13	4
16	1	1	4	60	4	0	0	500	33	6	8
17	1	2	8	61	4	1	4	600	40	0	0
18	1	4	0	62	4	2	8	700	46	13	4
19	1	5	4	63	4	4	0	800	53	6	8
20	1	6	8	64	4	5	4	900	60	0	0
21	1	8	0	65	4	6	8	1000	66	13	4
22	1	9	4	66	4	8	0	2000	133	6	8
23	1	10	8	67	4	9	4	3000	200	0	0
24	1	12	0	68	4	10	8	4000	266	13	4
25	1	13	4	69	4	12	0	5000	333	6	8
26	1	14	8	70	4	13	4	6000	400	0	0
27	1	16	0	71	4	14	8	7000	466	13	4
[28]	1	17	4	72	4	16	0	8000	533	6	8
29	1	18	8	73	4	17	4	9000	600	0	0
30	2	0	0	74	4	18	8	10000	666	13	4
31	2	1	4	75	5	0	0				
32	2	2	8	76	5	1	4				
33	2	4	0	77	5	2	8	Great Hundred			
34	2	5	4	78	5	4	0	112	7	9	4
35	2	6	8	79	5	5	4	Gross			
36	2	8	0	80	5	6	8	144	9	12	0
37	2	9	4	81	5	8	0	Hay.			
38	2	10	8	82	5	9	4	256	17	1	4
39	2	12	0	83	5	10	8	Days in a Year			
40	2	13	4	[84]	5	12	0	365	24	6	8
41	2	14	8	85	5	13	4	Feet in a Rod			
42	2	16	0	86	5	14	8	272	18	2	8
43	2	17	4	87	5	16	0				
44	2	18	8	88	5	17	4				

N.	l.	s.	d.	q.	N.	l.	s.	d.	q.	N.	l.	s.	d.	q.
1	0	1	4	1	45	3	0	11	1	89	6	0	6	1
2	0	2	8	2	46	3	2	3	2	90	6	1	10	2
3	0	4	0	3	47	3	3	7	3	91	6	3	2	3
4	0	5	5	0	48	3	5	0	0	92	6	4	7	0
5	0	6	9	1	49	3	6	4	1	93	6	5	11	1
6	0	8	1	2	50	3	7	8	2	94	6	7	3	2
7	0	9	5	3	51	3	9	0	3	95	6	8	7	3
8	0	10	10	0	52	3	10	5	0	96	6	10	0	0
9	0	12	2	1	53	3	11	9	1	97	6	11	4	1
10	0	13	6	2	54	3	13	1	2	98	6	12	8	2
11	0	14	10	3	55	3	14	5	3	99	6	14	0	3
12	0	16	3	0	[56]	3	15	10	0	100	6	15	5	0
13	0	17	7	1	57	3	17	2	1	200	13	10	10	0
14	0	18	11	2	58	3	18	6	2	300	20	6	3	0
15	1	0	3	3	59	3	19	10	3	400	27	1	8	0
16	1	1	8	0	60	4	1	3	0	500	33	17	1	0
17	1	3	0	1	61	4	2	7	1	600	40	12	6	0
18	1	4	4	2	62	4	3	11	2	700	47	7	11	0
19	1	5	8	3	63	4	5	3	3	800	54	3	4	0
20	1	7	1	0	64	4	6	8	0	900	60	18	9	0
21	1	8	5	1	65	4	8	0	1	1000	67	14	2	0
22	1	9	9	2	66	4	9	4	2	2000	135	8	4	0
23	1	11	1	3	67	4	10	8	3	3000	203	2	6	0
24	1	12	6	0	68	4	12	1	0	4000	270	16	8	0
25	1	13	10	1	69	4	13	5	1	5000	338	10	10	0
26	1	15	2	2	70	4	14	9	2	6000	406	5	0	0
27	1	16	6	3	71	4	16	1	3	7000	473	19	2	0
[28]	1	17	11	0	72	4	17	6	0	8000	541	13	4	0
29	1	19	3	1	73	4	18	10	1	9000	609	7	6	0
30	2	0	7	2	74	5	0	2	2	10000	677	1	8	0
31	2	1	11	3	75	5	1	6	3					
32	2	3	4	0	76	5	2	11	0					
33	2	4	8	1	77	5	4	3	1	Great Hundred				
34	2	6	0	2	78	5	5	7	2	112	7	11	8	0
35	2	7	4	3	79	5	6	11	3	Grofs				
36	2	8	9	0	80	5	8	4	0	144	9	15	0	0
37	2	10	1	1	81	5	9	8	1	Wey				
38	2	11	5	2	82	5	11	0	2	256	17	6	8	0
39	2	12	9	3	83	5	12	4	3	Days in a Year				
40	2	14	2	0	[84]	5	13	9	0	365	24	14	3	1
41	2	15	6	1	85	5	15	1	1	Feet in a Rod				
42	2	16	10	2	86	5	16	5	2	272	18	8	4	0
43	2	18	2	3	87	5	17	9	3					
44	2	19	7	0	88	5	19	2	0					

N.	l.	s.	d.	q.	N.	l.	s.	d.	q.	N.	l.	s.	d.	q.
1	0	1	4	2	45	3	1	10	2	89	6	2	4	2
2	0	2	9	0	46	3	3	3	0	90	6	3	9	0
3	0	4	1	2	47	3	4	7	2	91	6	5	1	2
4	0	5	6	0	48	3	6	0	0	92	6	6	6	0
5	0	6	10	2	49	3	7	4	2	93	6	7	10	2
6	0	8	3	0	50	3	8	9	0	94	6	9	3	0
7	0	9	7	2	51	3	10	1	2	95	6	10	7	2
8	0	11	0	0	52	3	11	6	0	96	6	12	0	0
9	0	12	4	2	53	3	12	10	2	97	6	13	4	2
10	0	13	9	0	54	3	14	3	0	98	6	14	9	0
11	0	15	1	2	55	3	15	7	2	99	6	16	1	2
12	0	16	6	0	[56]	3	17	0	0	100	6	17	6	0
13	0	17	10	2	57	3	18	4	2	200	13	15	0	0
14	0	19	3	0	58	3	19	9	0	300	20	12	6	0
15	1	0	7	2	59	4	1	1	2	400	27	10	0	0
16	1	2	0	0	60	4	2	6	0	500	34	7	6	0
17	1	3	4	2	61	4	3	10	2	600	41	5	0	0
18	1	4	9	0	62	4	5	3	0	700	48	2	6	0
19	1	6	1	2	63	4	6	7	2	800	55	0	0	0
20	1	7	6	0	64	4	8	0	0	900	61	17	6	0
21	1	8	10	2	65	4	9	4	2	1000	68	15	0	0
22	1	10	3	0	66	4	10	9	0	2000	137	10	0	0
23	1	11	7	2	67	4	12	1	2	3000	206	5	0	0
24	1	13	0	0	68	4	13	6	0	4000	275	0	0	0
25	1	14	4	2	69	4	14	10	2	5000	343	15	0	0
26	1	15	9	0	70	4	16	3	0	6000	412	10	0	0
27	1	17	1	2	71	4	17	7	2	7000	481	5	0	0
[28]	1	18	6	0	72	4	19	0	0	8000	550	0	0	0
29	1	19	10	2	73	5	0	4	2	9000	618	15	0	0
30	2	1	3	0	74	5	1	9	0	10000	687	10	0	0
31	2	2	7	2	75	5	3	1	2					
32	2	4	0	0	76	5	4	6	0					
33	2	5	4	2	77	5	5	10	2	Great Hundred				
34	2	6	9	0	78	5	7	3	0	112 |	7	14	0	0
35	2	8	1	2	79	5	8	7	2	Grofs				
36	2	9	6	0	80	5	10	0	0	144 |	9	18	0	0
37	2	10	10	2	81	5	11	4	2	Wey				
38	2	12	3	0	82	5	12	9	0	256 |	17	12	0	0
39	2	13	7	2	83	5	14	1	2	Days in a Year				
40	2	15	0	0	[84]	5	15	6	0	365 |	25	1	10	2
41	2	16	4	2	85	5	16	10	2	Feet in a Rod				
42	2	17	9	0	86	5	18	3	0	272 |	18	14	0	0
43	2	19	1	2	87	5	19	7	2					
44	3	0	6	0	88	6	1	0	0					

N.	l.	s.	d.	q.	N.	l.	s.	d.	q.	N.	l.	s.	d.	q.
1	0	1	4	3	45	3	2	9	3	89	6	4	2	3
2	0	2	9	2	46	3	4	2	2	90	6	5	7	2
3	0	4	2	1	47	3	5	7	1	91	6	7	0	1
4	0	5	7	0	48	3	7	0	0	92	6	8	5	0
5	0	6	11	3	49	3	8	4	3	93	6	9	9	3
6	0	8	4	2	50	3	9	9	2	94	6	11	2	2
7	0	9	9	1	51	3	11	2	1	95	6	12	7	1
8	0	11	2	0	52	3	12	7	0	96	6	14	0	0
9	0	12	6	3	53	3	13	11	3	97	6	15	4	3
10	0	13	11	2	54	3	15	4	2	98	6	16	9	2
11	0	15	4	1	55	3	16	9	1	99	6	18	2	1
12	0	16	9	0	[56]	3	18	2	0	100	6	19	7	0
13	0	18	1	3	57	3	19	6	3	200	13	19	2	0
14	0	19	6	2	58	4	0	11	2	300	20	18	9	0
15	1	0	11	1	59	4	2	4	1	400	27	18	4	0
16	1	2	4	0	60	4	3	9	0	500	34	17	11	0
17	1	3	8	3	61	4	5	1	3	600	41	17	6	0
18	1	5	1	2	62	4	6	6	2	700	48	17	1	0
19	1	6	6	1	63	4	7	11	1	800	55	16	8	0
20	1	7	11	0	64	4	9	4	0	900	62	16	3	0
21	1	9	3	3	65	4	10	8	3	1000	69	15	10	0
22	1	10	8	2	66	4	12	1	2	2000	139	11	8	0
23	1	12	1	1	67	4	13	6	1	3000	209	7	6	0
24	1	13	6	0	68	4	14	11	0	4000	279	3	4	0
25	1	14	10	3	69	4	16	3	3	5000	348	19	2	0
26	1	16	3	2	70	4	17	8	2	6000	418	15	0	0
27	1	17	8	1	71	4	19	1	1	7000	488	10	10	0
[28]	1	19	1	0	72	5	0	6	0	8000	558	6	8	0
29	2	0	5	3	73	5	1	10	3	9000	628	2	6	0
30	2	1	10	2	74	5	3	3	2	10000	697	18	4	0
31	2	3	3	1	75	5	4	8	1					
32	2	4	8	0	76	5	6	1	0					
33	2	6	0	3	77	5	7	5	3	Great Hundred				
34	2	7	5	2	78	5	8	10	2	112	7	16	4	0
35	2	8	10	1	79	5	10	3	1	Grofs				
36	2	10	3	0	80	5	11	8	0	144	10	1	0	0
37	2	11	7	3	81	5	13	0	3	Wey				
38	2	13	0	2	82	5	14	5	2	256	17	17	4	0
39	2	14	5	1	83	5	15	10	1	Days in a Year				
40	2	15	10	0	[84]	5	17	3	0	365	25	9	5	3
41	2	17	2	3	85	5	18	7	3	Feet in a Rod				
42	2	18	7	2	86	6	0	0	2	272	18	19	8	0
43	3	0	0	1	87	6	1	5	1					
44	3	1	5	0	88	6	2	10	0					

N.	l.	s.	d.
1	0	1	5
2	0	2	10
3	0	4	3
4	0	5	8
5	0	7	1
6	0	8	6
7	0	9	11
8	0	11	4
9	0	12	9
10	0	14	2
11	0	15	7
12	0	17	0
13	0	18	5
14	0	19	10
15	1	1	3
16	1	2	8
17	1	4	1
18	1	5	6
19	1	6	11
20	1	8	4
21	1	9	9
22	1	11	2
23	1	12	7
24	1	14	0
25	1	15	5
26	1	16	10
27	1	18	3
[28]	1	19	8
29	2	1	1
30	2	2	6
31	2	3	11
32	2	5	4
33	2	6	9
34	2	8	2
35	2	9	7
36	2	11	0
37	2	12	5
38	2	13	10
39	2	15	3
40	2	16	8
41	2	18	1
42	2	19	6
43	3	0	11
44	3	2	4

N.	l.	s.	d.
45	3	3	9
46	3	5	2
47	3	6	7
48	3	8	0
49	3	9	5
50	3	10	10
51	3	12	3
52	3	13	8
53	3	15	1
54	3	16	6
55	3	17	11
[56]	3	19	4
57	4	0	9
58	4	2	2
59	4	3	7
60	4	5	0
61	4	6	5
62	4	7	10
63	4	9	3
64	4	10	8
65	4	12	1
66	4	13	6
67	4	14	11
68	4	16	4
69	4	17	9
70	4	19	2
71	5	0	7
72	5	2	0
73	5	3	5
74	5	4	10
75	5	6	3
76	5	7	8
77	5	9	1
78	5	10	6
79	5	11	11
80	5	13	4
81	5	14	9
82	5	16	2
83	5	17	7
[84]	5	19	0
85	6	0	5
86	6	1	10
87	6	3	3
88	6	4	8

N.	l.	s.	d.
89	6	6	1
90	6	7	6
91	6	8	11
92	6	10	4
93	6	11	9
94	6	13	2
95	6	14	7
96	6	16	0
97	6	17	5
98	6	18	10
99	7	0	3
100	7	1	8
200	14	3	4
300	21	5	0
400	28	6	8
500	35	8	4
600	42	10	0
700	49	11	8
800	56	13	4
900	63	15	0
1000	70	16	8
2000	141	13	4
3000	212	10	0
4000	283	6	8
5000	354	3	4
6000	425	0	0
7000	495	16	8
8000	566	13	4
9000	637	10	0
10000	708	6	8

Great Hundred

112 | 7 18 8

Greſs

144 | 10 4 0

Wey

256 | 18 2 8

Days in a Year

365 | 25 17 1

Feet in a Rod

272 | 19 5 4

N.	l.	s.	d.	q.
1	0	1	5	1
2	0	2	10	2
3	0	4	3	3
4	0	5	9	0
5	0	7	2	1
6	0	8	7	2
7	0	10	0	3
8	0	11	6	0
9	0	12	11	1
10	0	14	4	2
11	0	15	9	3
12	0	17	3	0
13	0	18	8	1
14	1	0	1	2
15	1	1	6	3
16	1	3	0	0
17	1	4	5	1
18	1	5	10	2
19	1	7	3	3
20	1	8	9	0
21	1	10	2	1
22	1	11	7	2
23	1	13	0	3
24	1	14	6	0
25	1	15	11	1
26	1	17	4	2
27	1	18	9	3
[28]	2	0	3	0
29	2	1	8	1
30	2	3	1	2
31	2	4	6	3
32	2	6	0	0
33	2	7	5	1
34	2	8	10	2
35	2	10	3	3
36	2	11	9	0
37	2	13	2	1
38	2	14	7	2
39	2	16	0	3
40	2	17	6	0
41	2	18	11	1
42	3	0	4	2
43	3	1	9	3
44	3	3	3	0

N.	l.	s.	d.	q.
45	3	4	8	1
46	3	6	1	2
47	3	7	6	3
48	3	9	0	0
49	3	10	5	1
50	3	11	10	2
51	3	13	3	3
52	3	14	9	0
53	3	16	2	1
54	3	17	7	2
55	3	19	0	3
[56]	4	0	6	0
57	4	1	11	1
58	4	3	4	2
59	4	4	9	3
60	4	6	3	0
61	4	7	8	1
62	4	9	1	2
63	4	10	6	3
64	4	12	0	0
65	4	13	5	1
66	4	14	10	2
67	4	16	3	3
68	4	17	9	0
69	4	19	2	1
70	5	0	7	2
71	5	2	0	3
72	5	3	6	0
73	5	4	11	1
74	5	6	4	2
75	5	7	9	3
76	5	9	3	0
77	5	10	8	1
78	5	12	1	2
79	5	13	6	3
80	5	15	0	0
81	5	16	5	1
82	5	17	10	2
83	5	19	3	3
[84]	6	0	9	0
85	6	2	2	1
86	6	3	7	2
87	6	5	0	3
88	6	6	6	0

N.	l.	s.	d.	q.
89	6	7	11	1
90	6	9	4	2
91	6	10	9	3
92	6	12	3	0
93	6	13	8	1
94	6	15	1	2
95	6	16	6	3
96	6	18	0	0
97	6	19	5	1
98	7	0	10	2
99	7	2	3	3
100	7	3	9	0
200	14	7	6	0
300	21	11	3	0
400	28	15	0	0
500	35	18	9	0
600	43	2	6	0
700	50	6	3	0
800	57	10	0	0
900	64	13	9	0
1000	71	17	6	0
2000	143	15	0	0
3000	215	12	6	0
4000	287	10	0	0
5000	359	7	6	0
6000	431	5	0	0
7000	503	2	6	0
8000	575	0	0	0
9000	646	17	6	0
10000	718	15	0	0

Great Hundred

112 | 8 | 1 | 0 | 0

Gross

144 | 10 | 7 | 0 | 0

Wey

256 | 18 | 8 | 0 | 0

Days in a Year

365 | 26 | 4 | 8 | 1

Feet in a Rod

272 | 19 | 11 | 0 | 0

N.	l.	s.	d.	q.
1	0	1	5	2
2	0	2	11	0
3	0	4	4	2
4	0	5	10	0
5	0	7	3	2
6	0	8	9	0
7	0	10	2	2
8	0	11	8	0
9	0	13	1	2
10	0	14	7	0
11	0	16	0	2
12	0	17	6	0
13	0	18	11	2
14	1	0	5	0
15	1	1	10	2
16	1	3	4	0
17	1	4	9	2
18	1	6	3	0
19	1	7	8	2
20	1	9	2	0
21	1	10	7	2
22	1	12	1	0
23	1	13	6	2
24	1	15	0	0
25	1	16	5	2
26	1	17	11	0
27	1	19	4	2
[28]	2	0	10	0
29	2	2	3	2
30	2	3	9	0
31	2	5	2	2
32	2	6	8	0
33	2	8	1	2
34	2	9	7	0
35	2	11	0	2
36	2	12	6	0
37	2	13	11	2
38	2	15	5	0
39	2	16	10	2
40	2	18	4	0
41	2	19	9	2
42	3	1	3	0
43	3	2	8	2
44	3	4	2	0

N.	l.	s.	d.	q.
45	3	5	7	2
46	3	7	1	0
47	3	8	6	2
48	3	10	0	0
49	3	11	5	2
50	3	12	11	0
51	3	14	4	2
52	3	15	10	0
53	3	17	3	2
54	3	18	9	0
55	4	0	2	2
[56]	4	1	8	0
57	4	3	1	2
58	4	4	7	0
59	4	6	0	2
60	4	7	6	0
61	4	8	11	2
62	4	10	5	0
63	4	11	10	2
64	4	13	4	0
65	4	14	9	2
66	4	16	3	0
67	4	17	8	2
68	4	19	2	0
69	5	0	7	2
70	5	2	1	0
71	5	3	6	2
72	5	5	0	0
73	5	6	5	2
74	5	7	11	0
75	5	9	4	2
76	5	10	10	0
77	5	12	3	2
78	5	13	9	0
79	5	15	2	2
80	5	16	8	0
81	5	18	1	2
82	5	19	7	0
83	6	1	0	2
[84]	6	2	6	0
85	6	3	11	2
86	6	5	5	0
87	6	6	10	2
88	6	8	4	0

N.	l.	s.	d.	q.
89	6	9	9	2
90	6	11	3	0
91	6	12	8	2
92	6	14	2	0
93	6	15	7	2
94	6	17	1	0
95	6	18	6	2
96	7	0	0	0
97	7	1	5	2
98	7	2	11	0
99	7	4	4	2
100	7	5	10	0
200	14	11	8	0
300	21	17	6	0
400	29	3	4	0
500	36	9	2	0
600	43	15	0	0
700	51	0	10	0
800	58	6	8	0
900	65	12	6	0
1000	72	18	4	0
2000	145	16	8	0
3000	218	15	0	0
4000	291	13	4	0
5000	364	11	8	0
6000	437	10	0	0
7000	510	8	4	0
8000	583	6	8	0
9000	656	5	0	0
10000	729	3	4	0

Great Hundred

112	8	3	4	0

Grofs

144	10	10	0	0

Wey

256	18	13	4	0

Days in a Year

365	26	12	3	2

Feet in a Rod

272	19	16	8	0

N.	l.	s.	d.	q.	N.	l.	s.	d.	q.	N.	l.	s.	d.	q.
1	0	1	5	3	45	3	6	6	3	89	6	11	7	3
2	0	2	11	2	46	3	8	0	2	90	6	13	1	2
3	0	4	5	1	47	3	9	6	1	91	6	14	7	1
4	0	5	11	0	48	3	11	0	0	92	6	16	1	0
5	0	7	4	3	49	3	12	5	3	93	6	17	6	3
6	0	8	10	2	50	3	13	11	2	94	6	19	0	2
7	0	10	4	1	51	3	15	5	1	95	7	0	6	1
8	0	11	10	0	52	3	16	11	0	96	7	2	0	0
9	0	13	3	3	53	3	18	4	3	97	7	3	5	3
10	0	14	9	2	54	3	19	10	2	98	7	4	11	2
11	0	16	3	1	55	4	1	4	1	99	7	6	5	1
12	0	17	9	0	[56]	4	2	10	0	100	7	7	11	0
13	0	19	2	3	57	4	4	3	3	200	14	15	10	0
14	1	0	8	2	58	4	5	9	2	300	22	3	9	0
15	1	2	2	1	59	4	7	3	1	400	29	11	8	0
16	1	3	8	0	60	4	8	9	0	500	36	19	7	0
17	1	5	1	3	61	4	10	2	3	600	44	7	6	0
18	1	6	7	2	62	4	11	8	2	700	51	15	5	0
19	1	8	1	1	63	4	13	2	1	800	59	3	4	0
20	1	9	7	0	64	4	14	8	0	900	66	11	3	0
21	1	11	0	3	65	4	16	1	3	1000	73	19	2	0
22	1	12	6	2	66	4	17	7	2	2000	147	18	4	0
23	1	14	0	1	67	4	19	1	1	3000	221	17	6	0
24	1	15	6	0	68	5	0	7	0	4000	295	16	8	0
25	1	16	11	3	69	5	2	0	3	5000	369	15	10	0
26	1	18	5	2	70	5	3	6	2	6000	443	15	0	0
27	1	19	11	1	71	5	5	0	1	7000	517	14	2	0
[28]	2	1	5	0	72	5	6	6	0	8000	591	13	4	0
29	2	2	10	3	73	5	7	11	3	9000	665	12	6	0
30	2	4	4	2	74	5	9	5	2	10000	739	11	8	0
31	2	5	10	1	75	5	10	11	1					
32	2	7	4	0	76	5	12	5	0					
33	2	8	9	3	77	5	13	10	3		*Great Hundred*			
34	2	10	3	2	78	5	15	4	2	112	8	5	8	0
35	2	11	9	1	79	5	16	10	1		*Grofs*			
36	2	13	3	0	80	5	18	4	0	144	10	13	0	0
37	2	14	8	3	81	5	19	9	3		*Wey*			
38	2	16	2	2	82	6	1	3	2	256	18	18	8	0
39	2	17	8	1	83	6	2	9	1		*Days in a Year*			
40	2	19	2	0	[84]	6	4	3	0	365	26	19	10	3
41	3	0	7	3	85	6	5	8	3		*Feet in a Rod*			
42	3	2	1	2	86	6	7	2	2	272	20	2	4	0
43	3	3	7	1	87	6	8	8	1					
44	3	5	1	0	88	6	10	2	0					

N.	l.	s.	d.
1	0	1	6
2	0	3	0
3	0	4	6
4	0	6	0
5	0	7	6
6	0	9	0
7	0	10	6
8	0	12	0
9	0	13	6
10	0	15	0
11	0	16	6
12	0	18	0
13	0	19	6
14	1	1	0
15	1	2	6
16	1	4	0
17	1	5	6
18	1	7	0
19	1	8	6
20	1	10	0
21	1	11	6
22	1	13	0
23	1	14	6
24	1	16	0
25	1	17	6
26	1	19	0
27	2	0	6
[28]	2	2	0
29	2	3	6
30	2	5	0
31	2	6	6
32	2	8	0
33	2	9	6
34	2	11	0
35	2	12	6
36	2	14	0
37	2	15	6
38	2	17	0
39	2	18	6
40	3	0	0
41	3	1	6
42	3	3	0
43	3	4	6
44	3	6	0

N.	l.	s.	d.
45	3	7	6
46	3	9	0
47	3	10	6
48	3	12	0
49	3	13	6
50	3	15	0
51	3	16	6
52	3	18	0
53	3	19	6
54	4	1	0
55	4	2	6
[56]	4	4	0
57	4	5	6
58	4	7	0
59	4	8	6
60	4	10	0
61	4	11	6
62	4	13	0
63	4	14	6
64	4	16	0
65	4	17	6
66	4	19	0
67	5	0	6
68	5	2	0
69	5	3	6
70	5	5	0
71	5	6	6
72	5	8	0
73	5	9	6
74	5	11	0
75	5	12	6
76	5	14	0
77	5	15	6
78	5	17	0
79	5	18	6
80	6	0	0
81	6	1	6
82	6	3	0
83	6	4	6
[84]	6	6	0
85	6	7	6
86	6	9	0
87	6	10	6
88	6	12	0

N.	l.	s.	d.
89	6	13	6
90	6	15	0
91	6	16	6
92	6	18	0
93	6	19	6
94	7	1	0
95	7	2	6
96	7	4	0
97	7	5	6
98	7	7	0
99	7	8	6
100	7	10	0
200	15	0	0
300	22	10	0
400	30	0	0
500	37	10	0
600	45	0	0
700	52	10	0
800	60	0	0
900	67	10	0
1000	75	0	0
2000	150	0	0
3000	225	0	0
4000	300	0	0
5000	375	0	0
6000	450	0	0
7000	525	0	0
8000	600	0	0
9000	675	0	0
10000	750	0	0

Great Hundred

112	8	8	0

Grofs

144	10	16	0

Wey

256	19	4	0

Days in a Year

365	27	7	6

Feet in a Rod

272	20	8	0

N.	l.	s.	d.	q.	N.	l.	s.	d.	q.	N.	l.	s.	d.	q.
1	0	1	6	1	45	3	8	5	1	89	6	15	4	1
2	0	3	0	2	46	3	9	11	2	90	6	16	10	2
3	0	4	6	3	47	3	11	5	3	91	6	18	4	3
4	0	6	1	0	48	3	13	0	0	92	6	19	11	0
5	0	7	7	1	49	3	14	6	1	93	7	1	5	1
6	0	9	1	2	50	3	16	0	2	94	7	2	11	2
7	0	10	7	3	51	3	17	6	3	95	7	4	5	3
8	0	12	2	0	52	3	19	1	0	96	7	6	0	0
9	0	13	8	1	53	4	0	7	1	97	7	7	6	1
10	0	15	2	2	54	4	2	1	2	98	7	9	0	2
11	0	16	8	3	55	4	3	7	3	99	7	10	6	3
12	0	18	3	0	[56]	4	5	2	0	100	7	12	1	0
13	0	19	9	1	57	4	6	8	1	200	15	4	2	0
14	1	1	3	2	58	4	8	2	2	300	22	16	3	0
15	1	2	9	3	59	4	9	8	3	400	30	8	4	0
16	1	4	4	0	60	4	11	3	0	500	38	0	5	0
17	1	5	10	1	61	4	12	9	1	600	45	12	6	0
18	1	7	4	2	62	4	14	3	2	700	53	4	7	0
19	1	8	10	3	63	4	15	9	3	800	60	16	8	0
20	1	10	5	0	64	4	17	4	0	900	68	8	9	0
21	1	11	11	1	65	4	18	10	1	1000	76	0	10	0
22	1	13	5	2	66	5	0	4	2	2000	152	1	8	0
23	1	14	11	3	67	5	1	10	3	3000	228	2	6	0
24	1	16	6	0	68	5	3	5	0	4000	304	3	4	0
25	1	18	0	1	69	5	4	11	1	5000	380	4	2	0
26	1	19	6	2	70	5	6	5	2	6000	456	5	0	0
27	2	1	0	3	71	5	7	11	3	7000	532	5	10	0
[28]	2	2	7	0	72	5	9	6	0	8000	608	6	8	0
29	2	4	1	1	73	5	11	0	1	9000	684	7	6	0
30	2	5	7	2	74	5	12	6	2	10000	760	8	4	0
31	2	7	1	3	75	5	14	0	3					
32	2	8	8	0	76	5	15	7	0					
33	2	10	2	1	77	5	17	1	1	Great Hundred				
34	2	11	8	2	78	5	18	7	2	112	8	10	4	0
35	2	13	2	3	79	6	0	1	3	Grofs				
36	2	14	9	0	80	6	1	8	0	144	10	19	0	0
37	2	16	3	1	81	6	3	2	1	Wey				
38	2	17	9	2	82	6	4	8	2	256	19	9	4	0
39	2	19	3	3	83	6	6	2	3	Days in a Year				
40	3	0	10	0	[84]	6	7	9	0	365	27	15	1	1
41	3	2	4	1	85	6	9	3	1	Feet in a Rod				
42	3	3	10	2	86	6	10	9	2	272	20	13	8	0
43	3	5	4	3	87	6	12	3	3					
44	3	6	11	0	88	6	13	10	0					

H

N.	l.	s.	d.	q.	N.	l.	s.	d.	q.	N.	l.	s.	d.	q.
1	0	1	6	2	45	3	9	4	2	89	6	17	2	2
2	0	3	1	0	46	3	10	11	0	90	6	18	9	0
3	0	4	7	2	47	3	12	5	2	91	7	0	3	2
4	0	6	2	0	48	3	14	0	0	92	7	1	10	0
5	0	7	8	2	49	3	15	6	2	93	7	3	4	2
6	0	9	3	0	50	3	17	1	0	94	7	4	11	0
7	0	10	9	2	51	3	18	7	2	95	7	6	5	2
8	0	12	4	0	52	4	0	2	0	96	7	8	0	0
9	0	13	10	2	53	4	1	8	2	97	7	9	6	2
10	0	15	5	0	54	4	3	3	0	98	7	11	1	0
11	0	16	11	2	55	4	4	9	2	99	7	12	7	2
12	0	18	6	0	[56]	4	6	4	0	100	7	14	2	0
13	1	0	0	2	57	4	7	10	2	200	15	8	4	0
14	1	1	7	0	58	4	9	5	0	300	23	2	6	0
15	1	3	1	2	59	4	10	11	2	400	30	16	8	0
16	1	4	8	0	60	4	12	6	0	500	38	10	10	0
17	1	6	2	2	61	4	14	0	2	600	46	5	0	0
18	1	7	9	0	62	4	15	7	0	700	53	19	2	0
19	1	9	3	2	63	4	17	1	2	800	61	13	4	0
20	1	10	10	0	64	4	18	8	0	900	69	7	6	0
21	1	12	4	2	65	5	0	2	2	1000	77	1	8	0
22	1	13	11	0	66	5	1	9	0	2000	154	3	4	0
23	1	15	5	2	67	5	3	3	2	3000	231	5	0	0
24	1	17	0	0	68	5	4	10	0	4000	308	6	8	0
25	1	18	6	2	69	5	6	4	2	5000	385	8	4	0
26	2	0	1	0	70	5	7	11	0	6000	462	10	0	0
27	2	1	7	2	71	5	9	5	2	7000	539	11	8	0
[28]	2	3	2	0	72	5	11	0	0	8000	616	13	4	0
29	2	4	8	2	73	5	12	6	2	9000	693	15	0	0
30	2	6	3	0	74	5	14	1	0	10000	770	16	8	0
31	2	7	9	2	75	5	15	7	2					
32	2	9	4	0	76	5	17	2	0					
33	2	10	10	2	77	5	18	8	2	**Great Hundred**				
34	2	12	5	0	78	6	0	3	0	112	8	12	8	0
35	2	13	11	2	79	6	1	9	2	*Grofs*				
36	2	15	6	0	80	6	3	4	0	144	11	2	0	0
37	2	17	0	2	81	6	4	10	2	*Wey*				
38	2	18	7	0	82	6	6	5	0	256	19	14	8	0
39	3	0	1	2	83	6	7	11	2	*Days in a Year*				
40	3	1	8	0	[84]	6	9	6	0	365	28	2	8	2
41	3	3	2	2	85	6	11	0	2	*Feet in a Rod*				
42	3	4	9	0	86	6	12	7	0	272	20	19	4	0
43	3	6	3	2	87	6	14	1	2					
44	3	7	10	0	88	6	15	8	0					

N.	l.	s.	d.	q.	N.	l.	s.	d.	q.	N.	l.	s.	d.	q.
1	0	1	6	3	45	3	10	3	3	89	6	19	0	3
2	0	3	1	2	46	3	11	10	2	90	7	0	7	2
3	0	4	8	1	47	3	13	5	1	91	7	2	2	1
4	0	6	3	0	48	3	15	0	0	92	7	3	9	0
5	0	7	9	3	49	3	16	6	3	93	7	5	3	3
6	0	9	4	2	50	3	18	1	2	94	7	6	10	2
7	0	10	11	1	51	3	19	8	1	95	7	8	5	1
8	0	12	6	0	52	4	1	3	0	96	7	10	0	0
9	0	14	0	3	53	4	2	9	3	97	7	11	6	3
10	0	15	7	2	54	4	4	4	2	98	7	13	1	2
11	0	17	2	1	55	4	5	11	1	99	7	14	8	1
12	0	18	9	0	[56]	4	7	6	0	100	7	16	3	0
13	1	0	3	3	57	4	9	0	3	200	15	12	6	0
14	1	1	10	2	58	4	10	7	2	300	23	8	9	0
15	1	3	5	1	59	4	12	2	1	400	31	5	0	0
16	1	5	0	0	60	4	13	9	0	500	39	1	3	0
17	1	6	6	3	61	4	15	3	3	600	46	17	6	0
18	1	8	1	2	62	4	16	10	2	700	54	13	9	0
19	1	9	8	1	63	4	18	5	1	800	62	10	0	0
20	1	11	3	0	64	5	0	0	0	900	70	6	3	0
21	1	12	9	3	65	5	1	6	3	1000	78	2	6	0
22	1	14	4	2	66	5	3	1	2	2000	156	5	0	0
23	1	15	11	1	67	5	4	8	1	3000	234	7	6	0
24	1	17	6	0	68	5	6	3	0	4000	312	10	0	0
25	1	19	0	3	69	5	7	9	3	5000	390	12	6	0
26	2	0	7	2	70	5	9	4	2	6000	468	15	0	0
27	2	2	2	1	71	5	10	11	1	7000	546	17	6	0
[28]	2	3	9	0	72	5	12	6	0	8000	625	0	0	0
29	2	5	3	3	73	5	14	0	3	9000	703	2	6	0
30	2	6	10	2	74	5	15	7	2	10000	781	5	0	0
31	2	8	5	1	75	5	17	2	1					
32	2	10	0	0	76	5	18	9	0					
33	2	11	6	3	77	6	0	3	3	*Great Hundred*				
34	2	13	1	2	78	6	1	10	2	112	8	15	0	0
35	2	14	8	1	79	6	3	5	1	*Grofs*				
36	2	16	3	0	80	6	5	0	0	144	11	5	0	0
37	2	17	9	3	81	6	6	6	3	*Wey*				
38	2	19	4	2	82	6	8	1	2	256	20	0	0	0
39	3	0	11	1	83	6	9	8	1	*Days in a Year*				
40	3	2	6	0	[84]	6	11	3	0	365	28	10	3	3
41	3	4	0	3	85	6	12	9	3	*Feet in a Rod*				
42	3	5	7	2	86	6	14	4	2	272	21	5	0	0
43	3	7	2	1	87	6	15	11	1					
44	3	8	9	0	88	6	17	6	0					

N.	l.	s.	d.	N.	l.	s.	d.	N.	l.	s.	d.
1	0	1	7	45	3	11	3	89	7	0	11
2	0	3	2	46	3	12	10	90	7	2	6
3	0	4	9	47	3	14	5	91	7	4	1
4	0	6	4	48	3	16	0	92	7	5	8
5	0	7	11	49	3	17	7	93	7	7	3
6	0	9	6	50	3	19	2	94	7	8	10
7	0	11	1	51	4	0	9	95	7	10	5
8	0	12	8	52	4	2	4	96	7	12	0
9	0	14	3	53	4	3	11	97	7	13	7
10	0	15	10	54	4	5	6	98	7	15	2
11	0	17	5	55	4	7	1	99	7	16	9
12	0	19	0	[56]	4	8	8	100	7	18	4
13	1	0	7	57	4	10	3	200	15	16	8
14	1	2	2	58	4	11	10	300	23	15	0
15	1	3	9	59	4	13	5	400	31	13	4
16	1	5	4	60	4	15	0	500	39	11	8
17	1	6	11	61	4	16	7	600	47	10	0
18	1	8	6	62	4	18	2	700	55	8	4
19	1	10	1	63	4	19	9	800	63	6	8
20	1	11	8	64	5	1	4	900	71	5	0
21	1	13	3	65	5	2	11	1000	79	3	4
22	1	14	10	66	5	4	6	2000	158	6	8
23	1	16	5	67	5	6	1	3000	237	10	0
24	1	18	0	68	5	7	8	4000	316	13	4
25	1	19	7	69	5	9	3	5000	395	16	8
26	2	1	2	70	5	10	10	6000	475	0	0
27	2	2	9	71	5	12	5	7000	554	3	4
[28]	2	4	4	72	5	14	0	8000	633	6	8
29	2	5	11	73	5	15	7	9000	712	10	0
30	2	7	6	74	5	17	2	10000	791	13	4
31	2	9	1	75	5	18	9				
32	2	10	8	76	6	0	4				
33	2	12	3	77	6	1	11				
34	2	13	10	78	6	3	6				
35	2	15	5	79	6	5	1				
36	2	17	0	80	6	6	8				
37	2	18	7	81	6	8	3				
38	3	0	2	82	6	9	10				
39	3	1	9	83	6	11	5				
40	3	3	4	[84]	6	13	0				
41	3	4	11	85	6	14	7				
42	3	6	6	86	6	16	2				
43	3	8	1	87	6	17	9				
44	3	9	8	88	6	19	4				

Great Hundred

112	8	17	4

Grofs

144	11	8	0

Wey

256	20	5	4

Days in a Year

365	28	17	11

Feet in a Rod

272	21	10	8

N.	l.	s.	d.	q.
1	0	1	7	1
2	0	3	2	2
3	0	4	9	3
4	0	6	5	0
5	0	8	0	1
6	0	9	7	2
7	0	11	2	3
8	0	12	10	0
9	0	14	5	1
10	0	16	0	2
11	0	17	7	3
12	0	19	3	0
13	1	0	10	1
14	1	2	5	2
15	1	4	0	3
16	1	5	8	0
17	1	7	3	1
18	1	8	10	2
19	1	10	5	3
20	1	12	1	0
21	1	13	8	1
22	1	15	3	2
23	1	16	10	3
24	1	18	6	0
25	2	0	1	1
26	2	1	8	2
27	2	3	3	3
[28]	2	4	11	0
29	2	6	6	1
30	2	8	1	2
31	2	9	8	3
32	2	11	4	0
33	2	12	11	1
34	2	14	6	2
35	2	16	1	3
36	2	17	9	0
37	2	19	4	1
38	3	0	11	2
39	3	2	6	3
40	3	4	2	0
41	3	5	9	1
42	3	7	4	2
43	3	8	11	3
44	3	10	7	0

N.	l.	s.	d.	q.
45	3	12	2	1
46	3	13	9	2
47	3	15	4	3
48	3	17	0	0
49	3	18	7	1
50	4	0	2	2
51	4	1	9	3
52	4	3	5	0
53	4	5	0	1
54	4	6	7	2
55	4	8	2	3
[56]	4	9	10	0
57	4	11	5	1
58	4	13	0	2
59	4	14	7	3
60	4	16	3	0
61	4	17	10	1
62	4	19	5	2
63	5	1	0	3
64	5	2	8	0
65	5	4	3	1
66	5	5	10	2
67	5	7	5	3
68	5	9	1	0
69	5	10	8	1
70	5	12	3	2
71	5	13	10	3
72	5	15	6	0
73	5	17	1	1
74	5	18	8	2
75	6	0	3	3
76	6	1	11	0
77	6	3	6	1
78	6	5	1	2
79	6	6	8	3
80	6	8	4	0
81	6	9	11	1
82	6	11	6	2
83	6	13	1	3
[84]	6	14	9	0
85	6	16	4	1
86	6	17	11	2
87	6	19	6	3
88	7	1	2	0

N.	l.	s.	d.	q.
89	7	2	9	1
90	7	4	4	2
91	7	5	11	3
92	7	7	7	0
93	7	9	2	1
94	7	10	9	2
95	7	12	4	3
96	7	14	0	0
97	7	15	7	1
98	7	17	2	2
99	7	18	9	3
100	8	0	5	0
200	16	0	10	0
300	24	1	3	0
400	32	1	8	0
500	40	2	1	0
600	48	2	6	0
700	56	2	11	0
800	64	3	4	0
900	72	3	9	0
1000	80	4	2	0
2000	160	8	4	0
3000	240	12	6	0
4000	320	16	8	0
5000	401	0	10	0
6000	481	5	0	0
7000	561	9	2	0
8000	641	13	4	0
9000	721	17	6	0
10000	802	1	8	0

Great Hundred

112	8	19	8	0

Grofs

144	11	11	0	0

Wey

256	20	10	8	0

Days in a Year

365	29	5	6	1

Feet in a Rod

272	21	16	4	0

N.	l.	s.	d.	q.	N.	l.	s.	d.	q.	N.	l.	s.	d.	q.
1	0	1	7	2	45	3	13	1	2	89	7	4	7	2
2	0	3	3	0	46	3	14	9	0	90	7	6	3	0
3	0	4	10	2	47	3	16	4	2	91	7	7	10	2
4	0	6	6	0	48	3	18	0	0	92	7	9	6	0
5	0	8	1	2	49	3	19	7	2	93	7	11	1	2
6	0	9	9	0	50	4	1	3	0	94	7	12	9	0
7	0	11	4	2	51	4	2	10	2	95	7	14	4	2
8	0	13	0	0	52	4	4	6	0	96	7	16	0	0
9	0	14	7	2	53	4	6	1	2	97	7	17	7	2
10	0	16	3	0	54	4	7	9	0	98	7	19	3	0
11	0	17	10	2	55	4	9	4	2	99	8	0	10	2
12	0	19	6	0	[56]	4	11	0	0	100	8	2	6	0
13	1	1	1	2	57	4	12	7	2	200	16	5	0	0
14	1	2	9	0	58	4	14	3	0	300	24	7	6	0
15	1	4	4	2	59	4	15	10	2	400	32	10	0	0
16	1	6	0	0	60	4	17	6	0	500	40	12	6	0
17	1	7	7	2	61	4	19	1	2	600	48	15	0	0
18	1	9	3	0	62	5	0	9	0	700	56	17	6	0
19	1	10	10	2	63	5	2	4	2	800	65	0	0	0
20	1	12	6	0	64	5	4	0	0	900	73	2	6	0
21	1	14	1	2	65	5	5	7	2	1000	81	5	0	0
22	1	15	9	0	66	5	7	3	0	2000	162	10	0	0
23	1	17	4	2	67	5	8	10	2	3000	243	15	0	0
24	1	19	0	0	68	5	10	6	0	4000	325	0	0	0
25	2	0	7	2	69	5	12	1	2	5000	406	5	0	0
26	2	2	3	0	70	5	13	9	0	6000	487	10	0	0
27	2	3	10	2	71	5	15	4	2	7000	568	15	0	0
[28]	2	5	6	0	72	5	17	0	0	8000	650	0	0	0
29	2	7	1	2	73	5	18	7	2	9000	731	5	0	0
30	2	8	9	0	74	6	0	3	0	10000	812	10	0	0
31	2	10	4	2	75	6	1	10	2					
32	2	12	0	0	76	6	3	6	0					
33	2	13	7	2	77	6	5	1	2	*Great Hundred*				
34	2	15	3	0	78	6	6	9	0	112	9	2	0	0
35	2	16	10	2	79	6	8	4	2	*Grofs*				
36	2	18	6	0	80	6	10	0	0	144	11	14	0	0
37	3	0	1	2	81	6	11	7	2	*Wy*				
38	3	1	9	0	82	6	13	3	0	256	20	16	0	0
39	3	3	4	2	83	6	14	10	2	*Days in a Year*				
40	3	5	0	0	[84]	6	16	6	0	365	29	13	1	2
41	3	6	7	2	85	6	18	1	2	*Feet in a Rod*				
42	3	8	3	0	86	6	19	9	0	272	22	2	0	0
43	3	9	10	2	87	7	1	4	2					
44	3	11	6	0	88	7	3	0	0					

N.	l.	s.	d.	q.
1	0	1	7	3
2	0	3	3	2
3	0	4	11	1
4	0	6	7	0
5	0	8	2	3
6	0	9	10	2
7	0	11	6	1
8	0	13	2	0
9	0	14	9	3
10	0	16	5	2
11	0	18	1	1
12	0	19	9	0
13	1	1	4	3
14	1	3	0	2
15	1	4	8	1
16	1	6	4	0
17	1	7	11	3
18	1	9	7	2
19	1	11	3	1
20	1	12	11	0
21	1	14	6	3
22	1	16	2	2
23	1	17	10	1
24	1	19	6	0
25	2	1	1	3
26	2	2	9	2
27	2	4	5	1
[28]	2	6	1	0
29	2	7	8	3
30	2	9	4	2
31	2	11	0	1
32	2	12	8	0
33	2	14	3	3
34	2	15	11	2
35	2	17	7	1
36	2	19	3	0
37	3	0	10	3
38	3	2	6	2
39	3	4	2	1
40	3	5	10	0
41	3	7	5	3
42	3	9	1	2
43	3	10	9	1
44	3	12	5	0

N.	l.	s.	d.	q.
45	3	14	0	3
46	3	15	8	2
47	3	17	4	1
48	3	19	0	0
49	4	0	7	3
50	4	2	3	2
51	4	3	11	1
52	4	5	7	0
53	4	7	2	3
54	4	8	10	2
55	4	10	6	1
[56]	4	12	2	0
57	4	13	9	3
58	4	15	5	2
59	4	17	1	1
60	4	18	9	0
61	5	0	4	3
62	5	2	0	2
63	5	3	8	1
64	5	5	4	0
65	5	6	11	3
66	5	8	7	2
67	5	10	3	1
68	5	11	11	0
69	5	13	6	3
70	5	15	2	2
71	5	16	10	1
72	5	18	6	0
73	6	0	1	3
74	6	1	9	2
75	6	3	5	1
76	6	5	1	0
77	6	6	8	3
78	6	8	4	2
79	6	10	0	1
80	6	11	8	0
81	6	13	3	3
82	6	14	11	2
83	6	16	7	1
[84]	6	18	3	0
85	6	19	10	3
86	7	1	6	2
87	7	3	2	1
88	7	4	10	0

N.	l.	s.	d.	q
89	7	6	5	3
90	7	8	1	2
91	7	9	9	1
92	7	11	5	0
93	7	13	0	3
94	7	14	8	2
95	7	16	4	1
96	7	18	0	0
97	7	19	7	3
98	8	1	3	2
99	8	2	11	1
100	8	4	7	0
200	16	9	2	0
300	24	13	9	0
400	32	18	4	0
500	41	2	11	0
600	49	7	6	0
700	57	12	1	0
800	65	16	8	0
900	74	1	3	0
1000	82	5	10	0
2000	164	11	8	0
3000	246	17	6	0
4000	329	3	4	0
5000	411	9	2	0
6000	493	15	0	0
7000	576	0	10	0
8000	658	6	8	0
9000	740	12	6	0
10000	822	18	4	0

Great Hundred

112 | 9 4 4 0

Gross

144 | 11 17 0 0

Wey

256 | 21 1 4 0

Days in a Year

365 | 30 0 8 3

Feet in a Rod

272 | 22 7 8 0

N.	l.	s.	d.	N.	l.	s.	d.	N.	l.	s.	d.
1	0	1	8	45	3	15	0	89	7	8	4
2	0	3	4	46	3	16	8	90	7	10	0
3	0	5	0	47	3	18	4	91	7	11	8
4	0	6	8	48	4	0	0	92	7	13	4
5	0	8	4	49	4	1	8	93	7	15	0
6	0	10	0	50	4	3	4	94	7	16	8
7	0	11	8	51	4	5	0	95	7	18	4
8	0	13	4	52	4	6	8	96	8	0	0
9	0	15	0	53	4	8	4	97	8	1	8
10	0	16	8	54	4	10	0	98	8	3	4
11	0	18	4	55	4	11	8	99	8	5	0
12	1	0	0	[56]	4	13	4	100	8	6	8
13	1	1	8	57	4	15	0	200	16	13	4
14	1	3	4	58	4	16	8	300	25	0	0
15	1	5	0	59	4	18	4	400	33	6	8
16	1	6	8	60	5	0	0	500	41	13	4
17	1	8	4	61	5	1	8	600	50	0	0
18	1	10	0	62	5	3	4	700	58	6	8
19	1	11	8	63	5	5	0	800	66	13	4
20	1	13	4	64	5	6	8	900	75	0	0
21	1	15	0	65	5	8	4	1000	83	6	8
22	1	16	8	66	5	10	0	2000	166	13	4
23	1	18	4	67	5	11	8	3000	250	0	0
24	2	0	0	68	5	13	4	4000	333	6	8
25	2	1	8	69	5	15	0	5000	416	13	4
26	2	3	4	70	5	16	8	6000	500	0	0
27	2	5	0	71	5	18	4	7000	583	6	8
[28]	2	6	8	72	6	0	0	8000	666	13	4
29	2	8	4	73	6	1	8	9000	750	0	0
30	2	10	0	74	6	3	4	10000	833	6	8
31	2	11	8	75	6	5	0				
32	2	13	4	76	6	6	8				
33	2	15	0	77	6	8	4	*Great Hundred*			
34	2	16	8	78	6	10	0	112	9	6	8
35	2	18	4	79	6	11	8	*Grofs*			
36	3	0	0	80	6	13	4	144	12	0	0
37	3	1	8	81	6	15	0	*Wey*			
38	3	3	4	82	6	16	8	256	21	6	8
39	3	5	0	83	6	18	4	*Days in a Year*			
40	3	6	8	[84]	7	0	0	365	30	8	4
41	3	8	4	85	7	1	8	*Feet in a Rod*			
42	3	10	0	86	7	3	4	272	22	13	4
43	3	11	8	87	7	5	0				
44	3	13	4	88	7	6	8				

N.	l.	s.	d.	q.
1	0	1	8	1
2	0	3	4	2
3	0	5	0	3
4	0	6	9	0
5	0	8	5	1
6	0	10	1	2
7	0	11	9	3
8	0	13	6	0
9	0	15	2	1
10	0	16	10	2
11	0	18	6	3
12	1	0	3	0
13	1	1	11	1
14	1	3	7	2
15	1	5	3	3
16	1	7	0	0
17	1	8	8	1
18	1	10	4	2
19	1	12	0	3
20	1	13	9	0
21	1	15	5	1
22	1	17	1	2
23	1	18	9	3
24	2	0	6	0
25	2	2	2	1
26	2	3	10	2
27	2	5	6	3
[28]	2	7	3	0
29	2	8	11	1
30	2	10	7	2
31	2	12	3	3
32	2	14	0	0
33	2	15	8	1
34	2	17	4	2
35	2	19	0	3
36	3	0	9	0
37	3	2	5	1
38	3	4	1	2
39	3	5	9	3
40	3	7	6	0
41	3	9	2	1
42	3	10	10	2
43	3	12	6	3
44	3	14	3	0

N.	l.	s.	d.	q.
45	3	15	11	1
46	3	17	7	2
47	3	19	3	3
48	4	1	0	0
49	4	2	8	1
50	4	4	4	2
51	4	6	0	3
52	4	7	9	0
53	4	9	5	1
54	4	11	1	2
55	4	12	9	3
[56]	4	14	6	0
57	4	16	2	1
58	4	17	10	2
59	4	19	6	3
60	5	1	3	0
61	5	2	11	1
62	5	4	7	2
63	5	6	3	3
64	5	8	0	0
65	5	9	8	1
66	5	11	4	2
67	5	13	0	3
68	5	14	9	0
69	5	16	5	1
70	5	18	1	2
71	5	19	9	3
72	6	1	6	0
73	6	3	2	1
74	6	4	10	2
75	6	6	6	3
76	6	8	3	0
77	6	9	11	1
78	6	11	7	2
79	6	13	3	3
80	6	15	0	0
81	6	16	8	1
82	6	18	4	2
83	7	0	0	3
[84]	7	1	9	0
85	7	3	5	1
86	7	5	1	2
87	7	6	9	3
88	7	8	6	0

N.	l.	s.	d.	q.
89	7	10	2	1
90	7	11	10	2
91	7	13	6	3
92	7	15	3	0
93	7	16	11	1
94	7	18	7	2
95	8	0	3	3
96	8	2	0	0
97	8	3	8	1
98	8	5	4	2
99	8	7	0	3
100	8	8	9	0
200	16	17	6	0
300	25	6	3	0
400	33	15	0	0
500	42	3	9	0
600	50	12	6	0
700	59	1	3	0
800	67	10	0	0
900	75	18	9	0
1000	84	7	6	0
2000	168	15	0	0
3000	253	2	6	0
4000	337	10	0	0
5000	421	17	6	0
6000	506	5	0	0
7000	590	12	6	0
8000	675	0	0	0
9000	759	7	6	0
10000	843	15	0	0

Great Hundred

112 | 9 9 0 0

Grofs

144 | 12 3 0 0

Wey

256 | 21 12 0 0

Days in a Year

365 | 30 15 11 1

Feet in a Rod.

272 | 22 19 0 0

N.	l.	s.	d.	q.	N.	l.	s.	d.	q.	N.	l.	s.	d.	q.
1	0	1	8	2	45	3	16	10	2	89	7	12	0	2
2	0	3	5	0	46	3	18	7	0	90	7	13	9	0
3	0	5	1	2	47	4	0	3	2	91	7	15	5	2
4	0	6	10	0	48	4	2	0	0	92	7	17	2	0
5	0	8	6	2	49	4	3	8	2	93	7	18	10	2
6	0	10	3	0	50	4	5	5	0	94	8	0	7	0
7	0	11	11	2	51	4	7	1	2	95	8	2	3	2
8	0	13	8	0	52	4	8	10	0	96	8	4	0	0
9	0	15	4	2	53	4	10	6	2	97	8	5	8	2
10	0	17	1	0	54	4	12	3	0	98	8	7	5	0
11	0	18	9	2	55	4	13	11	2	99	8	9	1	2
12	1	0	6	0	[56]	4	15	8	0	100	8	10	10	0
13	1	2	2	2	57	4	17	4	2	200	17	1	8	0
14	1	3	11	0	58	4	19	1	0	300	25	12	6	0
15	1	5	7	2	59	5	0	9	2	400	34	3	4	0
16	1	7	4	0	60	5	2	6	0	500	42	14	2	0
17	1	9	0	2	61	5	4	2	2	600	51	5	0	0
18	1	10	9	0	62	5	5	11	0	700	59	15	10	0
19	1	12	5	2	63	5	7	7	2	800	68	6	8	0
20	1	14	2	0	64	5	9	4	0	900	76	17	6	0
21	1	15	10	2	65	5	11	0	2	1000	85	8	4	0
22	1	17	7	0	66	5	12	9	0	2000	170	16	8	0
23	1	19	3	2	67	5	14	5	2	3000	256	5	0	0
24	2	1	0	0	68	5	16	2	0	4000	341	13	4	0
25	2	2	8	2	69	5	17	10	2	5000	427	1	8	0
26	2	4	5	0	70	5	19	7	0	6000	512	10	0	0
27	2	6	1	2	71	6	1	3	2	7000	597	18	4	0
[28]	2	7	10	0	72	6	3	0	0	8000	683	6	8	0
29	2	9	6	2	73	6	4	8	2	9000	768	15	0	0
30	2	11	3	0	74	6	6	5	0	10000	854	3	4	0
31	2	12	11	2	75	6	8	1	2					
32	2	14	8	0	76	6	9	10	0					
33	2	16	4	2	77	6	11	6	2	Great Hundred				
34	2	18	1	0	78	6	13	3	0	112	9	11	4	0
35	2	19	9	2	79	6	14	11	2	Gross				
36	3	1	6	0	80	6	16	8	0	144	12	6	0	0
37	3	3	2	2	81	6	18	4	2	Wey				
38	3	4	11	0	82	7	0	1	0	256	21	17	4	0
39	3	6	7	2	83	7	1	9	2	Days in a Year				
40	3	8	4	0	[84]	7	3	6	0	365	31	3	6	2
41	3	10	0	2	85	7	5	2	2	Feet in a Rod				
42	3	11	9	0	86	7	6	11	0	272	23	4	8	0
43	3	13	5	2	87	7	8	7	2					
44	3	15	2	0	88	7	10	4	0					

N.	l.	s.	d.	q.	N.	l.	s.	d.	q.	N.	l.	s.	d.	q.
1	0	1	8	3	45	3	17	9	3	89	7	13	10	3
2	0	3	5	2	46	3	19	6	2	90	7	15	7	2
3	0	5	2	1	47	4	1	3	1	91	7	17	4	1
4	0	6	11	0	48	4	3	0	0	92	7	19	1	0
5	0	8	7	3	49	4	4	8	3	93	8	0	9	3
6	0	10	4	2	50	4	6	5	2	94	8	2	6	2
7	0	12	1	1	51	4	8	2	1	95	8	4	3	1
8	0	13	10	0	52	4	9	11	0	96	8	6	0	0
9	0	15	6	3	53	4	11	7	3	97	8	7	8	3
10	0	17	3	2	54	4	13	4	2	98	8	9	5	2
11	0	19	0	1	55	4	15	1	1	99	8	11	2	1
12	1	0	9	0	[56]	4	16	10	0	100	8	12	11	0
13	1	2	5	3	57	4	18	6	3	200	17	5	10	0
14	1	4	2	2	58	5	0	3	2	300	25	18	9	0
15	1	5	11	1	59	5	2	0	1	400	34	11	8	0
16	1	7	8	0	60	5	3	9	0	500	43	4	7	0
17	1	9	4	3	61	5	5	5	3	600	51	17	6	0
18	1	11	1	2	62	5	7	2	2	700	60	10	5	0
19	1	12	10	1	63	5	8	11	1	800	69	3	4	0
20	1	14	7	0	64	5	10	8	0	900	77	16	3	0
21	1	16	3	3	65	5	12	4	3	1000	86	9	2	0
22	1	18	0	2	66	5	14	1	2	2000	172	18	4	0
23	1	19	9	1	67	5	15	10	1	3000	259	7	6	0
24	2	1	6	0	68	5	17	7	0	4000	345	16	8	0
25	2	3	2	3	69	5	19	3	3	5000	432	5	10	0
26	2	4	11	2	70	6	1	0	2	6000	518	15	0	0
27	2	6	8	1	71	6	2	9	1	7000	605	4	2	0
[28]	2	8	5	0	72	6	4	6	0	8000	691	13	4	0
29	2	10	1	3	73	6	6	2	3	9000	778	2	6	0
30	2	11	10	2	74	6	7	11	2	10000	864	11	8	0
31	2	13	7	1	75	6	9	8	1					
32	2	15	4	0	76	6	11	5	0					
33	2	17	0	3	77	6	13	1	3					
34	2	18	9	2	78	6	14	10	2					
35	3	0	6	1	79	6	16	7	1					
36	3	2	3	0	80	6	18	4	0					
37	3	3	11	3	81	7	0	0	3					
38	3	5	8	2	82	7	1	9	2					
39	3	7	5	1	83	7	3	6	1					
40	3	9	2	0	[84]	7	5	3	0					
41	3	10	10	3	85	7	6	11	3					
42	3	12	7	2	86	7	8	8	2					
43	3	14	4	1	87	7	10	5	1					
44	3	16	1	0	88	7	12	2	0					

Great Hundred

112	9	13	8	0

Grofs

144	12	9	0	0

Wey

256	22	2	8	0

Days in a Year

365	31	11	1	3

Feet in a Rod

272	23	10	4	0

N.	l.	s.	d.	N.	l.	s.	d.	N.	l.	s.	d.
1	0	1	9	45	3	18	9	89	7	15	9
2	0	3	6	46	4	0	6	90	7	17	6
3	0	5	3	47	4	2	3	91	7	19	3
4	0	7	0	48	4	4	0	92	8	1	0
5	0	8	9	49	4	5	9	93	8	2	9
6	0	10	6	50	4	7	6	94	8	4	6
7	0	12	3	51	4	9	3	95	8	6	3
8	0	14	0	52	4	11	0	96	8	8	0
9	0	15	9	53	4	12	9	97	8	9	9
10	0	17	6	54	4	14	6	98	8	11	6
11	0	19	3	55	4	16	3	99	8	13	3
12	1	1	0	[56]	4	18	0	100	8	15	0
13	1	2	9	57	4	19	9	200	17	10	0
14	1	4	6	58	5	1	6	300	26	5	0
15	1	6	3	59	5	3	3	400	35	0	0
16	1	8	0	60	5	5	0	500	43	15	0
17	1	9	9	61	5	6	9	600	52	10	0
18	1	11	6	62	5	8	6	700	61	5	0
19	1	13	3	63	5	10	3	800	70	0	0
20	1	15	0	64	5	12	0	900	78	15	0
21	1	16	9	65	5	13	9	1000	87	10	0
22	1	18	6	66	5	15	6	2000	175	0	0
23	2	0	3	67	5	17	3	3000	262	10	0
24	2	2	0	68	5	19	0	4000	350	0	0
25	2	3	9	69	6	0	9	5000	437	10	0
26	2	5	6	70	6	2	6	6000	525	0	0
27	2	7	3	71	6	4	3	7000	612	10	0
[28]	2	9	0	72	6	6	0	8000	700	0	0
29	2	10	9	73	6	7	9	9000	787	10	0
30	2	12	6	74	6	9	6	10000	875	0	0
31	2	14	3	75	6	11	3				
32	2	16	0	76	6	13	0				
33	2	17	9	77	6	14	9				
34	2	19	6	78	6	16	6				
35	3	1	3	79	6	18	3				
36	3	3	0	80	7	0	0				
37	3	4	9	81	7	1	9				
38	3	6	6	82	7	3	6				
39	3	8	3	83	7	5	3				
40	3	10	0	[84]	7	7	0				
41	3	11	9	85	7	8	9				
42	3	13	6	86	7	10	6				
43	3	15	3	87	7	12	3				
44	3	17	0	88	7	14	0				

Great Hundred

112 | 9 16 0

Gross

144 | 12 12 0

Wey

256 | 22 8 0

Days in a Year

365 | 31 18 9

Feet in a Rod

272 | 23 16 0

N.	l.	s.	d.	q.	N.	l.	s.	d.	q.	N.	l.	s.	d.	q.
1	0	1	9	1	45	3	19	8	1	89	7	17	7	1
2	0	3	6	2	46	4	1	5	2	90	7	19	4	2
3	0	5	3	3	47	4	3	2	3	91	8	1	1	3
4	0	7	1	0	48	4	5	0	0	92	8	2	11	0
5	0	8	10	1	49	4	6	9	1	93	8	4	8	1
6	0	10	7	2	50	4	8	6	2	94	8	6	5	2
7	0	12	4	3	51	4	10	3	3	95	8	8	2	3
8	0	14	2	0	52	4	12	1	0	96	8	10	0	0
9	0	15	11	1	53	4	13	10	1	97	8	11	9	1
10	0	17	8	2	54	4	15	7	2	98	8	13	6	2
11	0	19	5	3	55	4	17	4	3	99	8	15	3	3
12	1	1	3	0	[56]	4	19	2	0	100	8	17	1	0
13	1	3	0	1	57	5	0	11	1	200	17	14	2	0
14	1	4	9	2	58	5	2	8	2	300	26	11	3	0
15	1	6	6	3	59	5	4	5	3	400	35	8	4	0
16	1	8	4	0	60	5	6	3	0	500	44	5	5	0
17	1	10	1	1	61	5	8	0	1	600	53	2	6	0
18	1	11	10	2	62	5	9	9	2	700	61	19	7	0
19	1	13	7	3	63	5	11	6	3	800	70	16	8	0
20	1	15	5	0	64	5	13	4	0	900	79	13	9	0
21	1	17	2	1	65	5	15	1	1	1000	88	10	10	0
22	1	18	11	2	66	5	16	10	2	2000	177	1	8	0
23	2	0	8	3	67	5	18	7	3	3000	265	12	6	0
24	2	2	6	0	68	6	0	5	0	4000	354	3	4	0
25	2	4	3	1	69	6	2	2	1	5000	442	14	2	0
26	2	6	0	2	70	6	3	11	2	6000	531	5	0	0
27	2	7	9	3	71	6	5	8	3	7000	619	15	10	0
[28]	2	9	7	0	72	6	7	6	0	8000	708	6	8	0
29	2	11	4	1	73	6	9	3	1	9000	796	17	6	0
30	2	13	1	2	74	6	11	0	2	10000	885	8	4	0
31	2	14	10	3	75	6	12	9	3					
32	2	16	8	0	76	6	14	7	0					
33	2	18	5	1	77	6	16	4	1					
34	3	0	2	2	78	6	18	1	2					
35	3	1	11	3	79	6	19	10	3					
36	3	3	9	0	80	7	1	8	0					
37	3	5	6	1	81	7	3	5	1					
38	3	7	3	2	82	7	5	2	2					
39	3	9	0	3	83	7	6	11	3					
40	3	10	10	0	[84]	7	8	9	0					
41	3	12	7	1	85	7	10	6	1					
42	3	14	4	2	86	7	12	3	2					
43	3	16	1	3	87	7	14	0	3					
44	3	17	11	0	88	7	15	10	0					

Great Hundred
112 | 9 18 4 0

Grofs
144 | 12 15 0 0

Wey
256 | 22 13 4 0

Days in a Year
365 | 32 6 4 1

Feet in a Rod
272 | 24 1 8 0

I

N.	l.	s.	d.	q.	N.	l.	s.	d.	q.	N.	l.	s.	d.	q.
1	0	1	9	2	45	4	0	7	2	89	7	19	5	2
2	0	3	7	0	46	4	2	5	0	90	8	1	3	0
3	0	5	4	2	47	4	4	2	2	91	8	3	0	2
4	0	7	2	0	48	4	6	0	0	92	8	4	10	0
5	0	8	11	2	49	4	7	9	2	93	8	6	7	2
6	0	10	9	0	50	4	9	7	0	94	8	8	5	0
7	0	12	6	2	51	4	11	4	2	95	8	10	2	2
8	0	14	4	0	52	4	13	2	0	96	8	12	0	0
9	0	16	1	2	53	4	14	11	2	97	8	13	9	2
10	0	17	11	0	54	4	16	9	0	98	8	15	7	0
11	0	19	8	2	55	4	18	6	2	99	8	17	4	2
12	1	1	6	0	[56]	5	0	4	0	100	8	19	2	0
13	1	3	3	2	57	5	2	1	2	200	17	18	4	0
14	1	5	1	0	58	5	3	11	0	300	26	17	6	0
15	1	6	10	2	59	5	5	8	2	400	35	16	8	0
16	1	8	8	0	60	5	7	6	0	500	44	15	10	0
17	1	10	5	2	61	5	9	3	2	600	53	15	0	0
18	1	12	3	0	62	5	11	1	0	700	62	14	2	0
19	1	14	0	2	63	5	12	10	2	800	71	13	4	0
20	1	15	10	0	64	5	14	8	0	900	80	12	6	0
21	1	17	7	2	65	5	16	5	2	1000	89	11	8	0
22	1	19	5	0	66	5	18	3	0	2000	179	3	4	0
23	2	1	2	2	67	6	0	0	2	3000	268	15	0	0
24	2	3	0	0	68	6	1	10	0	4000	358	6	8	0
25	2	4	9	2	69	6	3	7	2	5000	447	18	4	0
26	2	6	7	0	70	6	5	5	0	6000	537	10	0	0
27	2	8	4	2	71	6	7	2	2	7000	627	1	8	0
[28]	2	10	2	0	72	6	9	0	0	8000	716	13	4	0
29	2	11	11	2	73	6	10	9	2	9000	806	5	0	0
30	2	13	9	0	74	6	12	7	0	10000	895	16	8	0
31	2	15	6	2	75	6	14	4	2					
32	2	17	4	0	76	6	16	2	0					
33	2	19	1	2	77	6	17	11	2	*Great Hundred*				
34	3	0	11	0	78	6	19	9	0	112	10	0	8	0
35	3	2	8	2	79	7	1	6	2	*Grofs*				
36	3	4	6	0	80	7	3	4	0	144	12	18	0	0
37	3	6	3	2	81	7	5	1	2	*Wey*				
38	3	8	1	0	82	7	6	11	0	256	22	18	8	0
39	3	9	10	2	83	7	8	8	2	*Days in a Year*				
40	3	11	8	0	[84]	7	10	6	0	365	32	13	11	2
41	3	13	5	2	85	7	12	3	2	*Feet in a Rod*				
42	3	15	3	0	86	7	14	1	0	272	24	7	4	0
43	3	17	0	2	87	7	15	10	2					
44	3	18	10	0	88	7	17	8	0					

N.	l.	s.	d.	q.	N.	l.	s.	d.	q.	N.	l.	s.	d.	q.
1	0	1	9	3	45	4	1	6	3	89	8	1	3	3
2	0	3	7	2	46	4	3	4	2	90	8	3	1	2
3	0	5	5	1	47	4	5	2	1	91	8	4	11	1
4	0	7	3	0	48	4	7	0	0	92	8	6	9	0
5	0	9	0	3	49	4	8	9	3	93	8	8	6	3
6	0	10	10	2	50	4	10	7	2	94	8	10	4	2
7	0	12	8	1	51	4	12	5	1	95	8	12	2	1
8	0	14	6	0	52	4	14	3	0	96	8	14	0	0
9	0	16	3	3	53	4	16	0	3	97	8	15	9	3
10	0	18	1	2	54	4	17	10	2	98	8	17	7	2
11	0	19	11	1	55	4	19	8	1	99	8	19	5	1
12	1	1	9	0	[56]	5	1	6	0	100	9	1	3	0
13	1	3	6	3	57	5	3	3	3	200	18	2	6	0
14	1	5	4	2	58	5	5	1	2	300	27	3	9	0
15	1	7	2	1	59	5	6	11	1	400	36	5	0	0
16	1	9	0	0	60	5	8	9	0	500	45	6	3	0
17	1	10	9	3	61	5	10	6	3	600	54	7	6	0
18	1	12	7	2	62	5	12	4	2	700	63	8	9	0
19	1	14	5	1	63	5	14	2	1	800	72	10	0	0
20	1	16	3	0	64	5	16	0	0	900	81	11	3	0
21	1	18	0	3	65	5	17	9	3	1000	90	12	6	0
22	1	19	10	2	66	5	19	7	2	2000	181	5	0	0
23	2	1	8	1	67	6	1	5	1	3000	271	17	6	0
24	2	3	6	0	68	6	3	3	0	4000	362	10	0	0
25	2	5	3	3	69	6	5	0	3	5000	453	2	6	0
26	2	7	1	2	70	6	6	10	2	6000	543	15	0	0
27	2	8	11	1	71	6	8	8	1	7000	634	7	6	0
[28]	2	10	9	0	72	6	10	6	0	8000	725	0	0	0
29	2	12	6	3	73	6	12	3	3	9000	815	12	6	0
30	2	14	4	2	74	6	14	1	2	10000	906	5	0	0
31	2	16	2	1	75	6	15	11	1					
32	2	18	0	0	76	6	17	9	0					
33	2	19	9	3	77	6	19	6	3	*Great Hundred*				
34	3	1	7	2	78	7	1	4	2	112	10	3	0	0
35	3	3	5	1	79	7	3	2	1	*Grofs*				
36	3	5	3	0	80	7	5	0	0	144	13	1	0	0
37	3	7	0	3	81	7	6	9	3	*Wey*				
38	3	8	10	2	82	7	8	7	2	256	23	4	0	0
39	3	10	8	1	83	7	10	5	1	*Days in a Year*				
40	3	12	6	0	[84]	7	12	3	0	365	33	1	6	3
41	3	14	3	3	85	7	14	0	3	*Feet in a Rod*				
42	3	16	1	2	86	7	15	10	2	272	24	13	0	0
43	3	17	11	1	87	7	17	8	1					
44	3	19	9	0	88	7	19	6	0					

N.	l.	s.	d.	N.	l.	s.	d.	N.	l.	s.	d.
1	0	1	10	45	4	2	6	89	8	3	2
2	0	3	8	46	4	4	4	90	8	5	0
3	0	5	6	47	4	6	2	91	8	6	10
4	0	7	4	48	4	8	0	92	8	8	8
5	0	9	2	49	4	9	10	93	8	10	6
6	0	11	0	50	4	11	8	94	8	12	4
7	0	12	10	51	4	13	6	95	8	14	2
8	0	14	8	52	4	15	4	96	8	16	0
9	0	16	6	53	4	17	2	97	8	17	10
10	0	18	4	54	4	19	0	98	8	19	8
11	1	0	2	55	5	0	10	99	9	1	6
12	1	2	0	[56]	5	2	8	100	9	3	4
13	1	3	10	57	5	4	6	200	18	6	8
14	1	5	8	58	5	6	4	300	27	10	0
15	1	7	6	59	5	8	2	400	36	13	4
16	1	9	4	60	5	10	0	500	45	16	8
17	1	11	2	61	5	11	10	600	55	0	0
18	1	13	0	62	5	13	8	700	64	3	4
19	1	14	10	63	5	15	6	800	73	6	8
20	1	16	8	64	5	17	4	900	82	10	0
21	1	18	6	65	5	19	2	1000	91	13	4
22	2	0	4	66	6	1	0	2000	183	6	8
23	2	2	2	67	6	2	10	3000	275	0	0
24	2	4	0	68	6	4	8	4000	366	13	4
25	2	5	10	69	6	6	6	5000	458	6	8
26	2	7	8	70	6	8	4	6000	550	0	0
27	2	9	6	71	6	10	2	7000	641	13	4
[28]	2	11	4	72	6	12	0	8000	733	6	8
29	2	13	2	73	6	13	10	9000	825	0	0
30	2	15	0	74	6	15	8	10000	916	13	4
31	2	16	10	75	6	17	6				
32	2	18	8	76	6	19	4				
33	3	0	6	77	7	1	2	Great Hundred			
34	3	2	4	78	7	3	0	112	10	5	4
35	3	4	2	79	7	4	10	Grofs			
36	3	6	0	80	7	6	8	144	13	4	0
37	3	7	10	81	7	8	6	Wey			
38	3	9	8	82	7	10	4	256	23	9	4
39	3	11	6	83	7	12	2	Days in a Year			
40	3	13	4	[84]	7	14	0	365	33	9	2
41	3	15	2	85	7	15	10	Feet in a Rod			
42	3	17	0	86	7	17	8	272	24	18	8
43	3	18	10	87	7	19	6				
44	4	0	8	88	8	1	4				

N.	l.	s.	d.	q.	N.	l.	s.	d.	q.	N.	l.	s.	d.	q.
1	0	1	10	1	45	4	3	5	1	89	8	5	0	1
2	0	3	8	2	46	4	5	3	2	90	8	6	10	2
3	0	5	6	3	47	4	7	1	3	91	8	8	8	3
4	0	7	5	0	48	4	9	0	0	92	8	10	7	0
5	0	9	3	1	49	4	10	10	1	93	8	12	5	1
6	0	11	1	2	50	4	12	8	2	94	8	14	3	2
7	0	12	11	3	51	4	14	6	3	95	8	16	1	3
8	0	14	10	0	52	4	16	5	0	96	8	18	0	0
9	0	16	8	1	53	4	18	3	1	97	8	19	10	1
10	0	18	6	2	54	5	0	1	2	98	9	1	8	2
11	1	0	4	3	55	5	1	11	3	99	9	3	6	3
12	1	2	3	0	[56]	5	3	10	0	100	9	5	5	0
13	1	4	1	1	57	5	5	8	1	200	18	10	10	0
14	1	5	11	2	58	5	7	6	2	300	27	16	3	0
15	1	7	9	3	59	5	9	4	3	400	37	1	8	0
16	1	9	8	0	60	5	11	3	0	500	46	7	1	0
17	1	11	6	1	61	5	13	1	1	600	55	12	6	0
18	1	13	4	2	62	5	14	11	2	700	64	17	11	0
19	1	15	2	3	63	5	16	9	3	800	74	3	4	0
20	1	17	1	0	64	5	18	8	0	900	83	8	9	0
21	1	18	11	1	65	6	0	6	1	1000	92	14	2	0
22	2	0	9	2	66	6	2	4	2	2000	185	8	4	0
23	2	2	7	3	67	6	4	2	3	3000	278	2	6	0
24	2	4	6	0	68	6	6	1	0	4000	370	16	8	0
25	2	6	4	1	69	6	7	11	1	5000	463	10	10	0
26	2	8	2	2	70	6	9	9	2	6000	556	5	0	0
27	2	10	0	3	71	6	11	7	3	7000	648	19	2	0
[28]	2	11	11	0	72	6	13	6	0	8000	741	13	4	0
29	2	13	9	1	73	6	15	4	1	9000	834	7	6	0
30	2	15	7	2	74	6	17	2	2	10000	927	1	8	0

N.	l.	s.	d.	q.	N.	l.	s.	d.	q.
31	2	17	5	3	75	6	19	0	3
32	2	19	4	0	76	7	0	11	0
33	3	1	2	1	77	7	2	9	1
34	3	3	0	2	78	7	4	7	2
35	3	4	10	3	79	7	6	5	3
36	3	6	9	0	80	7	8	4	0
37	3	8	7	1	81	7	10	2	1
38	3	10	5	2	82	7	12	0	2
39	3	12	3	3	83	7	13	10	3
40	3	14	2	0	[84]	7	15	9	0
41	3	16	0	1	85	7	17	7	1
42	3	17	10	2	86	7	19	5	2
43	3	19	8	3	87	8	1	3	3
44	4	1	7	0	88	8	3	2	0

Great Hundred

112	10	7	8	0

Gross

144	13	7	0	0

Wey

256	23	14	8	0

Days in a Year

365	33	16	9	1

Feet in a Rod

272	25	4	4	0

N.	l.	s.	d.	q.
1	0	1	10	2
2	0	3	9	0
3	0	5	7	2
4	0	7	6	0
5	0	9	4	2
6	0	11	3	0
7	0	13	1	2
8	0	15	0	0
9	0	16	10	2
10	0	18	9	0
11	1	0	7	2
12	1	2	6	0
13	1	4	4	2
14	1	6	3	0
15	1	8	1	2
16	1	10	0	0
17	1	11	10	2
18	1	13	9	0
19	1	15	7	2
20	1	17	6	0
21	1	19	4	2
22	2	1	3	0
23	2	3	1	2
24	2	5	0	0
25	2	6	10	2
26	2	8	9	0
27	2	10	7	2
[28]	2	12	6	0
29	2	14	4	2
30	2	16	3	0
31	2	18	1	2
32	3	0	0	0
33	3	1	10	2
34	3	3	9	0
35	3	5	7	2
36	3	7	6	0
37	3	9	4	2
38	3	11	3	0
39	3	13	1	2
40	3	15	0	0
41	3	16	10	2
42	3	18	9	0
43	4	0	7	2
44	4	2	6	0

N.	l.	s.	d.	q.
45	4	4	4	2
46	4	6	3	0
47	4	8	1	2
48	4	10	0	0
49	4	11	10	2
50	4	13	9	0
51	4	15	7	2
52	4	17	6	0
53	4	19	4	2
54	5	1	3	0
55	5	3	1	2
[56]	5	5	0	0
57	5	6	10	2
58	5	8	9	0
59	5	10	7	2
60	5	12	6	0
61	5	14	4	2
62	5	16	3	0
63	5	18	1	2
64	6	0	0	0
65	6	1	10	2
66	6	3	9	0
67	6	5	7	2
68	6	7	6	0
69	6	9	4	2
70	6	11	3	0
71	6	13	1	2
72	6	15	0	0
73	6	16	10	2
74	6	18	9	0
75	7	0	7	2
76	7	2	6	0
77	7	4	4	2
78	7	6	3	0
79	7	8	1	2
80	7	10	0	0
81	7	11	10	2
82	7	13	9	0
83	7	15	7	2
[84]	7	17	6	0
85	7	19	4	2
86	8	1	3	0
87	8	3	1	2
88	8	5	0	0

N.	l.	s.	d.	q.
89	8	6	10	2
90	8	8	9	0
91	8	10	7	2
92	8	12	6	0
93	8	14	4	2
94	8	16	3	0
95	8	18	1	2
96	9	0	0	0
97	9	1	10	2
98	9	3	9	0
99	9	5	7	2
100	9	7	6	0
200	18	15	0	0
300	28	2	6	0
400	37	10	0	0
500	46	17	6	0
600	56	5	0	0
700	65	12	6	0
800	75	0	0	0
900	84	7	6	0
1000	93	15	0	0
2000	187	10	0	0
3000	281	5	0	0
4000	375	0	0	0
5000	468	15	0	0
6000	562	10	0	0
7000	656	5	0	0
8000	750	0	0	0
9000	843	15	0	0
10000	937	10	0	0

Great Hundred

112	10	10	0	0

Grofs

144	13	10	0	0

Wey

256	24	0	0	0

Days in a Year

365	34	4	4	2

Feet in a Rod

272	25	10	0	0

N.	l.	s.	d.	q.	N.	l.	s.	d.	q.	N.	l.	s.	d.	q.
1	0	1	10	3	45	4	5	3	3	89	8	8	8	3
2	0	3	9	2	46	4	7	2	2	90	8	10	7	2
3	0	5	8	1	47	4	9	1	1	91	8	12	6	1
4	0	7	7	0	48	4	11	0	0	92	8	14	5	0
5	0	9	5	3	49	4	12	10	3	93	8	16	3	3
6	0	11	4	2	50	4	14	9	2	94	8	18	2	2
7	0	13	3	1	51	4	16	8	1	95	9	0	1	1
8	0	15	2	0	52	4	18	7	0	96	9	2	0	0
9	0	17	0	3	53	5	0	5	3	97	9	3	10	3
10	0	18	11	2	54	5	2	4	2	98	9	5	9	2
11	1	0	10	1	55	5	4	3	1	99	9	7	8	1
12	1	2	9	0	[56]	5	6	2	0	100	9	9	7	0
13	1	4	7	3	57	5	8	0	3	200	18	19	2	0
14	1	6	6	2	58	5	9	11	2	300	28	8	9	0
15	1	8	5	1	59	5	11	10	:	400	37	18	4	0
16	1	10	4	0	60	5	13	9	0	500	47	7	11	0
17	1	12	2	3	61	5	15	7	3	600	56	17	6	0
18	1	14	1	2	62	5	17	6	2	700	66	7	1	0
19	1	16	0	1	63	5	19	5	1	800	75	16	8	0
20	1	17	11	0	64	6	1	4	0	900	85	6	3	0
21	1	19	9	3	65	6	3	2	3	1000	94	15	10	0
22	2	1	8	2	66	6	5	1	2	2000	189	11	8	0
23	2	3	7	1	67	6	7	0	1	3000	284	7	6	0
24	2	5	6	0	68	6	8	11	0	4000	379	3	4	0
25	2	7	4	3	69	6	10	9	3	5000	473	19	2	0
26	2	9	3	2	70	6	12	8	2	6000	568	15	0	0
27	2	11	2	1	71	6	14	7	1	7000	663	10	10	0
[28]	2	13	1	0	72	6	16	6	0	8000	758	6	8	0
29	2	14	11	3	73	6	18	4	3	9000	853	2	6	0
30	2	16	10	2	74	7	0	3	2	10000	947	18	4	0
31	2	18	9	1	75	7	2	2	1					
32	3	0	8	0	76	7	4	1	0					
33	3	2	6	3	77	7	5	11	3	**Great Hundred**				
34	3	4	5	2	78	7	7	10	2	112	10	12	4	0
35	3	6	4	1	79	7	9	9	1	*Grofs*				
36	3	8	3	0	80	7	11	8	0	144	13	13	0	0
37	3	10	1	3	81	7	13	6	3	*Wey*				
38	3	12	0	2	82	7	15	5	2	256	24	5	4	0
39	3	13	11	1	83	7	17	4	1	*Days in a Year*				
40	3	15	10	0	[84]	7	19	3	0	365	34	11	11	3
41	3	17	8	3	85	8	1	1	3	*Feet in a Rod*				
42	3	19	7	2	86	8	3	0	2	272	25	15	8	0
43	4	1	6	1	87	8	4	11	1					
44	4	3	5	0	88	8	6	10	0					

N.	l.	s.	d.	N.	l.	s.	d.	N.	l.	s.	d.
1	0	1	11	45	4	6	3	89	8	10	7
2	0	3	10	46	4	8	2	90	8	12	6
3	0	5	9	47	4	10	1	91	8	14	5
4	0	7	8	48	4	12	0	92	8	16	4
5	0	9	7	49	4	13	11	93	8	18	3
6	0	11	6	50	4	15	10	94	9	0	2
7	0	13	5	51	4	17	9	95	9	2	1
8	0	15	4	52	4	19	8	96	9	4	0
9	0	17	3	53	5	1	7	97	9	5	11
10	0	19	2	54	5	3	6	98	9	7	10
11	1	1	1	55	5	5	5	99	9	9	9
12	1	3	0	[56]	5	7	4	100	9	11	8
13	1	4	11	57	5	9	3	200	19	3	4
14	1	6	10	58	5	11	2	300	28	15	0
15	1	8	9	59	5	13	1	400	38	6	8
16	1	10	8	60	5	15	0	500	47	18	4
17	1	12	7	61	5	16	11	600	57	10	0
18	1	14	6	62	5	18	10	700	67	1	8
19	1	16	5	63	6	0	9	800	76	13	4
20	1	18	4	64	6	2	8	900	86	5	0
21	2	0	3	65	6	4	7	1000	95	16	8
22	2	2	2	66	6	6	6	2000	191	13	4
23	2	4	1	67	6	8	5	3000	287	10	0
24	2	6	0	68	6	10	4	4000	383	6	8
25	2	7	11	69	6	12	3	5000	479	3	4
26	2	9	10	70	6	14	2	6000	575	0	0
27	2	11	9	71	6	16	1	7000	670	16	8
[28	2	13	8	72	6	18	0	8000	766	13	4
29	2	15	7	73	6	19	11	9000	862	10	0
30]	2	17	6	74	7	1	10	10000	958	6	8
31	2	19	5	75	7	3	9				
32	3	1	4	76	7	5	8				
33	3	3	3	77	7	7	7				
34	3	5	2	78	7	9	6				
35	3	7	1	79	7	11	5				
36	3	9	0	80	7	13	4				
37	3	10	11	81	7	15	3				
38	3	12	10	82	7	17	2				
39	3	14	9	83	7	19	1				
40	3	16	8	[84]	8	1	0				
41	3	18	7	85	8	2	11				
42	4	0	6	86	8	4	10				
43	4	2	5	87	8	6	9				
44	4	4	4	88	8	8	8				

Great Hundred

112	10	14	8

Grofs

144	13	16	0

Wey

256	24	10	8

Days in a Year

365	34	19	7

Feet in a Rod

272	26	1	4

N.	l.	s.	d.	q.	N.	l.	s.	d.	q.	N.	l.	s.	d.	q.
1	0	1	11	1	45	4	7	2	1	89	8	12	5	1
2	0	3	10	2	46	4	9	1	2	90	8	14	4	2
3	0	5	9	3	47	4	11	0	3	91	8	16	3	3
4	0	7	9	0	48	4	13	0	0	92	8	18	3	0
5	0	9	8	1	49	4	14	11	1	93	9	0	2	1
6	0	11	7	2	50	4	16	10	2	94	9	2	1	2
7	0	13	6	3	51	4	18	9	3	95	9	4	0	3
8	0	15	6	0	52	5	0	9	0	96	9	6	0	0
9	0	17	5	1	53	5	2	8	1	97	9	7	11	1
10	0	19	4	2	54	5	4	7	2	98	9	9	10	2
11	1	1	3	3	55	5	6	6	3	99	9	11	9	3
12	1	3	3	0	[56]	5	8	6	0	100	9	13	9	0
13	1	5	2	1	57	5	10	5	1	200	19	7	6	0
14	1	7	1	2	58	5	12	4	2	300	29	1	3	0
15	1	9	0	3	59	5	14	3	3	400	38	15	0	0
16	1	11	0	0	60	5	16	3	0	500	48	8	9	0
17	1	12	11	1	61	5	18	2	1	600	58	2	6	0
18	1	14	10	2	62	6	0	1	2	700	67	16	3	0
19	1	16	9	3	63	6	2	0	3	800	77	10	0	0
20	1	18	9	0	64	6	4	0	0	900	87	3	9	0
21	2	0	8	1	65	6	5	11	1	1000	96	17	6	0
22	2	2	7	2	66	6	7	10	2	2000	193	15	0	0
23	2	4	6	3	67	6	9	9	3	3000	290	12	6	0
24	2	6	6	0	68	6	11	9	0	4000	387	10	0	0
25	2	8	5	1	69	6	13	8	1	5000	484	7	6	0
26	2	10	4	2	70	6	15	7	2	6000	581	5	0	0
27	2	12	3	3	71	6	17	6	3	7000	678	2	6	0
[28]	2	14	3	0	72	6	19	6	0	8000	775	0	0	0
29	2	16	2	1	73	7	1	5	1	9000	871	17	6	0
30	2	18	1	2	74	7	3	4	2	10000	968	15	0	0
31	3	0	0	3	75	7	5	3	3					
32	3	2	0	0	76	7	7	3	0					
33	3	3	11	1	77	7	9	2	1	**Great Hundred**				
34	3	5	10	2	78	7	11	1	2	112	10	17	0	0
35	3	7	9	3	79	7	13	0	3	*Grofs*				
36	3	9	9	0	80	7	15	0	0	144	13	19	0	0
37	3	11	8	1	81	7	16	11	1	*Wey*				
38	3	13	7	2	82	7	18	10	2	256	24	16	0	0
39	3	15	6	3	83	8	0	9	3	*Days in a Year*				
40	3	17	6	0	[84]	8	2	9	0	365	35	7	2	1
41	3	19	5	1	85	8	4	8	3	*Feet in a Rod*				
42	4	1	4	2	86	8	6	7	2	272	26	7	0	0
43	4	3	3	3	87	8	8	6	3					
44	4	5	3	0	88	8	10	6	0					

N.	l.	s.	d.	q.	N.	l.	s.	d.	q.	N.	l.	s.	d.	q.
1	0	1	11	2	45	4	8	1	2	89	8	14	3	2
2	0	3	11	0	46	4	10	1	0	90	8	16	3	0
3	0	5	10	2	47	4	12	0	2	91	8	18	2	2
4	0	7	10	0	48	4	14	0	0	92	9	0	2	0
5	0	9	9	2	49	4	15	11	2	93	9	2	1	2
6	0	11	9	0	50	4	17	11	0	94	9	4	1	0
7	0	13	8	2	51	4	19	10	2	95	9	6	0	2
8	0	15	8	0	52	5	1	10	0	96	9	8	0	0
9	0	17	7	2	53	5	3	9	2	97	9	9	11	2
10	0	19	7	0	54	5	5	9	0	98	9	11	11	0
11	1	1	6	2	55	5	7	8	2	99	9	13	10	2
12	1	3	6	0	[56]	5	9	8	0	100	9	15	10	0
13	1	5	5	2	57	5	11	7	2	200	19	11	8	0
14	1	7	5	0	58	5	13	7	0	300	29	7	6	0
15	1	9	4	2	59	5	15	6	2	400	39	3	4	0
16	1	11	4	0	60	5	17	6	0	500	48	19	2	0
17	1	13	3	2	61	5	19	5	2	600	58	15	0	0
18	1	15	3	0	62	6	1	5	0	700	68	10	10	0
19	1	17	2	2	63	6	3	4	2	800	78	6	8	0
20	1	19	2	0	64	6	5	4	0	900	88	2	6	0
21	2	1	1	2	65	6	7	3	2	1000	97	18	4	0
22	2	3	1	0	66	6	9	3	0	2000	195	16	8	0
23	2	5	0	2	67	6	11	2	2	3000	293	15	0	0
24	2	7	0	0	68	6	13	2	0	4000	391	13	4	0
25	2	8	11	2	69	6	15	1	2	5000	489	11	8	0
26	2	10	11	0	70	6	17	1	0	6000	587	10	0	0
27	2	12	10	2	71	6	19	0	2	7000	685	8	4	0
[28]	2	14	10	0	72	7	1	0	0	8000	783	6	8	0
29	2	16	9	2	73	7	2	11	2	9000	881	5	0	0
30	2	18	9	0	74	7	4	11	0	10000	979	3	4	0
31	3	0	8	2	75	7	6	10	2					
32	3	2	8	0	76	7	8	10	0					
33	3	4	7	2	77	7	10	9	2					
34	3	6	7	0	78	7	12	9	0					
35	3	8	6	2	79	7	14	8	2					
36	3	10	6	0	80	7	16	8	0					
37	3	12	5	2	81	7	18	7	2					
38	3	14	5	0	82	8	0	7	0					
39	3	16	4	2	83	8	2	6	2					
40	3	18	4	0	[84]	8	4	6	0					
41	4	0	3	2	85	8	6	5	2					
42	4	2	3	0	86	8	8	5	0					
43	4	4	2	2	87	8	10	4	2					
44	4	6	2	0	88	8	12	4	0					

Great Hundred

112 | 10 19 4 0

Gross

144 | 14 2 0 0

Wey

256 | 25 1 4 0

Days in a Year

365 | 35 14 9 2

Feet in a Rod

272 | 26 12 8 0

N.	l.	s.	d.	q.	N.	l.	s.	d.	q.	N.	l.	s.	d.	q.
1	0	1	11	3	45	4	9	0	3	89	8	16	1	3
2	0	3	11	2	46	4	11	0	2	90	8	18	1	2
3	0	5	11	1	47	4	13	0	1	91	9	0	1	1
4	0	7	11	0	48	4	15	0	0	92	9	2	1	0
5	0	9	10	3	49	4	16	11	3	93	9	4	0	3
6	0	11	10	2	50	4	18	11	2	94	9	6	0	2
7	0	13	10	1	51	5	0	11	1	95	9	8	0	1
8	0	15	10	0	52	5	2	11	0	96	9	10	0	0
9	0	17	9	3	53	5	4	10	3	97	9	11	11	3
10	0	19	9	2	54	5	6	10	2	98	9	13	11	2
11	1	1	9	1	55	5	8	10	1	99	9	15	11	1
12	1	3	9	0	[56]	5	10	10	0	100	9	17	11	0
13	1	5	8	3	57	5	12	9	3	200	19	15	10	0
14	1	7	8	2	58	5	14	9	2	300	29	13	9	0
15	1	9	8	1	59	5	16	9	1	400	39	11	8	0
16	1	11	8	0	60	5	18	9	0	500	49	9	7	0
17	1	13	7	3	61	6	0	8	3	600	59	7	6	0
18	1	15	7	2	62	6	2	8	2	700	69	5	5	0
19	1	17	7	1	63	6	4	8	1	800	79	3	4	0
20	1	19	7	0	64	6	6	8	0	900	89	1	3	0
21	2	1	6	3	65	6	8	7	3	1000	98	19	2	0
22	2	3	6	2	66	6	10	7	2	2000	197	18	4	0
23	2	5	6	1	67	6	12	7	1	3000	296	17	6	0
24	2	7	6	0	68	6	14	7	0	4000	395	16	8	0
25	2	9	5	3	69	6	16	6	3	5000	494	15	10	0
26	2	11	5	2	70	6	18	6	2	6000	593	15	0	0
27	2	13	5	1	71	7	0	6	1	7000	692	14	2	0
[28]	2	15	5	0	72	7	2	6	0	8000	791	13	4	0
29	2	17	4	3	73	7	4	5	3	9000	890	12	6	0
30	2	19	4	2	74	7	6	5	2	10000	989	11	8	0
31	3	1	4	1	75	7	8	5	1					
32	3	3	4	0	76	7	10	5	0					
33	3	5	3	3	77	7	12	4	3	*Great Hundred*				
34	3	7	3	2	78	7	14	4	2	112	11	11	8	0
35	3	9	3	1	79	7	16	4	1	*Grofs*				
36	3	11	3	0	80	7	18	4	0	144	14	5	0	0
37	3	13	2	3	81	8	0	3	3	*Wey*				
38	3	15	2	2	82	8	2	3	2	256	25	6	8	0
39	3	17	2	1	83	8	4	3	1	*Days in a Year*				
40	3	19	2	0	[84]	8	6	3	0	365	36	2	4	3
41	4	1	1	3	85	8	8	2	3	*Feet in a Rod*				
42	4	3	1	2	86	8	10	2	2	272	26	18	4	0
43	4	5	1	1	87	8	12	2	1					
44	4	7	1	0	88	8	14	2	0					

N.	l.	s.	d.
1	0	2	0
2	0	4	0
3	0	6	0
4	0	8	0
5	0	10	0
6	0	12	0
7	0	14	0
8	0	16	0
9	0	18	0
10	1	0	0
11	1	2	0
12	1	4	0
13	1	6	0
14	1	8	0
15	1	10	0
16	1	12	0
17	1	14	0
18	1	16	0
19	1	18	0
20	2	0	0
21	2	2	0
22	2	4	0
23	2	6	0
24	2	8	0
25	2	10	0
26	2	12	0
27	2	14	0
[28]	2	16	0
29	2	18	0
30	3	0	0
31	3	2	0
32	3	4	0
33	3	6	0
34	3	8	0
35	3	10	0
36	3	12	0
37	3	14	0
38	3	16	0
39	3	18	0
40	4	0	0
41	4	2	0
42	4	4	0
43	4	6	0
44	4	8	0

N.	l.	s.	d.
45	4	10	0
46	4	12	0
47	4	14	0
48	4	16	0
49	4	18	0
50	5	0	0
51	5	2	0
52	5	4	0
53	5	6	0
54	5	8	0
55	5	10	0
[56]	5	12	0
57	5	14	0
58	5	16	0
59	5	18	0
60	6	0	0
61	6	2	0
62	6	4	0
63	6	6	0
64	6	8	0
65	6	10	0
66	6	12	0
67	6	14	0
68	6	16	0
69	6	18	0
70	7	0	0
71	7	2	0
72	7	4	0
73	7	6	0
74	7	8	0
75	7	10	0
76	7	12	0
77	7	14	0
78	7	16	0
79	7	18	0
80	8	0	0
81	8	2	0
82	8	4	0
83	8	6	0
[84]	8	8	0
85	8	10	0
86	8	12	0
87	8	14	0
88	8	16	0

N.	l.	s.	d.
89	8	18	0
90	9	0	0
91	9	2	0
92	9	4	0
93	9	6	0
94	9	8	0
95	9	10	0
96	9	12	0
97	9	14	0
98	9	16	0
99	9	18	0
100	10	0	0
200	20	0	0
300	30	0	0
400	40	0	0
500	50	0	0
600	60	0	0
700	70	0	0
800	80	0	0
900	90	0	0
1000	100	0	0
2000	200	0	0
3000	300	0	0
4000	400	0	0
5000	500	0	0
6000	600	0	0
7000	700	0	0
8000	800	0	0
9000	900	0	0
10000	1000	0	0

Great Hundred

112 | 11   4   0

Gross

144 | 14   8   0

Wey

256 | 25   12   0

Days in a Year

365 | 36   10   0

Feet in a Rod

272 | 27   4   0

N.	l.	s.	d.	q.	N.	l.	s.	d.	q.	N.	l.	s.	d.	q.
1	0	2	0	2	45	4	11	10	2	89	9	1	8	2
2	0	4	1	0	46	4	13	11	0	90	9	3	9	0
3	0	6	1	2	47	4	15	11	2	91	9	5	9	2
4	0	8	2	0	48	4	18	0	0	92	9	7	10	0
5	0	10	2	2	49	5	0	0	2	93	9	9	10	2
6	0	12	3	0	50	5	2	1	0	94	9	11	11	0
7	0	14	3	2	51	5	4	1	2	95	9	13	11	2
8	0	16	4	0	52	5	6	2	0	96	9	16	0	0
9	0	18	4	2	53	5	8	2	2	97	9	18	0	2
10	1	0	5	0	54	5	10	3	0	98	10	0	1	0
11	1	2	5	2	55	5	12	3	2	99	10	2	1	2
12	1	4	6	0	[56]	5	14	4	0	100	10	4	2	0
13	1	6	6	2	57	5	16	4	2	200	20	8	4	0
14	1	8	7	0	58	5	18	5	0	300	30	12	6	0
15	1	10	7	2	59	6	0	5	2	400	40	16	8	0
16	1	12	8	0	60	6	2	6	0	500	51	0	10	0
17	1	14	8	2	61	6	4	6	2	600	61	5	0	0
18	1	16	9	0	62	6	6	7	0	700	71	9	2	0
19	1	18	9	2	63	6	8	7	2	800	81	13	4	0
20	2	0	10	0	64	6	10	8	0	900	91	17	6	0
21	2	2	10	2	65	6	12	8	2	1000	102	1	8	0
22	2	4	11	0	66	6	14	9	0	2000	204	3	4	0
23	2	6	11	2	67	6	16	9	2	3000	306	5	0	0
24	2	9	0	0	68	6	18	10	0	4000	408	6	8	0
25	2	11	0	2	69	7	0	10	2	5000	510	8	4	0
26	2	13	1	0	70	7	2	11	0	6000	612	10	0	0
27	2	15	1	2	71	7	4	11	2	7000	714	11	8	0
[28]	2	17	2	0	72	7	7	0	0	8000	816	13	4	0
29	2	19	2	2	73	7	9	0	2	9000	918	15	0	0
30	3	1	3	0	74	7	11	1	0	10000	1020	16	8	0
31	3	3	3	2	75	7	13	1	2					
32	3	5	4	0	76	7	15	2	0					
33	3	7	4	2	77	7	17	2	2	Great Hundred				
34	3	9	5	0	78	7	19	3	0	112	11	8	8	0
35	3	11	5	2	79	8	1	3	2					
36	3	13	6	0	80	8	3	4	0	Grofs				
37	3	15	6	2	81	8	5	4	2	144	14	14	0	0
38	3	17	7	0	82	8	7	5	0	Wey				
39	3	19	7	2	83	8	9	5	2	256	26	2	8	0
40	4	1	8	0	[84]	8	11	6	0	Days in a Year				
41	4	3	8	2	85	8	13	6	2	365	37	5	2	2
42	4	5	9	0	86	8	15	7	0	Feet in a Rod				
43	4	7	9	2	87	8	17	7	2	272	27	15	4	0
44	4	9	10	0	88	8	19	8	0					

K

N.	l.	s.	d.
1	0	2	1
2	0	4	2
3	0	6	3
4	0	8	4
5	0	10	5
6	0	12	6
7	0	14	7
8	0	16	8
9	0	18	9
10	1	0	10
11	1	2	11
12	1	5	0
13	1	7	1
14	1	9	2
15	1	11	3
16	1	13	4
17	1	15	5
18	1	17	6
19	1	19	7
20	2	1	8
21	2	3	9
22	2	5	10
23	2	7	11
24	2	10	0
25	2	12	1
26	2	14	2
27	2	16	3
[28]	2	18	4
29	3	0	5
30	3	2	6
31	3	4	7
32	3	6	8
33	3	8	9
34	3	10	10
35	3	12	11
36	3	15	0
37	3	17	1
38	3	19	2
39	4	1	3
40	4	3	4
41	4	5	5
42	4	7	6
43	4	9	7
44	4	11	8

N.	l.	s.	d.
45	4	13	9
46	4	15	10
47	4	17	11
48	5	0	0
49	5	2	1
50	5	4	2
51	5	6	3
52	5	8	4
53	5	10	5
54	5	12	6
55	5	14	7
[56]	5	16	8
57	5	18	9
58	6	0	10
59	6	2	11
60	6	5	0
61	6	7	1
62	6	9	2
63	6	11	3
64	6	13	4
65	6	15	5
66	6	17	6
67	6	19	7
68	7	1	8
69	7	3	9
70	7	5	10
71	7	7	11
72	7	10	0
73	7	12	1
74	7	14	2
75	7	16	4
76	7	18	3
77	8	0	5
78	8	2	6
79	8	4	7
80	8	6	8
81	8	8	9
82	8	10	10
83	8	12	11
[84]	8	15	0
85	8	17	1
86	8	19	2
87	9	1	3
88	9	3	4

N.	l.	s.	d.
89	9	5	5
90	9	7	6
91	9	9	7
92	9	11	8
93	9	13	9
94	9	15	10
95	9	17	11
96	10	0	0
97	10	2	1
98	10	4	2
99	10	6	3
100	10	8	4
200	20	16	8
300	31	5	0
400	41	13	4
500	52	1	8
600	62	10	0
700	72	18	4
800	83	6	8
900	93	15	0
1000	104	3	4
2000	208	6	8
3000	312	10	0
4000	416	13	4
5000	520	16	8
6000	625	0	0
7000	729	3	4
8000	833	6	8
9000	937	10	0
10000	1041	13	4

Great Hundred

112	11	13	4

Grofs

144	15	0	0

Wey

256	26	13	4

Days in a Year

365	38	0	5

Feet in a Rod

272	28	6	8

N.	l.	s.	d.	q.
1	0	2	1	2
2	0	4	3	0
3	0	6	4	2
4	0	8	6	0
5	0	10	7	2
6	0	12	9	0
7	0	14	10	2
8	0	17	0	0
9	0	19	1	2
10	1	1	3	0
11	1	3	4	2
12	1	5	6	0
13	1	7	7	2
14	1	9	9	0
15	1	11	10	2
16	1	14	0	0
17	1	16	1	2
18	1	18	3	0
19	2	0	4	2
20	2	2	6	0
21	2	4	7	2
22	2	6	9	0
23	2	8	10	2
24	2	11	0	0
25	2	13	1	2
26	2	15	3	0
27	2	17	4	2
[28]	2	19	6	0
29	3	1	7	2
30	3	3	9	0
31	3	5	10	2
32	3	8	0	0
33	3	10	1	2
34	3	12	3	0
35	3	14	4	2
36	3	16	6	0
37	3	18	7	2
38	4	0	9	0
39	4	2	10	2
40	4	5	0	0
41	4	7	1	2
42	4	9	3	0
43	4	11	4	2
44	4	13	6	0

N.	l.	s.	d.	q.
45	4	15	7	2
46	4	17	9	0
47	4	19	10	2
48	5	2	0	0
49	5	4	1	2
50	5	6	3	0
51	5	8	4	2
52	5	10	6	0
53	5	12	7	2
54	5	14	9	0
55	5	16	10	2
[56]	5	19	0	0
57	6	1	1	2
58	6	3	3	0
59	6	5	4	2
60	6	7	6	0
61	6	9	7	2
62	6	11	9	0
63	6	13	10	2
64	6	16	0	0
65	6	18	1	2
66	7	0	3	0
67	7	2	4	2
68	7	4	6	0
69	7	6	7	2
70	7	8	9	0
71	7	10	10	2
72	7	13	0	0
73	7	15	1	2
74	7	17	3	0
75	7	19	4	2
76	8	1	6	0
77	8	3	7	2
78	8	5	9	0
79	8	7	10	2
80	8	10	0	0
81	8	12	1	2
82	8	14	3	0
83	8	16	4	2
[84]	8	18	6	0
85	9	0	7	2
86	9	2	9	0
87	9	4	10	2
88	9	7	0	0

N	l.	s.	d.	q.
89	9	9	1	2
90	9	11	3	0
91	9	13	4	2
92	9	15	6	0
93	9	17	7	2
94	9	19	9	0
95	10	1	10	2
96	10	4	0	0
97	10	6	1	2
98	10	8	3	0
99	10	10	4	2
100	10	12	6	0
200	21	5	0	0
300	31	17	6	0
400	42	10	0	0
500	53	2	6	0
600	63	15	0	0
700	74	7	6	0
800	85	0	0	0
900	95	12	6	0
1000	106	5	0	0
2000	212	10	0	0
3000	318	15	0	0
4000	425	0	0	0
5000	531	5	0	0
6000	637	10	0	0
7000	743	15	0	0
8000	850	0	0	0
9000	956	5	0	0
10000	1062	10	0	0

Great Hundred

112	11	18	0	0

Grofs

144	15	6	0	0

Wey

256	27	4	0	0

Days in a Year

365	38	15	7	2

Feet in a Rod

272	28	18	0	0

N.	l.	s.	d.	N.	l.	s.	d.	N.	l.	s.	d.
1	0	2	2	45	4	17	6	89	9	12	10
2	0	4	4	46	4	19	8	90	9	15	0
3	0	6	6	47	5	1	10	91	9	17	2
4	0	8	8	48	5	4	0	92	9	19	4
5	0	10	10	49	5	6	2	93	10	1	6
6	0	13	0	50	5	8	4	94	10	3	8
7	0	15	2	51	5	10	6	95	10	5	10
8	0	17	4	52	5	12	8	96	10	8	0
9	0	19	6	53	5	14	10	97	10	10	2
10	1	1	8	54	5	17	0	98	10	12	4
11	1	3	10	55	5	19	2	99	10	14	6
12	1	6	0	[56]	6	1	4	100	10	16	8
13	1	8	2	57	6	3	6	200	21	13	4
14	1	10	4	58	6	5	8	300	32	10	0
15	1	12	6	59	6	7	10	400	43	6	8
16	1	14	8	60	6	10	0	500	54	3	4
17	1	16	10	61	6	12	2	600	65	0	0
18	1	19	0	62	6	14	4	700	75	16	8
19	2	1	2	63	6	16	6	800	86	13	4
20	2	3	4	64	6	18	8	900	97	10	0
21	2	5	6	65	7	0	10	1000	108	6	8
22	2	7	8	66	7	3	0	2000	216	13	4
23	2	9	10	67	7	5	2	3000	325	0	0
24	2	12	0	68	7	7	4	4000	433	6	8
25	2	14	2	69	7	9	6	5000	541	13	4
26	2	16	4	70	7	11	8	6000	650	0	0
27	2	18	6	71	7	13	10	7000	758	6	8
[28]	3	0	8	72	7	16	0	8000	866	13	4
29	3	2	10	73	7	18	2	9000	975	0	0
30	3	5	0	74	8	0	4	10000	1083	6	8
31	3	7	2	75	8	2	6				
32	3	9	4	76	8	4	8				
33	3	11	6	77	8	6	10	Great Hundred			
34	3	13	8	78	8	9	0	112	12	2	8
35	3	15	10	79	8	11	2	Grofs			
36	3	18	0	80	8	13	4	144	15	12	0
37	4	0	2	81	8	15	6	Wey			
38	4	2	4	82	8	17	8	256	27	14	8
39	4	4	6	83	8	19	10	Days in a Year			
40	4	6	8	[84]	9	2	0	365	39	10	10
41	4	8	10	85	9	4	2	Feet in a Rod			
42	4	11	0	86	9	6	4	272	29	9	4
43	4	13	2	87	9	8	6				
44	4	15	4	88	9	10	8				

N.	l.	s.	d.	q.
1	0	2	2	2
2	0	4	5	0
3	0	6	7	2
4	0	8	10	0
5	0	11	0	2
6	0	13	3	0
7	0	15	5	2
8	0	17	8	0
9	0	19	10	2
10	1	2	1	0
11	1	4	3	2
12	1	6	6	0
13	1	8	8	2
14	1	10	11	0
15	1	13	1	2
16	1	15	4	0
17	1	17	6	2
18	1	19	9	0
19	2	1	11	2
20	2	4	2	0
21	2	6	4	2
22	2	8	7	0
23	2	10	9	2
24	2	13	0	0
25	2	15	2	2
26	2	17	5	0
27	2	19	7	2
[28]	3	1	10	0
29	3	4	0	2
30	3	6	3	0
31	3	8	5	2
32	3	10	8	0
33	3	12	10	2
34	3	15	1	0
35	3	17	3	2
36	3	19	6	0
37	4	1	8	2
38	4	3	11	0
39	4	6	1	2
40	4	8	4	0
41	4	10	6	2
42	4	12	9	0
43	4	14	11	2
44	4	17	2	0

N.	l.	s.	d.	q.
45	4	19	4	2
46	5	1	7	0
47	5	3	9	2
48	5	6	0	0
49	5	8	2	2
50	5	10	5	0
51	5	12	7	2
52	5	14	10	0
53	5	17	0	2
54	5	19	3	0
55	6	1	5	2
[56]	6	3	8	0
57	6	5	10	2
58	6	8	1	0
59	6	10	3	2
60	6	12	6	0
61	6	14	8	2
62	6	16	11	0
63	6	19	1	2
64	7	1	4	0
65	7	3	6	2
66	7	5	9	0
67	7	7	11	2
68	7	10	2	0
69	7	12	4	2
70	7	14	7	0
71	7	16	9	2
72	7	19	0	0
73	8	1	2	2
74	8	3	5	0
75	8	5	7	2
76	8	7	10	0
77	8	10	0	2
78	8	12	3	0
79	8	14	5	2
80	8	16	8	0
81	8	18	10	2
82	9	1	1	0
83	9	3	3	2
[84]	9	5	6	0
85	9	7	8	2
86	9	9	11	0
87	9	12	1	2
88	9	14	4	0

N.	l.	s.	d.	q.
89	9	16	6	2
90	9	18	9	0
91	10	0	11	2
92	10	3	2	0
93	10	5	4	2
94	10	7	7	0
95	10	9	9	2
96	10	12	0	0
97	10	14	2	2
98	10	16	5	0
99	10	18	7	2
100	11	0	10	0
200	22	1	8	0
300	33	2	6	0
400	44	3	4	0
500	55	4	2	0
600	66	5	0	0
700	77	5	10	0
800	88	6	8	0
900	99	7	6	0
1000	110	8	4	0
2000	220	16	8	0
3000	331	5	0	0
4000	441	13	4	0
5000	552	1	8	0
6000	662	10	0	0
7000	772	18	4	0
8000	883	6	8	0
9000	993	15	0	0
10000	1104	3	4	0

Great Hundred

112	12	7	4	0

Grofs

144	15	18	0	0

Wey

256	28	5	4	0

Days in a Year

365	40	6	0	2

Feet in a Rod

272	30	0	8	0

K 3

N.	l.	s.	d.
1	0	2	3
2	0	4	6
3	0	6	9
4	0	9	0
5	0	11	3
6	0	13	6
7	0	15	9
8	0	18	0
9	1	0	3
10	1	2	6
11	1	4	9
12	1	7	0
13	1	9	3
14	1	11	6
15	1	13	9
16	1	16	0
17	1	18	3
18	2	0	6
19	2	2	9
20	2	5	0
21	2	7	3
22	2	9	6
23	2	11	9
24	2	14	0
25	2	16	3
26	1	18	6
27	3	0	9
[28]	3	3	0
29	3	5	3
30	3	7	6
31	3	9	9
32	3	12	0
33	3	14	3
34	3	16	6
35	3	18	9
36	4	1	0
37	4	3	3
38	4	5	6
39	4	7	9
40	4	10	0
41	4	12	3
42	4	14	6
43	4	16	9
44	4	19	0

N.	l.	s.	d.
45	5	1	3
46	5	3	6
47	5	5	9
48	5	8	0
49	5	10	3
50	5	12	6
51	5	14	9
52	5	17	0
53	5	19	3
54	6	1	6
55	6	3	9
[56]	6	6	0
57	6	8	3
58	6	10	6
59	6	12	9
60	6	15	0
61	6	17	3
62	6	19	6
63	7	1	9
64	7	4	0
65	7	6	3
66	7	8	6
67	7	10	9
68	7	13	0
69	7	15	3
70	7	17	6
71	7	19	9
72	8	2	0
73	8	4	3
74	8	6	6
75	8	8	9
76	8	11	0
77	8	13	3
78	8	15	6
79	8	17	9
80	9	0	0
81	9	2	3
82	9	4	6
83	9	6	9
[84]	9	9	0
85	9	11	3
86	9	13	6
87	9	15	9
88	9	18	0

N.	l.	s.	d.
89	10	0	3
90	10	2	6
91	10	4	9
92	10	7	0
93	10	9	3
94	10	11	6
95	10	13	9
96	10	16	0
97	10	18	3
98	11	0	6
99	11	2	9
100	11	5	0
200	22	10	0
300	33	15	0
400	45	0	0
500	56	5	0
600	67	10	0
700	78	15	0
800	90	0	0
900	101	5	0
1000	112	10	0
2000	225	0	0
3000	337	10	0
4000	450	0	0
5000	562	10	0
6000	675	0	0
7000	787	10	0
8000	900	0	0
9000	1012	10	0
10000	1125	0	0

Great Hundred

112	12	12	0

Grefs

144	16	4	0

Wey

256	28	16	0

Days in a Year

365	41	1	3

Feet in a Rod

272	30	12	0

N.	l.	s.	d.	q.	N.	l.	s.	d.	q.	N.	l.	s.	d.	q.
1	0	2	3	2	45	5	3	1	2	89	10	3	11	2
2	0	4	7	0	46	5	5	5	0	90	10	6	3	0
3	0	6	10	2	47	5	7	8	2	91	10	8	6	2
4	0	9	2	0	48	5	10	0	0	92	10	10	10	0
5	0	11	5	2	49	5	12	3	2	93	10	13	1	2
6	0	13	9	0	50	5	14	7	0	94	10	15	5	0
7	0	16	0	2	51	5	16	10	2	95	10	17	8	2
8	0	18	4	0	52	5	19	2	0	96	11	0	0	0
9	1	0	7	2	53	6	1	5	2	97	11	2	3	2
10	1	2	11	0	54	6	3	9	0	98	11	4	7	0
11	1	5	2	2	55	6	6	0	2	99	11	6	10	2
12	1	7	6	0	[56]	6	8	4	0	100	11	9	2	0
13	1	9	9	2	57	6	10	7	2	200	22	18	4	0
14	1	12	1	0	58	6	12	11	0	300	34	7	6	0
15	1	14	4	2	59	6	15	2	2	400	45	16	8	0
16	1	16	8	0	60	6	17	6	0	500	57	5	10	0
17	1	18	11	2	61	6	19	9	2	600	68	15	0	0
18	2	1	3	0	62	7	2	1	0	700	80	4	2	0
19	2	3	6	2	63	7	4	4	2	800	91	13	4	0
20	2	5	10	0	64	7	6	8	0	900	103	2	6	0
21	2	8	1	2	65	7	8	11	2	1000	114	11	8	0
22	2	10	5	0	66	7	11	3	0	2000	229	3	4	0
23	2	12	8	2	67	7	13	6	2	3000	343	15	0	0
24	2	15	0	0	68	7	15	10	0	4000	458	6	8	0
25	2	17	3	2	69	7	18	1	2	5000	572	18	4	0
26	2	19	7	0	70	8	0	5	0	6000	687	10	0	0
27	3	1	10	2	71	8	2	8	2	7000	802	1	8	0
[28]	3	4	2	0	72	8	5	0	0	8000	916	13	4	0
29	3	6	5	2	73	8	7	3	2	9000	1031	5	0	0
30	3	8	9	0	74	8	9	7	0	10000	1145	16	8	0
31	3	11	0	2	75	8	11	10	2					
32	3	13	4	0	76	8	14	2	0					
33	3	15	7	2	77	8	16	5	2	*Great Hundred*				
34	3	17	11	0	78	8	18	9	0	112	12	16	8	0
35	4	0	2	2	79	9	1	0	2	*Grofs*				
36	4	2	6	0	80	9	3	4	0	144	16	10	0	0
37	4	4	9	2	81	9	5	7	2	*Wey*				
38	4	7	1	0	82	9	7	11	0	256	29	6	8	0
39	4	9	4	2	83	9	10	2	2	*Days in a Year*				
40	4	11	8	0	[84]	9	12	6	0	365	41	16	5	2
41	4	13	11	2	85	9	14	9	2	*Feet in a Rod*				
42	4	16	3	0	86	9	17	1	0	272	31	3	4	0
43	4	18	6	2	87	9	19	4	2					
44	5	0	10	0	88	10	1	8	0					

N.	l.	s.	d.	N.	l.	s.	d.	N.	l.	s.	d.
1	0	2	4	45	5	5	0	89	10	7	8
2	0	4	8	46	5	7	4	90	10	10	0
3	0	7	0	47	5	9	8	91	10	12	4
4	0	9	4	48	5	12	0	92	10	14	8
5	0	11	8	49	5	14	4	93	10	17	0
6	0	14	0	50	5	16	8	94	10	19	4
7	0	16	4	51	5	19	0	95	11	1	8
8	0	18	8	52	6	1	4	96	11	4	0
9	1	1	0	53	6	3	8	97	11	6	4
10	1	3	4	54	6	6	0	98	11	8	8
11	1	5	8	55	6	8	4	99	11	11	0
12	1	8	0	[56]	6	10	8	100	11	13	4
13	1	10	4	57	6	13	0	200	23	6	8
14	1	12	8	58	6	15	4	300	35	0	0
15	1	15	0	59	6	17	8	400	46	13	4
16	1	17	4	60	7	0	0	500	58	6	8
17	1	19	8	61	7	2	4	600	70	0	0
18	2	2	0	62	7	4	8	700	81	13	4
19	2	4	4	63	7	7	0	800	93	6	8
20	2	6	8	64	7	9	4	900	105	0	0
21	2	9	0	65	7	11	8	1000	116	13	4
22	2	11	4	66	7	14	0	2000	233	6	8
23	2	13	8	67	7	16	4	3000	350	0	0
24	2	16	0	68	7	18	8	4000	466	13	4
25	2	18	4	69	8	1	0	5000	583	6	8
26	3	0	8	70	8	3	4	6000	700	0	0
27	3	3	0	71	8	5	8	7000	816	13	4
[28]	3	5	4	72	8	8	0	8000	933	6	8
29	3	7	8	73	8	10	4	9000	1050	0	0
30	3	10	0	74	8	12	8	10000	1166	13	4
31	3	12	4	75	8	15	0				
32	3	14	8	76	8	17	4				
33	3	17	0	77	8	19	8	*Great Hundred*			
34	3	19	4	78	9	2	0	112	13	1	4
35	4	1	8	79	9	4	4	*Grofs*			
36	4	4	0	80	9	6	8	144	16	16	0
37	4	6	4	81	9	9	0	*Wey*			
38	4	8	8	82	9	11	4	256	29	17	4
39	4	11	0	83	9	13	8	*Days in a Year*			
40	4	13	4	[84]	9	16	0	365	42	11	8
41	4	15	8	85	9	18	4	*Feet in a Rod*			
42	4	18	0	86	10	0	8	272	31	14	8
43	5	0	4	87	10	3	0				
44	5	2	8	88	10	5	4				

N.	l.	s.	d.	q.	N.	l.	s.	d.	q.	N.	l.	s.	d.	q.
1	0	2	4	2	45	5	6	10	2	89	10	11	4	2
2	0	4	9	0	46	5	9	3	0	90	10	13	9	0
3	0	7	1	2	47	5	11	7	2	91	10	16	1	2
4	0	9	6	0	48	5	14	0	0	92	10	18	6	0
5	0	11	10	2	49	5	16	4	2	93	11	0	10	2
6	0	14	3	0	50	5	18	9	0	94	11	3	3	0
7	0	16	7	2	51	6	1	1	2	95	11	5	7	2
8	0	19	0	0	52	6	3	6	0	96	11	8	0	0
9	1	1	4	2	53	6	5	10	2	97	11	10	4	2
10	1	3	9	0	54	6	8	3	0	98	11	12	9	0
11	1	6	1	2	55	6	10	7	2	99	11	15	1	2
12	1	8	6	0	[56]	6	13	0	0	100	11	17	6	0
13	1	10	10	2	57	6	15	4	2	200	23	15	0	0
14	1	13	3	0	58	6	17	9	0	300	35	12	6	0
15	1	15	7	2	59	7	0	1	2	400	47	10	0	0
16	1	18	0	0	60	7	2	6	0	500	59	7	6	0
17	2	0	4	2	61	7	4	10	2	600	71	5	0	0
18	2	2	9	0	62	7	7	3	0	700	83	2	6	0
19	2	5	1	2	63	7	9	7	2	800	95	0	0	0
20	2	7	6	0	64	7	12	0	0	900	106	17	6	0
21	2	9	10	2	65	7	14	4	2	1000	118	15	0	0
22	2	12	3	0	66	7	16	9	0	2000	237	10	0	0
23	2	14	7	2	67	7	19	1	2	3000	356	5	0	0
24	2	17	0	0	68	8	1	6	0	4000	475	0	0	0
25	2	19	4	2	69	8	3	10	2	5000	593	15	0	0
26	3	1	9	0	70	8	6	3	0	6000	712	10	0	0
27	3	4	1	2	71	8	8	7	2	7000	831	5	0	0
[28]	3	6	6	0	72	8	11	0	0	8000	950	0	0	0
29	3	8	10	2	73	8	13	4	2	9000	1068	15	0	0
30	3	11	3	0	74	8	15	9	0	10000	1187	10	0	0
31	3	13	7	2	75	8	18	1	2					
32	3	16	0	0	76	9	0	6	0					
33	3	18	4	2	77	9	2	10	2		*Great Hundred*			
34	4	0	9	0	78	9	5	3	0	112	13	6	0	0
35	4	3	1	2	79	9	7	7	2		*Grofs*			
36	4	5	6	0	80	9	10	0	0	144	17	2	0	0
37	4	7	10	2	81	9	12	4	2		*Wey*			
38	4	10	3	0	82	9	14	9	0	256	30	8	0	0
39	4	12	7	2	83	9	17	1	2		*Days in a Year*			
40	4	15	0	0	[84]	9	19	6	0	365	43	6	10	2
41	4	17	4	2	85	10	1	10	2		*Feet in a Rod*			
42	4	19	9	0	86	10	4	3	0	272	32	6	0	0
43	5	2	1	2	87	10	6	7	2					
44	5	4	6	0	88	10	9	0	0					

N.	l.	s.	d.	N.	l.	s.	d.	N.	l.	s.	d.
1	0	2	5	45	5	8	9	89	10	15	1
2	0	4	10	46	5	11	2	90	10	17	6
3	0	7	3	47	5	13	7	91	10	19	11
4	0	9	8	48	5	16	0	92	11	2	4
5	0	12	1	49	5	18	5	93	11	4	9
6	0	14	6	50	6	0	10	94	11	7	2
7	0	16	11	51	6	3	3	95	11	9	7
8	0	19	4	52	6	5	8	96	11	12	0
9	1	1	9	53	6	8	1	97	11	14	5
10	1	4	2	54	6	10	6	98	11	16	10
11	1	6	7	55	6	12	11	99	11	19	3
12	1	9	0	[56]	6	15	4	100	12	1	8
13	1	11	5	57	6	17	9	200	24	3	4
14	1	13	10	58	7	0	2	300	36	5	0
15	1	16	3	59	7	2	7	400	48	6	8
16	1	18	8	60	7	5	0	500	60	8	4
17	2	1	1	61	7	7	5	600	72	10	0
18	2	3	6	62	7	9	10	700	84	11	8
19	2	5	11	63	7	12	3	800	96	13	4
20	2	8	4	64	7	14	8	900	108	15	0
21	2	10	9	65	7	17	1	1000	120	16	8
22	2	13	2	66	7	19	6	2000	241	13	4
23	2	15	7	67	8	1	11	3000	362	10	0
24	2	18	0	68	8	4	4	4000	483	6	8
25	3	0	5	69	8	6	9	5000	604	3	4
26	3	2	10	70	8	9	2	6000	725	0	0
27	3	5	3	71	8	11	7	7000	845	16	8
[28]	3	7	0	72	8	14	0	8000	966	13	4
29	3	10	1	73	8	16	5	9000	1087	10	0
30	3	12	6	74	8	18	10	10000	1208	6	8
31	3	14	11	75	9	1	3				
32	3	17	4	76	9	3	8				
33	3	19	9	77	9	6	1	Great Hundred			
34	4	2	2	78	9	8	6	112	13	10	8
35	4	4	7	79	9	10	11	Grofs			
36	4	7	0	80	9	13	4	144	17	8	0
37	4	9	5	81	9	15	9	Wey			
38	4	11	10	82	9	18	2	256	30	18	8
39	4	14	3	83	10	0	7	Days in a Year			
40	4	16	8	[84]	10	3	0	365	44	2	1
41	4	19	1	85	10	5	5	Feet in a Rod			
42	5	1	6	86	10	7	10	272	32	17	4
43	5	3	11	87	10	10	3				
44	5	6	4	88	10	12	8				

N.	l.	s.	d.	q.
1	0	2	5	2
2	0	4	11	0
3	0	7	4	2
4	0	9	10	0
5	0	12	3	2
6	0	14	9	0
7	0	17	2	2
8	0	19	8	0
9	1	2	1	2
10	1	4	7	0
11	1	7	0	2
12	1	9	6	0
13	1	11	11	2
14	1	14	5	0
15	1	16	10	2
16	1	19	4	0
17	2	1	9	2
18	2	4	3	0
19	2	6	8	2
20	2	9	2	0
21	2	11	7	2
22	2	14	1	0
23	2	16	6	2
24	2	19	0	0
25	3	1	5	2
26	3	3	11	0
27	3	6	4	2
[28]	3	8	10	0
29	3	11	3	2
30	3	13	9	0
31	3	16	2	2
32	3	18	8	0
33	4	1	1	2
34	4	3	7	0
35	4	6	0	2
36	4	8	6	0
37	4	10	11	2
38	4	13	5	0
39	4	15	10	2
40	4	18	4	0
41	5	0	9	2
42	5	3	3	0
43	5	5	8	2
44	5	8	2	0

N.	l.	s.	d.	q.
45	5	10	7	2
46	5	13	1	0
47	5	15	6	2
48	5	18	0	0
49	6	0	5	2
50	6	2	11	0
51	6	5	4	2
52	6	7	10	0
53	6	10	3	2
54	6	12	9	0
55	6	15	2	2
[56]	6	17	8	0
57	7	0	1	2
58	7	2	7	0
59	7	5	0	2
60	7	7	6	0
61	7	9	11	2
62	7	12	5	0
63	7	14	10	2
64	7	17	4	0
65	7	19	9	2
66	8	2	3	0
67	8	4	8	2
68	8	7	2	0
69	8	9	7	2
70	8	12	1	0
71	8	14	6	2
72	8	17	0	0
73	8	19	5	2
74	9	1	11	0
75	9	4	4	2
76	9	6	10	0
77	9	9	3	2
78	9	11	9	0
79	9	14	2	2
80	9	16	8	0
81	9	19	1	2
82	10	1	7	0
83	10	4	0	2
[84]	10	6	6	0
85	10	8	11	2
86	10	11	5	0
87	10	13	10	2
88	10	16	4	0

N.	l.	s.	d.	q.
89	10	18	9	2
90	11	1	3	0
91	11	3	8	2
92	11	6	2	0
93	11	8	7	2
94	11	11	1	0
95	11	13	6	2
96	11	16	0	0
97	11	18	5	2
98	12	0	11	0
99	12	3	4	2
100	12	5	10	0
200	24	11	8	0
300	36	17	6	0
400	49	3	4	0
500	61	9	2	0
600	73	15	0	0
700	86	0	10	0
800	98	6	8	0
900	110	12	6	0
1000	122	18	4	0
2000	245	16	8	0
3000	368	15	0	0
4000	491	13	4	0
5000	614	11	8	0
6000	737	10	0	0
7000	860	8	4	0
8000	983	6	8	0
9000	1106	5	0	0
10000	1229	3	4	0

Great Hundred

112	13	15	4	0

Gross

144	17	14	0	0

Wey

256	31	9	4	0

Days in a Year

365	44	17	3	2

Feet in a Rod

272	33	8	8	0

N.	l.	s.	d.	N.	l.	s.	d.	N.	l.	s.	d.
1	0	2	6	45	5	12	6	89	11	2	6
2	0	5	0	46	5	15	0	90	11	5	0
3	0	7	6	47	5	17	6	91	11	7	6
4	0	10	0	48	6	0	0	92	11	10	0
5	0	12	6	49	6	2	6	93	11	12	6
6	0	15	0	50	6	5	0	94	11	15	0
7	0	17	6	51	6	7	6	95	11	17	6
8	1	0	0	52	6	10	0	96	12	0	0
9	1	2	6	53	6	12	6	97	12	2	6
10	1	5	0	54	6	15	0	98	12	5	0
11	1	7	6	55	6	17	6	99	12	7	6
12	1	10	0	[56]	7	0	0	100	12	10	0
13	1	12	6	57	7	2	6	200	25	0	0
14	1	15	0	58	7	5	0	300	37	10	0
15	1	17	6	59	7	7	6	400	50	0	0
16	2	0	0	60	7	10	0	500	62	10	0
17	2	2	6	61	7	12	6	600	75	0	0
18	2	5	0	62	7	15	0	700	87	10	0
19	2	7	6	63	7	17	6	800	100	0	0
20	2	10	0	64	8	0	0	900	112	10	0
21	2	12	6	65	8	2	6	1000	125	0	0
22	2	15	0	66	8	5	0	2000	250	0	0
23	2	17	6	67	8	7	6	3000	375	0	0
24	3	0	0	68	8	10	0	4000	500	0	0
25	3	2	6	69	8	12	6	5000	625	0	0
26	3	5	0	70	8	15	0	6000	750	0	0
27	3	7	6	71	8	17	6	7000	875	0	0
[28]	3	10	0	72	9	0	0	8000	1000	0	0
29	3	12	6	73	9	2	6	9000	1125	0	0
30	3	15	0	74	9	5	0	10000	1250	0	0
31	3	17	6	75	9	7	6				
32	4	0	0	76	9	10	0				
33	4	2	6	77	9	12	6	Great Hundred			
34	4	5	0	78	9	15	6	112	14	0	0
35	4	7	6	79	9	17	6	Gross			
36	4	10	0	80	10	0	0	144	18	0	0
37	4	12	6	81	10	2	6	Wey			
38	4	15	0	82	10	5	0	256	32	0	0
39	4	17	6	83	10	7	6	Days in a Year			
40	5	0	0	[84]	10	10	0	365	45	12	6
41	5	2	6	85	10	12	6	Feet in a Rod			
42	5	5	0	86	10	15	0	272	34	0	0
43	5	7	6	87	10	17	6				
44	5	10	0	88	11	0	0				

N.	l.	s.	d.	q.
1	0	2	6	2
2	0	5	1	0
3	0	7	7	2
4	0	10	2	0
5	0	12	8	2
6	0	15	3	0
7	0	17	9	2
8	1	0	4	0
9	1	2	10	2
10	1	5	5	0
11	1	7	11	2
12	1	10	6	0
13	1	13	0	2
14	1	15	7	0
15	1	18	1	2
16	2	0	8	0
17	2	3	2	2
18	2	5	9	0
19	2	8	3	2
20	2	10	10	0
21	2	13	4	2
22	2	15	11	0
23	2	18	5	2
24	3	1	0	0
25	3	3	6	2
26	3	6	1	0
27	3	8	7	2
[28]	3	11	2	0
29	3	13	8	2
30	3	16	3	0
31	3	18	9	2
32	4	1	4	0
33	4	3	10	2
34	4	6	5	0
35	4	8	11	2
36	4	11	6	0
37	4	14	0	2
38	4	16	7	0
39	4	19	1	2
40	5	1	8	0
41	5	4	2	2
42	5	6	9	0
43	5	9	3	2
44	5	11	10	0

N.	l.	s.	d.	q.
45	5	14	4	2
46	5	16	11	0
47	5	19	5	2
48	6	2	0	0
49	6	4	6	2
50	6	7	1	0
51	6	9	7	2
52	6	12	2	0
53	6	14	8	2
54	6	17	3	0
55	6	19	9	2
[56]	7	2	4	0
57	7	4	10	2
58	7	7	5	0
59	7	9	11	2
60	7	12	6	0
61	7	15	0	2
62	7	17	7	0
63	8	0	1	2
64	8	2	8	0
65	8	5	2	2
66	8	7	9	0
67	8	10	3	2
68	8	12	10	0
69	8	15	4	2
70	8	17	11	0
71	9	0	5	2
72	9	3	0	0
73	9	5	6	2
74	9	8	1	0
75	9	10	7	2
76	9	13	2	0
77	9	15	8	2
78	9	18	3	0
79	10	0	9	2
80	10	3	4	0
81	10	5	10	2
82	10	8	5	0
83	10	10	11	2
[84]	10	13	6	0
85	10	16	0	2
86	10	18	7	0
87	11	1	1	2
88	11	3	8	0

N.	l.	s.	d.	q.
89	11	6	2	2
90	11	8	9	0
91	11	11	3	2
92	11	13	10	0
93	11	16	4	2
94	11	18	11	0
95	12	1	5	2
96	12	4	0	0
97	12	6	6	2
98	12	9	1	0
99	12	11	7	2
100	12	14	2	0
200	25	8	4	0
300	38	2	6	0
400	50	16	8	0
500	63	10	10	0
600	76	5	0	0
700	88	19	2	0
800	101	13	4	0
900	114	7	6	0
1000	127	1	8	0
2000	254	3	4	0
3000	381	5	0	0
4000	508	6	8	0
5000	635	8	4	0
6000	762	10	0	0
7000	889	11	8	0
8000	1016	13	4	0
9000	1143	15	0	0
10000	1270	16	8	0

Great Hundred

112	14	4	8	0

Grofs

144	18	6	0	0

Wey

256	32	10	8	0

Days in a Year

365	46	7	8	2

Feet in a Rod

272	34	11	4	0

N.	l.	s.	d.	N.	l.	s.	d.	N.	l.	s.	d.
1	0	2	7	45	5	16	3	89	11	9	11
2	0	5	2	46	5	18	10	90	11	12	6
3	0	7	9	47	6	1	5	91	11	15	1
4	0	10	4	48	6	4	0	92	11	17	8
5	0	12	11	49	6	6	7	93	14	0	3
6	0	15	6	50	6	9	2	94	12	2	10
7	0	18	1	51	6	11	9	95	12	5	5
8	1	0	8	52	6	14	4	96	12	8	0
9	1	3	3	53	6	16	11	97	12	10	7
10	1	5	10	54	6	19	6	98	12	13	2
11	1	8	5	55	7	2	1	99	12	15	9
12	1	11	0	[56]	7	4	8	100	12	18	4
13	1	13	7	57	7	7	3	200	25	16	8
14	1	16	2	58	7	9	10	300	38	15	0
15	1	18	9	59	7	12	5	400	51	13	4
16	2	1	4	60	7	15	0	500	64	11	8
17	2	3	11	61	7	17	7	600	77	10	0
18	2	6	6	62	8	0	2	700	90	8	4
19	2	9	1	63	8	2	9	800	103	6	8
20	2	11	8	64	8	5	4	900	116	5	0
21	2	14	3	65	8	7	11	1000	129	3	4
22	2	16	10	66	8	10	6	2000	258	6	8
23	2	19	5	67	8	13	1	3000	387	10	0
24	3	2	0	68	8	15	8	4000	516	13	4
25	3	4	7	69	8	18	3	5000	645	16	8
26	3	7	2	70	9	0	10	6000	775	0	0
27	3	9	9	71	9	3	5	7000	904	3	4
[28]	3	12	4	72	9	6	0	8000	1033	6	8
29	3	14	11	73	9	8	7	9000	1162	10	0
30	3	17	6	74	9	11	2	10000	1291	13	4
31	4	0	1	75	9	13	9				
32	4	2	8	76	9	16	4				
33	4	5	3	77	9	18	11				
34	4	7	10	78	10	1	6				
35	4	10	5	79	10	4	1				
36	4	13	0	80	10	6	8				
37	4	15	7	81	10	9	3				
38	4	18	2	82	10	11	10				
39	5	0	9	83	10	14	5				
40	5	3	4	[84]	10	17	0				
41	5	5	11	85	10	19	7				
42	5	8	6	86	11	2	2				
43	5	11	1	87	11	4	9				
44	5	13	8	88	11	7	4				

Great Hundred

112	14	9	4

Grofs

144	18	12	0

Wey

256	33	1	4

Days in a Year

365	47	2	11

Feet in a Rod

272	35	2	8

N.	l.	s.	d.	q.	N.	l.	s.	d.	q.	N.	l.	s.	d.	q.
1	0	2	7	2	45	5	18	1	2	89	11	13	7	2
2	0	5	3	0	46	6	0	9	0	90	11	16	3	0
3	0	7	10	2	47	6	3	4	2	91	11	18	10	2
4	0	10	6	0	48	6	6	0	0	92	12	1	6	0
5	0	13	1	2	49	6	8	7	2	93	12	4	1	2
6	0	15	9	0	50	6	11	3	0	94	12	6	9	0
7	0	18	4	2	51	6	13	10	2	95	12	9	4	2
8	1	1	0	0	52	6	16	6	0	96	12	12	0	0
9	1	3	7	2	53	6	19	1	2	97	12	14	7	2
10	1	6	3	0	54	7	1	9	0	98	12	17	3	0
11	1	8	10	2	55	7	4	4	2	99	12	19	10	2
12	1	11	6	0	[56]	7	7	0	0	100	13	2	6	0
13	1	14	1	2	57	7	9	7	2	200	26	5	0	0
14	1	16	9	0	58	7	12	3	0	300	39	7	6	0
15	1	19	4	2	59	7	14	10	2	400	52	10	0	0
16	2	2	0	0	60	7	17	6	0	500	65	12	6	0
17	2	4	7	2	61	8	0	1	2	600	78	15	0	0
18	2	7	3	0	62	8	2	9	0	700	91	17	6	0
19	2	9	10	2	63	8	5	4	2	800	105	0	0	0
20	2	12	6	0	64	8	8	0	0	900	118	2	6	0
21	2	15	1	2	65	8	10	7	2	1000	131	5	0	0
22	2	17	9	0	66	8	13	3	0	2000	262	10	0	0
23	3	0	4	2	67	8	15	10	2	3000	393	15	0	0
24	3	3	0	0	68	8	18	6	0	4000	525	0	0	0
25	3	5	7	2	69	9	1	1	2	5000	956	5	0	0
26	3	8	3	0	70	9	3	9	0	6000	787	10	0	0
27	3	10	10	2	71	9	6	4	2	7000	918	15	0	0
[28]	3	13	6	0	72	9	9	0	0	8000	1050	0	0	0
29	3	16	1	2	73	9	11	7	2	9000	1181	5	0	0
30	3	18	9	0	74	9	14	3	0	10000	1312	10	0	0
31	4	1	4	2	75	9	16	10	2					
32	4	4	0	0	76	9	19	6	0					
33	4	6	7	2	77	10	2	1	2					
34	4	9	3	0	78	10	4	9	0					
35	4	11	10	2	79	10	7	4	2					
36	4	14	6	0	80	10	10	0	0					
37	4	17	1	2	81	10	12	7	2					
38	4	19	9	0	82	10	15	3	0					
39	5	2	4	2	83	10	17	10	2					
40	5	5	0	0	[84]	11	0	6	0					
41	5	7	7	2	85	11	3	1	2					
42	5	10	3	0	86	11	5	9	0					
43	5	12	10	2	87	11	8	4	2					
44	5	15	6	0	88	11	11	0	0					

Great Hundred

112	14	14	0	0

Grofs

144	18	18	0	0

Wey

256	33	12	0	0

Days in a Year

365	47	18	1	2

Feet in a Rod

272	35	14	0	0

N.	l.	s.	d.	N.	l.	s.	d.	N.	l.	s.	d.
1	0	2	8	45	6	0	0	89	11	17	4
2	0	5	4	46	6	2	8	90	12	0	0
3	0	8	0	47	6	5	4	91	12	2	8
4	0	10	8	48	6	8	0	92	12	5	4
5	0	13	4	49	6	10	8	93	12	8	0
6	0	16	0	50	6	13	4	94	12	10	8
7	0	18	8	51	6	16	0	95	12	13	4
8	1	1	4	52	6	18	8	96	12	16	0
9	1	4	0	53	7	1	4	97	12	18	8
10	1	6	8	54	7	4	0	98	13	1	4
11	1	9	4	55	7	6	8	99	13	4	0
12	1	12	0	[56]	7	9	4	100	13	6	8
13	1	14	8	57	7	12	0	200	26	13	4
14	1	17	4	58	7	14	8	300	40	0	0
15	2	0	0	59	7	17	4	400	53	6	8
16	2	2	8	60	8	0	0	500	66	13	4
17	2	5	4	61	8	2	8	600	80	0	0
18	2	8	0	62	8	5	4	700	93	6	8
19	2	10	8	63	8	8	0	800	106	13	4
20	2	13	4	64	8	10	8	900	120	0	0
21	2	16	0	65	8	13	4	1000	133	6	8
22	2	18	8	66	8	16	0	2000	266	13	4
23	3	1	4	67	8	18	8	3000	400	0	0
24	3	4	0	68	9	1	4	4000	533	6	8
25	3	6	8	69	9	4	0	5000	666	13	4
26	3	9	4	70	9	6	8	6000	800	0	0
27	3	12	0	71	9	9	4	7000	933	6	8
[28]	3	14	8	72	9	12	0	8000	1066	13	4
29	3	17	4	73	9	14	8	9000	1200	0	0
30	4	0	0	74	9	17	4	10000	1333	6	8
31	4	2	8	75	10	0	0				
32	4	5	4	76	10	2	8				
33	4	8	0	77	10	5	4	Great Hundred			
34	4	10	8	78	10	8	0	112	14	18	8
35	4	13	4	79	10	10	8	Grofs			
36	4	16	0	80	10	13	4	144	19	4	0
37	4	18	8	81	10	16	0	Wey			
38	5	1	4	82	10	18	8	256	34	2	8
39	5	4	0	83	11	1	4	Days in a Year			
40	5	6	8	[84]	11	4	0	365	48	13	4
41	5	9	4	85	11	6	8	Feet in a Rod			
42	5	12	0	86	11	9	4	272	36	5	4
43	5	14	8	87	11	12	0				
44	5	17	4	88	11	14	8				

N.	l.	s.	d.	q.
1	0	2	8	2
2	0	5	5	0
3	0	8	1	2
4	0	10	10	0
5	0	13	6	2
6	0	16	3	0
7	0	18	11	2
8	1	1	8	0
9	1	4	4	2
10	1	7	1	0
11	1	9	9	2
12	1	12	6	0
13	1	15	2	2
14	1	17	11	0
15	2	0	7	2
16	2	3	4	0
17	2	6	0	2
18	2	8	9	0
19	2	11	5	2
20	2	14	2	0
21	2	16	10	2
22	2	19	7	0
23	3	2	3	2
24	3	5	0	0
25	3	7	8	2
26	3	10	5	0
27	3	13	1	2
[28]	3	15	10	0
29	3	18	6	2
30	4	1	3	0
31	4	3	11	2
32	4	6	8	0
33	4	9	4	2
34	4	12	1	0
35	4	14	9	2
36	4	17	6	0
37	5	0	2	2
38	5	2	11	0
39	5	5	7	2
40	5	8	4	0
41	5	11	0	2
42	5	13	9	0
43	5	16	5	2
44	5	19	2	0

N.	l.	s.	d.	q.
45	6	1	10	2
46	6	4	7	0
47	6	7	3	2
48	6	10	0	0
49	6	12	8	2
50	6	15	5	0
51	6	18	1	2
52	7	0	10	0
53	7	3	6	2
54	7	6	3	0
55	7	8	11	2
[56]	7	11	8	0
57	7	14	4	2
58	7	17	1	0
59	7	19	9	2
60	8	2	6	0
61	8	5	2	2
62	8	7	11	0
63	8	10	7	2
64	8	13	4	0
65	8	16	0	2
66	8	18	9	0
67	9	1	5	2
68	9	4	2	0
69	9	6	10	2
70	9	9	7	0
71	9	12	3	2
72	9	15	0	0
73	9	17	8	2
74	10	0	5	0
75	10	3	1	2
76	10	5	10	0
77	10	8	6	2
78	10	11	3	0
79	10	13	11	2
80	10	16	8	0
81	10	19	4	2
82	11	2	1	0
83	11	4	9	2
[84]	11	7	6	0
85	11	10	2	2
86	11	12	11	0
87	11	15	7	2
88	11	18	4	0

N.	l.	s.	d.	q.
89	12	1	0	2
90	12	3	9	0
91	12	6	5	2
92	12	9	2	0
93	12	11	10	2
94	12	14	7	0
95	12	17	3	2
96	13	0	0	0
97	13	2	8	2
98	13	5	5	0
99	13	8	1	2
100	13	10	10	0
200	27	1	8	0
300	40	12	6	0
400	54	3	4	0
500	67	14	2	0
600	81	5	0	0
700	94	15	10	0
800	108	6	8	0
900	121	17	6	0
1000	135	8	4	0
2000	270	16	8	0
3000	406	5	0	0
4000	541	13	4	0
5000	677	1	8	0
6000	812	10	0	0
7000	947	18	4	0
8000	1083	6	8	0
9000	1218	15	0	0
10000	1354	3	4	0

Great Hundred

112	15	3	4	0

Grofs

144	19	10	0	0

Wey

256	34	13	4	0

Days in a Year

365	49	8	6	2

Feet in a Rod

272	36	16	8	0

N.	l.	s.	d.	N.	l.	s.	d.	N.	l.	s.	d.
1	0	2	9	45	6	3	9	89	12	4	9
2	0	5	6	46	6	6	6	90	12	7	6
3	0	8	3	47	6	9	3	91	12	10	3
4	0	11	0	48	6	12	0	92	12	13	0
5	0	13	9	49	6	14	9	93	12	15	9
6	0	16	6	50	6	17	6	94	12	18	6
7	0	19	3	51	7	0	3	95	13	1	3
8	1	2	0	52	7	3	0	96	13	4	0
9	1	4	9	53	7	5	9	97	13	6	9
10	1	7	6	54	7	8	6	98	13	9	6
11	1	10	3	55	7	11	3	99	13	12	3
12	1	13	0	[56]	7	14	0	100	13	15	0
13	1	15	9	57	7	16	9	200	27	10	0
14	1	18	6	58	7	19	6	300	41	5	0
15	2	1	3	59	8	2	3	400	55	0	0
16	2	4	0	60	8	5	0	500	68	15	0
17	2	6	9	61	8	7	9	600	82	10	0
18	2	9	6	62	8	10	6	700	96	5	0
19	2	12	3	63	8	13	3	800	110	0	0
20	2	15	0	64	8	16	0	900	123	15	0
21	2	17	9	65	8	18	9	1000	137	10	0
22	3	0	6	66	9	1	6	2000	275	0	0
23	3	3	3	67	9	4	3	3000	412	10	0
24	3	6	0	68	9	7	0	4000	550	0	0
25	3	8	9	69	9	9	9	5000	687	10	0
26	3	11	6	70	9	12	6	6000	825	0	0
27	3	14	3	71	9	15	3	7000	962	10	0
[28]	3	17	0	72	9	18	0	8000	1100	0	0
29	3	19	9	73	10	0	9	9000	1237	10	0
30	4	2	6	74	10	3	6	10000	1375	0	0
31	4	5	3	75	10	6	3				
32	4	8	0	76	10	9	0				
33	4	10	9	77	10	11	9				
34	4	13	6	78	10	14	6				
35	4	16	3	79	10	17	3				
36	4	19	0	80	11	0	0				
37	5	1	9	81	11	2	9				
38	5	4	6	82	11	5	6				
39	5	7	3	83	11	8	3				
40	5	10	0	[84]	11	11	0				
41	5	12	9	85	11	13	9				
42	5	15	6	86	11	16	6				
43	5	18	3	87	11	19	3				
44	6	1	0	88	12	2	0				

Great Hundred

112	15	8	0

Grefs

144	19	16	0

Wey

256	35	4	0

Days in a Year

365	50	3	9

Feet in a Rod

272	37	8	0

4	0	11	2	0
5	0	13	11	2
6	0	16	9	0
7	0	19	6	2
8	1	2	4	0
9	1	5	1	2
10	1	7	11	0
11	1	10	8	2
12	1	13	6	0
13	1	16	3	2
14	1	19	1	0
15	2	1	10	2
16	2	4	8	0
17	2	7	5	2
18	2	10	3	0
19	2	13	0	2
20	2	15	10	0
21	2	18	7	2
22	3	1	5	0
23	3	4	2	2
24	3	7	0	0
25	3	9	9	2
26	3	12	7	0
27	3	15	4	2
[28]	3	18	2	0
29	4	0	11	2
30	4	3	9	0
31	4	6	6	2
32	4	9	4	0
33	4	12	1	2
34	4	14	11	0
35	4	17	8	2
36	5	0	6	0
37	5	3	3	2
38	5	6	1	0
39	5	8	10	2
40	5	11	8	0
41	5	14	5	2
42	5	17	3	0
43	6	0	0	2
44	6	2	10	0

48	6	14	0	0
49	6	16	9	2
50	6	19	7	0
51	7	2	4	2
52	7	5	2	0
53	7	7	11	2
54	7	10	9	0
55	7	13	6	2
[56]	7	16	4	0
57	7	19	1	2
58	8	1	11	0
59	8	4	8	2
60	8	7	6	0
61	8	10	3	2
62	8	13	1	0
63	8	15	10	2
64	8	18	8	0
65	9	1	5	2
66	9	4	3	0
67	9	7	0	2
68	9	9	10	0
69	9	12	7	2
70	9	15	5	0
71	9	18	2	2
72	10	1	0	0
73	10	3	9	2
74	10	6	7	0
75	10	9	4	2
76	10	12	2	0
77	10	14	11	2
78	10	17	9	0
79	11	0	6	2
80	11	3	4	0
81	11	6	1	2
82	11	8	11	0
83	11	11	8	2
[84]	11	14	6	0
85	11	17	3	2
86	12	0	1	0
87	12	2	10	2
88	12	5	8	0

92	12	16	10	0
93	12	19	7	2
94	13	2	5	0
95	13	5	2	2
96	13	8	0	0
97	13	10	9	2
98	13	13	7	0
99	13	16	4	2
100	13	19	2	0
200	27	18	4	0
300	41	17	6	0
400	55	16	8	0
500	69	15	10	0
600	83	15	0	0
700	97	14	2	0
800	111	13	4	0
900	125	12	6	0
1000	139	11	8	0
2000	279	3	4	0
3000	418	15	0	0
4000	558	6	8	0
5000	697	18	4	0
6000	837	10	0	0
7000	977	1	8	0
8000	1116	13	4	0
9000	1256	5	0	0
10000	1395	16	8	0

Great Hundred

112	15	12	8	0

Grofs

144	20	2	0	0

Wey

256	35	14	8	0

Days in a Year

365	50	18	11	2

Feet in a Rod

272	37	19	4	0

N.	l.	s.	d.	N.	l.	s.	d	N.	l.	s.	d.
1	0	2	10	45	6	7	6	89	12	12	2
2	0	5	8	46	6	10	4	90	12	15	0
3	0	8	6	47	6	13	2	91	12	17	10
4	0	11	4	48	6	16	0	92	13	0	8
5	0	14	2	49	6	18	10	93	13	3	6
6	0	17	0	50	7	1	8	94	13	6	4
7	0	19	10	51	7	4	6	95	13	9	2
8	1	2	8	52	7	7	4	96	13	12	0
9	1	5	6	53	7	10	2	97	13	14	10
10	1	8	4	54	7	13	0	98	13	17	8
11	1	11	2	55	7	15	10	99	14	0	6
12	1	14	0	[56]	7	18	8	100	14	3	4
13	1	16	10	57	8	1	6	200	28	6	8
14	1	19	8	58	8	4	4	300	42	10	0
15	2	2	6	59	8	7	2	400	56	13	4
16	2	5	4	60	8	10	0	500	70	16	8
17	2	8	2	61	8	12	10	600	85	0	0
18	2	11	0	62	8	15	8	700	99	3	4
19	2	13	10	63	8	18	6	800	113	6	8
20	2	16	8	64	9	1	4	900	127	10	0
21	2	19	6	65	9	4	2	1000	141	13	4
22	3	2	4	66	9	7	0	2000	283	6	8
23	3	5	2	67	9	9	10	3000	425	0	0
24	3	8	0	68	9	12	8	4000	566	13	4
25	3	10	10	69	9	15	6	5000	708	6	8
26	3	13	8	70	9	18	4	6000	850	0	0
27	3	16	6	71	10	1	2	7000	991	13	4
[28]	3	19	4	72	10	4	0	8000	1133	6	8
29	4	2	2	73	10	6	10	9000	1275	0	0
30	4	5	0	74	10	9	8	10000	1416	13	4
31	4	7	10	75	10	12	6				
32	4	10	8	76	10	15	4				
33	4	13	6	77	10	18	2	*Great Hundred*			
34	4	16	4	78	11	1	0	112	15	17	4
35	4	19	2	79	11	3	10	*Gross*			
36	5	2	0	80	11	6	8	144	20	8	0
37	5	4	10	81	11	9	6	*Wey*			
38	5	7	8	82	11	12	4	256	36	5	4
39	5	10	6	83	11	15	2	*Days in a Year*			
40	5	13	4	[84]	11	18	0	365	51	14	2
41	5	16	2	85	12	0	10	*Feet in a Rod*			
42	5	19	0	86	12	3	8	272	38	10	8
43	6	1	10	87	12	6	6				
44	6	4	8	88	12	9	4				

N.	l.	s.	d.	q.	N.	l.	s.	d.	q.	N.	l.	s.	d.	q.
1	0	2	10	2	45	6	9	4	2	89	12	15	10	2
2	0	5	9	0	46	6	12	3	0	90	12	18	9	0
3	0	8	7	2	47	6	15	1	2	91	13	1	7	2
4	0	11	6	0	48	6	18	0	0	92	13	4	6	0
5	0	14	4	2	49	7	0	10	2	93	13	7	4	2
6	0	17	3	0	50	7	3	9	0	94	13	10	3	0
7	1	0	1	2	51	7	6	7	2	95	13	13	1	2
8	1	3	0	0	52	7	9	6	0	96	13	16	0	0
9	1	5	10	2	53	7	12	4	2	97	13	18	10	2
10	1	8	9	0	54	7	15	3	0	98	14	1	9	0
11	1	11	7	2	55	7	18	1	2	99	14	4	7	2
12	1	14	6	0	[56]	8	1	0	0	100	14	7	6	0
13	1	17	4	2	57	8	3	10	2	200	28	15	0	0
14	2	0	3	0	58	8	6	9	0	300	43	2	6	0
15	2	3	1	2	59	8	9	7	2	400	57	10	0	0
16	2	6	0	0	60	8	12	6	0	500	71	17	6	0
17	2	8	10	2	61	8	15	4	2	600	86	5	0	0
18	2	11	9	0	62	8	18	3	0	700	100	12	6	0
19	2	14	7	2	63	9	1	1	2	800	115	0	0	0
20	2	17	6	0	64	9	4	0	0	900	129	7	6	0
21	3	0	4	2	65	9	6	10	2	1000	143	15	0	0
22	3	3	3	0	66	9	9	9	0	2000	287	10	0	0
23	3	6	1	2	67	9	12	7	2	3000	431	5	0	0
24	3	9	0	0	68	9	15	6	0	4000	575	0	0	0
25	3	11	10	2	69	9	18	4	2	5000	718	15	0	0
26	3	14	9	0	70	10	1	3	0	6000	862	10	0	0
27	3	17	7	2	71	10	4	1	2	7000	1006	5	0	0
[28]	4	0	6	0	72	10	7	0	0	8000	1150	0	0	0
29	4	3	4	2	73	10	9	10	2	9000	1293	15	0	0
30	4	6	3	0	74	10	12	9	0	10000	1437	10	0	0
31	4	9	1	2	75	10	15	7	2					
32	4	12	0	0	76	10	18	6	0					
33	4	14	10	2	77	11	1	4	2					
34	4	17	9	0	78	11	4	3	0					
35	5	0	7	2	79	11	7	1	2					
36	5	3	6	0	80	11	10	0	0					
37	5	6	4	2	81	11	12	10	2					
38	5	9	3	0	82	11	15	9	0					
39	5	12	1	2	83	11	18	7	2					
40	5	15	0	0	[84]	12	1	6	0					
41	5	17	10	2	85	12	4	4	2					
42	6	0	9	0	86	12	7	3	0					
43	6	3	7	2	87	12	10	1	2					
44	6	6	6	0	88	12	13	0	0					

Great Hundred

112 | 16 2 0 0

Grofs

144 | 20 14 0 0

Wey

256 | 36 16 0 0

Days in a Year

365 | 52 9 4 2

Feet in a Rod

272 | 39 2 0 0

N.	l.	s.	d.
1	0	2	11
2	0	5	10
3	0	8	9
4	0	11	8
5	0	14	7
6	0	17	6
7	1	0	5
8	1	3	4
9	1	6	3
10	1	9	2
11	1	12	1
12	1	15	0
13	1	17	11
14	2	0	10
15	2	3	9
16	2	6	8
17	2	9	7
18	2	12	6
19	2	15	5
20	2	18	4
21	3	1	3
22	3	4	2
23	3	7	1
24	3	10	0
25	3	12	11
26	3	15	10
27	3	18	9
[28]	4	1	8
29	4	4	7
30	4	7	6
31	4	10	5
32	4	13	8
33	4	16	3
34	4	19	2
35	5	2	1
36	5	5	0
37	5	7	11
38	5	10	10
39	5	13	9
40	5	16	8
41	5	19	7
42	6	2	6
43	6	5	5
44	6	8	4

N.	l.	s.	d.
45	6	11	3
46	6	14	2
47	6	17	1
48	7	0	0
49	7	2	11
50	7	5	10
51	7	8	9
52	7	11	8
53	7	14	7
54	7	17	6
55	8	0	5
[56]	8	3	4
57	8	6	3
58	8	9	2
59	8	12	1
60	8	15	0
61	8	17	11
62	9	0	10
63	9	3	9
64	9	6	8
65	9	9	7
66	9	12	6
67	9	15	5
68	9	18	4
69	10	1	3
70	10	4	2
71	10	7	1
72	10	10	0
73	10	12	11
74	10	15	10
75	10	18	9
76	11	1	8
77	11	4	7
78	11	7	6
79	11	10	5
80	11	13	4
81	11	16	3
82	11	19	2
83	12	2	1
[84]	12	5	0
85	12	7	11
86	12	10	10
87	12	13	9
88	12	16	8

N.	l.	s.	d.
89	12	19	7
90	13	2	6
91	13	5	5
92	13	8	4
93	13	11	3
94	13	14	2
95	13	17	1
96	14	0	0
97	14	2	11
98	14	5	10
99	14	8	9
100	14	11	8
200	29	3	4
300	43	15	0
400	58	6	8
500	72	18	4
600	87	10	0
700	102	1	8
800	116	13	4
900	131	5	0
1000	145	16	8
2000	291	13	4
3000	437	10	0
4000	583	6	8
5000	729	3	4
6000	875	0	0
7000	1020	16	8
8000	1166	13	4
9000	1312	10	0
10000	1458	6	8

Great Hundred

112	16	6	8

Gross

144	21	0	0

Wey

256	37	6	8

Days in a Year

365	53	4	7

Feet in a Rod

272	39	13	4

N.	l.	s.	d.	q.
1	0	2	11	2
2	0	5	11	0
3	0	8	10	2
4	0	11	10	0
5	0	14	9	2
6	0	17	9	0
7	1	0	8	2
8	1	3	8	0
9	1	6	7	2
10	1	9	7	0
11	1	12	6	2
12	1	15	6	0
13	1	18	5	2
14	2	1	5	0
15	2	4	4	2
16	2	7	4	0
17	2	10	3	2
18	2	13	3	0
19	2	16	2	2
20	2	19	2	0
21	3	2	1	2
22	3	5	1	0
23	3	8	0	2
24	3	11	0	0
25	3	13	11	2
26	3	16	11	0
27	3	19	10	2
[28]	4	2	10	0
29	4	5	9	2
30	4	8	9	0
31	4	11	8	2
32	4	14	8	0
33	4	17	7	2
34	5	0	7	0
35	5	3	6	2
36	5	6	6	0
37	5	9	5	2
38	5	12	5	0
39	5	15	4	2
40	5	18	4	0
41	6	1	3	2
42	6	4	3	0
43	6	7	2	2
44	6	10	2	0

N.	l.	s.	d.	q.
45	6	13	1	2
46	6	16	1	0
47	6	19	0	2
48	7	2	0	0
49	7	4	11	2
50	7	7	11	0
51	7	10	10	2
52	7	13	10	0
53	7	16	9	2
54	7	19	9	0
55	8	2	8	2
[56]	8	5	8	0
57	8	8	7	2
58	8	11	7	0
59	8	14	6	2
60	8	17	6	0
61	9	0	5	2
62	9	3	5	0
63	9	6	4	2
64	9	9	4	0
65	9	12	3	2
66	9	15	3	0
67	9	18	2	2
68	10	1	2	0
69	10	4	1	2
70	10	7	1	0
71	10	10	0	2
72	10	13	0	0
73	10	15	11	2
74	10	18	11	0
75	11	1	10	2
76	11	4	10	0
77	11	7	9	2
78	11	10	9	0
79	11	13	8	2
80	11	16	8	0
81	11	19	7	2
82	12	2	7	0
83	12	5	6	2
[84]	12	8	6	0
85	12	11	5	2
86	12	14	5	0
87	12	17	4	2
88	13	0	4	0

N.	l.	s.	d.	q.
89	13	3	3	2
90	13	6	3	0
91	13	9	2	2
92	13	12	2	0
93	13	15	1	2
94	13	18	1	0
95	14	1	0	2
96	14	4	0	0
97	14	6	11	2
98	14	9	11	0
99	14	12	10	2
100	14	15	10	0
200	29	11	8	0
300	44	7	6	0
400	59	3	4	0
500	73	19	2	0
600	88	15	0	0
700	103	10	10	0
800	118	6	8	0
900	133	2	6	0
1000	147	18	4	0
2000	295	16	8	0
3000	443	15	0	0
4000	591	13	4	0
5000	739	11	8	0
6000	887	10	0	0
7000	1035	8	4	0
8000	1183	6	8	0
9000	1331	5	0	0
10000	1479	3	4	0

Great Hundred

112	16	11	4	0

Gross

144	21	6	0	0

Wey

256	37	17	4	0

Days in a Year

365	53	19	9	2

Feet in a Rod

272	40	4	8	0

N.	l.	s.	d.	N.	l.	s.	d.	N.	l.	s.	d.
1	0	3	0	45	6	15	0	89	13	7	0
2	0	6	0	46	6	18	0	90	13	10	0
3	0	9	0	47	7	1	0	91	13	13	0
4	0	12	0	48	7	4	0	92	13	16	0
5	0	15	0	49	7	7	0	93	13	19	0
6	0	18	0	50	7	10	0	94	14	2	0
7	1	1	0	51	7	13	0	95	14	5	0
8	1	4	0	52	7	16	0	96	14	8	0
9	1	7	0	53	7	19	0	97	14	11	0
10	1	10	0	54	8	2	0	98	14	14	0
11	1	13	0	55	8	5	0	99	14	17	0
12	1	16	0	[56]	8	8	0	100	15	0	0
13	1	19	0	57	8	11	0	200	30	0	0
14	2	2	0	58	8	14	0	300	45	0	0
15	2	5	0	59	8	17	0	400	60	0	0
16	2	8	0	60	9	0	0	500	75	0	0
17	2	11	0	61	9	3	0	600	90	0	0
18	2	14	0	62	9	6	0	700	105	0	0
19	2	17	0	63	9	9	0	800	120	0	0
20	3	0	0	64	9	12	0	900	135	0	0
21	3	3	0	65	9	15	0	1000	150	0	0
22	3	6	0	66	9	18	0	2000	300	0	0
23	3	9	0	67	10	1	0	3000	450	0	0
24	3	12	0	68	10	4	0	4000	600	0	0
25	3	15	0	69	10	7	0	5000	750	0	0
26	3	18	0	70	10	10	0	6000	900	0	0
27	4	1	0	71	10	13	0	7000	1050	0	0
[28]	4	4	0	72	10	16	0	8000	1200	0	0
29	4	7	0	73	10	19	0	9000	1350	0	0
30	4	10	0	74	11	2	0	10000	1500	0	0
31	4	13	0	75	11	5	0				
32	4	16	0	76	11	8	0				
33	4	19	0	77	11	11	0	*Great Hundred*			
34	5	2	0	78	11	14	0	112	16	16	0
35	5	5	0	79	11	17	0	*Grofs*			
36	5	8	0	80	12	0	0	144	21	12	0
37	5	11	0	81	12	3	0	*Wey*			
38	5	14	0	82	12	6	0	256	38	8	0
39	5	17	0	83	12	9	0	*Days in a Year*			
40	6	0	0	[84]	12	12	0	365	54	15	0
41	6	3	0	85	12	15	0	*Feet in a Rod*			
42	6	6	0	86	12	18	0	272	40	16	0
43	6	9	0	87	13	1	0				
44	6	12	0	88	13	4	0				

N.	l.	s.	d.	N.	l.	s.	d.	N.	l.	s.	d.
1	0	3	1	45	6	18	9	89	13	14	5
2	0	6	2	46	7	1	10	90	13	17	6
3	0	9	3	47	7	4	11	91	14	0	7
4	0	12	4	48	7	8	0	92	14	3	8
5	0	15	5	49	7	11	1	93	14	6	9
6	0	18	6	50	7	14	2	94	14	9	10
7	1	1	7	51	7	17	3	95	14	12	11
8	1	4	8	52	8	0	4	96	14	16	0
9	1	7	9	53	8	3	5	97	14	19	1
10	1	10	10	54	8	6	6	98	15	2	2
11	1	13	11	55	8	9	7	99	15	5	3
12	1	17	0	[56]	8	12	8	100	15	8	4
13	2	0	1	57	8	15	9	200	30	16	8
14	2	3	2	58	8	18	10	300	46	5	0
15	2	6	3	59	9	1	11	400	61	13	4
16	2	9	4	60	9	5	0	500	77	1	8
17	2	12	5	61	9	8	1	600	92	10	0
18	2	15	6	62	9	11	2	700	107	18	4
19	2	18	7	63	9	14	3	800	123	6	8
20	3	1	8	64	9	17	4	900	138	15	0
21	3	4	9	65	10	0	5	1000	154	3	4
22	3	7	10	66	10	3	6	2000	308	6	8
23	3	10	11	67	10	6	7	3000	462	10	0
24	3	14	0	68	10	9	8	4000	616	13	4
25	3	17	1	69	10	12	9	5000	770	16	8
26	4	0	2	70	10	15	10	6000	925	0	0
27	4	3	3	71	10	18	11	7000	1079	3	4
[28]	4	6	4	72	11	2	6	8000	1233	6	8
29	4	9	5	73	11	5	1	9000	1387	10	0
30	4	12	6	74	11	8	2	10000	1541	13	4
31	4	15	7	75	11	11	3				
32	4	18	8	76	11	14	4				
33	5	1	9	77	11	17	5				
34	5	4	10	78	12	0	6				
35	5	7	11	79	12	3	7				
36	5	11	0	80	12	6	8				
37	5	14	1	81	12	9	9				
38	5	17	2	82	12	12	10				
39	6	0	3	83	12	15	11				
40	6	3	4	[84]	12	19	0				
41	6	6	5	85	13	2	1				
42	6	9	6	86	13	5	2				
43	6	12	7	87	13	8	3				
44	6	15	8	88	13	11	4				

Great Hundred

112	17	5	4

Grofs

144	22	4	0

Wey

256	39	9	4

Days in a Year

365	56	5	5

Feet in a Rod

272	41	18	8

M

N.	l.	s.	d.	N.	l.	s.	d.	N.	l.	s.	d.
1	0	3	2	45	7	2	6	89	14	1	10
2	0	6	4	46	7	5	8	90	14	5	0
3	0	9	6	47	7	8	10	91	14	8	2
4	0	12	8	48	7	12	0	92	14	11	4
5	0	15	10	49	7	15	2	93	14	14	6
6	0	19	0	50	7	18	4	94	14	17	8
7	1	2	2	51	8	1	6	95	15	0	10
8	1	5	4	52	8	4	8	96	15	4	0
9	1	8	6	53	8	7	10	97	15	7	2
10	1	11	8	54	8	11	0	98	15	10	4
11	1	14	10	55	8	14	2	99	15	13	6
12	1	18	0	[56]	8	17	4	100	15	16	8
13	2	1	2	57	9	0	6	200	31	13	4
14	2	4	4	58	9	3	8	300	47	10	0
15	2	7	6	59	9	6	10	400	63	6	8
16	2	10	8	60	9	10	0	500	79	3	4
17	2	13	10	61	9	13	2	600	95	0	0
18	2	17	0	62	9	16	4	700	110	16	8
19	3	0	2	63	9	19	6	800	126	13	4
20	3	3	4	64	10	2	8	900	142	10	0
21	3	6	6	65	10	5	10	1000	158	6	8
22	3	9	8	66	10	9	0	2000	316	13	4
23	3	12	10	67	10	12	2	3000	475	0	0
24	3	16	0	68	10	15	4	4000	633	6	8
25	3	19	2	69	10	18	6	5000	791	13	4
26	4	2	4	70	11	1	8	6000	950	0	0
27	4	5	6	71	11	4	10	7000	1108	6	8
[28]	4	8	8	72	11	8	0	8000	1266	13	4
29	4	11	10	73	11	11	2	9000	1425	0	0
30	4	15	0	74	11	14	4	10000	1583	6	8
31	4	18	2	75	11	17	6				
32	5	1	4	76	12	0	8				
33	5	4	6	77	12	3	10	Great Hundred			
34	5	7	8	78	12	7	0	112	17	14	8
35	5	10	10	79	12	10	2	Grofs			
36	5	14	0	80	12	13	4	144	22	16	0
37	5	17	2	81	12	16	6	Wey			
38	6	0	4	82	12	19	8	256	40	10	8
39	6	3	6	83	13	2	10	Days in a Year			
40	6	6	8	[84]	13	6	0	365	57	15	10
41	6	9	10	85	13	9	2	Feet in a Rod			
42	6	13	0	86	13	12	4	272	43	1	4
43	6	16	2	87	13	15	6				
44	6	19	4	88	13	18	8				

N.	l.	s.	d.
1	0	3	3
2	0	6	6
3	0	9	9
4	0	13	0
5	0	16	3
6	0	19	6
7	1	2	9
8	1	6	0
9	1	9	3
10	1	12	6
11	1	15	9
12	1	19	0
13	2	2	3
14	2	5	6
15	2	8	9
16	2	12	0
17	2	15	3
18	2	18	6
19	3	1	9
20	3	5	0
21	3	8	3
22	3	11	6
23	3	14	9
24	3	18	0
25	4	1	3
26	4	4	6
27	4	7	9
[28]	4	11	0
29	4	14	3
30	4	17	6
31	5	0	9
32	5	4	0
33	5	7	3
34	5	10	6
35	5	13	9
36	5	17	0
37	6	0	3
38	6	3	6
39	6	6	9
40	6	10	0
41	6	13	3
42	6	16	6
43	6	19	9
44	7	3	0

N.	l.	s.	d.
45	7	6	3
46	7	9	6
47	7	12	9
48	7	16	0
49	7	19	3
50	8	2	6
51	8	5	9
52	8	9	0
53	8	12	3
54	8	15	6
55	8	18	9
[56]	9	2	0
57	9	5	3
58	9	8	6
59	9	11	9
60	9	15	0
61	9	18	3
62	10	1	6
63	10	4	9
64	10	8	0
65	10	11	3
66	10	14	6
67	10	17	9
68	11	1	0
69	11	4	3
70	11	7	6
71	11	10	9
72	11	14	0
73	11	17	3
74	12	0	6
75	12	3	9
76	12	7	0
77	12	10	3
78	12	13	6
79	12	16	9
80	13	0	0
81	13	3	3
82	13	6	6
83	13	9	9
[84]	13	13	0
85	13	16	3
86	13	19	6
87	14	2	9
88	14	6	0

N.	l.	s.	d.
89	14	9	3
90	14	12	6
91	14	15	9
92	14	19	0
93	15	2	3
94	15	5	6
95	15	8	9
96	15	12	0
97	15	15	3
98	15	18	6
99	16	1	9
100	16	5	0
200	32	10	0
300	48	15	0
400	65	0	0
500	81	5	0
600	97	10	0
700	113	15	0
800	130	0	0
900	146	5	0
1000	162	10	0
2000	325	0	0
3000	487	10	0
4000	650	0	0
5000	812	10	0
6000	975	0	0
7000	1137	10	0
8000	1300	0	0
9000	1462	10	0
10000	1625	0	0

Great Hundred

112	18	4	0

Grofs

144	23	8	0

Wey

256	41	12	0

Days in a Year

365	59	6	3

Feet in a Rod

272	44	4	0

N.	l.	s.	d.	N.	l.	s.	d.	N.	l.	s.	d.
1	0	3	4	45	7	10	0	89	14	16	8
2	0	6	8	46	7	13	4	90	15	0	0
3	0	10	0	47	7	16	8	91	15	3	4
4	0	13	4	48	8	0	0	92	15	6	8
5	0	16	8	49	8	3	4	93	15	10	0
6	1	0	0	50	8	6	8	94	15	13	4
7	1	3	4	51	8	10	0	95	15	16	8
8	1	6	8	52	8	13	4	96	16	0	0
9	1	10	0	53	8	16	8	97	16	3	4
10	1	13	4	54	9	0	0	98	16	6	8
11	1	16	8	55	9	3	4	99	16	10	0
12	2	0	0	[56]	9	6	8	100	16	13	4
13	2	3	4	57	9	10	0	200	33	6	8
14	2	6	8	58	9	13	4	300	50	0	0
15	2	10	0	59	9	16	8	400	66	13	4
16	2	13	4	60	10	0	0	500	83	6	8
17	2	16	8	61	10	3	4	600	100	0	0
18	3	0	0	62	10	6	8	700	116	13	4
19	3	3	4	63	10	10	0	800	133	6	8
20	3	6	8	64	10	13	4	900	150	0	0
21	3	10	0	65	10	16	8	1000	166	13	4
22	3	13	4	66	11	0	0	2000	333	6	8
23	3	16	8	67	11	3	4	3000	500	0	0
24	4	0	0	68	11	6	8	4000	666	13	4
25	4	3	4	69	11	10	0	5000	833	6	8
26	4	6	8	70	11	13	4	6000	1000	0	0
27	4	10	0	71	11	16	8	7000	1166	13	4
[28]	4	13	4	72	12	0	0	8000	1333	6	8
29	4	16	8	73	12	3	4	9000	1500	0	0
30	5	0	0	74	12	6	8	10000	1666	13	4
31	5	3	4	75	12	10	0				
32	5	6	8	76	12	13	4				
33	5	10	0	77	12	16	8				
34	5	13	4	78	13	0	0				
35	5	16	8	79	13	3	4				
36	6	0	0	80	13	6	8				
37	6	3	4	81	13	10	0				
38	6	6	8	82	13	13	4				
39	6	10	0	83	13	16	8				
40	6	13	4	[84]	14	0	0				
41	6	16	8	85	14	3	4				
42	7	0	0	86	14	6	8				
43	7	3	4	87	14	10	0				
44	7	6	8	88	14	13	4				

Great Hundred

112	18	13	4

Grofs

144	24	0	0

Wey

256	42	13	4

Days in a Year

365	60	16	8

Feet in a Rod

272	45	6	8

N.	l.	s.	d.	N.	l.	s.	d.	N.	l.	s.	d.
1	0	3	5	45	7	13	9	89	15	4	1
2	0	6	10	46	7	17	2	90	15	7	6
3	0	10	3	47	8	0	7	91	15	10	11
4	0	13	8	48	8	4	0	92	15	14	4
5	0	17	1	49	8	7	5	93	15	17	9
6	1	0	6	50	8	10	10	94	16	1	2
7	1	3	11	51	8	14	3	95	16	4	7
8	1	7	4	52	8	17	8	96	16	8	0
9	1	10	9	53	9	1	1	97	16	11	5
10	1	14	2	54	9	4	6	98	16	14	10
11	1	17	7	55	9	7	11	99	16	18	3
12	2	1	0	[56]	9	11	4	100	17	1	8
13	2	4	5	57	9	14	9	200	34	3	4
14	2	7	10	58	9	18	2	300	51	5	0
15	2	11	3	59	10	1	7	400	68	6	8
16	2	14	8	60	10	5	0	500	85	8	4
17	2	18	1	61	10	8	5	600	102	10	0
18	3	1	6	62	10	11	10	700	119	11	8
19	3	4	11	63	10	15	3	800	136	13	4
20	3	8	4	64	10	18	8	900	153	15	0
21	3	11	9	65	11	2	1	1000	170	16	8
22	3	15	2	66	11	5	6	2000	341	13	4
23	3	18	7	67	11	8	11	3000	512	10	0
24	4	2	0	68	11	12	4	4000	683	6	8
25	4	5	5	69	11	15	9	5000	854	3	4
26	4	8	10	70	11	19	2	6000	1025	0	0
27	4	12	3	71	12	2	7	7000	1195	16	8
[28]	4	15	8	72	12	6	0	8000	1366	13	4
29	4	19	1	73	12	9	5	9000	1537	10	0
30	5	2	6	74	12	12	10	10000	1708	6	8
31	5	5	11	75	12	16	3				
32	5	9	4	76	12	19	8				
33	5	12	9	77	13	3	1				
34	5	16	2	78	13	6	6				
35	5	19	7	79	13	9	11				
36	6	3	0	80	13	13	4				
37	6	6	5	81	13	16	9				
38	6	9	10	82	14	0	2				
39	6	13	3	83	14	3	7				
40	6	16	8	[84]	14	7	0				
41	7	0	1	85	14	10	5				
42	7	3	6	86	14	13	10				
43	7	6	11	87	14	17	3				
44	7	10	4	88	15	0	8				

Great Hundred

112 | 19 2 8

Gross

144 | 24 12 0

Wey

256 | 43 14 8

Days in a Year

365 | 62 7 1

Feet in a Rod

272 | 46 9 4

M 3

N.	l.	s.	d.
1	0	3	6
2	0	7	0
3	0	10	6
4	0	14	0
5	0	17	6
6	1	1	0
7	1	4	6
8	1	8	0
9	1	11	6
10	1	15	0
11	1	18	6
12	2	2	0
13	2	5	6
14	2	9	0
15	2	12	6
16	2	16	0
17	2	19	6
18	3	3	0
19	3	6	6
20	3	10	0
21	3	13	6
22	3	17	0
23	4	0	6
24	4	4	0
25	4	7	6
26	4	11	0
27	4	14	6
[28]	4	18	0
29	5	1	6
30	5	5	0
31	5	8	6
32	5	12	0
33	5	15	6
34	5	19	0
35	6	2	6
36	6	6	0
37	6	9	6
38	6	13	0
39	6	16	6
40	7	0	0
41	7	3	6
42	7	7	0
43	7	10	6
44	7	14	0

N.	l.	s.	d.
45	7	17	6
46	8	1	0
47	8	4	6
48	8	8	0
49	8	11	6
50	8	15	0
51	8	18	6
52	9	2	0
53	9	5	6
54	9	9	0
55	9	12	6
[56]	9	16	0
57	9	19	6
58	10	3	0
59	10	6	6
60	10	10	0
61	10	13	6
62	10	17	0
63	11	0	6
64	11	4	0
65	11	7	6
66	11	11	0
67	11	14	6
68	11	18	0
69	12	1	6
70	12	5	0
71	12	8	6
72	12	12	0
73	12	15	6
74	12	19	0
75	13	2	6
76	13	6	0
77	13	9	6
78	13	13	0
79	13	16	6
80	14	0	0
81	14	3	6
82	14	7	0
83	14	10	6
[84]	14	14	0
85	14	17	6
86	15	1	0
87	15	4	6
88	15	8	0

N.	l.	s.	d.
89	15	11	6
90	15	15	0
91	15	18	6
92	16	2	0
93	16	5	6
94	16	9	0
95	16	12	6
96	16	16	0
97	16	19	6
98	17	3	0
99	17	6	6
100	17	10	0
200	35	0	0
300	52	10	0
400	70	0	0
500	87	10	0
600	105	0	0
700	122	10	0
800	140	0	0
900	157	10	0
1000	175	0	0
2000	350	0	0
3000	525	0	0
4000	700	0	0
5000	875	0	0
6000	1050	0	0
7000	1225	0	0
8000	1400	0	0
9000	1575	0	0
10000	1750	0	0

Great Hundred

112 | 19 12 0

Gross

144 | 25 4 0

Wey

256 | 44 16 0

Days in a Year

365 | 63 17 6

Feet in a Rod

272 | 47 12 0

N.	l.	s.	d.	N.	l.	s.	d.	N.	l.	s.	d.
1	0	3	7	45	8	1	3	89	15	18	11
2	0	7	2	46	8	4	10	90	16	2	6
3	0	10	9	47	8	8	5	91	16	6	1
4	0	14	4	48	8	12	0	92	16	9	8
5	0	17	11	49	8	15	7	93	16	13	3
6	1	1	6	50	8	19	2	94	16	16	10
7	1	5	1	51	9	2	9	95	17	0	5
8	1	8	8	52	9	6	4	96	17	4	0
9	1	12	3	53	9	9	11	97	17	7	7
10	1	15	10	54	9	13	6	98	17	11	2
11	1	19	5	55	9	17	1	99	17	14	9
12	2	3	0	[56]	10	0	8	100	17	18	4
13	2	6	7	57	10	4	3	200	35	16	8
14	2	10	2	58	10	7	10	300	53	15	0
15	2	13	9	59	10	11	5	400	71	13	4
16	2	17	4	60	10	15	0	500	89	11	8
17	3	0	11	61	10	18	7	600	107	10	0
18	3	4	6	62	11	2	2	700	125	8	4
19	3	8	1	63	11	5	9	800	143	6	8
20	3	11	8	64	11	9	4	900	161	5	0
21	3	15	3	65	11	12	11	1000	179	3	4
22	3	18	10	66	11	16	6	2000	358	6	8
23	4	2	5	67	12	0	1	3000	537	10	0
24	4	6	0	68	12	3	8	4000	716	13	4
25	4	9	7	69	12	7	3	5000	895	16	8
26	4	13	2	70	12	10	10	6000	1075	0	0
27	4	16	9	71	12	14	5	7000	1254	3	4
[28]	5	0	4	72	12	18	0	8000	1433	6	8
29	5	3	11	73	13	1	7	9000	1612	10	0
30	5	7	6	74	13	5	2	10000	1791	13	4
31	5	11	1	75	13	8	9				
32	5	14	8	76	13	12	4				
33	5	18	3	77	13	15	11				
34	6	1	10	78	13	19	6				
35	6	5	5	79	14	3	1				
36	6	9	0	80	14	6	8				
37	6	12	7	81	14	10	3				
38	6	16	2	82	14	13	10				
39	6	19	9	83	14	17	5				
40	7	3	4	[84]	15	1	0				
41	7	6	11	85	15	4	7				
42	7	10	6	86	15	8	2				
43	7	14	1	87	15	11	9				
44	7	17	8	88	15	15	4				

Great Hundred

112	20	1	4

Grofs

144	25	16	0

Wey

256	45	17	4

Days in a Year

365	65	7	11

Feet in a Rod

272	48	14	8

N.	l.	s.	d.	N.	l.	s.	d.	N.	l.	s.	d.
1	0	3	8	45	8	5	0	89	16	6	4
2	0	7	4	46	8	8	8	90	16	10	0
3	0	11	0	47	8	12	4	91	16	13	8
4	0	14	8	48	8	16	0	92	16	17	4
5	0	18	4	49	8	19	8	93	17	1	0
6	1	2	0	50	9	3	4	94	17	4	8
7	1	5	8	51	9	7	0	95	17	8	4
8	1	9	4	52	9	10	8	96	17	12	0
9	1	13	0	53	9	14	4	97	17	15	8
10	1	16	8	54	9	18	0	98	17	19	4
11	2	0	4	55	10	1	8	99	18	3	0
12	2	4	0	[56]	10	5	4	100	18	6	8
13	2	7	8	57	10	9	0	200	36	13	4
14	2	11	4	58	10	12	8	300	55	0	0
15	2	15	0	59	10	16	4	400	73	6	8
16	2	18	8	60	11	0	0	500	91	13	4
17	3	2	4	61	11	3	8	600	110	0	0
18	3	6	0	62	11	7	4	700	128	6	8
19	3	9	8	63	11	11	0	800	146	13	4
20	3	13	4	64	11	14	8	900	165	0	0
21	3	17	0	65	11	18	4	1000	183	6	8
22	4	0	8	66	12	2	0	2000	366	13	4
23	4	4	4	67	12	5	8	3000	550	0	0
24	4	8	0	68	12	9	4	4000	733	6	8
25	4	11	8	69	12	13	0	5000	916	13	4
26	4	15	4	70	12	16	8	6000	1100	0	0
27	4	19	0	71	13	0	4	7000	1283	6	8
[28]	5	2	8	72	13	4	0	8000	1466	13	4
29	5	6	4	73	13	7	8	9000	1650	0	0
30	5	10	0	74	13	11	4	10000	1833	6	8
31	5	13	8	75	13	15	0				
32	5	17	4	76	13	18	8				
33	6	1	0	77	14	2	4	*Great Hundred*			
34	6	4	8	78	14	6	0	112	20	10	8
35	6	8	4	79	14	9	8	*Grofs*			
36	6	12	0	80	14	13	4	144	26	8	0
37	6	15	8	81	14	17	0	*Wey*			
38	6	19	4	82	15	0	8	256	46	18	8
39	7	3	0	83	15	4	4	*Days in a Year*			
40	7	6	8	[84]	15	8	0	365	66	18	4
41	7	10	4	85	15	11	8	*Feet in a Rod*			
42	7	14	0	86	15	15	4	272	49	17	4
43	7	17	8	87	15	19	0				
44	8	1	4	88	16	2	8				

N.	l.	s.	d.
1	0	3	9
2	0	7	6
3	0	11	3
4	0	15	0
5	0	18	9
6	1	2	6
7	1	6	3
8	1	10	0
9	1	13	9
10	1	17	6
11	2	1	3
12	2	5	0
13	2	8	9
14	2	12	6
15	2	16	3
16	3	0	0
17	3	3	9
18	3	7	6
19	3	11	3
20	3	15	0
21	3	18	9
22	4	2	6
23	4	6	3
24	4	10	0
25	4	13	9
26	4	17	6
27	5	1	3
[28]	5	5	0
29	5	8	9
30	5	12	6
31	5	16	3
32	6	0	0
33	6	3	9
34	6	7	6
35	6	11	3
36	6	15	0
37	6	18	9
38	7	2	6
39	7	6	3
40	7	10	0
41	7	13	9
42	7	17	6
43	8	1	3
44	8	5	0

N.	l.	s.	d.
45	8	8	9
46	8	12	6
47	8	16	3
48	9	0	0
49	9	3	9
50	9	7	6
51	9	11	3
52	9	15	0
53	9	18	9
54	10	2	6
55	10	6	3
[56]	10	10	0
57	10	13	9
58	10	17	6
59	11	1	3
60	11	5	0
61	11	8	9
62	11	12	6
63	11	16	3
64	12	0	0
65	12	3	9
66	12	7	6
67	12	11	3
68	12	15	0
69	12	18	9
70	13	2	6
71	13	6	3
72	13	10	0
73	13	13	9
74	13	17	6
75	14	1	3
76	14	5	0
77	14	8	9
78	14	12	6
79	14	16	3
80	15	0	0
81	15	3	9
82	15	7	6
83	15	11	3
[84]	15	15	0
85	15	18	9
86	16	2	6
87	16	6	3
88	16	10	0

N.	l.	s.	d.
89	16	13	9
90	16	17	6
91	17	1	3
92	17	5	0
93	17	8	9
94	17	12	6
95	17	16	3
96	18	0	0
97	18	3	9
98	18	7	6
99	18	11	3
100	18	15	0
200	37	10	0
300	56	5	0
400	75	0	0
500	93	15	0
600	112	10	0
700	131	5	0
800	150	0	0
900	168	15	0
1000	187	10	0
2000	375	0	0
3000	562	10	0
4000	750	0	0
5000	937	10	0
6000	1125	0	0
7000	1312	10	0
8000	1500	0	0
9000	1687	10	0
10000	1875	0	0

Great Hundred

112	21	0	0

Grofs

144	27	0	0

Wey

256	48	0	0

Days in a Year

365	68	8	9

Feet in a Rod

272	51	0	0

N.	l.	s.	d.	N.	l.	s.	d.	N.	l.	s.	d.
1	0	3	10	45	8	12	6	89	17	1	2
2	0	7	8	46	8	16	4	90	17	5	0
3	0	11	6	47	9	0	2	91	17	8	10
4	0	15	4	48	9	4	0	92	17	12	8
5	0	19	2	49	9	7	10	93	17	16	6
6	1	3	0	50	9	11	8	94	18	0	4
7	1	6	10	51	9	15	6	95	18	4	2
8	1	10	8	52	9	19	4	96	18	8	0
9	1	14	6	53	10	3	2	97	18	11	10
10	1	18	4	54	10	7	0	98	18	15	8
11	2	2	2	55	10	10	10	99	18	19	6
12	2	6	0	[56]	10	14	8	100	19	3	4
13	2	9	10	57	10	18	6	200	38	6	8
14	2	13	8	58	11	2	4	300	57	10	0
15	2	17	6	59	11	6	2	400	76	13	4
16	3	1	4	60	11	10	0	500	95	16	8
17	3	5	2	61	11	13	10	600	115	0	0
18	3	9	0	62	11	17	8	700	134	3	4
19	3	12	10	63	12	1	6	800	153	6	8
20	3	16	8	64	12	5	4	900	172	10	0
21	4	0	6	65	12	9	2	1000	191	13	4
22	4	4	4	66	12	13	0	2000	383	6	8
23	4	8	2	67	12	16	10	3000	575	0	0
24	4	12	0	68	13	0	8	4000	766	13	4
25	4	15	10	69	13	4	6	5000	958	6	8
26	4	19	8	70	13	8	4	6000	1150	0	0
27	5	3	6	71	13	12	2	7000	1341	13	4
[28]	5	7	4	72	13	16	0	8000	1533	6	8
29	5	11	2	73	13	19	10	9000	1725	0	0
30	5	15	0	74	14	3	8	10000	1916	13	4
31	5	18	10	75	14	7	6				
32	6	2	8	76	14	11	4				
33	6	6	6	77	14	15	2				
34	6	10	4	78	14	19	0				
35	6	14	2	79	15	2	10				
36	6	18	0	80	15	6	8				
37	7	1	10	81	15	10	6				
38	7	5	8	82	15	14	4				
39	7	9	6	83	15	18	2				
40	7	13	4	[84]	16	2	0				
41	7	17	2	85	16	5	10				
42	8	1	0	86	16	9	8				
43	8	4	10	87	16	13	6				
44	8	8	8	88	16	17	4				

Great Hundred

112	21	9	4

Grofs

144	27	12	0

Wey

256	49	1	4

Days in a Year

365	69	19	2

Feet in a Rod

272	52	2	8

N.	l.	s.	d.
1	0	3	11
2	0	7	10
3	0	11	9
4	0	15	8
5	0	19	7
6	1	3	6
7	1	7	5
8	1	11	4
9	1	15	3
10	1	19	2
11	2	3	1
12	2	7	0
13	2	10	11
14	2	14	10
15	2	18	9
16	3	2	8
17	3	6	7
18	3	10	6
19	3	14	5
20	3	18	4
21	4	2	3
22	4	6	2
23	4	10	1
24	4	14	0
25	4	17	11
26	5	1	10
27	5	5	9
[28]	5	9	8
29	5	13	7
30	5	17	6
31	6	1	5
32	6	5	4
33	6	9	3
34	6	13	2
35	6	17	1
36	7	1	0
37	7	4	11
38	7	8	10
39	7	12	9
40	7	16	8
41	8	0	7
42	8	4	6
43	8	8	5
44	8	12	4

N.	l.	s.	d.
45	8	16	3
46	9	0	2
47	9	4	1
48	9	8	0
49	9	11	11
50	9	15	10
51	9	19	9
52	10	3	8
53	10	7	7
54	10	11	6
55	10	15	5
[56]	10	19	4
57	11	3	3
58	11	7	2
59	11	11	1
60	11	15	0
61	11	18	11
62	12	2	10
63	12	6	9
64	12	10	8
65	12	14	7
66	12	18	6
67	13	2	5
68	13	6	4
69	13	10	3
70	13	14	2
71	13	18	1
72	14	2	0
73	14	5	11
74	14	9	10
75	14	13	9
76	14	17	8
77	15	1	7
78	15	5	6
79	15	9	5
80	15	13	4
81	15	17	3
82	16	1	2
83	16	5	1
[84]	16	9	0
85	16	12	11
86	16	16	10
87	17	0	9
88	17	4	8

N.	l.	s.	d.
89	17	8	7
90	17	12	6
91	17	16	5
92	18	0	4
93	18	4	3
94	18	8	2
95	18	12	1
96	18	16	0
97	18	19	11
98	19	3	10
99	19	7	9
100	19	11	8
200	39	3	4
300	58	15	0
400	78	6	8
500	97	18	4
600	117	10	0
700	137	1	8
800	156	13	4
900	176	5	0
1000	195	16	8
2000	391	13	4
3000	587	10	0
4000	783	6	8
5000	979	3	4
6000	1175	0	0
7000	1350	16	8
8000	1566	13	4
9000	1762	10	0
10000	1958	6	8

Great Hundred

112	21	18	8

Grofs

144	28	4	0

Wey

256	50	2	8

Days in a Year

365	71	9	7

Feet in a Rod

272	53	5	4

N.	l.	s.	d.	N.	l.	s.	d.	N.	l.	s.	d.
1	0	4	0	45	9	0	0	89	17	16	0
2	0	8	0	46	9	4	0	90	18	0	0
3	0	12	0	47	9	8	0	91	18	4	0
4	0	16	0	48	9	12	0	92	18	8	0
5	1	0	0	49	9	16	0	93	18	12	0
6	1	4	0	50	10	0	0	94	18	16	0
7	1	8	0	51	10	4	0	95	19	0	0
8	1	12	0	52	10	8	0	96	19	4	0
9	1	16	0	53	10	12	0	97	19	8	0
10	2	0	0	54	10	16	0	98	19	12	0
11	2	4	0	55	11	0	0	99	19	16	0
12	2	8	0	[56]	11	4	0	100	20	0	0
13	2	12	0	57	11	8	0	200	40	0	0
14	2	16	0	58	11	12	0	300	60	0	0
15	3	0	0	59	11	16	0	400	80	0	0
16	3	4	0	60	12	0	0	500	100	0	0
17	3	8	0	61	12	4	0	600	120	0	0
18	3	12	0	62	12	8	0	700	140	0	0
19	3	16	0	63	12	12	0	800	160	0	0
20	4	0	0	64	12	16	0	900	180	0	0
21	4	4	0	65	13	0	0	1000	200	0	0
22	4	8	0	66	13	4	0	2000	400	0	0
23	4	12	0	67	13	8	0	3000	600	0	0
24	4	16	0	68	13	12	0	4000	800	0	0
25	5	0	0	69	13	16	0	5000	1000	0	0
26	5	4	0	70	14	0	0	6000	1200	0	0
27	5	8	0	71	14	4	0	7000	1400	0	0
[28]	5	12	0	72	14	8	0	8000	1600	0	0
29	5	16	0	73	14	12	0	9000	1800	0	0
30	6	0	0	74	14	16	0	10000	2000	0	0
31	6	4	0	75	15	0	0				
32	6	8	0	76	15	4	0				
33	6	12	0	77	15	8	0	*Great Hundred*			
34	6	16	0	78	15	12	0	112	22	8	0
35	7	0	0	79	15	16	0	*Gross*			
36	7	4	0	80	16	0	0	144	28	16	0
37	7	8	0	81	16	4	0	*Wey*			
38	7	12	0	82	16	8	0	256	51	4	0
39	7	16	0	83	16	12	0	*Days in a Year*			
40	8	0	0	[84]	16	16	0	365	73	0	0
41	8	4	0	85	17	0	0	*Feet in a Rod*			
42	8	8	0	86	17	4	0	272	54	8	0
43	8	12	0	87	17	8	0				
44	8	16	0	88	17	12	0				

N.	l.	s.	d.	N.	l.	s.	d.	N.	l.	s.	d.
1	0	4	1	45	9	3	9	89	18	3	5
2	0	8	2	46	9	7	10	90	18	7	6
3	0	12	3	47	9	11	11	91	18	11	7
4	0	16	4	48	9	16	0	92	18	15	8
5	1	0	5	49	10	0	1	93	18	19	9
6	1	4	6	50	10	4	2	94	19	3	10
7	1	8	7	51	10	8	3	95	19	7	11
8	1	12	8	52	10	12	4	96	19	12	0
9	1	16	9	53	10	16	5	97	19	16	1
10	2	0	10	54	11	0	6	98	20	0	2
11	2	4	11	55	11	4	7	99	20	4	3
12	2	9	0	[56]	11	8	8	100	20	8	4
13	2	13	1	57	11	12	9	200	40	16	8
14	2	17	2	58	11	16	10	300	61	5	0
15	3	1	3	59	12	0	11	400	81	13	4
16	3	5	4	60	12	5	0	500	102	1	8
17	3	9	5	61	12	9	1	600	122	10	0
18	3	13	6	62	12	13	2	700	142	18	4
19	3	17	7	63	12	17	3	800	163	6	8
20	4	1	8	64	13	1	4	900	183	15	0
21	4	5	9	65	13	5	5	1000	204	3	4
22	4	9	10	66	13	9	6	2000	408	6	8
23	4	13	11	67	13	13	7	3000	612	10	0
24	4	18	0	68	13	17	8	4000	816	13	4
25	5	2	1	69	14	1	9	5000	1020	16	8
26	5	6	2	70	14	5	10	6000	1225	0	0
27	5	10	3	71	14	9	11	7000	1429	3	4
[28]	5	14	4	72	14	14	0	8000	1633	6	8
29	5	18	5	73	14	18	1	9000	1837	10	0
30	6	2	6	74	15	2	2	10000	2041	13	4
31	6	6	7	75	15	6	3				
32	6	10	8	76	15	10	4				
33	6	14	9	77	15	14	5				
34	6	18	10	78	15	18	6				
35	7	2	11	79	16	2	7				
36	7	7	0	80	16	6	8				
37	7	11	1	81	16	10	9				
38	7	15	2	82	16	14	10				
39	7	19	3	83	16	18	11				
40	8	3	4	[84]	17	3	0				
41	8	7	5	85	17	7	1				
42	8	11	6	86	17	11	2				
43	8	15	7	87	17	15	3				
44	8	19	8	88	17	19	4				

Great Hundred

112	22	17	4

Grofs

144	29	8	0

Way

256	52	5	4

Days in a Year

365	74	10	5

Feet in a Rod

272	55	10	8

N

N.	l.	s.	d.	N.	l.	s.	d.	N.	l.	s.	d.
1	0	4	2	45	9	7	6	89	18	10	10
2	0	8	4	46	9	11	8	90	18	15	0
3	0	12	6	47	9	15	10	91	18	19	2
4	0	16	8	48	10	0	0	92	19	3	4
5	1	0	10	49	10	4	2	93	19	7	6
6	1	5	0	50	10	8	4	94	19	11	8
7	1	9	2	51	10	12	6	95	19	15	10
8	1	13	4	52	10	16	8	96	20	0	0
9	1	17	6	53	11	0	10	97	20	4	2
10	2	1	8	54	11	5	0	98	20	8	4
11	2	5	10	55	11	9	2	99	20	12	6
12	2	10	0	[56]	11	13	4	100	20	16	8
13	2	14	2	57	11	17	6	200	41	13	4
14	2	18	4	58	12	1	8	300	62	10	0
15	3	2	6	59	12	5	10	400	83	6	8
16	3	6	8	60	12	10	0	500	104	3	4
17	3	10	10	61	12	14	2	600	125	0	0
18	3	15	0	62	12	18	4	700	145	16	8
19	3	19	2	63	13	2	6	800	166	13	4
20	4	3	4	64	13	6	8	900	187	10	0
21	4	7	6	65	13	10	10	1000	208	6	8
22	4	11	8	66	13	15	0	2000	416	13	4
23	4	15	10	67	13	19	2	3000	625	0	0
24	5	0	0	68	14	3	4	4000	833	6	8
25	5	4	2	69	14	7	6	5000	1041	13	4
26	5	8	4	70	14	11	8	6000	1250	0	0
27	5	12	6	71	14	15	10	7000	1458	6	8
[28]	5	16	8	72	15	0	0	8000	1666	13	4
29	6	0	10	73	15	4	2	9000	1875	0	0
30	6	5	0	74	15	8	4	10000	2083	6	8
31	6	9	2	75	15	12	6				
32	6	13	4	76	15	16	8				
33	6	17	6	77	16	0	10	Great Hundred			
34	7	1	8	78	16	5	0	112	23	6	8
35	7	5	10	79	16	9	2	Grofs			
36	7	10	0	80	16	13	4	144	30	0	0
37	7	14	2	81	16	17	6	Wey			
38	7	18	4	82	17	1	8	256	53	6	8
39	8	2	6	83	17	5	10	Days in a Year			
40	8	6	8	[84]	17	10	0	365	76	0	10
41	8	10	10	85	17	14	2	Feet in a Rod			
42	8	15	0	86	17	18	4	272	56	13	4
43	8	19	2	87	18	2	6				
44	9	3	4	88	18	6	8				

N.	l.	s.	d.	N.	l.	s.	d.	N.	l.	s.	d.
1	0	4	3	45	9	11	3	89	18	18	3
2	0	8	6	46	9	15	6	90	19	2	6
3	0	12	9	47	9	19	9	91	19	6	9
4	0	17	0	48	10	4	0	92	19	11	0
5	1	1	3	49	10	8	3	93	19	15	3
6	1	5	6	50	10	12	6	94	19	19	6
7	1	9	9	51	10	16	9	95	20	3	9
8	1	14	0	52	11	1	0	96	20	8	0
9	1	18	3	53	11	5	3	97	20	12	3
10	2	2	6	54	11	9	6	98	20	16	6
11	2	6	9	55	11	13	9	99	21	0	9
12	2	11	0	[56]	11	18	0	100	21	5	0
13	2	15	3	57	12	2	3	200	42	10	0
14	2	19	6	58	12	6	6	300	63	15	0
15	3	3	9	59	12	10	9	400	85	0	0
16	3	8	0	60	12	15	0	500	106	5	0
17	3	12	3	61	12	19	3	600	127	10	0
18	3	16	6	62	13	3	6	700	148	15	0
19	4	0	9	63	13	7	9	800	170	0	0
20	4	5	0	64	13	12	0	900	191	5	0
21	4	9	3	65	13	16	3	1000	212	10	0
22	4	13	6	66	14	0	6	2000	425	0	0
23	4	17	9	67	14	4	9	3000	637	10	0
24	5	2	0	68	14	9	0	4000	850	0	0
25	5	6	3	69	14	13	3	5000	1062	10	0
26	5	10	6	70	14	17	6	6000	1275	0	0
27	5	14	9	71	15	1	9	7000	1487	10	0
[28]	5	19	0	72	15	6	0	8000	1700	0	0
29	6	3	3	73	15	10	3	9000	1912	10	0
30	6	7	6	74	15	14	6	10000	2125	0	0
31	6	11	9	75	15	18	9				
32	6	16	0	76	16	3	0				
33	7	0	3	77	16	7	3				
34	7	4	6	78	16	11	6				
35	7	8	9	79	16	15	9				
36	7	13	0	80	17	0	0				
37	7	17	3	81	17	4	3				
38	8	1	6	82	17	8	6				
39	8	5	9	83	17	12	9				
40	8	10	0	[84]	17	17	0				
41	8	14	3	85	18	1	3				
42	8	18	6	86	18	5	6				
43	9	2	9	87	18	9	9				
44	9	7	0	88	18	14	0				

Great Hundred

112 | 23 16 0

Grofs

144 | 30 12 0

Wey

256 | 54 8 0

Days in a Year

365 | 77 11 3

Feet in a Rod

272 | 57 16 0

N.	l.	s.	d.	N.	l.	s.	d.	N	l.	s.	d.
1	0	4	4	45	9	15	0	89	19	5	8
2	0	8	8	46	9	19	4	90	19	10	0
3	0	13	0	47	10	3	8	91	19	14	4
4	0	17	4	48	10	8	0	92	19	18	8
5	1	1	8	49	10	12	4	93	20	3	0
6	1	6	0	50	10	16	8	94	20	7	4
7	1	10	4	51	11	1	0	95	20	11	8
8	1	14	8	52	11	5	4	96	20	16	0
9	1	19	0	53	11	9	8	97	21	0	4
10	2	3	4	54	11	14	0	98	21	4	8
11	2	7	8	55	11	18	4	99	21	9	0
12	2	12	0	[56]	12	2	8	100	21	13	4
13	2	16	4	57	12	7	0	200	43	6	8
14	3	0	8	58	12	11	4	300	65	0	0
15	3	5	0	59	12	15	8	400	86	13	4
16	3	9	4	60	13	0	0	500	108	6	8
17	3	13	8	61	13	4	4	600	130	0	0
18	3	18	0	62	13	8	8	700	151	13	4
19	4	2	4	63	13	13	0	800	173	6	8
20	4	6	8	64	13	17	4	900	195	0	0
21	4	11	0	65	14	1	8	1000	216	13	4
22	4	15	4	66	14	6	0	2000	433	6	8
23	4	19	8	67	14	10	4	3000	650	0	0
24	5	4	0	68	14	14	8	4000	866	13	4
25	5	8	4	69	14	19	0	5000	1083	6	8
26	5	12	8	70	15	3	4	6000	1300	0	0
27	5	17	0	71	15	7	8	7000	1516	13	4
[28]	6	1	4	72	15	12	0	8000	1733	6	8
29	6	5	8	73	15	16	4	9000	1950	0	0
30	6	10	0	74	16	0	8	10000	2166	13	4
31	6	14	4	75	16	5	0				
32	6	18	8	76	16	9	4				
33	7	3	0	77	16	13	8	*Great Hundred*			
34	7	7	4	78	16	18	0	112	24	5	4
35	7	11	8	79	17	2	4	*Grofs*			
36	7	16	0	80	17	6	8	144	31	4	0
37	8	0	4	81	17	11	0	*Wey*			
38	8	4	8	82	17	15	4	256	55	9	4
39	8	9	0	83	17	19	8	*Days in a Year*			
40	8	13	4	[84]	18	4	0	365	79	1	8
41	8	17	8	85	18	8	4	*Feet in a Rod*			
42	9	2	0	86	18	12	8	272	58	18	8
43	9	6	4	87	18	17	0				
44	9	10	8	88	19	1	4				

N.	l.	s.	d.	N.	l.	s.	d.	N.	l.	s.	d.
1	0	4	5	45	9	18	9	89	19	13	1
2	0	8	10	46	10	3	2	90	19	17	6
3	0	13	3	47	10	7	7	91	20	1	11
4	0	17	8	48	10	12	0	92	20	6	4
5	1	2	1	49	10	16	5	93	20	10	9
6	1	6	6	50	11	0	10	94	20	15	2
7	1	10	11	51	11	5	3	95	20	19	7
8	1	15	4	52	11	9	8	96	21	4	0
9	1	19	9	53	11	14	1	97	21	8	5
10	2	4	2	54	11	18	6	98	21	12	10
11	2	8	7	55	12	2	11	99	21	17	3
12	2	13	0	[56]	12	7	4	100	22	1	8
13	2	17	5	57	12	11	9	200	44	3	4
14	3	1	10	58	12	16	2	300	66	5	0
15	3	6	3	59	13	0	7	400	88	6	8
16	3	10	8	60	13	5	0	500	110	8	4
17	3	15	1	61	13	9	5	600	132	10	0
18	3	19	6	62	13	13	10	700	154	11	8
19	4	3	11	63	13	18	3	800	176	13	4
20	4	8	4	64	14	2	8	900	198	15	0
21	4	12	9	65	14	7	1	1000	220	16	8
22	4	17	2	66	14	11	6	2000	441	13	4
23	5	1	7	67	14	15	11	3000	662	10	0
24	5	6	0	68	15	0	4	4000	883	6	8
25	5	10	5	69	15	4	9	5000	1104	3	4
26	5	14	10	70	15	9	2	6000	1325	0	0
27	5	19	3	71	15	13	7	7000	1545	16	8
[28]	6	3	8	72	15	18	0	8000	1766	13	4
29	6	8	1	73	16	2	5	9000	1987	10	0
30	6	12	6	74	16	6	10	10000	2208	6	8
31	6	16	11	75	16	11	3				
32	7	1	4	76	16	15	8				
33	7	5	9	77	17	0	1	Great *Hundred*			
34	7	10	2	78	17	4	6	112	24	14	8
35	7	14	7	79	17	8	11	*Grofs*			
36	7	19	0	80	17	13	4	144	31	16	0
37	8	3	5	81	17	17	9	*Wey*			
38	8	7	10	82	18	2	2	256	56	10	8
39	8	12	3	83	18	6	7	*Days in a Year*			
40	8	16	8	[84]	18	11	0	365	80	12	1
41	9	1	1	85	18	15	5	*Feet in a Rod*			
42	9	5	6	86	18	19	10	272	60	1	4
43	9	9	11	87	19	4	3				
44	9	14	4	88	19	8	8				

N.	l.	s.	d.	N.	l.	s.	d.	N.	l.	s.	d.
1	0	4	6	45	10	2	6	89	20	0	6
2	0	9	0	46	10	7	0	90	20	5	0
3	0	13	6	47	10	11	6	91	20	9	6
4	0	18	0	48	10	16	0	92	20	14	0
5	1	2	6	49	11	0	6	93	20	18	6
6	1	7	0	50	11	5	0	94	21	3	0
7	1	11	6	51	11	9	6	95	21	7	6
8	1	16	0	52	11	14	0	96	21	12	0
9	2	0	6	53	11	18	6	97	21	16	6
10	2	5	0	54	12	3	0	98	22	1	0
11	2	9	6	55	12	7	6	99	22	5	6
12	2	14	0	[56]	12	12	0	100	22	10	0
13	2	18	6	57	12	16	6	200	45	0	0
14	3	3	0	58	13	1	0	300	67	10	0
15	3	7	6	59	13	5	6	400	90	0	0
16	3	12	0	60	13	10	0	500	112	10	0
17	3	16	6	61	13	14	6	600	135	0	0
18	4	1	0	62	13	19	0	700	157	10	0
19	4	5	6	63	14	3	6	800	180	0	0
20	4	10	0	64	14	8	0	900	202	10	0
21	4	14	6	65	14	12	6	1000	225	0	0
22	4	19	0	66	14	17	0	2000	450	0	0
23	5	3	6	67	15	1	6	3000	675	0	0
24	5	8	0	68	15	6	0	4000	900	0	0
25	5	12	6	69	15	10	6	5000	1125	0	0
26	5	17	0	70	15	15	0	6000	1350	0	0
27	6	1	6	71	15	19	6	7000	1575	0	0
[28]	6	6	0	72	16	4	0	8000	1800	0	0
29	6	10	6	73	16	8	6	9000	2025	0	0
30	6	15	0	74	16	13	0	10000	2250	0	0
31	6	19	6	75	16	17	6				
32	7	4	0	76	17	2	0				
33	7	8	6	77	17	6	6				
34	7	13	0	78	17	11	0				
35	7	17	6	79	17	15	6				
36	8	2	0	80	18	0	0				
37	8	6	6	81	18	4	6				
38	8	11	0	82	18	9	0				
39	8	15	6	83	18	13	6				
40	9	0	0	[84]	18	18	0				
41	9	4	6	85	19	2	6				
42	9	9	0	86	19	7	0				
43	9	13	6	87	19	11	6				
44	9	18	0	88	19	16	0				

Great Hundred

112	25	4	0

Gross

144	32	8	0

Wey

256	57	12	0

Days in a Year

365	82	2	6

Feet in a Rod

272	61	4	0

N.	l.	s.	d.	N.	l.	s.	d.	N.	l.	s.	d.
1	0	4	7	45	10	6	3	89	20	7	11
2	0	9	2	46	10	10	10	90	20	12	6
3	0	13	9	47	10	15	5	91	20	17	1
4	0	18	4	48	11	0	0	92	21	1	8
5	1	2	11	49	11	4	7	93	21	6	3
6	1	7	6	50	11	9	2	94	21	10	10
7	1	12	1	51	11	13	9	95	21	15	5
8	1	16	8	52	11	18	4	96	22	0	0
9	2	1	3	53	12	2	11	97	22	4	7
10	2	5	10	54	12	7	6	98	22	9	2
11	2	10	5	55	12	12	1	99	22	13	9
12	2	15	0	[56]	12	16	8	100	22	18	4
13	2	19	7	57	13	1	3	200	45	16	8
14	3	4	2	58	13	5	10	300	68	15	0
15	3	8	9	59	13	10	5	400	91	13	4
16	3	13	4	60	13	15	0	500	114	11	8
17	3	17	11	61	13	19	7	600	137	10	0
18	4	2	6	62	14	4	2	700	160	8	4
19	4	7	1	63	14	8	9	800	183	6	8
20	4	11	8	64	14	13	4	900	206	5	0
21	4	16	3	65	14	17	11	1000	229	3	4
22	5	0	10	66	15	2	6	2000	458	6	8
23	5	5	5	67	15	7	1	3000	687	10	0
24	5	10	0	68	15	11	8	4000	916	13	4
25	5	14	7	69	15	16	3	5000	1145	16	8
26	5	19	2	70	16	0	10	6000	1375	0	0
27	6	3	9	71	16	5	5	7000	1604	3	4
[28]	6	8	4	72	16	10	0	8000	1833	6	8
29	6	12	11	73	16	14	7	9000	2062	10	0
30	6	17	6	74	16	19	2	10000	2291	13	4
31	7	2	1	75	17	3	9				
32	7	6	8	76	17	8	4				
33	7	11	3	77	17	12	11				
34	7	15	10	78	17	17	6				
35	8	0	5	79	18	2	1				
36	8	5	0	80	18	6	8				
37	8	9	7	81	18	11	3				
38	8	14	2	82	18	15	10				
39	8	18	9	83	19	0	5				
40	9	3	4	[84]	19	5	0				
41	9	7	11	85	19	9	7				
42	9	12	6	86	19	14	2				
43	9	17	1	87	19	18	9				
44	10	1	8	88	20	3	4				

Great Hundred			
112	25	13	4

Gross			
144	33	0	0

Wey			
256	58	13	4

Days in a Year			
365	83	12	11

Feet in a Rod			
272	62	6	8

N.	l.	s.	d.	N.	l.	s.	d.	N.	l.	s.	d.
1	0	4	8	45	10	10	0	89	20	15	4
2	0	9	4	46	10	14	8	90	21	0	0
3	0	14	0	47	10	19	4	91	21	4	8
4	0	18	8	48	11	4	0	92	21	9	4
5	1	3	4	49	11	8	8	93	21	14	0
6	1	8	0	50	11	13	4	94	21	18	8
7	1	12	8	51	11	18	0	95	22	3	4
8	1	17	4	52	12	2	8	96	22	8	0
9	2	2	0	53	12	7	4	97	22	12	8
10	2	6	8	54	12	12	0	98	22	17	4
11	2	11	4	55	12	16	8	99	23	2	0
12	2	16	0	[56]	13	1	4	100	23	6	8
13	3	0	8	57	13	6	0	200	46	13	4
14	3	5	4	58	13	10	8	300	70	0	0
15	3	10	0	59	13	15	4	400	93	6	8
16	3	14	8	60	14	0	0	500	116	13	4
17	3	19	4	61	14	4	8	600	140	0	0
18	4	4	0	62	14	9	4	700	163	6	8
19	4	8	8	63	14	14	0	800	186	13	4
20	4	13	4	64	14	18	8	900	210	0	0
21	4	18	0	65	15	3	4	1000	233	6	8
22	5	2	8	66	15	8	0	2000	466	13	4
23	5	7	4	67	15	12	8	3000	700	0	0
24	5	12	0	68	15	17	4	4000	933	6	8
25	5	16	8	69	16	2	0	5000	1166	13	4
26	6	1	4	70	16	6	8	6000	1400	0	0
27	6	6	0	71	16	11	4	7000	1633	6	8
[28]	6	10	8	72	16	16	0	8000	1866	13	4
29	6	15	4	73	17	0	8	9000	2100	0	0
30	7	0	0	74	17	5	4	10000	2333	6	8
31	7	4	8	75	17	10	0				
32	7	9	4	76	17	14	8				
33	7	14	0	77	17	19	4	*Great Hundred*			
34	7	18	8	78	18	4	0	112	26	2	8
35	8	3	4	79	18	8	8	*Grofs*			
36	8	8	0	80	18	13	4	144	33	12	0
37	8	12	8	81	18	18	0	*Wey*			
38	8	17	4	82	19	2	8	256	59	14	8
39	9	2	0	83	19	7	4	*Days in a Year*			
40	9	6	8	[84]	19	12	0	365	85	3	4
41	9	11	4	85	19	16	8	*Feet in a Rod*			
42	9	16	0	86	20	1	4	272	63	9	4
43	10	0	8	87	20	6	0				
44	10	5	4	88	20	10	8				

N.	l.	s.	d.	N.	l.	s.	d.	N.	l.	s.	d.
1	0	4	9	45	10	13	9	89	21	2	9
2	0	9	6	46	10	18	6	90	21	7	6
3	0	14	3	47	11	3	3	91	21	12	3
4	0	19	0	48	11	8	0	92	21	17	0
5	1	3	9	49	11	12	9	93	22	1	9
6	1	8	6	50	11	17	6	94	22	6	6
7	1	13	3	51	12	2	3	95	22	11	3
8	1	18	0	52	12	7	0	96	22	16	0
9	2	2	9	53	12	11	9	97	23	0	9
10	2	7	6	54	12	16	6	98	23	5	6
11	2	12	3	55	13	1	3	99	23	10	3
12	2	17	0	[56]	13	6	0	100	23	15	0
13	3	1	9	57	13	10	9	200	47	10	0
14	3	6	6	58	13	15	6	300	71	5	0
15	3	11	3	59	14	0	3	400	95	0	0
16	3	16	0	60	14	5	0	500	118	15	0
17	4	0	9	61	14	9	9	600	142	10	0
18	4	5	6	62	14	14	6	700	166	5	0
19	4	10	3	63	14	19	3	800	190	0	0
20	4	15	0	64	15	4	0	900	213	15	0
21	4	19	9	65	15	8	9	1000	237	10	0
22	5	4	6	66	15	13	6	2000	475	0	0
23	5	9	3	67	15	18	3	3000	712	10	0
24	5	14	0	68	16	3	0	4000	950	0	0
25	5	18	9	69	16	7	9	5000	1187	10	0
26	6	3	6	70	16	12	6	6000	1425	0	0
27	6	8	3	71	16	17	3	7000	1662	10	0
[28]	6	13	0	72	17	2	0	8000	1900	0	0
29	6	17	9	73	17	6	9	9000	2137	10	0
30	7	2	6	74	17	11	6	10000	2375	0	0
31	7	7	3	75	17	16	3				
32	7	12	0	76	18	1	0				
33	7	16	9	77	18	5	9	Great Hundred			
34	8	1	6	78	18	10	6	112	26	12	0
35	8	6	3	79	18	15	3	Grofs			
36	8	11	0	80	19	0	0	144	34	4	0
37	8	15	9	81	19	4	9	Wey			
38	9	0	6	82	19	9	6	256	60	16	0
39	9	5	3	83	19	14	3	Days in a Year			
40	9	10	0	[84]	19	19	0	365	86	13	9
41	9	14	9	85	20	3	9	Feet in a Rod			
42	9	19	6	86	20	8	6	272	64	12	0
43	10	4	3	87	20	13	3				
44	10	9	0	88	20	18	0				

N.	l.	s.	d.	N.	l.	s.	d.	N.	l.	s.	d.
1	0	4	10	45	10	17	6	89	21	10	2
2	0	9	8	46	11	2	4	90	21	15	0
3	0	14	6	47	11	7	2	91	21	19	10
4	0	19	4	48	11	12	0	92	22	4	8
5	1	4	2	49	11	16	10	93	22	9	6
6	1	9	0	50	12	1	8	94	22	14	4
7	1	13	10	51	12	6	6	95	22	19	2
8	1	18	8	52	12	11	4	96	23	4	0
9	2	3	6	53	12	16	2	97	23	8	10
10	2	8	4	54	13	1	0	98	23	13	8
11	2	13	2	55	13	5	10	99	23	18	6
12	2	18	0	[56]	13	10	8	100	24	3	4
13	3	2	10	57	13	15	6	200	48	6	8
14	3	7	8	58	14	0	4	300	72	10	0
15	3	12	6	59	14	5	2	400	96	13	4
16	3	17	4	60	14	10	0	500	120	16	8
17	4	2	2	61	14	14	10	600	145	0	0
18	4	7	0	62	14	19	8	700	169	3	4
19	4	11	10	63	15	4	6	800	193	6	8
20	4	16	8	64	15	9	4	900	217	10	0
21	5	1	6	65	15	14	2	1000	241	13	4
22	5	6	4	66	15	19	0	2000	483	6	8
23	5	11	2	67	16	3	10	3000	725	0	0
24	5	16	0	68	16	8	8	4000	966	13	4
25	6	0	10	69	16	13	6	5000	1208	6	8
26	6	5	8	70	16	18	4	6000	1450	0	0
27	6	10	6	71	17	3	2	7000	1691	13	4
[28]	6	15	4	72	17	8	0	8000	1933	6	8
29	7	0	2	73	17	12	10	9000	2175	0	0
30	7	5	0	74	17	17	8	10000	2416	13	4
31	7	9	10	75	18	2	6				
32	7	14	8	76	18	7	4				
33	7	19	6	77	18	12	2	Great Hundred			
34	8	4	4	78	18	17	0	112	27	1	4
35	8	9	2	79	19	1	10	Grofs			
36	8	14	0	80	19	6	8	144	34	16	0
37	8	18	10	81	19	11	6	Wey			
38	9	3	8	82	19	16	4	256	61	17	4
39	9	8	6	83	20	1	2	Days in a Year			
40	9	13	4	[84]	20	6	0	365	88	4	2
41	9	18	2	85	20	10	10	Feet in a Rod			
42	10	3	0	86	20	15	8	272	65	14	8
43	10	7	10	87	21	0	6				
44	10	12	8	88	21	5	4				

N.	l.	s.	d.	N.	l.	s.	d.	N.	l.	s.	d.
1	0	4	11	45	11	1	3	89	21	17	7
2	0	9	10	46	11	6	2	90	22	2	6
3	0	14	9	47	11	11	1	91	22	7	5
4	0	19	8	48	11	16	0	92	22	12	4
5	1	4	7	49	12	0	11	93	22	17	3
6	1	9	6	50	12	5	10	94	23	2	2
7	1	14	5	51	12	10	9	95	23	7	1
8	1	19	4	52	12	15	8	96	23	12	0
9	2	4	3	53	13	0	7	97	23	16	11
10	2	9	2	54	13	5	6	98	24	1	10
11	2	14	1	55	13	10	5	99	24	6	9
12	2	19	0	[56]	13	15	4	100	24	11	8
13	3	3	11	57	14	0	3	200	49	3	4
14	3	8	10	58	14	5	2	300	73	15	0
15	3	13	9	59	14	10	1	400	98	6	8
16	3	18	8	60	14	15	0	500	122	18	4
17	4	3	7	61	14	19	11	600	147	10	0
18	4	8	6	62	15	4	10	700	172	1	8
19	4	13	5	63	15	9	9	800	196	13	4
20	4	18	4	64	15	14	8	900	221	5	0
21	5	3	3	65	15	19	7	1000	245	16	8
22	5	8	2	66	16	4	6	2000	491	13	4
23	5	13	1	67	16	9	5	3000	737	10	0
24	5	18	0	68	16	14	4	4000	983	6	8
25	6	2	11	69	16	19	3	5000	1229	3	4
26	6	7	10	70	17	4	2	6000	1475	0	0
27	6	12	9	71	17	9	1	7000	1720	16	8
[28]	6	17	8	72	17	14	0	8000	1966	13	4
29	7	2	7	73	17	18	11	9000	2212	10	0
30	7	7	6	74	18	3	10	10000	2458	6	8
31	7	12	5	75	18	8	9				
32	7	17	4	76	18	13	8				
33	8	2	3	77	18	18	7	*Great Hundred*			
34	8	7	2	78	19	3	6	112	27	10	8
35	8	12	1	79	19	8	5	*Grofs*			
36	8	17	0	80	19	13	4	144	35	8	0
37	9	1	11	81	19	18	3	*Wey*			
38	9	6	10	82	20	3	2	256	62	18	8
39	9	11	9	83	20	8	1	*Days in a Year*			
40	9	16	8	[84]	20	13	0	365	89	14	7
41	10	1	7	85	20	17	11	*Feet in a Rod*			
42	10	6	6	86	21	2	10	272	66	17	4
43	10	11	5	87	21	7	9				
44	10	16	4	88	21	12	8				

N.	l.	s.	d.	N.	l.	s.	d.	N.	l.	s.	d.
1	0	5	0	45	11	5	0	89	22	5	0
2	0	10	0	46	11	10	0	90	22	10	0
3	0	15	0	47	11	15	0	91	22	15	0
4	1	0	0	48	12	0	0	92	23	0	0
5	1	5	0	49	12	5	0	93	23	5	0
6	1	10	0	50	12	10	0	94	23	10	0
7	1	15	0	51	12	15	0	95	23	15	0
8	2	0	0	52	13	0	0	96	24	0	0
9	2	5	0	53	13	5	0	97	24	5	0
10	2	10	0	54	13	10	0	98	24	10	0
11	2	15	0	55	13	15	0	99	24	15	0
12	3	0	0	[56]	14	0	0	100	25	0	0
13	3	5	0	57	14	5	0	200	50	0	0
14	3	10	0	58	14	10	0	300	75	0	0
15	3	15	0	59	14	15	0	400	100	0	0
16	4	0	0	60	15	0	0	500	125	0	0
17	4	5	0	61	15	5	0	600	150	0	0
18	4	10	0	62	15	10	0	700	175	0	0
19	4	15	0	63	15	15	0	800	200	0	0
20	5	0	0	64	16	0	0	900	225	0	0
21	5	5	0	65	16	5	0	1000	250	0	0
22	5	10	0	66	16	10	0	2000	500	0	0
23	5	15	0	67	16	15	0	3000	750	0	0
24	6	0	0	68	17	0	0	4000	1000	0	0
25	6	5	0	69	17	5	0	5000	1250	0	0
26	6	10	0	70	17	10	0	6000	1500	0	0
27	6	15	0	71	17	15	0	7000	1750	0	0
[28]	7	0	0	72	18	0	0	8000	2000	0	0
29	7	5	0	73	18	5	0	9000	2250	0	0
30	7	10	0	74	18	10	0	10000	2500	0	0
31	7	15	0	75	18	15	0				
32	8	0	0	76	19	0	0				
33	8	5	0	77	19	5	0	*Great Hundred*			
34	8	10	0	78	19	10	0	112	28	0	0
35	8	15	0	79	19	15	0	*Grofs*			
36	9	0	0	80	20	0	0	144	36	0	0
37	9	5	0	81	20	5	0	*Wey*			
38	9	10	0	82	20	10	0	256	64	0	0
39	9	15	0	83	20	15	0	*Days in a Year*			
40	10	0	0	[84]	21	0	0	365	91	5	0
41	10	5	0	85	21	5	0	*Feet in a Rod*			
42	10	10	0	86	21	10	0	272	68	0	0
43	10	15	0	87	21	15	0				
44	11	0	0	88	22	0	0				

N.	l.	s.	d.	N.	l.	s.	d.	N.	l.	s.	d.
1	0	5	1	45	11	8	9	89	22	12	5
2	0	10	2	46	11	13	10	90	22	17	6
3	0	15	3	47	11	18	11	91	23	2	7
4	1	0	4	48	12	4	0	92	23	7	8
5	1	5	5	49	12	9	1	93	23	12	9
6	1	10	6	50	12	14	2	94	23	17	10
7	1	15	7	51	12	19	3	95	24	2	11
8	2	0	8	52	13	4	4	96	24	8	0
9	2	5	9	53	13	9	5	97	24	13	1
10	2	10	10	54	13	14	6	98	24	18	2
11	2	15	11	55	13	19	7	99	25	3	3
12	3	1	0	[56]	14	4	8	100	25	8	4
13	3	6	1	57	14	9	9	200	50	16	8
14	3	11	2	58	14	14	10	300	76	5	0
15	3	16	3	59	14	19	11	400	101	13	4
16	4	1	4	60	15	5	0	500	127	1	8
17	4	6	5	61	15	10	1	600	152	10	0
18	4	11	6	62	15	15	2	700	177	18	4
19	4	16	7	63	16	0	3	800	203	6	8
20	5	1	8	64	16	5	4	900	228	15	0
21	5	6	9	65	16	10	5	1000	254	3	4
22	5	11	10	66	16	15	6	2000	508	6	8
23	5	16	11	67	17	0	7	3000	762	10	0
24	6	2	0	68	17	5	8	4000	1016	13	4
25	6	7	1	69	17	10	9	5000	1270	16	8
26	6	12	2	70	17	15	10	6000	1525	0	0
27	6	17	3	71	18	0	11	7000	1779	3	4
[28]	7	2	4	72	18	6	0	8000	2033	6	8
29	7	7	5	73	18	11	1	9000	2287	10	0
30	7	12	6	74	18	16	2	10000	2541	13	4
31	7	17	7	75	19	1	3				
32	8	2	8	76	19	6	4				
33	8	7	9	77	19	11	5				
34	8	12	10	78	19	16	6				
35	8	17	11	79	20	1	7				
36	9	3	0	80	20	6	8				
37	9	8	1	81	20	11	9				
38	9	13	2	82	20	16	10				
39	9	18	3	83	21	1	11				
40	10	3	4	[84]	21	7	0				
41	10	8	5	85	21	12	1				
42	10	13	6	86	21	17	2				
43	10	18	7	87	22	2	3				
44	11	3	8	88	22	7	4				

Great Hundred

112	28	9	4

Grofs

144	36	12	0

Wey

256	65	1	4

Days in a Year

365	92	15	5

Feet in a Rod

272	69	2	8

O

N.	l.	s.	d.	N.	l.	s.	d.	N.	l.	s.	d.
1	0	5	2	45	11	12	6	89	22	19	10
2	0	10	4	46	11	17	8	90	23	5	0
3	0	15	6	47	12	2	10	91	23	10	2
4	1	0	8	48	12	8	0	92	23	15	4
5	1	5	10	49	12	13	2	93	24	0	6
6	1	11	0	50	12	18	4	94	24	5	8
7	1	16	2	51	13	3	6	95	24	10	10
8	2	1	4	52	13	8	8	96	24	16	0
9	2	6	6	53	13	13	10	97	25	1	2
10	2	11	8	54	13	19	0	98	25	6	4
11	2	16	10	55	14	4	2	99	25	11	6
12	3	2	0	[56]	14	9	4	100	25	16	8
13	3	7	2	57	14	14	6	200	51	13	4
14	3	12	4	58	14	19	8	300	77	10	0
15	3	17	6	59	15	4	10	400	103	6	8
16	4	2	8	60	15	10	0	500	129	3	4
17	4	7	10	61	15	15	2	600	155	0	0
18	4	13	0	62	16	0	4	700	180	16	8
19	4	18	2	63	16	5	6	800	206	13	4
20	5	3	4	64	16	10	8	900	232	10	0
21	5	8	6	65	16	15	10	1000	258	6	8
22	5	13	8	66	17	1	0	2000	516	13	4
23	5	18	10	67	17	6	2	3000	775	0	0
24	6	4	0	68	17	11	4	4000	1033	6	8
25	6	9	2	69	17	16	6	5000	1291	13	4
26	6	14	4	70	18	1	8	6000	1550	0	0
27	6	19	6	71	18	6	10	7000	1808	6	8
[28]	7	4	8	72	18	12	0	8000	2066	13	4
29	7	9	10	73	18	17	2	9000	2325	0	0
30	7	15	0	74	19	2	4	10000	2583	6	8
31	8	0	2	75	19	7	6				
32	8	5	4	76	19	12	8				
33	8	10	6	77	19	17	10				
34	8	15	8	78	20	3	0				
35	9	0	10	79	20	8	2				
36	9	6	0	80	20	13	4				
37	9	11	2	81	20	18	6				
38	9	16	4	82	21	3	8				
39	10	1	6	83	21	8	10				
40	10	6	8	[84]	21	14	0				
41	10	11	10	85	21	19	2				
42	10	17	0	86	22	4	4				
43	11	2	2	87	22	9	6				
44	11	7	4	88	22	14	8				

Great Hundred

112	28	18	8

Grofs

144	37	4	0

Wey

256	66	2	8

Days in a Year

365	94	5	10

Feet in a Rod

272	70	5	4

N.	l.	s.	d.	N.	l.	s.	d.	N.	l.	s.	d.
1	0	5	3	45	11	16	3	89	23	7	3
2	0	10	6	46	12	1	6	90	23	12	6
3	0	15	9	47	12	6	9	91	23	17	9
4	1	1	0	48	12	12	0	92	24	3	0
5	1	6	3	49	12	17	3	93	24	8	3
6	1	11	6	50	13	2	6	94	24	13	6
7	1	16	9	51	13	7	9	95	24	18	9
8	2	2	0	52	13	13	0	96	25	4	0
9	2	7	3	53	13	18	3	97	25	9	3
10	2	12	6	54	14	3	6	98	25	14	6
11	2	17	9	55	14	8	9	99	25	19	9
12	3	3	0	[56]	14	14	0	100	26	5	0
13	3	8	3	57	14	19	3	200	52	10	0
14	3	13	6	58	15	4	6	300	78	15	0
15	3	18	9	59	15	9	9	400	105	0	0
16	4	4	0	60	15	15	0	500	131	5	0
17	4	9	3	61	16	0	3	600	157	10	0
18	4	14	6	62	16	5	6	700	183	15	0
19	4	19	9	63	16	10	9	800	210	0	0
20	5	5	0	64	16	16	0	900	236	5	0
21	5	10	3	65	17	1	3	1000	262	10	0
22	5	15	6	66	17	6	6	2000	525	0	0
23	6	0	9	67	17	11	9	3000	787	10	0
24	6	6	0	68	17	17	0	4000	1050	0	0
25	6	11	3	69	18	2	3	5000	1312	10	0
26	6	16	6	70	18	7	6	6000	1575	0	0
27	7	1	9	71	18	12	9	7000	1837	10	0
[28]	7	7	0	72	18	18	0	8000	2100	0	0
29	7	12	3	73	19	3	3	9000	2362	10	0
30	7	17	6	74	19	8	6	10000	2625	0	0
31	8	2	9	75	19	13	9				
32	8	8	0	76	19	19	0				
33	8	13	3	77	20	4	3	Great Hundred			
34	8	18	6	78	20	9	6	112	29	8	0
35	9	3	9	79	20	14	9	Grofs			
36	9	9	0	80	21	0	0	144	37	16	0
37	9	14	3	81	21	5	3	Wey			
38	9	19	6	82	21	10	6	256	67	4	0
39	10	4	9	83	21	15	9	Days in a Year			
40	10	10	0	[84]	22	1	0	365	95	16	3
41	10	15	3	85	22	6	3	Feet in a Rod			
42	11	0	6	86	22	11	6	272	71	8	0
43	11	5	9	87	22	16	9				
44	11	11	0	88	23	2	0				

N.	l.	s.	d.	N.	l.	s.	d.	N	l.		d.
1	0	5	4	45	12	0	0	89	23	14	8
2	0	10	8	46	12	5	4	90	24	0	0
3	0	16	0	47	12	10	8	91	24	5	4
4	1	1	4	48	12	16	0	92	24	10	8
5	1	6	8	49	13	1	4	93	24	16	0
6	1	12	0	50	13	6	8	94	25	1	4
7	1	17	4	51	13	12	0	95	25	6	8
8	2	2	8	52	13	17	4	96	25	12	0
9	2	8	0	53	14	2	8	97	25	17	4
10	2	13	4	54	14	8	0	98	26	2	8
11	2	18	8	55	14	13	4	99	26	8	0
12	3	4	0	[56]	14	18	8	100	26	13	4
13	3	9	4	57	15	4	0	200	53	6	8
14	3	14	8	58	15	9	4	300	80	0	0
15	4	0	0	59	15	14	8	400	106	13	4
16	4	5	4	60	16	0	0	500	133	6	8
17	4	10	8	61	16	5	4	600	160	0	0
18	4	16	0	62	16	10	8	700	186	13	4
19	5	1	4	63	16	16	0	800	213	6	8
20	5	6	8	64	17	1	4	900	240	0	0
21	5	12	0	65	17	6	8	1000	266	13	4
22	5	17	4	66	17	12	0	2000	533	6	8
23	6	2	8	67	17	17	4	3000	800	0	0
24	6	8	0	68	18	2	8	4000	1066	13	4
25	6	13	4	69	18	8	0	5000	1333	6	8
26	6	18	8	70	18	13	4	6000	1600	0	0
27	7	4	0	71	18	18	8	7000	1866	13	4
[28]	7	9	4	72	19	4	0	8000	2133	6	8
29	7	14	8	73	19	9	4	9000	2400	0	0
30	8	0	0	74	19	14	8	10000	2666	13	4
31	8	5	4	75	20	0	0				
32	8	10	8	76	20	5	4				
33	8	16	0	77	20	10	8	*Great Hundred*			
34	9	1	4	78	20	16	0	112	29	17	4
35	9	6	8	79	21	1	4	*Gross*			
36	9	12	0	80	21	6	8	144	38	8	0
37	9	17	4	81	21	12	0	*Wey* -			
38	10	2	8	82	21	17	4	256	68	5	4
39	10	8	0	83	22	2	8	*Days in a Year*			
40	10	13	4	[84]	22	8	0	365	97	6	8
41	10	18	8	85	22	13	4	*Feet in a Rod*			
42	11	4	0	86	22	18	8	272	72	10	8
43	11	9	4	87	23	4	0				
44	11	14	8	88	23	9	4				

N.	l.	s.	d.	N.	l.	s.	d.	N.	l.	s.	d.
1	0	5	5	45	12	3	9	89	24	2	1
2	0	10	10	46	12	9	2	90	24	7	6
3	0	16	3	47	12	14	7	91	24	12	11
4	1	1	8	48	13	0	0	92	24	18	4
5	1	7	1	49	13	5	5	93	25	3	9
6	1	12	6	50	13	10	10	94	25	9	2
7	1	17	11	51	13	16	3	95	25	14	7
8	2	3	4	52	14	1	8	96	26	0	0
9	2	8	9	53	14	7	1	97	26	5	5
10	2	14	2	54	14	12	6	98	26	10	10
11	2	19	7	55	14	17	11	99	26	16	3
12	3	5	0	[56]	15	3	4	100	27	1	8
13	3	10	5	57	15	8	9	200	54	3	4
14	3	15	10	58	15	14	2	300	81	5	0
15	4	1	3	59	15	19	7	400	108	6	8
16	4	6	8	60	16	5	0	500	135	8	4
17	4	12	1	61	16	10	5	600	162	10	0
18	4	17	6	62	16	15	10	700	189	11	8
19	5	2	11	63	17	1	3	800	216	13	4
20	5	8	4	64	17	6	8	900	243	15	0
21	5	13	9	65	17	12	1	1000	270	16	8
22	5	19	2	66	17	17	6	2000	541	13	4
23	6	4	7	67	18	2	11	3000	812	10	0
24	6	10	0	68	18	8	4	4000	1083	6	8
25	6	15	5	69	18	13	9	5000	1354	3	4
26	7	0	10	70	18	19	2	6000	1625	0	0
27	7	6	3	71	19	4	7	7000	1895	16	8
[28]	7	11	8	72	19	10	0	8000	2166	13	4
29	7	17	1	73	19	15	5	9000	2437	10	0
30	8	2	6	74	20	0	10	10000	2708	6	8
31	8	7	11	75	20	6	3				
32	8	13	4	76	20	11	8				
33	8	18	9	77	20	17	1	Great Hundred			
34	9	4	2	78	21	2	6	112	30	6	8
35	9	9	7	79	21	7	11	Grofs			
36	9	15	0	80	21	13	4	144	39	0	0
37	10	0	5	81	21	18	9	Wey			
38	10	5	10	82	22	4	2	256	69	6	8
39	10	11	3	83	22	9	7	Days in a Year			
40	10	16	8	[84]	22	15	0	365	98	17	1
41	11	2	1	85	23	0	5	Feet in a Rod			
42	11	7	6	86	23	5	10	272	73	13	4
43	11	12	11	87	23	11	3				
44	11	18	4	88	23	16	8				

N.	l.	s.	d.
1	0	5	6
2	0	11	0
3	0	16	6
4	1	2	0
5	1	7	6
6	1	13	0
7	1	18	6
8	2	4	0
9	2	9	6
10	2	15	0
11	3	0	6
12	3	6	0
13	3	11	6
14	3	17	0
15	4	2	6
16	4	8	0
17	4	13	6
18	4	19	0
19	5	4	6
20	5	10	0
21	5	15	6
22	6	1	0
23	6	6	6
24	6	12	0
25	6	17	6
26	7	3	0
27	7	8	6
[28]	7	14	0
29	7	19	6
30	8	5	0
31	8	10	6
32	8	16	0
33	9	1	6
34	9	7	0
35	9	12	6
36	9	18	0
37	10	3	6
38	10	9	0
39	10	14	6
40	11	0	0
41	11	5	6
42	11	11	0
43	11	16	6
44	12	2	0

N.	l.	s.	d.
45	12	7	6
46	12	13	0
47	12	18	6
48	13	4	0
49	13	9	6
50	13	15	0
51	14	0	6
52	14	6	0
53	14	11	6
54	14	17	0
55	15	2	6
[56]	15	8	0
57	15	13	6
58	15	19	0
59	16	4	6
60	16	10	0
61	16	15	6
62	17	1	0
63	17	6	6
64	17	12	0
65	17	17	6
66	18	3	0
67	18	8	6
68	18	14	0
69	18	19	6
70	19	5	0
71	19	10	6
72	19	16	0
73	20	1	6
74	20	7	0
75	20	12	6
76	20	18	0
77	21	3	6
78	21	9	0
79	21	14	6
80	22	0	0
81	22	5	6
82	22	11	0
83	22	16	6
[84]	23	2	0
85	23	7	6
86	23	13	0
87	23	18	6
88	24	4	0

N.	l.	s.	d.
89	24	9	6
90	24	15	0
91	25	0	6
92	25	6	0
93	25	11	6
94	25	17	0
95	26	2	6
96	26	8	0
97	26	13	6
98	26	19	0
99	27	4	6
100	27	10	0
200	55	0	0
300	82	10	0
400	110	0	0
500	137	10	0
600	165	0	0
700	192	10	0
800	220	0	0
900	247	10	0
1000	275	0	0
2000	550	0	0
3000	825	0	0
4000	1100	0	0
5000	1375	0	0
6000	1650	0	0
7000	1925	0	0
8000	2200	0	0
9000	2475	0	0
10000	2750	0	0

Great Hundred

112	30	16	0

Gross

144	39	12	0

Wey

256	70	8	0

Days in a Year

365	100	7	6

Feet in a Rod

272	74	16	0

N.	l.	s.	d.	N.	l.	s.	d.	N.	l.	s.	d.
1	0	5	7	45	12	11	3	89	24	16	11
2	0	11	2	46	12	16	10	90	25	2	6
3	0	16	9	47	13	2	5	91	25	8	1
4	1	2	4	48	13	8	0	92	25	13	8
5	1	7	11	49	13	13	7	93	25	19	3
6	1	13	6	50	13	19	2	94	26	4	10
7	1	19	1	51	14	4	9	95	26	10	5
8	2	4	8	52	14	10	4	96	26	16	0
9	2	10	3	53	14	15	11	97	27	1	7
10	2	15	10	54	15	1	6	98	27	7	2
11	3	1	5	55	15	7	1	99	27	12	9
12	3	7	0	[56]	15	12	8	100	27	18	4
13	3	12	7	57	15	18	3	200	55	16	8
14	3	18	2	58	16	3	10	300	83	15	0
15	4	3	9	59	16	9	5	400	111	13	4
16	4	9	4	60	16	15	0	500	139	11	8
17	4	14	11	61	17	0	7	600	167	10	0
18	5	0	6	62	17	6	2	700	195	8	4
19	5	6	1	63	17	11	9	800	223	6	8
20	5	11	8	64	17	17	4	900	251	5	0
21	5	17	3	65	18	2	11	1000	279	3	4
22	6	2	10	66	18	8	6	2000	558	6	8
23	6	8	5	67	18	14	1	3000	837	10	0
24	6	14	0	68	18	19	8	4000	1116	13	4
25	6	19	7	69	19	5	3	5000	1395	16	8
26	7	5	2	70	19	10	10	6000	1675	0	0
27	7	10	9	71	19	16	5	7000	1954	3	4
[28]	7	16	4	72	20	2	0	8000	2233	6	8
29	8	1	11	73	20	7	7	9000	2512	10	0
30	8	7	6	74	20	13	2	10000	2791	13	4
31	8	13	1	75	20	18	9				
32	8	18	8	76	21	4	4				
33	9	4	3	77	21	9	11		Great Hundred		
34	9	9	10	78	21	15	6	112	31	5	4
35	9	15	5	79	22	1	1		Gross		
36	10	1	0	80	22	6	8	144	40	4	0
37	10	6	7	81	22	12	3		Wey		
38	10	12	2	82	22	17	10	256	71	9	4
39	10	17	9	83	23	3	5		Days in a Year		
40	11	3	4	[84]	23	9	0	365	101	17	11
41	11	8	11	85	23	14	7		Feet in a Rod		
42	11	14	6	86	24	0	2	272	75	18	8
43	12	0	1	87	24	5	9				
44	12	5	8	88	24	11	4				

N.	l.	s.	d.	N.	l.	s.	d.	N.	l.	s.	d.
1	0	5	8	45	12	15	0	89	25	4	4
2	0	11	4	46	13	0	8	90	25	10	0
3	0	17	0	47	13	6	4	91	25	15	8
4	1	2	8	48	13	12	0	92	26	1	4
5	1	8	4	49	13	17	8	93	26	7	0
6	1	14	0	50	14	3	4	94	26	12	8
7	1	19	8	51	14	9	0	95	26	18	4
8	2	5	4	52	14	14	8	96	27	4	0
9	2	11	0	53	15	0	4	97	27	9	8
10	2	16	8	54	15	6	0	98	27	15	4
11	3	2	4	55	15	11	8	99	28	1	0
12	3	8	0	[56]	15	17	4	100	28	6	8
13	3	13	8	57	16	3	0	200	56	13	4
14	3	19	4	58	16	8	8	300	85	0	0
15	4	5	0	59	16	14	4	400	113	6	8
16	4	10	8	60	17	0	0	500	141	13	4
17	4	16	4	61	17	5	8	600	170	0	0
18	5	2	0	62	17	11	4	700	198	6	8
19	5	7	8	63	17	17	0	800	226	13	4
20	5	13	4	64	18	2	8	900	255	0	0
21	5	19	0	65	18	8	4	1000	283	6	8
22	6	4	8	66	18	14	0	2000	566	13	4
23	6	10	4	67	18	19	8	3000	850	0	0
24	6	16	0	68	19	5	4	4000	1133	6	8
25	7	1	8	69	19	11	0	5000	1416	13	4
26	7	7	4	70	19	16	8	6000	1700	0	0
27	7	13	0	71	20	2	4	7000	1983	6	8
[28]	7	18	8	72	20	8	0	8000	2266	13	4
29	8	4	4	73	20	13	8	9000	2550	0	0
30	8	10	0	74	20	19	4	10000	2833	6	8
31	8	15	8	75	21	5	0				
32	9	1	4	76	21	10	8				
33	9	7	0	77	21	16	4	Great Hundred			
34	9	12	8	78	22	2	0	112	31	14	8
35	9	18	4	79	22	7	8	Grofs			
36	10	4	0	80	22	13	4	144	40	16	8
37	10	9	8	81	22	19	0	Wey			
38	10	15	4	82	23	4	8	256	72	10	8
39	11	1	0	83	23	10	4	Days in a Year			
40	11	6	8	[84]	23	16	0	365	103	8	4
41	11	12	4	85	24	1	8	Feet in a Rod			
42	11	18	0	86	24	7	4	272	77	1	4
43	12	3	8	87	24	13	0				
44	12	9	4	88	24	18	8				

N.	l.	s.	d.	N.	l.	s.	d.	N.	l.	s.	d.
1	0	5	9	45	12	18	9	89	25	11	9
2	0	11	6	46	13	4	6	90	25	17	6
3	0	17	3	47	13	10	3	91	26	3	3
4	1	3	0	48	13	16	0	92	26	9	0
5	1	8	9	49	14	1	9	93	26	14	9
6	1	14	6	50	14	7	6	94	27	0	6
7	2	0	3	51	14	13	3	95	27	6	3
8	2	6	0	52	14	19	0	96	27	12	0
9	2	11	9	53	15	4	9	97	27	17	9
10	2	17	6	54	15	10	6	98	28	3	6
11	3	3	3	55	15	16	3	99	28	9	3
12	3	9	0	[56]	16	2	0	100	28	15	0
13	3	14	9	57	16	7	9	200	57	10	0
14	4	0	6	58	16	13	6	300	86	5	0
15	4	6	3	59	16	19	3	400	115	0	0
16	4	12	0	60	17	5	0	500	143	15	0
17	4	17	9	61	17	10	9	600	172	10	0
18	5	3	6	62	17	16	6	700	201	5	0
19	5	9	3	63	18	2	3	800	230	0	0
20	5	15	0	64	18	8	0	900	258	15	0
21	6	0	9	65	18	13	9	1000	287	10	0
22	6	6	6	66	18	19	6	2000	575	0	0
23	6	12	3	67	19	5	3	3000	862	10	0
24	6	18	0	68	19	11	0	4000	1150	0	0
25	7	3	9	69	19	16	9	5000	1437	10	0
26	7	9	6	70	20	2	6	6000	1725	0	0
27	7	15	3	71	20	8	3	7000	2012	10	0
[28]	8	1	0	72	20	14	0	8000	2300	0	0
29	8	6	9	73	20	19	9	9000	2587	10	0
30	8	12	6	74	21	5	6	10000	2875	0	0
31	8	18	3	75	21	11	3				
32	9	4	0	76	21	17	0				
33	9	9	9	77	22	2	9				
34	9	15	6	78	22	8	6				
35	10	1	3	79	22	14	3				
36	10	7	0	80	23	0	0				
37	10	12	9	81	23	5	9				
38	10	18	6	82	23	11	6				
39	11	4	3	83	23	17	3				
40	11	10	0	[84]	24	3	0				
41	11	15	9	85	24	8	9				
42	12	1	6	86	24	14	6				
43	12	7	3	87	25	0	3				
44	12	13	0	88	25	6	0				

Great Hundred

112		32	4	0

Grofs

144		41	8	0

Wey

256		73	12	0

Days in a Year

365		104	18	9

Feet in a Rod

272		78	4	0

N.	l.	s.	d.	N.	l.	s.	d.	N.	l.	s.	d.
1	0	5	10	45	13	2	6	89	25	19	2
2	0	11	8	46	13	8	4	90	26	5	0
3	0	17	6	47	13	14	2	91	26	10	10
4	1	3	4	48	14	0	0	92	26	16	8
5	1	9	2	49	14	5	10	93	27	2	6
6	1	15	0	50	14	11	8	94	27	8	4
7	2	0	10	51	14	17	6	95	27	14	2
8	2	6	8	52	15	3	4	96	28	0	0
9	2	12	6	53	15	9	2	97	28	5	10
10	2	18	4	54	15	15	0	98	28	11	8
11	3	4	2	55	16	0	10	99	28	17	6
12	3	10	0	[56]	16	6	8	100	29	3	4
13	3	15	10	57	16	12	6	200	58	6	8
14	4	1	8	58	16	18	4	300	87	10	0
15	4	7	6	59	17	4	2	400	116	13	4
16	4	13	4	60	17	10	0	500	145	16	8
17	4	19	2	61	17	15	10	600	175	0	0
18	5	5	0	62	18	1	8	700	204	3	4
19	5	10	10	63	18	7	6	800	233	6	8
20	5	16	8	64	18	13	4	900	262	10	0
21	6	2	6	65	18	19	2	1000	291	13	4
22	6	8	4	66	19	5	0	2000	583	6	8
23	6	14	2	67	19	10	10	3000	175	0	0
24	7	0	0	68	19	16	8	4000	1166	13	4
25	7	5	10	69	20	2	6	5000	1458	6	8
26	7	11	8	70	20	8	4	6000	1750	0	0
27	7	17	6	71	20	14	2	7000	2041	13	4
[28]	8	3	4	72	21	0	0	8000	2333	6	8
29	8	9	2	73	21	5	10	9000	2625	0	0
30	8	15	0	74	21	11	8	10000	2916	13	4
31	9	0	10	75	21	17	6				
32	9	6	8	76	22	3	4				
33	9	12	6	77	22	9	2	*Great Hundred*			
34	9	18	4	78	22	15	0	112	32	13	4
35	10	4	2	79	23	0	10	*Grofs*			
36	10	10	0	80	23	6	8	144	42	0	0
37	10	15	10	81	23	12	6	*Wey*			
38	11	1	8	82	23	18	4	256	74	13	4
39	11	7	6	83	24	4	2	*Days in a Year*			
40	11	13	4	[84]	24	10	0	365	106	9	2
41	11	19	2	85	24	15	10	*Feet in a Rod*			
42	12	5	0	86	25	1	8	272	79	6	8
43	12	10	10	87	25	7	6				
44	12	16	8	88	25	13	4				

N.	l.	s.	d.	N.	l.	s.	d.	N.	l.	s.	d.
1	0	5	11	45	13	6	3	89	26	6	7
2	0	11	10	46	13	12	2	90	26	12	6
3	0	17	9	47	13	18	1	91	26	18	5
4	1	3	8	48	14	4	0	92	27	4	4
5	1	9	7	49	14	9	11	93	27	10	3
6	1	15	6	50	14	15	10	94	27	16	2
7	2	1	5	51	15	1	9	95	28	2	1
8	2	7	4	52	15	7	8	96	28	8	0
9	2	13	3	53	15	13	7	97	28	13	11
10	2	19	2	54	15	19	6	98	28	19	10
11	3	5	1	55	16	5	5	99	29	5	9
12	3	11	0	[56]	16	11	4	100	29	11	8
13	3	16	11	57	16	17	3	200	59	3	4
14	4	2	10	58	17	3	2	300	88	15	0
15	4	8	9	59	17	9	1	400	118	6	8
16	4	14	8	60	17	15	0	500	147	18	4
17	5	0	7	61	18	0	11	600	177	10	0
18	5	6	6	62	18	6	10	700	207	1	8
19	5	12	5	63	18	12	9	800	236	13	4
20	5	18	4	64	18	18	8	900	266	5	e
21	6	4	3	65	19	4	7	1000	295	16	8
22	6	10	2	66	19	10	6	2000	591	13	4
23	6	16	1	67	19	16	5	3000	887	10	0
24	7	2	0	68	20	2	4	4000	1183	6	8
25	7	7	11	69	20	8	3	5000	1479	3	4
26	7	13	10	70	20	14	2	6000	1775	0	0
27	7	19	9	71	21	0	1	7000	2070	16	8
[28]	8	5	8	72	21	6	0	8000	2366	13	4
29	8	11	7	73	21	11	11	9000	2662	10	0
30	8	17	6	74	21	17	10	10000	2958	6	8
31	9	3	5	75	22	3	9				
32	9	9	4	76	22	9	8				
33	9	15	3	77	22	15	7	*Great Hundred*			
34	10	1	2	78	23	1	6	112	33	2	8
35	10	7	1	79	23	7	5	*Gross*			
36	10	13	0	80	23	13	4	144	42	12	0
37	10	18	11	81	23	19	3	*Wey*			
38	11	4	10	82	24	5	2	256	75	14	8
39	11	10	9	83	24	11	1	*Days in a Year*			
40	11	16	8	[84]	24	17	0	365	107	19	7
41	12	2	7	85	25	2	11	*Feet in a Rod*			
42	12	8	6	86	25	8	10	272	80	9	4
43	12	14	5	87	25	14	9				
44	13	0	4	88	26	0	8				

N.	l.	s.	d.	N.	l.	s.	d.	N.	l.	s.	d.
1	0	6	0	45	13	10	0	89	26	14	0
2	0	12	0	46	13	16	0	90	27	0	0
3	0	18	0	47	14	2	0	91	27	6	0
4	1	4	0	48	14	8	0	92	27	12	0
5	1	10	0	49	14	14	0	93	27	18	0
6	1	16	0	50	15	0	0	94	28	4	0
7	2	2	0	51	15	6	0	95	28	10	0
8	2	8	0	52	15	12	0	96	28	16	0
9	2	14	0	53	15	18	0	97	29	2	0
10	3	0	0	54	16	4	0	98	29	8	0
11	3	6	0	55	16	10	0	99	29	14	0
12	3	12	0	[56]	16	16	0	100	30	0	0
13	3	18	0	57	17	2	0	200	60	0	0
14	4	4	0	58	17	8	0	300	90	0	0
15	4	10	0	59	17	14	0	400	120	0	0
16	4	16	0	60	18	0	0	500	150	0	0
17	5	2	0	61	18	6	0	600	180	0	0
18	5	8	0	62	18	12	0	700	210	0	0
19	5	14	0	63	18	18	0	800	240	0	0
20	6	0	0	64	19	4	0	900	270	0	0
21	6	6	0	65	19	10	0	1000	300	0	0
22	6	12	0	66	19	16	0	2000	600	0	0
23	6	18	0	67	20	2	0	3000	900	0	0
24	7	4	0	68	20	8	0	4000	1200	0	0
25	7	10	0	69	20	14	0	5000	1500	0	0
26	7	16	0	70	21	0	0	6000	1800	0	0
27	8	2	0	71	21	6	0	7000	2100	0	0
[28]	8	8	0	72	21	12	0	8000	2400	0	0
29	8	14	0	73	21	18	0	9000	2700	0	0
30	9	0	0	74	22	4	0	10000	3000	0	0
31	9	6	0	75	22	10	0				
32	9	12	0	76	22	16	0				
33	9	18	0	77	23	2	0	Great Hundred			
34	10	4	0	78	23	8	0	112	33	12	0
35	10	10	0	79	23	14	0	Gross			
36	10	16	0	80	24	0	0	144	43	4	0
37	11	2	0	81	24	6	0	Wey			
38	11	8	0	82	24	12	0	256	76	16	0
39	11	14	0	83	24	18	0	Days in a Year			
40	12	0	0	[84]	25	4	0	365	109	10	0
41	12	6	0	85	25	10	0	Feet in a Rod			
42	12	12	0	86	25	16	0	272	81	12	0
43	12	18	0	87	26	2	0				
44	13	4	0	88	26	8	0				

N.	l.	s.	d.	N.	l.	s.	d.	N.	l.	s.	d.
1	0	6	1	45	13	13	9	89	27	1	5
2	0	12	2	46	13	19	10	90	27	7	6
3	0	18	3	47	14	5	11	91	27	13	7
4	1	4	4	48	14	12	0	92	27	19	8
5	1	10	5	49	14	18	1	93	28	5	9
6	1	16	6	50	15	4	2	94	28	11	10
7	2	2	7	51	15	10	3	95	28	17	11
8	2	8	8	52	15	16	4	96	29	4	0
9	2	14	9	53	16	2	5	97	29	10	1
10	3	0	10	54	16	8	6	98	29	16	2
11	3	6	11	55	16	14	7	99	30	2	3
12	3	13	0	[56]	17	0	8	100	30	8	4
13	3	19	1	57	17	6	9	200	60	16	8
14	4	5	2	58	17	12	10	300	91	5	0
15	4	11	3	59	17	18	11	400	121	13	4
16	4	17	4	60	18	5	0	500	152	1	8
17	5	3	5	61	18	11	1	600	182	10	0
18	5	9	6	62	18	17	2	700	212	18	4
19	5	15	7	63	19	3	3	800	243	6	8
20	6	1	8	64	19	9	4	900	273	15	0
21	6	7	9	65	19	15	5	1000	304	3	4
22	6	13	10	66	20	1	6	2000	608	6	8
23	6	19	11	67	20	7	7	3000	912	10	0
24	7	6	0	68	20	13	8	4000	1216	13	4
25	7	12	1	69	20	19	9	5000	1520	16	8
26	7	18	2	70	21	5	10	6000	1825	0	0
27	8	4	3	71	21	11	11	7000	2129	3	4
[28]	8	10	4	72	21	18	0	8000	2433	6	8
29	8	16	5	73	22	4	1	9000	2737	10	0
30	9	2	6	74	22	10	2	10000	3041	13	4
31	9	8	7	75	22	16	3				
32	9	14	8	76	23	2	4				
33	10	0	9	77	23	8	5	Great Hundred			
34	10	6	10	78	23	14	6	112	34	1	4
35	10	12	11	79	24	0	7	Grofs			
36	10	19	0	80	24	6	8	144	43	16	0
37	11	5	1	81	24	12	9	Wey			
38	11	11	2	82	24	18	10	256	77	17	4
39	11	17	3	83	25	4	11	Days in a Year			
40	12	3	4	[84]	25	11	0	365	111	0	5
41	12	9	5	85	25	17	1	Feet in a Rod			
42	12	15	6	86	26	3	2	272	82	14	8
43	13	1	7	87	26	9	3				
44	13	7	8	88	26	15	4				

P

N.	l.	s.	d.	N.	l.	s.	d.	N.	l.	s.	d.
1	0	6	2	45	13	17	6	89	27	8	10
2	0	12	4	46	14	3	8	90	27	15	0
3	0	18	6	47	14	9	10	91	28	1	2
4	1	4	8	48	14	16	0	92	28	7	4
5	1	10	10	49	15	2	2	93	28	13	6
6	1	17	0	50	15	8	4	94	28	19	8
7	2	3	2	51	15	14	6	95	29	5	10
8	2	9	4	52	16	0	8	96	29	12	0
9	2	15	6	53	16	6	10	97	29	18	2
10	3	1	8	54	16	13	0	98	30	4	4
11	3	7	10	55	16	19	2	99	30	10	6
12	3	14	0	[56]	17	5	4	100	30	16	8
13	4	0	2	57	17	11	6	200	61	13	4
14	4	6	4	58	17	17	8	300	92	10	0
15	4	12	6	59	18	3	10	400	123	6	8
16	4	18	8	60	18	10	0	500	154	3	4
17	5	4	10	61	18	16	2	600	185	0	0
18	5	11	0	62	19	2	4	700	215	16	8
19	5	17	2	63	19	8	6	800	246	13	4
20	6	3	4	64	19	14	8	900	277	10	0
21	6	9	6	65	20	0	10	1000	308	6	8
22	6	15	8	66	20	7	0	2000	616	13	4
23	7	1	10	67	20	13	2	3000	925	0	0
24	7	8	0	68	20	19	4	4000	1233	6	8
25	7	14	2	69	21	5	6	5000	1541	13	4
26	8	0	4	70	21	11	8	6000	1850	0	0
27	8	6	6	71	21	17	10	7000	2158	6	8
[28]	8	12	8	72	22	4	0	8000	2466	13	4
29	8	18	10	73	22	10	2	9000	2775	0	0
30	9	5	0	74	22	16	4	10000	3083	6	8
31	9	11	2	75	23	2	6				
32	9	17	4	76	23	8	8				
33	10	3	6	77	23	14	10				
34	10	9	8	78	24	1	0				
35	10	15	10	79	24	7	2				
36	11	2	0	80	24	13	4				
37	11	8	2	81	24	19	6				
38	11	14	4	82	25	5	8				
39	12	0	6	83	25	11	10				
40	12	6	8	[84]	25	18	0				
41	12	12	10	85	26	4	2				
42	12	19	0	86	26	10	4				
43	13	5	2	87	26	16	6				
44	13	11	4	88	27	2	8				

Great Hundred
112 | 34 10 8

Grofs
144 | 44 8 0

Wey
256 | 78 18 8

Days in a Year
365 | 112 10 10

Feet in a Rod
272 | 83 17 4

N.	l.	s.	d.
1	0	6	3
2	0	12	6
3	0	18	9
4	1	5	0
5	1	11	3
6	1	17	6
7	2	3	9
8	2	10	0
9	2	16	3
10	3	2	6
11	3	8	9
12	3	15	0
13	4	1	3
14	4	7	6
15	4	13	9
16	5	0	0
17	5	6	3
18	5	12	6
19	5	18	9
20	6	5	0
21	6	11	3
22	6	17	6
23	7	3	9
24	7	10	0
25	7	16	3
26	8	2	6
27	8	8	9
[28]	8	15	0
29	9	1	3
30	9	7	6
31	9	13	9
32	10	0	0
33	10	6	3
34	10	12	6
35	10	18	9
36	11	5	0
37	11	11	3
38	11	17	6
39	12	3	9
40	12	10	0
41	12	16	3
42	13	2	6
43	13	8	9
44	13	15	0

N.	l.	s.	d.
45	14	1	3
46	14	7	6
47	14	13	9
48	15	0	0
49	15	6	3
50	15	12	6
51	15	18	9
52	16	5	0
53	16	11	3
54	16	17	6
55	17	3	9
[56]	17	10	0
57	17	16	3
58	18	2	6
59	18	8	9
60	18	15	0
61	19	1	3
62	19	7	6
63	19	13	9
64	20	0	0
65	20	6	3
66	20	12	6
67	20	18	9
68	21	5	0
69	21	11	3
70	21	17	6
71	22	3	9
72	22	10	0
73	22	16	3
74	23	2	6
75	23	8	9
76	23	15	0
77	24	1	3
78	24	7	6
79	24	13	9
80	25	0	0
81	25	6	3
82	25	12	6
83	25	18	9
[84]	26	5	0
85	26	11	3
86	26	17	6
87	27	3	9
88	27	10	0

N.	l.	s.	d.
89	27	16	3
90	28	2	6
91	28	8	9
92	28	15	0
93	29	1	3
94	29	7	6
95	29	13	9
96	30	0	0
97	30	6	3
98	30	12	6
99	30	18	9
100	31	5	0
200	62	10	0
300	93	15	0
400	125	0	0
500	156	5	0
600	187	10	0
700	218	15	0
800	250	0	0
900	281	5	0
1000	312	10	0
2000	625	0	0
3000	937	10	0
4000	1250	0	0
5000	1562	10	0
6000	1875	0	0
7000	2187	10	0
8000	2500	0	0
9000	2812	10	0
10000	3125	0	0

Great Hundred

112	35	0	0

Grofs

144	45	0	0

Wey

256	80	0	0

Days in a Year

365	114	1	3

Feet in a Rod

272	85	0	0

N.	l.	s.	d.	N.	l.	s.	d.	N	l.	s.	d.
1	0	6	4	45	14	5	0	89	28	3	8
2	0	12	8	46	14	11	4	90	28	10	0
3	0	19	0	47	14	17	8	91	28	16	4
4	1	5	4	48	15	4	0	92	29	2	8
5	1	11	8	49	15	10	4	93	29	9	0
6	1	18	0	50	15	16	8	94	29	15	4
7	2	4	4	51	16	3	0	95	30	1	8
8	2	10	8	52	16	9	4	96	30	8	0
9	2	17	0	53	16	15	8	97	30	14	4
10	3	3	4	54	17	2	0	98	31	0	8
11	3	9	8	55	17	8	4	99	31	7	0
12	3	16	0	[56]	17	14	8	100	31	13	4
13	4	2	4	57	18	1	0	200	63	6	8
14	4	8	8	58	18	7	4	300	95	0	0
15	4	15	0	59	18	13	8	400	126	13	4
16	5	1	4	60	19	0	0	500	158	6	8
17	5	7	8	61	19	6	4	600	190	0	0
18	5	14	0	62	19	12	8	700	221	13	4
19	6	0	4	63	19	19	0	800	253	6	8
20	6	6	8	64	20	5	4	900	285	0	0
21	6	13	0	65	20	11	8	1000	316	13	4
22	6	19	4	66	20	18	0	2000	633	6	8
23	7	5	8	67	21	4	4	3000	950	0	0
24	7	12	0	68	21	10	8	4000	1266	13	4
25	7	18	4	69	21	17	0	5000	1583	6	8
26	8	4	8	70	22	3	4	6000	1900	0	0
27	8	11	0	71	22	9	8	7000	2216	13	4
[28]	8	17	4	72	22	16	0	8000	2533	6	8
29	9	3	8	73	23	2	4	9000	2850	0	0
30	9	10	0	74	23	8	8	10000	3166	13	4
31	9	16	4	75	23	15	0				
32	10	2	8	76	24	1	4				
33	10	9	0	77	24	7	8				
34	10	15	4	78	24	14	0				
35	10	1	8	79	25	0	4				
36	11	8	0	80	25	6	8				
37	11	14	4	81	25	13	0				
38	12	0	8	82	25	19	4				
39	12	7	0	83	26	5	8				
40	12	13	4	[84]	26	12	0				
41	12	19	8	85	26	18	4				
42	13	6	0	86	27	4	8				
43	13	12	4	87	27	11	0				
44	13	18	8	88	27	17	4				

Great Hundred

112	35	9	4

Gross

144	45	12	0

Wey

256	81	1	4

Days in a Year

365	115	11	8

Feet in a Rod

272	86	2	8

N.	l.	s.	d.	N.	l.	s.	d.	N.	l.	s.	d.
1	0	6	5	45	14	8	9	89	28	11	1
2	0	12	10	46	14	15	2	90	28	17	6
3	0	19	3	47	15	1	7	91	29	3	11
4	1	5	8	48	15	8	0	92	29	10	4
5	1	12	1	49	15	14	5	93	29	16	9
6	1	18	6	50	16	0	10	94	30	3	2
7	2	4	11	51	16	7	3	95	30	9	7
8	2	11	4	52	16	13	8	96	30	16	0
9	2	17	9	53	17	0	1	97	31	2	5
10	3	4	2	54	17	6	6	98	31	8	10
11	3	10	7	55	17	12	11	99	31	15	3
12	3	17	0	[56]	17	19	4	100	32	1	8
13	4	3	5	57	18	5	9	200	64	3	4
14	4	9	10	58	18	12	2	300	96	5	0
15	4	16	3	59	18	18	7	400	128	6	8
16	5	2	8	60	19	5	0	500	160	8	4
17	5	9	1	61	19	11	5	600	192	10	0
18	5	15	6	62	19	17	10	700	224	11	8
19	6	1	11	63	20	4	3	800	256	13	4
20	6	8	4	64	20	10	8	900	288	15	0
21	6	14	9	65	20	17	1	1000	320	16	8
22	7	1	2	66	21	3	6	2000	641	13	4
23	7	7	7	67	21	9	11	3000	962	10	0
24	7	14	0	68	21	16	4	4000	1283	6	8
25	8	0	5	69	22	2	9	5000	1604	3	4
26	8	6	10	70	22	9	2	6000	1925	0	0
27	8	13	3	71	22	15	7	7000	2245	16	8
[28]	8	19	8	72	23	2	0	8000	2566	13	4
29	9	6	1	73	23	8	5	9000	2887	10	0
30	9	12	6	74	23	14	10	10000	3208	6	8
31	9	18	11	75	24	1	3				
32	10	5	4	76	24	7	8				
33	10	11	9	77	24	14	1		*Great Hundred*		
34	10	18	2	78	25	0	6	112	35	18	8
35	11	4	7	79	25	6	11		*Grofs*		
36	11	11	0	80	25	13	4	144	46	4	0
37	11	17	5	81	25	19	9		*Wey*		
38	12	3	10	82	26	6	2	256	82	2	8
39	12	10	3	83	26	12	7		*Days in a Year*		
40	12	16	8	[84]	26	19	0	365	117	2	1
41	13	3	1	85	27	5	5		*Feet in a Rod*		
42	13	9	6	86	27	11	10	272	87	5	4
43	13	15	11	87	27	18	3				
44	14	2	4	88	28	4	8				

N.	l.	s.	d.
1	0	6	6
2	0	13	0
3	0	19	6
4	1	6	0
5	1	12	6
6	1	19	0
7	2	5	6
8	2	12	0
9	2	18	6
10	3	5	0
11	3	11	6
12	3	18	0
13	4	4	6
14	4	11	0
15	4	17	6
16	5	4	0
17	5	10	6
18	5	17	0
19	6	3	6
20	6	10	0
21	6	16	6
22	7	3	0
23	7	9	6
24	7	16	0
25	8	2	6
26	8	9	0
27	8	15	6
[28]	9	2	0
29	9	8	6
30	9	15	0
31	10	1	6
32	10	8	0
33	10	14	6
34	11	1	0
35	11	7	6
36	11	14	0
37	12	0	6
38	12	7	0
39	12	13	6
40	13	0	0
41	13	6	6
42	13	13	0
43	13	19	6
44	14	6	0

N.	l.	s.	d.
45	14	12	6
46	14	19	0
47	15	5	6
48	15	12	0
49	15	18	6
50	16	5	0
51	16	11	6
52	16	18	0
53	17	4	6
54	17	11	0
55	17	17	6
56	18	4	0
57	18	10	6
58	18	17	0
59	19	3	6
60	19	10	0
61	19	16	6
62	20	3	0
63	20	9	6
64	20	16	0
65	21	2	6
66	21	9	0
67	21	15	6
68	22	2	0
69	22	8	6
70	22	15	0
71	23	1	6
72	23	8	0
73	23	14	6
74	24	1	0
75	24	7	6
76	24	14	0
77	25	0	6
78	25	7	0
79	25	13	6
80	26	0	0
81	26	6	6
82	26	13	0
83	26	19	6
[84]	27	6	0
85	27	12	6
86	27	19	0
87	28	5	6
88	28	12	0

N.	l.	s.	d.
89	28	18	6
90	29	5	0
91	29	11	6
92	29	18	0
93	30	4	6
94	30	11	0
95	30	17	6
96	31	4	0
97	31	10	6
98	31	17	0
99	32	3	6
100	32	10	0
200	65	0	0
300	97	10	0
400	130	0	0
500	162	10	0
600	195	0	0
700	227	10	0
800	260	0	0
900	292	10	0
1000	325	0	0
2000	650	0	0
3000	975	0	0
4000	1300	0	0
5000	1625	0	0
6000	1950	0	0
7000	2275	0	0
8000	2600	0	0
9000	2925	0	0
10000	3250	0	0

Great Hundred

112	36	8	0

Grofs

144	46	16	0

Wey

256	83	4	0

Days in a Year

365	118	12	6

Feet in a Rod

272	89	8	0

N.	l.	s.	d.	N.	l.	s.	d.	N.	l.	s.	d.
1	0	6	7	45	14	16	3	89	29	5	11
2	0	13	2	46	15	2	10	90	29	12	6
3	0	19	9	47	15	9	5	91	29	19	1
4	1	6	4	48	15	16	0	92	30	5	8
5	1	12	11	49	16	2	7	93	30	12	3
6	1	19	6	50	16	9	2	94	30	18	10
7	2	6	1	51	16	15	9	95	31	5	5
8	2	12	8	52	17	2	4	96	31	12	0
9	2	19	3	53	17	8	11	97	31	18	7
10	3	5	10	54	17	15	6	98	32	5	2
11	3	12	5	55	18	2	1	99	32	11	9
12	3	19	0	56	18	8	8	100	32	18	4
13	4	5	7	57	18	15	3	200	65	16	8
14	4	12	2	58	19	1	10	300	98	15	0
15	4	18	9	59	19	8	5	400	131	13	4
16	5	5	4	60	19	15	0	500	164	11	8
17	5	11	11	61	20	1	7	600	197	10	0
18	5	18	6	62	20	8	2	700	230	8	4
19	6	5	1	63	20	14	9	800	263	6	8
20	6	11	8	64	21	1	4	900	296	5	0
21	6	18	3	65	21	7	11	1000	329	3	4
22	7	4	10	66	21	14	6	2000	658	6	8
23	7	11	5	67	22	1	1	3000	987	10	0
24	7	18	0	68	22	7	8	4000	1316	13	4
25	8	4	7	69	22	14	3	5000	1645	16	8
26	8	11	2	70	23	0	10	6000	1975	0	0
27	8	17	9	71	23	7	5	7000	2304	3	4
[28]	9	4	4	72	23	14	0	8000	2633	6	8
29	9	10	11	73	24	0	7	9000	2962	10	0
30	9	17	6	74	24	7	2	10000	3291	13	4
31	10	4	1	75	24	13	9				
32	10	10	8	76	25	0	4				
33	10	17	3	77	25	6	11				
34	11	3	10	78	25	13	6				
35	11	10	5	79	26	0	1				
36	11	17	0	80	26	6	8				
37	12	3	7	81	26	13	3				
38	12	10	2	82	26	19	10				
39	12	16	9	83	27	6	5				
40	13	3	4	[84]	27	13	0				
41	13	9	11	85	27	19	7				
42	13	16	6	86	28	6	2				
43	14	3	1	87	28	12	9				
44	14	9	8	88	28	19	4				

Great Hundred

112	36	17	4

Grofs

144	47	8	0

Wey

256	84	5	4

Days in a Year

365	120	2	11

Feet in a Rod

272	89	10	8

N.	l.	s.	d.	N.	l.	s.	d.	N.	l.	s.	d.
1	0	6	8	45	15	0	0	89	29	13	4
2	0	13	4	46	15	6	8	90	30	0	0
3	1	0	0	47	15	13	4	91	30	6	8
4	1	6	8	48	16	0	0	92	30	13	4
5	1	13	4	49	16	6	8	93	31	0	0
6	2	0	0	50	16	13	4	94	31	6	8
7	2	6	8	51	17	0	0	95	31	13	4
8	2	13	4	52	17	6	8	96	32	0	0
9	3	0	0	53	17	13	4	97	32	6	8
10	3	6	8	54	18	0	0	98	32	13	4
11	3	13	4	55	18	6	8	99	33	0	0
12	4	0	0	[56]	18	13	4	100	33	6	8
13	4	6	8	57	19	0	0	200	66	13	4
14	4	13	4	58	19	6	8	300	100	0	0
15	5	0	0	59	19	13	4	400	133	6	8
16	5	6	8	60	20	0	0	500	166	13	4
17	5	13	4	61	20	6	8	600	200	0	0
18	6	0	0	62	20	13	4	700	233	6	8
19	6	6	8	63	21	0	0	800	266	13	4
20	6	13	4	64	21	6	8	900	300	0	0
21	7	0	0	65	21	13	4	1000	333	6	8
22	7	6	8	66	22	0	0	2000	666	13	4
23	7	13	4	67	22	6	8	3000	1000	0	0
24	8	0	0	68	22	13	4	4000	1333	6	8
25	8	6	8	69	23	0	0	5000	1666	13	4
26	8	13	4	70	23	6	8	6000	2000	0	0
27	9	0	0	71	23	13	4	7000	2333	6	8
[28]	9	6	8	72	24	0	0	8000	2666	13	4
29	9	13	4	73	24	6	8	9000	3000	0	0
30	10	0	0	74	24	13	4	10000	3333	6	8
31	10	6	8	75	25	0	0				
32	10	13	4	76	25	6	8				
33	11	0	0	77	25	13	4	*Great Hundred*			
34	11	6	8	78	26	0	0	112	37	6	8
35	11	13	4	79	26	6	8	*Grofs*			
36	12	0	0	80	26	13	4	144	48	0	0
37	12	6	8	81	27	0	0	*Wey*			
38	12	13	4	82	27	6	8	256	85	6	8
39	13	0	0	83	27	13	4	*Days in a Year*			
40	13	6	8	[84]	28	0	0	365	121	13	4
41	13	13	4	85	28	6	8	*Feet in a Rod*			
42	14	0	0	86	28	13	4	272	90	13	4
43	14	6	8	87	29	0	0				
44	14	13	4	88	29	6	8				

N.	l.	s.	d.	N.	l.	s.	d.	N.	l.	s.	d.
1	0	6	9	45	15	3	9	89	30	0	9
2	0	13	6	46	15	10	6	90	30	7	6
3	1	0	3	47	15	17	3	91	30	14	3
4	1	7	0	48	16	4	0	92	31	1	0
5	1	13	9	49	16	10	9	93	31	7	9
6	2	0	6	50	16	17	6	94	31	14	6
7	2	7	3	51	17	4	3	95	32	1	3
8	2	14	0	52	17	11	0	96	32	8	0
9	3	0	9	53	17	17	9	97	32	14	9
10	3	7	6	54	18	4	6	98	33	1	6
11	3	14	3	55	18	11	3	99	33	8	3
12	4	1	0	[56]	18	18	0	100	33	15	0
13	4	7	9	57	19	4	9	200	67	10	0
14	4	14	6	58	19	11	6	300	101	5	0
15	5	1	3	59	19	18	3	400	135	0	0
16	5	8	0	60	20	5	0	500	168	15	0
17	5	14	9	61	20	11	9	600	202	10	0
18	6	1	6	62	20	18	6	700	236	5	0
19	6	8	3	63	21	5	3	800	270	0	0
20	6	15	0	64	21	12	0	900	303	15	0
21	7	1	9	65	21	18	9	1000	337	10	0
22	7	8	6	66	22	5	6	2000	675	0	0
23	7	15	3	67	22	12	3	3000	1012	10	0
24	8	2	0	68	22	19	0	4000	1350	0	0
25	8	8	9	69	23	5	9	5000	1687	10	0
26	8	15	6	70	23	12	6	6000	2025	0	0
27	9	2	3	71	23	19	3	7000	2362	10	0
[28]	9	9	0	72	24	6	0	8000	2700	0	0
29	9	15	9	73	24	12	9	9000	3037	10	0
30	10	2	6	74	24	19	6	10000	3375	0	0
31	10	9	3	75	25	6	3				
32	10	16	0	76	25	13	0				
33	11	2	9	77	25	19	9				
34	11	9	6	78	26	6	6				
35	11	16	3	79	26	13	3				
36	12	3	0	80	27	0	0				
37	12	9	9	81	27	6	9				
38	12	16	6	82	27	13	6				
39	13	3	3	83	28	0	3				
40	13	10	0	[84]	28	7	0				
41	13	16	9	85	28	13	9				
42	14	3	6	86	29	0	6				
43	14	10	3	87	29	7	3				
44	14	17	0	88	29	14	0				

Great Hundred

112	37	16	0

Grofs

144	48	12	0

Wey

256	86	8	0

Days in a Year

365	123	3	9

Feet in a Rod

272	91	16	0

N.	l.	s.	d.	N.	l.	s.	d.	N.	l.	s.	d.
1	0	6	10	45	15	7	6	89	30	8	2
2	0	13	8	46	15	14	4	90	30	15	0
3	1	0	6	47	16	1	2	91	31	1	10
4	1	7	4	48	16	8	0	92	31	8	8
5	1	14	2	49	16	14	10	93	31	15	6
6	2	1	0	50	17	1	8	94	32	2	4
7	2	7	10	51	17	8	6	95	32	9	2
8	2	14	8	52	17	15	4	96	32	16	0
9	3	1	6	53	18	2	2	97	33	2	10
10	3	8	4	54	18	9	0	98	33	9	8
11	3	15	2	55	18	15	10	99	33	16	6
12	4	2	0	[56]	19	2	8	100	34	3	4
13	4	8	10	57	19	9	6	200	68	6	8
14	4	15	8	58	19	16	4	300	102	10	0
15	5	2	6	59	20	3	2	400	136	13	4
16	5	9	4	60	20	10	0	500	170	16	8
17	5	16	2	61	20	16	10	600	205	0	0
18	6	3	0	62	21	3	8	700	239	3	4
19	6	9	10	63	21	10	6	800	273	6	8
20	6	16	8	64	21	17	4	900	307	10	0
21	7	3	6	65	22	4	2	1000	341	13	4
22	7	10	4	66	22	11	0	2000	683	6	8
23	7	17	2	67	22	17	10	3000	1025	0	0
24	8	4	0	68	23	4	8	4000	1366	13	4
25	8	10	10	69	23	11	6	5000	1708	6	8
26	8	17	8	70	23	18	4	6000	2050	0	0
27	9	4	6	71	24	5	2	7000	2391	13	4
[28]	9	11	4	72	24	12	0	8000	2733	6	8
29	9	18	2	73	24	18	10	9000	3075	0	0
30	10	5	0	74	25	5	8	10000	3416	13	4
31	10	11	10	75	25	12	6				
32	10	18	8	76	25	19	4				
33	11	5	6	77	26	6	2				
34	11	12	4	78	26	13	0				
35	11	19	2	79	26	19	10				
36	12	6	0	80	27	6	8				
37	12	12	10	81	27	13	6				
38	12	19	8	82	28	0	4				
39	13	6	6	83	28	7	2				
40	13	13	4	[84]	28	14	0				
41	14	0	2	85	29	0	10				
42	14	7	0	86	29	7	8				
43	14	13	10	87	29	14	6				
44	15	0	8	88	30	1	4				

Great Hundred

112	38	5	4

Grofs

144	49	4	0

Wey

256	87	9	4

Days in a Year

365	124	14	2

Feet in a Rod

272	92	18	8

N.	l.	s.	d.	N.	l.	s.	d.	N.	l.	s.	d.
1	0	6	11	45	15	11	3	89	30	15	7
2	0	13	10	46	15	18	2	90	31	2	6
3	1	0	9	47	16	5	1	91	31	9	5
4	1	7	8	48	16	12	0	92	31	16	4
5	1	14	7	49	16	18	11	93	32	3	3
6	2	1	6	50	17	5	10	94	32	10	2
7	2	8	5	51	17	12	9	95	32	17	1
8	2	15	4	52	17	19	8	96	33	4	0
9	3	2	3	53	18	6	7	97	33	10	11
10	3	9	2	54	18	13	6	98	33	17	10
11	3	16	1	55	19	0	5	99	34	4	9
12	4	3	0	[56]	19	7	4	100	34	11	8
13	4	9	11	57	19	14	3	200	69	3	4
14	4	16	10	58	20	1	2	300	103	15	0
15	5	3	9	59	20	8	1	400	138	6	8
16	5	10	8	60	20	15	0	500	172	18	4
17	5	17	7	61	21	1	11	600	207	10	0
18	6	4	6	62	21	8	10	700	242	1	8
19	6	11	5	63	21	15	9	800	276	13	4
20	6	18	4	64	22	2	8	900	311	5	0
21	7	5	3	65	22	9	7	1000	345	16	8
22	7	12	2	66	22	16	6	2000	691	13	4
23	7	19	1	67	23	3	5	3000	1037	10	0
24	8	6	0	68	23	10	4	4000	1383	6	8
25	8	12	11	69	23	17	3	5000	1729	3	4
26	8	19	10	70	24	4	2	6000	2075	0	0
27	9	6	9	71	24	11	1	7000	2420	16	8
[28]	9	13	8	72	24	18	0	8000	2766	13	4
29	10	0	7	73	25	4	11	9000	3112	10	0
30	10	7	6	74	25	11	10	10000	3458	6	8
31	10	14	5	75	25	18	9				
32	11	1	4	76	26	5	8				
33	11	8	3	77	26	12	7	*Great Hundred*			
34	11	15	2	78	26	19	6	112	38	14	8
35	12	2	1	79	27	6	5	*Gross*			
36	12	9	0	80	27	13	4	144	49	16	0
37	12	15	11	81	28	0	3	*Wey*			
38	13	2	10	82	28	7	2	256	88	10	8
39	13	9	9	83	28	14	1	*Days in a Year*			
40	13	16	8	[84]	29	1	0	365	126	4	7
41	14	3	7	85	29	7	11	*Feet in a Rod*			
42	14	10	6	86	29	14	10	272	94	1	4
43	14	17	5	87	30	1	9				
44	15	4	4	88	30	8	8				

N.	l.	s.	d.	N.	l.	s.	d.	N.	l.	s.	d.
1	0	7	0	45	15	15	0	89	31	3	0
2	0	14	0	46	16	2	0	90	31	10	0
3	1	1	0	47	16	9	0	91	31	17	0
4	1	8	0	48	16	16	0	92	32	4	0
5	1	15	0	49	17	3	0	93	32	11	0
6	2	2	0	50	17	10	0	94	32	18	0
7	2	9	0	51	17	17	0	95	33	5	0
8	2	16	0	52	18	4	0	96	33	12	0
9	3	3	0	53	18	11	0	97	33	19	0
10	3	10	0	54	18	18	0	98	34	6	0
11	3	17	0	55	19	5	0	99	34	13	0
12	4	4	0	[56]	19	12	0	100	35	0	0
13	4	11	0	57	19	19	0	200	70	0	0
14	4	18	0	58	20	6	0	300	105	0	0
15	5	5	0	59	20	13	0	400	140	0	0
16	5	12	0	60	21	0	0	500	175	0	0
17	5	19	0	61	21	7	0	600	210	0	0
18	6	6	0	62	21	14	0	700	245	0	0
19	6	13	0	63	22	1	0	800	280	0	0
20	7	0	0	64	22	8	0	900	315	0	0
21	7	7	0	65	22	15	0	1000	350	0	0
22	7	14	0	66	23	2	0	2000	700	0	0
23	8	1	0	67	23	9	0	3000	1050	0	0
24	8	8	0	68	23	16	0	4000	1400	0	0
25	8	15	0	69	24	3	0	5000	1750	0	0
26	9	2	0	70	24	10	0	6000	2100	0	0
27	9	9	0	71	24	17	0	7000	2450	0	0
[28]	9	16	0	72	25	4	0	8000	2800	0	0
29	10	3	0	73	25	11	0	9000	3150	0	0
30	10	10	0	74	25	18	0	10000	3500	0	0
31	10	17	0	75	26	5	0				
32	11	4	0	76	26	12	0				
33	11	11	0	77	26	19	0	*Great Hundred*			
34	11	18	0	78	27	6	0	112	39	4	0
35	12	5	0	79	27	13	0	*Grofs*			
36	12	12	0	80	28	0	0	144	50	8	0
37	12	19	0	81	28	7	0	*Wey*			
38	13	6	0	82	28	14	0	256	89	12	0
39	13	13	0	83	29	1	0	*Days in a Year*			
40	14	0	0	[84]	29	8	0	365	127	15	0
41	14	7	0	85	29	15	0	*Feet in a Rod*			
42	14	14	0	86	30	2	0	272	95	4	0
43	15	1	0	87	30	9	0				
44	15	8	0	88	30	16	0				

N.	l.	s.	d.	N.	l.	s.	d.	N.	l.	s.	d.
1	0	7	1	45	15	18	9	89	31	10	5
2	0	14	2	46	16	5	10	90	31	17	6
3	1	1	3	47	16	12	11	91	32	4	7
4	1	8	4	48	17	0	0	92	32	11	8
5	1	15	5	49	17	7	1	93	32	18	9
6	2	2	6	50	17	14	2	94	33	5	10
7	2	9	7	51	18	1	3	95	33	12	11
8	2	16	8	52	18	8	4	96	34	0	0
9	3	3	9	53	18	15	5	97	34	7	1
10	3	10	10	54	19	2	6	98	34	14	2
11	3	17	11	55	19	9	7	99	35	1	3
12	4	5	0	[56]	19	16	8	100	35	8	4
13	4	12	1	57	20	3	9	200	70	16	8
14	4	19	2	58	20	10	10	300	106	5	0
15	5	6	3	59	20	17	11	400	141	13	4
16	5	13	4	60	21	5	0	500	177	1	8
17	6	0	5	61	21	12	1	600	212	10	0
18	6	7	6	62	21	19	2	700	247	18	4
19	6	14	7	63	22	6	3	800	283	6	8
20	7	1	8	64	22	13	4	900	318	15	0
21	7	8	9	65	23	0	5	1000	354	3	4
22	7	15	10	66	23	7	6	2000	708	6	8
23	8	2	11	67	23	14	7	3000	1062	10	0
24	8	10	0	68	24	1	8	4000	1416	13	4
25	8	17	1	69	24	8	9	5000	1770	16	8
26	9	4	2	70	24	15	10	6000	2125	0	0
27	9	11	3	71	25	2	11	7000	2479	3	4
[28]	9	18	4	72	25	10	0	8000	2833	6	8
29	10	5	5	73	25	17	1	9000	3187	10	0
30	10	12	6	74	26	4	2	10000	3541	13	4
31	10	19	7	75	26	11	3				
32	11	6	8	76	26	18	4				
33	11	13	9	77	27	5	5	Great Hundred			
34	12	0	10	78	27	12	6	112	39	13	4
35	12	7	11	79	27	19	7	Grofs			
36	12	15	0	80	28	6	8	144	51	0	0
37	13	2	1	81	28	13	9	Wey			
38	13	9	2	82	29	0	10	256	90	13	4
39	13	16	3	83	29	7	11	Days in a Year			
40	14	3	4	[84]	29	15	0	365	129	5	5
41	14	10	5	85	30	2	1	Feet in a Rod			
42	14	17	6	86	30	9	2	272	96	6	8
43	15	4	7	87	30	16	3				
44	15	11	8	88	31	3	4				

Q

N.	l.	s.	d.	N.	l.	s.	d.	N.	l.	s.	d.
1	0	7	2	45	16	2	6	89	31	17	10
2	0	14	4	46	16	9	8	90	32	5	0
3	1	1	6	47	16	16	10	91	32	12	2
4	1	8	8	48	17	4	0	92	32	19	4
5	1	15	10	49	17	11	2	93	33	6	6
6	2	3	0	50	17	18	4	94	33	13	8
7	2	10	2	51	18	5	6	95	34	0	10
8	2	17	4	52	18	12	8	96	34	8	0
9	3	4	6	53	18	19	10	97	34	15	2
10	3	11	8	54	19	7	0	98	35	2	4
11	3	18	10	55	19	14	2	99	35	9	6
12	4	6	0	[56]	20	1	4	100	35	16	8
13	4	13	2	57	20	8	6	200	71	13	4
14	5	0	4	58	20	15	8	300	107	10	0
15	5	7	6	59	21	2	10	400	143	6	8
16	5	14	8	60	21	10	0	500	179	3	4
17	6	1	10	61	21	17	2	600	215	0	0
18	6	9	0	62	22	4	4	700	250	16	8
19	6	16	2	63	22	11	6	800	286	13	4
20	7	3	4	64	22	18	8	900	322	10	0
21	7	10	6	65	23	5	10	1000	358	6	8
22	7	17	8	66	23	13	0	2000	716	13	4
23	8	4	10	67	24	0	2	3000	1075	0	0
24	8	12	0	68	24	7	4	4000	1433	6	8
25	8	19	2	69	24	14	6	5000	1791	13	4
26	9	6	4	70	25	1	8	6000	2150	0	0
27	9	13	6	71	25	8	10	7000	2508	6	8
[28]	10	0	8	72	25	16	0	8000	2866	13	4
29	10	7	10	73	26	3	2	9000	3225	0	0
30	10	15	0	74	26	10	4	10000	3583	6	8
31	11	2	2	75	20	17	6				
32	11	9	4	76	27	4	8				
33	11	16	6	77	27	11	10				
34	12	3	8	78	27	19	0				
35	12	10	10	79	28	6	2				
36	12	18	0	80	28	13	4				
37	13	5	2	81	29	0	6				
38	13	12	4	82	29	7	8				
39	13	19	6	83	29	14	10				
40	14	6	8	[84]	30	2	0				
41	14	13	10	85	30	9	2				
42	15	1	0	86	30	16	4				
43	15	8	2	87	31	3	6				
44	15	15	4	88	31	10	8				

Great Hundred

112	40	2	8

Gross

144	51	12	0

Wey

256	91	14	8

Days in a Year

365	130	15	10

Feet in a Rod

272	97	9	4

N.	l.	s.	d.	N.	l.	s.	d.	N.	l.	s.	d.
1	0	7	3	45	16	6	3	89	32	5	3
2	0	14	6	46	16	13	6	90	32	12	6
3	1	1	9	47	17	0	9	91	32	19	9
4	1	9	0	48	17	8	0	92	33	7	0
5	1	16	3	49	17	15	3	93	33	14	3
6	2	3	6	50	18	2	6	94	34	1	6
7	2	10	9	51	18	9	9	95	34	8	9
8	2	18	0	52	18	17	0	96	34	16	0
9	3	5	3	53	19	4	3	97	35	3	3
10	3	12	6	54	19	11	6	98	35	10	6
11	3	19	9	55	19	18	9	99	35	17	9
12	4	7	0	[56]	20	6	0	100	36	5	0
13	4	14	3	57	20	13	3	200	72	10	0
14	5	1	6	58	21	0	6	300	108	15	0
15	5	8	9	59	21	7	9	400	145	0	0
16	5	16	0	60	21	15	0	500	181	5	0
17	6	3	3	61	22	2	3	600	217	10	0
18	6	10	6	62	22	9	6	700	253	15	0
19	6	17	9	63	22	16	9	800	290	0	0
20	7	5	0	64	23	4	0	900	326	5	0
21	7	12	3	65	23	11	3	1000	362	10	0
22	7	19	6	66	23	18	6	2000	725	0	0
23	8	6	9	67	24	5	9	3000	1087	10	0
24	8	14	0	68	24	13	0	4000	1450	0	0
25	9	1	3	69	25	0	3	5000	1812	10	0
26	9	8	6	70	25	7	6	6000	2175	0	0
27	9	15	9	71	25	14	9	7000	2537	10	0
[28]	10	3	0	72	26	2	0	8000	2900	0	0
29	10	10	3	73	26	9	3	9000	3262	10	0
30	10	17	6	74	26	16	6	10000	3625	0	0
31	11	4	9	75	27	3	9				
32	11	12	0	76	27	11	0				
33	11	19	3	77	27	18	3				
34	12	6	6	78	28	5	6				
35	12	13	9	79	28	12	9				
36	13	1	0	80	29	0	0				
37	13	8	3	81	29	7	3				
38	13	15	6	82	29	14	6				
39	14	2	9	83	30	1	9				
40	14	10	0	[84]	30	9	0				
41	14	17	3	85	30	16	3				
42	15	4	6	86	31	3	6				
43	15	11	9	87	31	10	9				
44	15	19	0	88	31	18	0				

Great Hundred

112	40	12	0

Grofs

144	52	4	0

Wey

256	92	16	0

Days in a Year

365	132	6	3

Feet in a Rod

272	98	12	0

N.	l.	s.	d.	N.	l.	s.	d.	N	l.	s.	d.
1	0	7	4	45	16	10	0	89	32	12	8
2	0	14	8	46	16	17	4	90	33	0	0
3	1	2	0	47	17	4	8	91	33	7	4
4	1	9	4	48	17	12	0	92	33	14	8
5	1	16	8	49	17	19	4	93	34	2	0
6	2	4	0	50	18	6	8	94	34	9	4
7	2	11	4	51	18	14	0	95	34	16	8
8	2	18	8	52	19	1	4	96	35	4	0
9	3	6	0	53	19	8	8	97	35	11	4
10	3	13	4	54	19	16	0	98	35	18	8
11	4	0	8	55	20	3	4	99	36	6	0
12	4	8	0	56	20	10	8	100	36	13	4
13	4	15	4	57	20	18	0	200	73	6	8
14	5	2	8	58	21	5	4	300	110	0	0
15	5	10	0	59	21	12	8	400	146	13	4
16	5	17	4	60	22	0	0	500	183	6	8
17	6	4	8	61	22	7	4	600	220	0	0
18	6	12	0	62	22	14	8	700	256	13	4
19	6	19	4	63	23	2	0	800	293	6	8
20	7	6	8	64	23	9	4	900	330	0	0
21	7	14	0	65	23	16	8	1000	366	13	4
22	8	1	4	66	24	4	0	2000	733	6	8
23	8	8	8	67	24	11	4	3000	1100	0	0
24	8	16	0	68	24	18	8	4000	1466	13	4
25	9	3	4	69	25	6	0	5000	1833	6	8
26	9	10	8	70	25	13	4	6000	2200	0	0
27	9	18	0	71	26	0	8	7000	2566	13	4
[28]	10	5	4	72	26	8	0	8000	2933	6	8
29	10	12	8	73	26	15	4	9000	3300	0	0
30	11	0	0	74	27	2	8	10000	3666	13	4
31	11	7	4	75	27	10	0				
32	11	14	8	76	27	17	4				
33	12	2	0	77	28	4	8				
34	12	9	4	78	28	12	0				
35	12	16	8	79	28	19	4				
36	13	4	0	80	29	6	8				
37	13	11	4	81	29	14	0				
38	13	18	8	82	30	1	4				
39	14	6	0	83	30	8	8				
40	14	13	4	[84]	30	16	0				
41	15	0	8	85	31	3	4				
42	15	8	0	86	31	10	8				
43	15	15	4	87	31	18	0				
44	16	2	8	88	32	5	4				

Great Hundred

112	41	1	4

Grofs

144	52	16	0

Wey

256	93	17	4

Days in a Year

365	133	16	8

Feet in a Rod

272	99	14	8

N.	l.	s.	d.	N.	l.	s.	d.	N.	l.	s.	d.
1	0	7	5	45	16	13	9	89	33	0	1
2	0	14	10	46	17	1	2	90	33	7	6
3	1	2	3	47	17	8	7	91	33	14	11
4	1	9	8	48	17	16	0	92	34	2	4
5	1	17	1	49	18	3	5	93	34	9	9
6	2	4	6	50	18	10	10	94	34	17	2
7	2	11	11	51	18	18	3	95	35	4	7
8	2	19	4	52	19	5	8	96	35	12	0
9	3	6	9	53	19	13	1	97	35	19	5
10	3	14	2	54	20	0	6	98	36	6	10
11	4	1	7	55	20	7	11	99	36	14	3
12	4	9	0	[56]	20	15	4	100	37	1	8
13	4	16	5	57	21	2	9	200	74	3	4
14	5	3	10	58	21	10	2	300	111	5	0
15	5	11	3	59	21	17	7	400	148	6	8
16	5	18	8	60	22	5	0	500	185	8	4
17	6	6	1	61	22	12	5	600	222	10	0
18	6	13	6	62	22	19	10	700	259	11	8
19	7	0	11	63	23	7	3	800	296	13	4
20	7	8	4	64	23	14	8	900	333	15	0
21	7	15	9	65	24	2	1	1000	370	16	8
22	8	3	2	66	24	9	6	2000	741	13	4
23	8	10	7	67	24	16	11	3000	1112	10	0
24	8	18	0	68	25	4	4	4000	1483	6	8
25	9	5	5	69	25	11	9	5000	1854	3	4
26	9	12	10	70	25	19	2	6000	2225	0	0
27	10	0	3	71	26	6	7	7000	2595	16	8
[28]	10	7	8	72	26	14	0	8000	2966	13	4
29	10	15	1	73	27	1	5	9000	3337	10	0
30	11	2	6	74	27	8	10	10000	3708	6	8
31	11	9	11	75	27	16	3				
32	11	17	4	76	28	3	8				
33	12	4	9	77	28	11	1	Great Hundred			
34	12	12	2	78	28	18	6	112	41	10	8
35	12	19	7	79	29	5	11	Grofs			
36	13	7	0	80	29	13	4	144	53	8	0
37	13	14	5	81	30	0	9	Wey			
38	14	1	10	82	30	8	2	256	94	18	8
39	14	9	3	83	30	15	7	Days in a Year			
40	14	16	8	[84]	31	3	0	365	135	7	1
41	15	4	1	85	31	10	5	Feet in a Rod			
42	15	11	6	86	31	17	10	272¼	100	17	4
43	15	18	11	87	32	5	3				
44	16	6	4	88	32	12	8				

Q 3

N.	l.	s.	d.	N.	l.	s.	d.	N.	l.	s.	d.
1	0	7	6	45	16	17	6	89	33	7	6
2	0	15	0	46	17	5	0	90	33	15	0
3	1	2	6	47	17	12	6	91	34	2	6
4	1	10	0	48	18	0	0	92	34	10	0
5	1	17	6	49	18	7	6	93	34	17	6
6	2	5	0	50	18	15	0	94	35	5	0
7	2	12	6	51	19	2	6	95	35	12	6
8	3	0	0	52	19	10	0	96	36	0	0
9	3	7	6	53	19	17	6	97	36	7	6
10	3	15	0	54	20	5	0	98	36	15	0
11	4	2	6	55	20	12	6	99	37	2	6
12	4	10	0	[56]	21	0	0	100	37	10	0
13	4	17	6	57	21	7	6	200	75	0	0
14	5	5	0	58	21	15	0	300	112	10	0
15	5	12	6	59	22	2	6	400	150	0	0
16	6	0	0	60	22	10	0	500	187	10	0
17	6	7	6	61	22	17	6	600	225	0	0
18	6	15	0	62	23	5	0	700	262	10	0
19	7	2	6	63	23	12	6	800	300	0	0
20	7	10	0	64	24	0	0	900	337	10	0
21	7	17	6	65	24	7	6	1000	375	0	0
22	8	5	0	66	24	15	0	2000	750	0	0
23	8	12	6	67	25	2	6	3000	1125	0	0
24	9	0	0	68	25	10	0	4000	1500	0	0
25	9	7	6	69	25	17	6	5000	1875	0	0
26	9	15	0	70	26	5	0	6000	2250	0	0
27	10	2	6	71	26	12	6	7000	2625	0	0
[28]	10	10	0	72	27	0	0	8000	3000	0	0
29	10	17	6	73	27	7	6	9000	3375	0	0
30	11	5	0	74	27	15	0	10000	3750	0	0
31	11	12	6	75	28	2	6				
32	12	0	0	76	28	10	0				
33	12	7	6	77	28	17	6				
34	12	15	0	78	29	5	0				
35	13	2	6	79	29	12	6				
36	13	10	0	80	30	0	0				
37	13	17	6	81	30	7	6				
38	14	5	0	82	30	15	0				
39	14	12	6	83	31	2	6				
40	15	0	0	[84]	31	10	0				
41	15	7	6	85	31	17	6				
42	15	15	0	86	32	5	0				
43	16	2	6	87	32	12	6				
44	16	10	0	88	33	0	0				

Great Hundred

112	42	0	0

Gross

144	54	0	0

Wey

256	96	0	0

Days in a Year

365	136	17	6

Feet in a Rod

272	102	0	0

N.	l.	s.	d.	N.	l.	s.	d.	N.	l.	s.	d.
1	0	7	7	45	17	1	3	89	33	14	11
2	0	15	2	46	17	8	10	90	34	2	6
3	1	2	9	47	17	16	5	91	34	10	1
4	1	10	4	48	18	4	0	92	34	17	8
5	1	17	11	49	18	11	7	93	35	5	3
6	2	5	6	50	18	19	2	94	35	12	10
7	2	13	1	51	19	6	9	95	36	0	5
8	3	0	8	52	19	14	4	96	36	8	0
9	3	8	3	53	20	1	11	97	36	15	7
10	3	15	10	54	20	9	6	98	37	3	2
11	4	3	5	55	20	17	1	99	37	10	9
12	4	11	0	[56]	21	4	8	100	37	18	4
13	4	18	7	57	21	12	3	200	75	16	8
14	5	6	2	58	21	19	10	300	113	15	0
15	5	13	9	59	22	7	5	400	151	13	4
16	6	1	4	60	22	15	0	500	189	11	8
17	6	8	11	61	23	2	7	600	227	10	0
18	6	16	6	62	23	10	2	700	265	8	4
19	7	4	1	63	23	17	9	800	303	6	8
20	7	11	8	64	24	5	4	900	341	5	0
21	7	19	3	65	24	12	11	1000	379	3	4
22	8	6	10	66	25	0	6	2000	758	6	8
23	8	14	5	67	25	8	1	3000	1137	10	0
24	9	2	0	68	25	15	8	4000	1516	13	4
25	9	9	7	69	26	3	3	5000	1895	16	8
26	9	17	2	70	26	10	10	6000	2275	0	0
27	10	4	9	71	26	18	5	7000	2654	3	4
[28]	10	12	4	72	27	6	0	8000	3033	6	8
29	10	19	11	73	27	13	7	9000	3412	10	0
30	11	7	6	74	28	1	2	10000	3791	13	4
31	11	15	1	75	28	8	9				
32	12	2	8	76	28	16	4				
33	12	10	3	77	29	3	11				
34	12	17	10	78	29	11	6				
35	13	5	5	79	29	19	1				
36	13	13	0	80	30	6	8				
37	14	0	7	81	30	14	3				
38	14	8	2	82	31	1	10				
39	14	15	9	83	31	9	5				
40	15	3	4	[84]	31	17	0				
41	15	10	11	85	32	4	7				
42	15	18	6	86	32	12	2				
43	16	6	1	87	32	19	9				
44	16	13	8	88	33	7	4				

Great Hundred

112 | 42 9 4

Grofs

144 | 54 12 0

Wey

256 | 97 1 4

Days in a Year

365 | 138 7 11

Feet in a Rod

272 | 103 2 8

N.	l.	s.	d.	N.	l.	s.	d.	N.	l.	s.	d.
1	0	7	8	45	17	5	0	89	34	2	4
2	0	15	4	46	17	12	8	90	34	10	0
3	1	3	0	47	18	0	4	91	34	17	8
4	1	10	8	48	18	8	0	92	35	5	4
5	1	18	4	49	18	15	8	93	35	13	0
6	2	6	0	50	19	3	4	94	36	0	8
7	2	13	8	51	19	11	0	95	36	8	4
8	3	1	4	52	19	18	8	96	36	16	0
9	3	9	0	53	20	6	4	97	37	3	8
10	3	16	8	54	20	14	0	98	37	11	4
11	4	4	4	55	21	1	8	99	37	19	0
12	4	12	0	[56]	21	9	4	100	38	6	8
13	4	19	8	57	21	17	0	200	76	13	4
14	5	7	4	58	22	4	8	300	115	0	0
15	5	15	0	59	22	12	4	400	153	6	8
16	6	2	8	60	23	0	0	500	191	13	4
17	6	10	4	61	23	7	8	600	230	0	0
18	6	18	0	62	23	15	4	700	268	6	8
19	7	5	8	63	24	3	0	800	306	13	4
20	7	13	4	64	24	10	8	900	345	0	0
21	8	1	0	65	24	18	4	1000	383	6	8
22	8	8	8	66	25	6	0	2000	766	13	4
23	8	16	4	67	25	13	8	3000	1150	0	0
24	9	4	0	68	26	1	4	4000	1533	6	8
25	9	11	8	69	26	9	0	5000	1916	13	4
26	9	19	4	70	26	16	8	6000	2300	0	0
27	10	7	0	71	27	4	4	7000	2683	6	8
[28]	10	14	8	72	27	12	0	8000	3066	13	4
29	11	2	4	73	27	19	8	9000	3450	0	0
30	11	10	0	74	28	7	4	10000	3833	6	8
31	11	17	8	75	28	15	0				
32	12	5	4	76	29	2	8				
33	12	13	0	77	29	10	4				
34	13	0	8	78	29	18	0				
35	13	8	4	79	30	5	8				
36	13	16	0	80	30	13	4				
37	14	3	8	81	31	1	0				
38	14	11	4	82	31	8	8				
39	14	19	0	83	31	16	4				
40	15	6	8	[84]	32	4	0				
41	15	14	4	85	32	11	8				
42	16	2	0	86	32	19	4				
43	16	9	8	87	33	7	0				
44	16	17	4	88	33	14	8				

Great Hundred

112	42	18	8

Grofs

144	55	4	0

Wey

256	98	2	8

Days in a Year

365	139	18	4

Feet in a Rod

272	104	5	4

N.	l.	s.	d.	N.	l.	s.	d.	N.	l.	s.	d.
1	0	7	9	45	17	8	9	89	34	9	9
2	0	15	6	46	17	16	6	90	34	17	6
3	1	3	3	47	18	4	3	91	35	5	3
4	1	11	0	48	18	12	0	92	35	13	0
5	1	18	9	49	18	19	9	93	36	0	9
6	2	6	6	50	19	7	6	94	36	8	6
7	2	14	3	51	19	15	3	95	36	16	3
8	3	2	0	52	20	3	0	96	37	4	0
9	3	9	9	53	20	10	9	97	37	11	9
10	3	17	6	54	20	18	6	98	37	19	6
11	4	5	3	55	21	6	3	99	38	7	3
12	4	13	0	[56]	21	14	0	100	38	15	0
13	5	0	9	57	22	1	9	200	77	10	0
14	5	8	6	58	22	9	6	300	116	5	0
15	5	16	3	59	22	17	3	400	155	0	0
16	6	4	0	60	23	5	0	500	193	15	0
17	6	11	9	61	23	12	9	600	232	10	0
18	6	19	6	62	24	0	6	700	271	5	0
19	7	7	3	63	24	8	3	800	310	0	0
20	7	15	0	64	24	16	0	900	348	15	0
21	8	2	9	65	25	3	9	1000	387	10	0
22	8	10	6	66	25	11	6	2000	775	0	0
23	8	18	3	67	25	19	3	3000	1162	10	0
24	9	6	0	68	26	7	0	4000	1550	0	0
25	9	13	9	69	26	14	9	5000	1937	10	0
26	10	1	6	70	27	2	6	6000	2325	0	0
27	10	9	3	71	27	10	3	7000	2712	10	0
[28]	10	17	0	72	27	18	0	8000	3100	0	0
29	11	4	9	73	28	5	9	9000	3487	10	0
30	11	12	6	74	28	13	6	10000	3875	0	0
31	12	0	3	75	29	1	3				
32	12	8	0	76	29	9	0				
33	12	15	9	77	29	16	9				
34	13	3	6	78	30	4	6				
35	13	11	3	79	30	12	3				
36	13	19	0	80	31	0	0				
37	14	6	9	81	31	7	9				
38	14	14	6	82	31	15	6				
39	15	2	3	83	32	3	3				
40	15	10	0	[84]	32	11	0				
41	15	17	9	85	32	18	9				
42	16	5	6	86	33	6	6				
43	16	13	3	87	33	14	3				
44	17	1	0	88	34	2	0				

Great Hundred

112 | 43 8 0

Grofs

144 | 55 16 0

Wey

256 | 99 4 0

Days in a Year

365 | 141 8 9

Feet in a Rod

272 | 105 8 0

N.	l.	s.	d.	N.	l.	s.	d.		N.	l.	s.	d.
1	0	7	10	45	17	12	6		89	34	17	2
2	0	15	8	46	18	0	4		90	35	5	0
3	1	3	6	47	18	8	2		91	35	12	10
4	1	11	4	48	18	16	0		92	36	0	8
5	1	19	2	49	19	3	10		93	36	8	6
6	2	7	0	50	19	11	8		94	36	16	4
7	2	14	10	51	19	19	6		95	37	4	2
8	3	2	8	52	20	7	4		96	37	12	0
9	3	10	6	53	20	15	2		97	37	19	10
10	3	18	4	54	21	3	0		98	38	7	8
11	4	6	2	55	21	10	10		99	38	15	6
12	4	14	0	[56]	21	18	8		100	39	3	4
13	5	1	10	57	22	6	6		200	78	6	8
14	5	9	8	58	22	14	4		300	117	10	0
15	5	17	6	59	23	2	2		400	156	13	4
16	6	5	4	60	23	10	0		500	195	16	8
17	6	13	2	61	23	17	10		600	235	0	0
18	7	1	0	62	24	5	8		700	274	3	4
19	7	8	10	63	24	13	6		800	313	6	8
20	7	16	8	64	25	1	4		900	352	10	0
21	8	4	6	65	25	9	2		1000	391	13	4
22	8	12	4	66	25	17	0		2000	783	6	8
23	9	0	2	67	26	4	10		3000	1175	0	0
24	9	8	0	68	26	12	8		4000	1566	13	4
25	9	15	10	69	27	0	6		5000	1958	6	8
26	10	3	8	70	27	8	4		6000	2350	0	0
27	10	11	6	71	27	16	2		7000	2741	13	4
[28]	10	19	4	72	28	4	0		8000	3133	6	8
29	11	7	2	73	28	11	10		9000	3525	0	0
30	11	15	0	74	28	19	8		10000	3916	13	4
31	12	2	10	75	29	7	6					
32	12	10	8	76	29	15	4					
33	12	18	6	77	30	3	2					
34	13	6	4	78	30	11	0					
35	13	14	2	79	30	18	10					
36	14	2	0	80	31	6	8					
37	14	9	10	81	31	14	6					
38	14	17	8	82	32	2	4					
39	15	5	6	83	32	10	2					
40	15	13	4	[84]	32	18	0					
41	16	1	2	85	33	5	10					
42	16	9	0	86	33	13	8					
43	16	16	10	87	34	1	6					
44	17	4	8	88	34	9	4					

	l.	s.	d.
Great Hundred			
112	43	17	4
Gross			
144	56	8	0
Wey			
236	100	5	4
Days in a Year			
365	142	19	2
Feet in a Rod			
272	106	10	8

N.	l.	s.	d.	N.	l.	s.	d.	N.	l.	s.	d.
1	0	7	11	45	17	16	3	89	35	4	7
2	0	15	10	46	18	4	2	90	35	12	6
3	1	3	9	47	18	12	1	91	36	0	5
4	1	11	8	48	19	0	0	92	36	8	4
5	1	19	7	49	19	7	11	93	36	16	3
6	2	7	6	50	19	15	10	94	37	4	2
7	2	15	5	51	20	3	9	95	37	12	1
8	3	3	4	52	20	11	8	96	38	0	0
9	3	11	3	53	20	19	7	97	38	7	11
10	3	19	2	54	21	7	6	98	38	15	10
11	4	7	1	55	21	15	5	99	39	3	9
12	4	15	0	[56]	22	3	4	100	39	11	8
13	5	2	11	57	22	11	3	200	79	3	4
14	5	10	10	58	22	19	2	300	118	15	0
15	5	18	9	59	23	7	1	400	158	6	8
16	6	6	8	60	23	15	0	500	197	18	4
17	6	14	7	61	24	2	11	600	237	10	0
18	7	2	6	62	24	10	10	700	277	1	8
19	7	10	5	63	24	18	9	800	316	13	4
20	7	18	4	64	25	6	8	900	356	5	0
21	8	6	3	65	25	14	7	1000	395	16	8
22	8	14	2	66	26	2	6	2000	791	13	4
23	9	2	1	67	26	10	5	3000	1187	10	0
24	9	10	0	68	26	18	4	4000	1583	6	8
25	9	17	11	69	27	6	3	5000	1979	3	4
26	10	5	10	70	27	14	2	6000	2375	0	0
27	10	13	9	71	28	2	1	7000	2770	16	8
[28]	11	1	8	72	28	10	0	8000	3166	13	4
29	11	9	7	73	28	17	11	9000	3562	10	0
30	11	17	6	74	29	5	10	10000	3958	6	8
31	12	5	5	75	29	13	9				
32	12	13	4	76	30	1	8				
33	13	1	3	77	30	9	7				
34	13	9	2	78	30	17	6				
35	13	17	1	79	31	5	5				
36	14	5	0	80	31	13	4				
37	14	12	11	81	32	1	3				
38	15	0	10	82	32	9	2				
39	15	8	9	83	32	17	1				
40	15	16	8	[84]	33	5	0				
41	16	4	7	85	33	12	11				
42	16	12	6	86	34	0	10				
43	17	0	5	87	34	8	9				
44	17	8	4	88	34	16	8				

Great Hundred

112	44	6	8

Grefs

144	57	0	0

Wey

256	101	6	8

Days in a Year

365	144	9	7

Feet in a Rod

272	107	13	4

N.	l.	s.	d.	N.	l.	s.	d.	N.	l.	s.	d.
1	0	8	0	45	18	0	0	89	35	12	0
2	0	16	0	46	18	8	0	90	36	0	0
3	1	4	0	47	18	16	0	91	36	8	0
4	1	12	0	48	19	4	0	92	36	16	0
5	2	0	0	49	19	12	0	93	37	4	0
6	2	8	0	50	20	0	0	94	37	12	0
7	2	16	0	51	20	8	0	95	38	0	0
8	3	4	0	52	20	16	0	96	38	8	0
9	3	12	0	53	21	4	0	97	38	16	0
10	4	0	0	54	21	12	0	98	39	4	0
11	4	8	0	55	22	0	0	99	39	12	0
12	4	16	0	[56]	22	8	0	100	40	0	0
13	5	4	0	57	22	16	0	200	80	0	0
14	5	12	0	58	23	4	0	300	120	0	0
15	6	0	0	59	23	12	0	400	160	0	0
16	6	8	0	60	24	0	0	500	200	0	0
17	6	16	0	61	24	8	0	600	240	0	0
18	7	4	0	62	24	16	0	700	280	0	0
19	7	12	0	63	25	4	0	800	320	0	0
20	8	0	0	64	25	12	0	900	360	0	0
21	8	8	0	65	26	0	0	1000	400	0	0
22	8	16	0	66	26	8	0	2000	800	0	0
23	9	4	0	67	26	16	0	3000	1200	0	0
24	9	12	0	68	27	4	0	4000	1600	0	0
25	10	0	0	69	27	12	0	5000	2000	0	0
26	10	8	0	70	28	0	0	6000	2400	0	0
27	10	16	0	71	28	8	0	7000	2800	0	0
[28]	11	4	0	72	28	16	0	8000	3200	0	0
29	11	12	0	73	29	4	0	9000	3600	0	0
30	12	0	0	74	29	12	0	10000	4000	0	0
31	12	8	0	75	30	0	0				
32	12	16	0	76	30	8	0				
33	13	4	0	77	30	16	0				
34	13	12	0	78	31	4	0				
35	14	0	0	79	31	12	0				
36	14	8	0	80	32	0	0				
37	14	16	0	81	32	8	0				
38	15	4	0	82	32	16	0				
39	15	12	0	83	33	4	0				
40	16	0	0	[84]	33	12	0				
41	16	8	0	85	34	0	0				
42	16	16	0	86	34	8	0				
43	17	4	0	87	34	16	0				
44	17	12	0	88	35	4	0				

Great Hundred

	l.	s.	d.
112	44	16	0

Grofs

	l.	s.	d.
144	57	12	0

Wey

	l.	s.	d.
256	102	8	0

Days in a Year

	l.	s.	d.
365	146	0	0

Feet in a Rod

	l.	s.	d.
272	108	16	0

N.	l.	s.	d.	N.	l.	s.	d.	N.	l.	s.	d.
1	0	8	1	45	18	3	9	89	35	19	5
2	0	16	2	46	18	11	10	90	36	7	6
3	1	4	3	47	18	19	11	91	36	15	7
4	1	12	4	48	19	8	0	92	37	3	8
5	2	0	5	49	19	16	1	93	37	11	9
6	2	8	6	50	20	4	2	94	37	19	10
7	2	16	7	51	20	12	3	95	38	7	11
8	3	4	8	52	21	0	4	96	38	16	0
9	3	12	9	53	21	8	5	97	39	4	1
10	4	0	10	54	21	16	6	98	39	12	2
11	4	8	11	55	22	4	7	99	40	0	3
12	4	17	0	[56]	22	12	8	100	40	8	4
13	5	5	1	57	23	0	9	200	80	16	8
14	5	13	2	58	23	8	10	300	121	5	0
15	6	1	3	59	23	16	11	400	161	13	4
16	6	9	4	60	24	5	0	500	202	1	8
17	6	17	5	61	24	13	1	600	242	10	0
18	7	5	6	62	25	1	2	700	282	18	4
19	7	13	7	63	25	9	3	800	323	6	8
20	8	1	8	64	25	17	4	900	363	15	0
21	8	9	9	65	26	5	5	1000	404	3	4
22	8	17	10	66	26	13	6	2000	808	6	8
23	9	5	11	67	27	1	7	3000	1212	10	0
24	9	14	0	68	27	9	8	4000	1616	13	4
25	10	2	1	69	27	17	9	5000	2020	16	8
26	10	10	2	70	28	5	10	6000	2425	0	0
27	10	18	3	71	28	13	11	7000	2829	3	4
[28]	11	6	4	72	29	2	0	8000	3233	6	8
29	11	14	5	73	29	10	1	9000	3637	10	0
30	12	2	6	74	29	18	2	10000	4041	13	4
31	12	10	7	75	30	6	3				
32	12	18	8	76	30	14	4				
33	13	6	9	77	31	2	5		*Great Hundred*		
34	13	14	10	78	31	10	6	112	45	5	4
35	14	2	11	79	31	18	7		*Gross*		
36	14	11	0	80	32	6	8	144	58	4	0
37	14	19	1	81	32	14	9		*Wey*		
38	15	7	2	82	33	2	10	256	103	9	4
39	15	15	3	83	33	10	11		*Days in a Year*		
40	16	3	4	[84]	33	19	0	365	147	10	5
41	16	11	5	85	34	7	1		*Feet in a Rod*		
42	16	19	6	86	34	15	2	272	109	18	8
43	17	7	7	87	35	3	3				
44	17	15	8	88	35	11	4				

R

N.	l.	s.	d.	N.	l.	s.	d.	N.	l.	s.	d.
1	0	8	2	45	18	7	6	89	36	6	10
2	0	16	4	46	18	15	8	90	36	15	0
3	1	4	6	47	19	3	10	91	37	3	2
4	1	12	8	48	19	12	0	92	37	11	4
5	2	0	10	49	20	0	2	93	37	19	6
6	2	9	0	50	20	8	4	94	38	7	8
7	2	17	2	51	20	16	6	95	38	15	10
8	3	5	4	52	21	4	8	96	39	4	0
9	3	13	6	53	21	12	10	97	39	12	2
10	4	1	8	54	22	1	0	98	40	0	4
11	4	9	10	55	22	9	2	99	40	8	6
12	4	18	0	[56]	22	17	4	100	40	16	8
13	5	6	2	57	23	5	6	200	81	13	4
14	5	14	4	58	23	13	8	300	122	10	0
15	6	2	6	59	24	1	10	400	163	6	8
16	6	10	8	60	24	10	0	500	204	3	4
17	6	18	10	61	24	18	2	600	245	0	0
18	7	7	0	62	25	6	4	700	285	16	8
19	7	15	2	63	25	14	6	800	326	13	4
20	8	3	4	64	26	2	8	900	367	10	0
21	8	11	6	65	26	10	10	1000	408	6	8
22	8	19	8	66	26	19	0	2000	816	13	4
23	9	7	10	67	27	7	2	3000	1225	0	0
24	9	16	0	68	27	15	4	4000	1633	6	8
25	10	4	2	69	28	3	6	5000	2041	13	4
26	10	12	4	70	28	11	8	6000	2450	0	0
27	11	0	6	71	28	19	10	7000	2858	6	8
[28]	11	8	8	72	29	8	0	8000	3266	13	4
29	11	16	10	73	29	16	2	9000	3675	0	0
30	12	5	0	74	30	4	4	10000	4083	6	8
31	12	13	2	75	30	12	6				
32	13	1	4	76	31	0	8				
33	13	9	6	77	31	8	10	*Great Hundred*			
34	13	17	8	78	31	17	0	112	45	14	8
35	14	5	10	79	32	5	2	*Grofs*			
36	14	14	0	80	32	13	4	144	58	16	0
37	15	2	2	81	33	1	6	*Wey*			
38	15	10	4	82	33	9	8	256	104	10	8
39	15	18	6	83	33	17	10	*Days in a Year*			
40	16	6	8	[84]	34	6	0	365	149	0	10
41	16	14	10	85	34	14	2	*Feet in a Rod*			
42	17	3	0	86	35	2	4	272	111	1	4
43	17	11	2	87	35	10	6				
44	17	19	4	88	35	18	8				

N.	L. s. d.			N.	l. s. d.			N.	l. s. d.		
1	0	8	3	45	18	11	3	89	36	14	3
2	0	16	6	46	18	19	6	90	37	2	6
3	1	4	9	47	19	7	9	91	37	10	9
4	1	13	0	48	19	16	0	92	37	19	0
5	2	1	3	49	20	4	3	93	38	7	3
6	2	9	6	50	20	12	6	94	38	15	6
7	2	17	9	51	21	0	9	95	39	3	9
8	3	6	0	52	21	9	0	96	39	12	0
9	3	14	3	53	21	17	3	97	40	0	3
10	4	2	6	54	22	5	6	98	40	8	6
11	4	10	9	55	22	13	9	99	40	16	9
12	4	19	0	[56]	23	2	0	100	41	5	0
13	5	7	3	57	23	10	3	200	82	10	0
14	5	15	6	58	23	18	6	300	123	15	0
15	6	3	9	59	24	6	9	400	165	0	0
16	6	12	0	60	24	15	0	500	206	5	0
17	7	0	3	61	25	3	3	600	247	10	0
18	7	8	6	62	25	11	6	700	288	15	0
19	7	16	9	63	25	19	9	800	330	0	0
20	8	5	0	64	26	8	0	900	371	5	0
21	8	13	3	65	26	16	3	1000	412	10	0
22	9	1	6	66	27	4	6	2000	825	0	0
23	9	9	9	67	27	12	9	3000	1237	10	0
24	9	18	0	68	28	1	0	4000	1650	0	0
25	10	6	3	69	28	9	3	5000	2062	10	0
26	10	14	6	70	28	17	6	6000	2475	0	0
27	11	2	9	71	29	5	9	7000	2887	10	0
[28]	11	11	0	72	29	14	0	8000	3300	0	0
29	11	19	3	73	30	2	3	9000	3712	10	0
30	12	7	6	74	30	10	6	10000	4125	0	0
31	12	15	9	75	30	18	9				
32	13	4	0	76	31	7	0				
33	13	12	3	77	31	15	3	Great Hundred			
34	14	0	6	78	32	3	6	112	46	4	0
35	14	8	9	79	32	11	9	Grefs			
36	14	17	0	80	33	0	0	144	59	8	0
37	15	5	3	81	33	8	3	Wey			
38	15	13	6	82	33	16	6	256	105	12	0
39	16	1	9	83	34	4	9	Days in a Year			
40	16	10	0	[84]	34	13	0	365	150	11	3
41	16	18	3	85	35	1	3	Feet in a Rod			
42	17	6	6	86	35	9	6	272	112	4	0
43	17	14	9	87	35	17	9				
44	18	3	0	88	36	6	0				

N.	l.	s.	d.	N.	l.	s.	d.	N.	l.	s.	d.
1	0	8	4	45	18	15	0	89	37	1	8
2	0	16	8	46	19	3	4	90	37	10	0
3	1	5	0	47	19	11	8	91	37	18	4
4	1	13	4	48	20	0	0	92	38	6	8
5	2	1	8	49	20	8	4	93	38	15	0
6	2	10	0	50	20	16	8	94	39	3	4
7	2	18	4	51	21	5	0	95	39	11	8
8	3	6	8	52	21	13	4	96	40	0	0
9	3	15	0	53	22	1	8	97	40	8	4
10	4	3	4	54	22	10	0	98	40	16	8
11	4	11	8	55	22	18	4	99	41	5	0
12	5	0	0	[56]	23	6	8	100	41	13	4
13	5	8	4	57	23	15	0	200	83	6	8
14	5	16	8	58	24	3	4	300	125	0	0
15	6	5	0	59	24	11	8	400	166	13	4
16	6	13	4	60	25	0	0	500	208	6	8
17	7	1	8	61	25	8	4	600	250	0	0
18	7	10	0	62	25	16	8	700	291	13	4
19	7	18	4	63	26	5	0	800	333	6	8
20	8	6	8	64	26	13	4	900	375	0	0
21	8	15	0	65	27	1	8	1000	416	13	4
22	9	3	4	66	27	10	0	2000	833	6	8
23	9	11	8	67	27	18	4	3000	1250	0	0
24	10	0	0	68	28	6	8	4000	1666	13	4
25	10	8	4	69	28	15	0	5000	2083	6	8
26	10	16	8	70	29	3	4	6000	2500	0	0
27	11	5	0	71	29	11	8	7000	2916	13	4
[28]	11	13	4	72	30	0	0	8000	3333	6	8
29	12	1	8	73	30	8	4	9000	3750	0	0
30	12	10	0	74	30	16	8	10000	4166	13	4
31	12	18	4	75	31	5	0				
32	13	6	8	76	31	13	4				
33	13	15	0	77	32	1	8				
34	14	3	4	78	32	10	0	*Great Hundred*			
35	14	11	8	79	32	18	4	112	46	13	4
36	15	0	0	80	33	6	8	*Gross*			
37	15	8	4	81	33	15	0	144	60	0	0
38	15	16	8	82	34	3	4	*Wey*			
39	16	5	0	83	34	11	8	256	106	13	4
40	16	13	4	[84]	35	0	0	*Days in a Year*			
41	17	1	8	85	35	8	4	365	152	1	8
42	17	10	0	86	35	16	8	*Feet in a Rod*			
43	17	18	4	87	36	5	0	272	113	6	8
44	18	6	8	88	36	13	4				

N.	l.	s.	d.	N.	l.	s.	d.	N.	l.	s.	d.
1	0	8	5	45	18	18	9	89	37	9	1
2	0	16	10	46	19	7	2	90	37	17	6
3	1	5	3	47	19	15	7	91	38	5	11
4	1	13	8	48	20	4	0	92	38	14	4
5	2	2	1	49	20	12	5	93	39	2	9
6	2	10	6	50	21	0	10	94	39	11	2
7	2	18	11	51	21	9	3	95	39	19	7
8	3	7	4	52	21	17	8	96	40	8	0
9	3	15	9	53	22	6	1	97	40	16	5
10	4	4	2	54	22	14	6	98	41	4	10
11	4	12	7	55	23	2	11	99	41	13	3
12	5	1	0	[56]	23	11	4	100	42	1	8
13	5	9	5	57	23	19	9	200	84	3	4
14	5	17	10	58	24	8	2	300	126	5	0
15	6	6	3	59	24	16	7	400	168	6	8
16	6	14	8	60	25	5	0	500	210	8	4
17	7	3	1	61	25	13	5	600	252	10	0
18	7	11	6	62	26	1	10	700	294	11	8
19	7	19	11	63	26	10	3	800	336	13	4
20	8	8	4	64	26	18	8	900	378	15	0
21	8	16	9	65	27	7	1	1000	420	16	8
22	9	5	2	66	27	15	6	2000	841	13	4
23	9	13	7	67	28	3	11	3000	1262	10	0
24	10	2	0	68	28	12	4	4000	1683	6	8
25	10	10	5	69	29	0	9	5000	2104	3	4
26	10	18	10	70	29	9	2	6000	2525	0	0
27	11	7	3	71	29	17	7	7000	2945	16	8
[28]	11	15	8	72	30	6	0	8000	3366	13	4
29	12	4	1	73	30	14	5	9000	3787	10	0
30	12	12	6	74	31	2	10	10000	4208	6	8
31	13	0	11	75	31	11	3				
32	13	9	4	76	31	19	8				
33	13	17	9	77	32	8	1				
34	14	6	2	78	32	16	6				
35	14	14	7	79	33	4	11				
36	15	3	0	80	33	13	4				
37	15	11	5	81	34	1	9				
38	15	19	10	82	34	10	2				
39	16	8	3	83	34	18	7				
40	16	16	8	[84]	35	7	0				
41	17	5	1	85	35	15	5				
42	17	13	6	86	36	3	10				
43	18	1	11	87	36	12	3				
44	18	10	4	88	37	0	8				

Great Hundred

112	47	2	8

Grofs

144	60	12	0

Wey

256	107	14	8

Days in a Year

365	153	12	1

Feet in a Rod

272	114	9	4

N.	l.	s.	d.	N.	l.	s.	d.	N.	l.	s.	d.
1	0	8	6	45	19	2	6	89	37	16	6
2	0	17	0	46	19	11	0	90	38	5	0
3	1	5	6	47	19	19	6	91	38	13	6
4	1	14	0	48	20	8	0	92	39	2	0
5	2	2	6	49	20	16	6	93	39	10	6
6	2	11	0	50	21	5	0	94	39	19	0
7	2	19	6	51	21	13	6	95	40	7	6
8	3	8	0	52	22	2	0	96	40	16	0
9	3	16	6	53	22	10	6	97	41	4	6
10	4	5	0	54	22	19	0	98	41	13	0
11	4	13	6	55	23	7	6	99	42	1	6
12	5	2	0	[56]	23	16	0	100	42	10	0
13	5	10	6	57	24	4	6	200	85	0	0
14	5	19	0	58	24	13	0	300	127	10	0
15	6	7	6	59	25	1	6	400	170	0	0
16	6	16	0	60	25	10	0	500	212	10	0
17	7	4	6	61	25	18	6	600	255	0	0
18	7	13	0	62	26	7	0	700	297	10	0
19	8	1	6	63	26	15	6	800	340	0	0
20	8	10	0	64	27	4	0	900	382	10	0
21	8	18	6	65	27	12	6	1000	425	0	0
22	9	7	0	66	28	1	0	2000	850	0	0
23	9	15	6	67	28	9	6	3000	1275	0	0
24	10	4	0	68	28	18	0	4000	1700	0	0
25	10	12	6	69	29	6	6	5000	2125	0	0
26	11	1	0	70	29	15	0	6000	2550	0	0
27	11	9	6	71	30	3	6	7000	2975	0	0
[28]	11	18	0	72	30	12	0	8000	3400	0	0
29	12	6	6	73	31	0	6	9000	3825	0	0
30	12	15	0	74	31	9	0	10000	4250	0	0
31	13	3	6	75	31	17	6				
32	13	12	0	76	32	6	0				
33	14	0	6	77	32	14	6				
34	14	9	0	78	33	3	0				
35	14	17	6	79	33	11	6				
36	15	6	0	80	34	0	0				
37	15	14	6	81	34	8	6				
38	16	3	0	82	34	17	0				
39	16	11	6	83	35	5	6				
40	17	0	0	[84]	35	14	0				
41	17	8	6	85	36	2	6				
42	17	17	0	86	36	11	0				
43	18	5	6	87	36	19	6				
44	18	14	0	88	37	8	0				

Great Hundred

112	47	12	0

Gross

144	61	4	0

Wey

256	108	16	0

Days in a Year

365	155	2	6

Feet in a Rod

272	115	12	0

N.	l.	s.	d.	N.	l.	s.	d.	N.	l.	s.	d.
1	0	8	7	45	19	6	3	89	38	3	11
2	0	17	2	46	19	14	10	90	38	12	6
3	1	5	9	47	20	3	5	91	39	1	1
4	1	14	4	48	20	12	0	92	39	9	8
5	2	2	11	49	21	0	7	93	39	18	3
6	2	11	6	50	21	9	2	94	40	6	10
7	3	0	1	51	21	17	9	95	40	15	5
8	3	8	8	52	22	6	4	96	41	4	0
9	3	17	3	53	22	14	11	97	41	12	7
10	4	5	10	54	23	3	6	98	42	1	2
11	4	14	5	55	23	12	1	99	42	9	9
12	5	3	0	56	24	0	8	100	42	18	4
13	5	11	7	57	24	9	3	200	85	16	8
14	6	0	2	58	24	17	10	300	128	15	0
15	6	8	9	59	25	6	5	400	171	14	4
16	6	17	4	60	25	15	0	500	214	11	8
17	7	5	11	61	26	3	7	600	257	10	0
18	7	14	6	62	26	12	2	700	300	8	4
19	8	3	1	63	27	0	9	800	343	6	8
20	8	11	8	64	27	9	4	900	386	5	0
21	9	0	3	65	27	17	11	1000	429	3	4
22	9	8	10	66	28	6	6	2000	858	6	8
23	9	17	5	67	28	15	1	3000	1287	10	0
24	10	6	0	68	29	3	8	4000	1716	13	4
25	10	14	7	69	29	12	3	5000	2145	16	8
26	11	3	2	70	30	0	10	6000	2575	0	0
27	11	11	9	71	30	9	5	7000	3004	3	4
[28]	12	0	4	72	30	18	0	8000	3433	6	8
29	12	8	11	73	31	6	7	9000	3862	10	0
30	12	17	6	74	31	15	2	10000	4291	13	4
31	13	6	1	75	32	3	9				
32	13	14	8	76	32	12	4				
33	14	3	3	77	33	0	11				
34	14	11	10	78	33	9	6				
35	15	0	5	79	33	18	1				
36	15	9	0	80	34	6	8				
37	15	17	7	81	34	15	3				
38	16	6	2	82	35	3	10				
39	16	14	9	83	35	12	5				
40	17	3	4	[84]	36	1	0				
41	17	11	11	85	36	9	7				
42	18	0	6	86	36	18	2				
43	18	9	1	87	37	6	9				
44	18	17	8	88	37	15	4				

Great Hundred

112	48	1	4

Grofs

144	61	16	0

Wey

256	109	17	4

Days in a Year

365	156	12	11

Feet in a Rod

272	116	14	8

N.	l.	s.	d.	N.	l.	s.	d.	N.	l.	s.	d.
1	0	8	8	45	19	10	0	89	38	11	4
2	0	17	4	46	19	18	8	90	39	0	0
3	1	6	0	47	20	7	4	91	39	8	8
4	1	14	8	48	20	16	0	92	39	17	4
5	2	3	4	49	21	4	8	93	40	6	0
6	2	12	0	50	21	13	4	94	40	14	8
7	3	0	8	51	22	2	0	95	41	3	4
8	3	9	4	52	22	10	8	96	41	12	0
9	3	18	0	53	22	19	4	97	42	0	8
10	4	6	8	54	23	8	0	98	42	9	4
11	4	15	4	55	23	16	8	99	42	18	0
12	5	4	0	[56]	24	5	4	100	43	6	8
13	5	12	8	57	24	14	0	200	86	13	4
14	6	1	4	58	25	2	8	300	130	0	0
15	6	10	0	59	25	11	4	400	173	6	8
16	6	18	8	60	26	0	0	500	216	13	4
17	7	7	4	61	26	8	8	600	260	0	0
18	7	16	0	62	26	17	4	700	303	6	8
19	8	4	8	63	27	6	0	800	346	13	4
20	8	13	4	64	27	14	8	900	390	0	0
21	9	2	0	65	28	3	4	1000	433	6	8
22	9	10	8	66	28	12	0	2000	866	13	4
23	9	19	4	67	29	0	8	3000	1300	0	0
24	10	8	0	68	29	9	4	4000	1733	6	8
25	10	16	8	69	29	18	0	5000	2166	13	4
26	11	5	4	70	30	6	8	6000	2600	0	0
27	11	14	0	71	30	15	4	7000	3033	6	8
[28]	12	2	8	72	31	4	0	8000	3466	13	4
29	12	11	4	73	31	12	8	9000	3900	0	0
30	13	0	0	74	32	1	4	10000	4333	6	8
31	13	8	8	75	32	10	0				
32	13	17	4	76	32	18	8				
33	14	6	0	77	33	7	4				
34	14	14	8	78	33	16	0				
35	15	3	4	79	34	4	8				
36	15	12	0	80	34	13	4				
37	16	0	8	81	35	2	0				
38	16	9	4	82	35	10	8				
39	16	18	0	83	35	19	4				
40	17	6	8	[84]	36	8	0				
41	17	15	4	85	36	16	8				
42	18	4	0	86	37	5	4				
43	18	12	8	87	37	14	0				
44	19	1	4	88	38	2	8				

Great Hundred

112	48	10	8

Grefs

144	62	8	0

Wey

256	110	18	8

Days in a Year

365	158	3	4

Feet in a Rod

272	117	17	4

N.	l.	s.	d.	N.	l.	s.	d.	N.	l.	s.	d.
1	0	8	9	45	19	13	9	89	38	18	9
2	0	17	6	46	20	2	6	90	39	7	6
3	1	6	3	47	20	11	3	91	39	16	3
4	1	15	0	48	21	0	0	92	40	5	0
5	2	3	0	49	21	8	9	93	40	13	9
6	2	12	6	50	21	17	6	94	41	2	6
7	3	1	3	51	22	6	3	95	41	11	3
8	3	10	0	52	22	15	0	96	42	0	0
9	3	18	9	53	23	3	9	97	42	8	9
10	4	7	6	54	23	12	6	98	42	17	6
11	4	16	3	55	24	1	3	99	43	6	3
12	5	5	0	[56]	24	10	0	100	43	15	0
13	5	13	9	57	24	18	9	200	87	10	0
14	6	2	6	58	25	7	6	300	131	5	0
15	6	11	3	59	25	16	3	400	175	0	0
16	7	0	0	60	26	5	0	500	218	15	0
17	7	8	9	61	26	13	9	600	262	10	0
18	7	17	6	62	27	2	6	700	306	5	0
19	8	6	3	63	27	11	3	800	350	0	0
20	8	15	0	64	28	0	0	900	393	15	0
21	9	3	9	65	28	8	9	1000	437	10	0
22	9	12	6	66	28	17	6	2000	875	0	0
23	10	1	3	67	29	6	3	3000	1312	10	0
24	10	10	0	68	29	15	0	4000	1750	0	0
25	10	18	9	69	30	3	9	5000	2187	10	0
26	11	7	6	70	30	12	6	6000	2625	0	0
27	11	16	3	71	31	1	3	7000	3062	10	0
[28]	12	5	0	72	31	10	0	8000	3500	0	0
29	12	13	9	73	31	18	9	9000	3937	10	0
30	13	2	6	74	32	7	6	10000	4375	0	0
31	13	11	3	75	32	16	3				
32	14	0	0	76	33	5	0				
33	14	8	9	77	33	13	9	*Great Hundred*			
34	14	17	6	78	34	2	6	112.	49	0	0
35	15	6	3	79	34	11	3	*Grofs*			
36	15	15	0	80	35	0	0	144	63	0	0
37	16	3	9	81	35	8	9	*Wey*			
38	16	12	6	82	35	17	6	256	112	0	0
39	17	1	3	83	36	6	3	*Days in a Year*			
40	17	10	0	[84]	36	15	0	365	159	13	9
41	17	18	9	85	37	3	9	*Feet in a Rod*			
42	18	7	6	86	37	12	6	272	119	0	0
43	18	16	3	87	38	1	3				
44	19	5	0	88	38	10	0				

N.	l.	s.	d.
1	0	8	10
2	0	17	8
3	1	6	6
4	1	15	4
5	2	4	2
6	2	13	0
7	3	1	10
8	3	10	8
9	3	19	6
10	4	8	4
11	4	17	2
12	5	6	0
13	5	14	10
14	6	3	8
15	6	12	6
16	7	1	4
17	7	10	2
18	7	19	0
19	8	7	10
20	8	16	8
21	9	5	6
22	9	14	4
23	10	3	2
24	10	12	0
25	11	0	10
26	11	9	8
27	11	18	6
[28]	12	7	4
29	12	16	2
30	13	5	0
31	13	13	10
32	14	2	8
33	14	11	6
34	15	0	4
35	15	9	2
36	15	18	0
37	16	6	10
38	16	15	8
39	17	4	6
40	17	13	4
41	18	2	2
42	18	11	0
43	18	19	10
44	19	8	8

N.	l.	s.	d.
45	19	17	6
46	20	6	4
47	20	15	2
48	21	4	0
49	21	12	10
50	22	1	8
51	22	10	6
52	22	19	4
53	23	8	2
54	23	17	0
55	24	5	10
[56]	24	14	8
57	25	3	6
58	25	12	4
59	26	1	2
60	26	10	0
61	26	18	10
62	27	7	8
63	27	16	6
64	28	5	4
65	28	14	2
66	29	3	0
67	29	11	10
68	30	0	8
69	30	9	6
70	30	18	4
71	31	7	2
72	31	16	0
73	32	4	10
74	32	13	8
75	33	2	6
76	33	11	4
77	34	0	2
78	34	9	0
79	34	17	10
80	35	6	8
81	35	15	6
82	36	4	4
83	36	13	2
[84]	37	2	0
85	37	10	10
86	37	19	8
87	38	8	6
88	38	17	4

N.	l.	s.	d.
89	39	6	2
90	39	15	0
91	40	3	10
92	40	12	8
93	41	1	6
94	41	10	4
95	41	19	2
96	42	8	0
97	42	16	10
98	43	5	8
99	43	14	6
100	44	3	4
200	88	6	8
300	132	10	0
400	179	13	4
500	220	16	8
600	265	0	0
700	309	3	4
800	353	6	8
900	397	10	0
1000	441	13	4
2000	883	6	8
3000	1325	0	0
4000	1766	13	4
5000	2208	6	8
6000	2650	0	0
7000	3091	13	4
8000	3533	6	8
9000	3975	0	0
10000	4416	13	4

Great Hundred

112	49	9	4

Grofs

144	63	12	0

Wey

256	113	1	4

Days in a Year

365	161	4	2

Feet in a Rod

272	120	2	8

N.	l.	s.	d.	N.	l.	s.	d.	N.	l.	s.	d.
1	0	8	11	45	20	1	3	89	39	13	7
2	0	17	10	46	20	10	2	90	40	2	6
3	1	6	9	47	20	19	1	91	40	11	5
4	1	15	8	48	21	8	0	92	41	0	4
5	2	4	7	49	21	16	11	93	41	9	3
6	2	13	6	50	22	5	10	94	41	18	2
7	3	2	5	51	22	14	9	95	42	7	1
8	3	11	4	52	23	3	8	96	42	16	0
9	4	0	3	53	23	12	7	97	43	4	11
10	4	9	2	54	24	1	6	98	43	13	10
11	4	18	1	55	24	10	5	99	44	2	9
12	5	7	0	[56]	24	19	4	100	44	11	8
13	5	15	11	57	25	8	3	200	89	3	4
14	6	4	10	58	25	17	2	300	133	15	0
15	6	13	9	59	26	6	1	400	178	6	8
16	7	2	8	60	26	15	0	500	222	18	4
17	7	11	7	61	27	3	11	600	267	10	0
18	8	0	6	62	27	12	10	700	312	1	8
19	8	9	5	63	28	1	9	800	356	13	4
20	8	18	4	64	28	10	8	900	401	5	0
21	9	7	3	65	28	19	7	1000	445	16	8
22	9	16	2	66	29	8	6	2000	891	13	4
23	10	5	1	67	29	17	5	3000	1337	10	0
24	10	14	0	68	30	6	4	4000	1783	6	8
25	11	2	11	69	30	15	3	5000	2229	3	4
26	11	11	10	70	31	4	2	6000	2675	0	0
27	12	0	9	71	31	13	1	7000	3120	16	8
[28]	12	9	8	72	32	2	0	8000	3566	13	4
29	12	18	7	73	32	10	11	9000	4012	10	0
30	13	7	6	74	32	19	10	10000	4458	6	8
31	13	16	5	75	33	8	9				
32	14	5	4	76	33	17	8				
33	14	14	3	77	34	6	7	Great Hundred			
34	15	3	2	78	34	15	6	112	49	18	8
35	15	12	1	79	35	4	5	Grofs			
36	16	1	0	80	35	13	4	144	64	4	0
37	16	9	11	81	36	2	3	Wey			
38	16	18	10	82	36	11	2	256	114	2	8
39	17	7	9	83	37	0	1	Days in a Year			
40	17	16	8	[84]	37	9	0	365	162	14	7
41	18	5	7	85	37	17	11	Feet in a Rod			
42	18	14	6	86	38	6	10	272	121	5	4
43	19	3	5	87	38	15	9				
44	19	12	4	88	39	4	8				

N.	l.	s.	d.	N.	l.	s.	d.	N.	l.	s.	d.
1	0	9	0	45	20	5	0	89	40	1	0
2	0	18	0	46	20	14	0	90	40	10	0
3	1	7	0	47	21	3	0	91	40	19	0
4	1	16	0	48	21	12	0	92	41	8	0
5	2	5	0	49	22	1	0	93	41	17	0
6	2	14	0	50	22	10	0	94	42	6	0
7	3	3	0	51	22	19	0	95	42	15	0
8	3	12	0	52	23	8	0	96	43	4	0
9	4	1	0	53	23	17	0	97	43	13	0
10	4	10	0	54	24	6	0	98	44	2	0
11	4	19	0	55	24	15	0	99	44	11	0
12	5	8	0	[56]	25	4	0	100	45	0	0
13	5	17	0	57	25	13	0	200	90	0	0
14	6	6	0	58	26	2	0	300	135	0	0
15	6	15	0	59	26	11	0	400	180	0	0
16	7	4	0	60	27	0	0	500	225	0	0
17	7	13	0	61	27	9	0	600	270	0	0
18	8	2	0	62	27	18	0	700	315	0	0
19	8	11	0	63	28	7	0	800	360	0	0
20	9	0	0	64	28	16	0	900	405	0	0
21	9	9	0	65	29	5	0	1000	450	0	0
22	9	18	0	66	29	14	0	2000	900	0	0
23	10	7	0	67	30	3	0	3000	1350	0	0
24	10	16	0	68	30	12	0	4000	1800	0	0
25	11	5	0	69	31	1	0	5000	2250	0	0
26	11	14	0	70	31	10	0	6000	2700	0	0
27	12	3	0	71	31	19	0	7000	3150	0	0
[28]	12	12	0	72	32	8	0	8000	3600	0	0
29	13	1	0	73	32	17	0	9000	4050	0	0
30	13	10	0	74	33	6	0	10000	4500	0	0
31	13	19	0	75	33	15	0				
32	14	8	0	76	34	4	0				
33	14	17	0	77	34	13	0	**Great Hundred**			
34	15	6	0	78	35	2	0	112	50	8	0
35	15	15	0	79	35	11	0	*Grofs*			
36	16	4	0	80	36	0	0	144	64	16	0
37	16	13	0	81	36	9	0	*Wey*			
38	17	2	0	82	36	18	0	256	115	4	0
39	17	11	0	83	37	7	0	*Days in a Year*			
40	18	0	0	[84]	37	16	0	365	164	5	0
41	18	9	0	85	38	5	0	*Feet in a Rod*			
42	18	18	0	86	38	14	0	272	122	8	0
43	19	7	0	87	39	3	0				
44	19	16	0	88	39	12	0				

N.	l.	s.	d.
1	0	9	1
2	0	18	2
3	1	7	3
4	1	16	4
5	2	5	5
6	2	14	6
7	3	3	7
8	3	12	8
9	4	1	9
10	4	10	10
11	4	19	11
12	5	9	0
13	5	18	1
14	6	7	2
15	6	16	3
16	7	5	4
17	7	14	5
18	8	3	6
19	8	12	7
20	9	1	8
21	9	10	9
22	9	19	10
23	10	8	11
24	10	18	0
25	11	7	1
26	11	16	2
27	12	5	3
[28]	12	14	4
29	13	3	5
30	13	12	6
31	14	1	7
32	14	10	8
33	14	19	9
34	15	8	10
35	15	17	11
36	16	7	0
37	16	16	1
38	17	5	2
39	17	14	3
40	18	3	4
41	18	12	5
42	19	1	6
43	19	10	7
44	19	19	8

N.	l.	s.	d.
45	20	8	9
46	20	17	10
47	21	6	11
48	21	16	0
49	22	5	1
50	22	14	2
51	23	3	3
52	23	12	4
53	24	1	5
54	24	10	6
55	24	19	7
[56]	25	8	8
57	25	17	9
58	26	6	10
59	26	15	11
60	27	5	0
61	27	14	1
62	28	3	2
63	28	12	3
64	29	1	4
65	29	10	5
66	29	19	6
67	30	8	7
68	30	17	8
69	31	6	9
70	31	15	10
71	32	4	11
72	32	14	0
73	33	3	1
74	33	12	2
75	34	1	3
76	34	10	4
77	34	19	5
78	35	8	6
79	35	17	7
80	36	6	8
81	36	15	9
82	37	4	10
83	37	13	11
[84]	38	3	0
85	38	12	1
86	39	1	2
87	39	10	3
88	39	19	4

N.	l.	s.	d.
89	40	8	5
90	40	17	6
91	41	6	7
92	41	15	8
93	42	4	9
94	42	13	10
95	43	2	11
96	43	12	0
97	44	1	1
98	44	10	2
99	44	19	3
100	45	8	4
200	90	16	8
300	136	5	0
400	181	13	4
500	227	1	8
600	272	10	0
700	317	18	4
800	363	6	8
900	408	15	0
1000	454	3	4
2000	908	6	8
3000	1362	10	0
4000	1816	13	4
5000	2270	16	8
6000	2725	0	0
7000	3179	3	4
8000	3633	6	8
9000	4087	10	0
10000	4541	13	4

Great Hundred

112	50	17	4

Grofs

144	65	8	0

Wey

256	116	5	4

Days in a Year

365	165	15	5

Feet in a Rod

272	123	10	8

S

N.	l.	s.	d.	N.	l.	s.	d.	N.	l.	s.	d.
1	0	9	2	45	20	12	6	89	40	15	10
2	0	18	4	46	21	1	8	90	41	5	0
3	1	7	6	47	21	10	10	91	41	14	2
4	1	16	8	48	22	0	0	92	42	3	4
5	2	5	10	49	22	9	2	93	42	12	6
6	2	15	0	50	22	18	4	94	43	1	8
7	3	4	2	51	23	7	6	95	43	10	10
8	3	13	4	52	23	16	8	96	44	0	0
9	4	2	6	53	24	5	10	97	44	9	2
10	4	11	8	54	24	15	0	98	44	18	4
11	5	0	10	55	25	4	2	99	45	7	6
12	5	10	0	[56]	25	13	4	100	45	16	8
13	5	19	2	57	26	2	6	200	91	13	4
14	6	8	4	58	26	11	8	300	137	10	0
15	6	17	6	59	27	0	10	400	183	6	8
16	7	6	8	60	27	10	0	500	229	3	4
17	7	15	10	61	27	19	2	600	275	0	0
18	8	5	0	62	28	8	4	700	320	16	8
19	8	14	2	63	28	17	6	800	366	13	4
20	9	3	4	64	29	6	8	900	412	10	0
21	9	12	6	65	29	15	10	1000	458	6	8
22	10	1	8	66	30	5	0	2000	916	13	4
23	10	10	10	67	30	14	2	3000	1375	0	0
24	11	0	0	68	31	3	4	4000	1833	6	8
25	11	9	2	69	31	12	6	5000	2291	13	4
26	11	18	4	70	32	1	8	6000	2750	0	0
27	12	7	6	71	32	10	10	7000	3208	6	8
[28]	12	16	8	72	33	0	0	8000	3666	13	4
29	13	5	10	73	33	9	2	9000	4125	0	0
30	13	15	0	74	33	18	4	10000	4583	6	8
31	14	4	2	75	34	7	6				
32	14	13	4	76	34	16	8				
33	15	2	6	77	35	5	10	*Great Hundred*			
34	15	11	8	78	35	15	0	112	51	6	8
35	16	0	10	79	36	4	2	*Grofs*			
36	16	10	0	80	36	13	4	144	66	0	0
37	16	19	2	81	37	2	6	*Wey*			
38	17	8	4	82	37	11	8	256	117	6	8
39	17	17	6	83	38	0	10	*Days in a Year*			
40	18	6	8	[84]	38	10	0	365	167	5	10
41	18	15	10	85	38	19	2	*Feet in a Rod*			
42	19	5	0	86	39	8	4	272	124	13	4
43	19	14	2	87	39	17	6				
44	20	3	4	88	40	6	8				

N.	l.	s.	d.	N.	l.	s.	d.	N.	l.	s.	d.
1	0	9	3	45	20	16	3	89	41	3	3
2	0	18	6	46	21	5	6	90	41	12	6
3	1	7	9	47	21	14	9	91	42	1	9
4	1	17	0	48	22	4	0	92	42	11	0
5	2	6	3	49	22	13	3	93	43	0	3
6	2	15	6	50	23	2	6	94	43	9	6
7	3	4	9	51	23	11	9	95	43	18	9
8	3	14	0	52	24	1	0	96	44	8	0
9	4	3	3	53	24	10	3	97	44	17	3
10	4	12	6	54	24	19	6	98	45	6	6
11	5	1	9	55	25	8	9	99	45	15	9
12	5	11	0	[56]	25	18	0	100	46	5	0
13	6	0	3	57	26	7	3	200	92	10	0
14	6	9	6	58	26	16	6	300	138	15	0
15	6	18	9	59	27	5	9	400	185	0	0
16	7	8	0	60	27	15	0	500	231	5	0
17	7	17	3	61	28	4	3	600	277	10	0
18	8	6	6	62	28	13	6	700	323	15	0
19	8	15	9	63	29	2	9	800	370	0	0
20	9	5	0	64	29	12	0	900	416	5	0
21	9	14	3	65	30	1	3	1000	462	10	0
22	10	3	6	66	30	10	6	2000	925	0	0
23	10	12	9	67	30	19	9	3000	1387	10	0
24	11	2	0	68	31	9	0	4000	1850	0	0
25	11	11	3	69	31	18	3	5000	2312	10	0
26	12	0	6	70	32	7	6	6000	2775	0	0
27	12	9	9	71	32	16	9	7000	3237	10	0
[28]	12	19	0	72	33	6	0	8000	3700	0	0
29	13	8	3	73	33	15	3	9000	4162	10	0
30	13	17	6	74	34	4	6	10000	4625	0	0
31	14	6	9	75	34	13	9				
32	14	16	0	76	35	3	0				
33	15	5	3	77	35	12	3	Great Hundred			
34	15	14	6	78	36	1	6	112	51	16	0
35	16	3	9	79	36	10	9	Grofs			
36	16	13	0	80	37	0	0	144	66	12	0
37	17	2	3	81	37	9	3	Wey			
38	17	11	6	82	37	18	6	256	118	8	0
39	18	0	9	83	38	7	9	Days in a Year			
40	18	10	0	[84]	38	17	0	365	168	16	3
41	18	19	3	85	39	6	3	Feet in a Rod			
42	19	8	6	86	39	15	6	272	125	16	0
43	19	17	9	87	40	4	9				
44	20	7	0	88	40	14	0				

N.	l.	s.	d.	N.	l.	s.	d.	N	l.	s.	d.
1	0	9	4	45	21	0	0	89	41	10	8
2	0	18	8	46	21	9	4	90	42	0	0
3	1	8	0	47	21	18	8	91	42	9	4
4	1	17	4	48	22	8	0	92	42	18	8
5	2	6	8	49	22	17	4	93	43	8	0
6	2	16	0	50	23	6	8	94	43	17	4
7	3	5	4	51	23	16	0	95	44	6	8
8	3	14	8	52	24	5	4	96	44	16	0
9	4	4	0	53	24	14	8	97	45	5	4
10	4	13	4	54	25	4	0	98	45	14	8
11	5	2	8	55	25	13	4	99	46	4	0
12	5	12	0	[56]	26	2	8	100	46	13	4
13	6	1	4	57	26	12	0	200	93	6	8
14	6	10	8	58	27	1	4	300	140	0	0
15	7	0	0	59	27	10	8	400	186	13	4
16	7	9	4	60	28	0	0	500	233	6	8
17	7	18	8	61	28	9	4	600	280	0	0
18	8	8	0	62	28	18	8	700	326	13	4
19	8	17	4	63	29	8	0	800	373	6	8
20	9	6	8	64	29	17	4	900	420	0	0
21	9	16	0	65	30	6	8	1000	466	13	4
22	10	5	4	66	30	16	0	2000	933	6	8
23	10	14	8	67	31	5	4	3000	1400	0	0
24	11	4	0	68	31	14	8	4000	1866	13	4
25	11	13	4	69	32	4	0	5000	2333	6	8
26	12	2	8	70	32	13	4	6000	2800	0	0
27	12	12	0	71	33	2	8	7000	3266	13	4
[28]	13	1	4	72	33	12	0	8000	3733	6	8
29	13	10	8	73	34	1	4	9000	4200	0	0
30	14	0	0	74	34	10	8	10000	4666	13	4
31	14	9	4	75	35	0	0				
32	14	18	8	76	35	9	4				
33	15	8	0	77	35	18	8	Great Hundred			
34	15	17	4	78	36	8	0	112	52	5	4
35	16	6	8	79	36	17	4	*Grofs*			
36	16	16	0	80	37	6	8	144	67	4	0
37	17	5	4	81	37	16	0	*Wey*			
38	17	14	8	82	38	5	4	256	119	9	4
39	18	4	0	83	38	14	8	Days in a Year			
40	18	13	4	[84]	39	4	0	365	170	6	8
41	19	2	8	85	39	13	4	Feet in a Rod			
42	19	12	0	86	40	2	8	272	126	18	8
43	20	1	4	87	40	12	0				
44	20	10	8	88	41	1	4				

N.	l.	s.	d.	N.	l.	s.	d.	N.	l.	s.	d.
1	0	9	5	45	21	3	9	89	41	18	1
2	0	18	10	46	21	13	2	90	42	7	6
3	1	8	3	47	22	2	7	91	42	16	11
4	1	17	8	48	22	12	0	92	43	6	4
5	2	7	1	49	23	1	5	93	43	15	9
6	2	16	6	50	23	10	10	94	44	5	2
7	3	5	11	51	24	0	3	95	44	14	7
8	3	15	4	52	24	9	8	96	45	4	0
9	4	4	9	53	24	19	1	97	45	13	5
10	4	14	2	54	25	8	6	98	46	2	10
11	5	3	7	55	25	17	11	99	46	12	3
12	5	13	0	[56]	26	7	4	100	47	1	8
13	6	2	5	57	26	16	9	200	94	3	4
14	6	11	10	58	27	6	2	300	141	5	0
15	7	1	3	59	27	15	7	400	188	6	8
16	7	10	8	60	28	5	0	500	235	8	4
17	8	0	1	61	28	14	5	600	282	10	0
18	8	9	6	62	29	3	10	700	329	11	8
19	8	18	11	63	29	13	3	800	376	13	4
20	9	8	4	64	30	2	8	900	423	15	0
21	9	17	9	65	30	12	1	1000	470	16	8
22	10	7	2	66	31	1	6	2000	941	13	4
23	10	16	7	67	31	10	11	3000	1412	10	0
24	11	6	0	68	32	0	4	4000	1883	6	8
25	11	15	5	69	32	9	9	5000	2354	3	4
26	12	4	10	70	32	19	2	6000	2825	0	0
27	12	14	3	71	33	8	7	7000	3295	16	8
[28]	13	3	8	72	33	18	0	8000	3766	13	4
29	13	13	1	73	34	7	5	9000	4237	10	0
30	14	2	6	74	34	16	10	10000	4708	6	8
31	14	11	11	75	35	6	3				
32	15	1	4	76	35	15	8				
33	15	10	9	77	36	5	1	Great Hundred			
34	16	0	2	78	36	14	6	112	52	14	8
35	16	9	7	79	37	3	11	Grofs			
36	16	19	0	80	37	13	4	144	67	16	0
37	17	8	5	81	38	2	9	Wey			
38	17	17	10	82	38	12	2	256	120	10	8
39	18	7	3	83	39	1	7	Days in a Year			
40	18	16	8	[84]	39	11	0	365	171	17	1
41	19	6	1	85	40	0	5	Feet in a Rod			
42	19	15	6	86	40	9	10	272	128	1	4
43	20	4	11	87	40	19	3				
44	20	14	4	88	41	8	8				

N.	l.	s.	d.	N.	l.	s.	d.	N.	l.	s.	d.
1	0	9	6	45	21	7	6	89	42	5	6
2	0	19	0	46	21	17	0	90	42	15	0
3	1	8	6	47	22	6	6	91	43	4	6
4	1	18	0	48	22	16	0	92	43	14	0
5	2	7	6	49	23	5	6	93	44	3	6
6	2	17	0	50	23	15	0	94	44	13	0
7	3	6	6	51	24	4	6	95	45	2	6
8	3	16	0	52	24	14	0	96	45	12	0
9	4	5	6	53	25	3	6	97	46	1	6
10	4	15	0	54	25	13	0	98	46	11	0
11	5	4	6	55	26	2	6	99	47	0	6
12	5	14	0	[56]	26	12	0	100	47	10	0
13	6	3	6	57	27	1	6	200	95	0	0
14	6	13	0	58	27	11	0	300	142	10	0
15	7	2	6	59	28	0	6	400	190	0	0
16	7	12	0	60	28	10	0	500	237	10	0
17	8	1	6	61	28	19	6	600	285	0	0
18	8	11	0	62	29	9	0	700	332	10	0
19	9	0	6	63	29	18	6	800	380	0	0
20	9	10	0	64	30	8	0	900	427	10	0
21	9	19	6	65	30	17	6	1000	475	0	0
22	10	9	0	66	31	7	0	2000	950	0	0
23	10	18	6	67	31	16	6	3000	1425	0	0
24	11	8	0	68	32	6	0	4000	1900	0	0
25	11	17	6	69	32	15	6	5000	2375	0	0
26	12	7	0	70	33	5	0	6000	2850	0	0
27	12	16	6	71	33	14	6	7000	3325	0	0
[28]	13	6	0	72	34	4	0	8000	3800	0	0
29	13	15	6	73	34	13	6	9000	4275	0	0
30	14	5	0	74	35	3	0	10000	4750	0	0
31	14	14	6	75	35	12	6				
32	15	4	0	76	36	2	0				
33	15	13	6	77	36	11	6				
34	16	3	0	78	37	1	0				
35	16	12	6	79	37	10	6				
36	17	2	0	80	38	0	0				
37	17	11	6	81	38	9	6				
38	18	1	0	82	38	19	0				
39	18	10	6	83	39	8	6				
40	19	0	0	[84]	39	18	0				
41	19	9	6	85	40	7	6				
42	19	19	0	86	40	17	0				
43	20	8	6	87	41	6	6				
44	20	18	0	88	41	16	0				

Great Hundred

112	53	4	0

Gross

144	68	8	0

Wey

256	121	12	0

Days in a Year

365	173	7	6

Feet in a Rod

272	129	4	0

N.	l.	s.	d.	N.	l.	s.	d.	N.	l.	s.	d.
1	0	9	7	45	21	11	3	89	42	12	11
2	0	19	2	46	22	0	10	90	43	2	6
3	1	8	9	47	22	10	5	91	43	12	1
4	1	18	4	48	23	0	0	92	44	1	8
5	2	7	11	49	23	9	7	93	44	11	3
6	2	17	6	50	23	19	2	94	45	0	10
7	3	7	1	51	24	8	9	95	45	10	5
8	3	16	8	52	24	18	4	96	46	0	0
9	4	6	3	53	25	7	11	97	46	9	7
10	4	15	10	54	25	17	6	98	46	19	2
11	5	5	5	55	26	7	1	99	47	8	9
12	5	15	0	[56]	26	16	8	100	47	18	4
13	6	4	7	57	27	6	3	200	95	16	8
14	6	14	2	58	27	15	10	300	143	15	0
15	7	3	9	59	28	5	5	400	191	13	4
16	7	13	4	60	28	15	0	500	239	11	8
17	8	2	11	61	29	4	7	600	287	10	0
18	8	12	6	62	29	14	2	700	335	8	4
19	9	2	1	63	30	3	9	800	383	6	8
20	9	11	8	64	30	13	4	900	431	5	0
21	10	1	3	65	31	2	11	1000	479	3	4
22	10	10	10	66	31	12	6	2000	958	6	8
23	11	0	5	67	32	2	1	3000	1437	10	0
24	11	10	0	68	32	11	8	4000	1916	13	4
25	11	19	7	69	33	1	3	5000	2395	16	8
26	12	9	2	70	33	10	10	6000	2875	0	0
27	12	18	9	71	34	0	5	7000	3354	3	4
[28]	13	8	4	72	34	10	0	8000	3833	6	8
29	13	17	11	73	34	19	7	9000	4312	10	0
30	14	7	6	74	35	9	2	10000	4791	13	4
31	14	17	1	75	35	18	9				
32	15	6	8	76	36	8	4				
33	15	16	3	77	36	17	11				
34	16	5	10	78	37	7	6				
35	16	15	5	79	37	17	1				
36	17	5	0	80	38	6	8				
37	17	14	7	81	38	16	3				
38	18	4	2	82	39	5	10				
39	18	13	9	83	39	15	5				
40	19	3	4	[84]	40	5	0				
41	19	12	11	85	40	14	7				
42	20	2	6	86	41	4	2				
43	20	12	1	87	41	13	9				
44	21	1	8	88	42	3	4				

Great Hundred
112 | 53 13 4

Grofs
144 | 69 0 0

Wey
256 | 122 13 4

Days in a Year
365 | 174 17 11

Feet in a Rod
272 | 130 6 8

N.	l.	s.	d.	N.	l.	s.	d.	N.	l.	s.	d.
1	0	9	8	45	21	15	0	89	43	0	4
2	0	19	4	46	22	4	8	90	43	10	0
3	1	9	0	47	22	14	4	91	43	19	8
4	1	18	8	48	23	4	0	92	44	9	4
5	2	8	4	49	23	13	8	93	44	19	0
6	2	18	0	50	24	3	4	94	45	8	8
7	3	7	8	51	24	13	0	95	45	18	4
8	3	17	4	52	25	2	8	96	46	8	0
9	4	7	0	53	25	12	4	97	46	17	8
10	4	16	8	54	26	2	0	98	47	7	4
11	5	6	4	55	26	11	8	99	47	17	0
12	5	16	0	[56]	27	1	4	100	48	6	8
13	6	5	8	57	27	11	0	200	96	13	4
14	6	15	4	58	28	0	8	300	145	0	0
15	7	5	0	59	28	10	4	400	193	6	8
16	7	14	8	60	29	0	0	500	241	13	4
17	8	4	4	61	29	9	8	600	290	0	0
18	8	14	0	62	29	19	4	700	338	6	8
19	9	3	8	63	30	9	0	800	386	13	4
20	9	13	4	64	30	18	8	900	435	0	0
21	10	3	0	65	31	8	4	1000	483	6	8
22	10	12	8	66	31	18	0	2000	966	13	4
23	11	2	4	67	32	7	8	3000	1450	0	0
24	11	12	0	68	32	17	4	4000	1933	6	8
25	12	1	8	69	33	7	0	5000	2416	13	4
26	12	11	4	70	33	16	8	6000	2900	0	0
27	13	1	0	71	34	6	4	7000	3383	6	8
[28]	13	10	8	72	34	16	0	8000	3866	13	4
29	14	0	4	73	35	5	8	9000	4350	0	0
30	14	10	0	74	35	15	4	10000	4833	6	8
31	14	19	8	75	36	5	0				
32	15	9	4	76	36	14	8				
33	15	19	0	77	37	4	4	Great Hundred			
34	16	8	8	78	37	14	0	112	54	2	8
35	16	18	4	79	38	3	8	Grofs			
36	17	8	0	80	38	13	4	144	69	12	0
37	17	17	8	81	39	3	0	Wey			
38	18	7	4	82	39	12	8	256	123	14	8
39	18	17	0	83	40	2	4	Days in a Year			
40	19	6	8	[84]	40	12	0	365	176	8	4
41	19	16	4	85	41	1	8	Feet in a Rod			
42	20	6	0	86	41	11	4	272	131	9	4
43	20	15	8	87	42	1	0				
44	21	5	4	88	42	10	8				

N.	l.	s.	d.	N.	l.	s.	d.	N.	l.	s.	d.
1	0	9	9	45	21	18	9	89	43	7	9
2	0	19	6	46	22	8	6	90	43	17	6
3	1	9	3	47	22	18	3	91	44	7	3
4	1	19	0	48	23	8	0	92	44	17	0
5	2	8	9	49	23	17	9	93	45	6	9
6	2	18	6	50	24	7	6	94	45	16	6
7	3	8	3	51	24	17	3	95	46	6	3
8	3	18	0	52	25	7	0	96	46	16	0
9	4	7	9	53	25	16	9	97	47	5	9
10	4	17	6	54	26	6	6	98	47	15	6
11	5	7	3	55	26	16	3	99	48	5	3
12	5	17	0	[56]	27	6	0	100	48	15	0
13	6	6	9	57	27	15	9	200	97	10	0
14	6	16	6	58	28	5	6	300	146	5	0
15	7	6	3	59	28	15	3	400	195	0	0
16	7	16	0	60	29	5	0	500	243	15	0
17	8	5	9	61	29	14	9	600	292	10	0
18	8	15	6	62	30	4	6	700	341	5	0
19	9	5	3	63	30	14	3	800	390	0	0
20	9	15	0	64	31	4	0	900	438	15	0
21	10	4	9	65	31	13	9	1000	487	10	0
22	10	14	6	66	32	3	6	2000	975	0	0
23	11	4	3	67	32	13	3	3000	1462	10	0
24	11	14	0	68	33	3	0	4000	1950	0	0
25	12	3	9	69	33	12	9	5000	2437	10	0
26	12	13	6	70	34	2	6	6000	2925	0	0
27	13	3	3	71	34	12	3	7000	3412	10	0
[28]	13	13	0	72	35	2	0	8000	3900	0	0
29	14	2	9	73	35	11	9	9000	4387	10	0
30	14	12	6	74	36	1	6	10000	4875	0	0
31	15	2	3	75	36	11	3				
32	15	12	0	76	37	1	0				
33	16	1	9	77	37	10	9	Great Hundred			
34	16	11	6	78	38	0	6	112	54	12	0
35	17	1	3	79	38	10	3	*Grofs*			
36	17	11	0	80	39	0	0	144	70	4	0
37	18	0	9	81	39	9	9	*Wey*			
38	18	10	6	82	39	19	6	256	124	16	0
39	19	0	3	83	40	9	3	*Days in a Year*			
40	19	10	0	[84]	40	19	0	365	177	18	9
41	19	19	9	85	41	8	9	*Feet in a Rod*			
42	20	9	6	86	41	18	6	272	132	12	0
43	20	19	3	87	42	8	3				
44	21	9	0	88	42	18	0				

N.	l.	s.	d.	N.	l.	s.	d.	N.	l.	s.	d.
1	0	9	10	45	22	2	6	89	43	15	2
2	0	19	8	46	22	12	4	90	44	5	0
3	1	9	6	47	23	2	2	91	44	14	10
4	1	19	4	48	23	12	0	92	45	4	8
5	2	9	2	49	24	1	10	93	45	14	6
6	2	19	0	50	24	11	8	94	46	4	4
7	3	8	10	51	25	1	6	95	46	14	2
8	3	18	8	52	25	11	4	96	47	4	0
9	4	8	6	53	26	1	2	97	47	13	10
10	4	18	4	54	26	11	0	98	48	3	8
11	5	8	2	55	27	0	10	99	48	13	6
12	5	18	0	[56]	27	10	8	100	49	3	4
13	6	7	10	57	28	0	6	200	98	6	8
14	6	17	8	58	28	10	4	300	147	10	0
15	7	7	6	59	29	0	2	400	196	13	4
16	7	17	4	60	29	10	0	500	245	16	8
17	8	7	2	61	29	19	10	600	295	0	0
18	8	17	0	62	30	9	8	700	344	3	4
19	9	6	10	63	30	19	6	800	393	6	8
20	9	16	8	64	31	9	4	900	442	10	0
21	10	6	6	65	31	19	2	1000	491	13	4
22	10	16	4	66	32	9	0	2000	983	6	8
23	11	6	2	67	32	18	10	3000	1475	0	0
24	11	16	0	68	33	8	8	4000	1966	13	4
25	12	5	10	69	33	18	6	5000	2458	6	8
26	12	15	8	70	34	8	4	6000	2950	0	0
27	13	5	6	71	34	18	2	7000	3441	13	4
[28]	13	15	4	72	35	8	0	8000	3933	6	8
29	14	5	2	73	35	17	10	9000	4425	0	0
30	14	15	0	74	36	7	8	10000	4916	13	4
31	15	4	10	75	36	17	6				
32	15	14	8	76	37	7	4				
33	16	4	6	77	37	17	2	Great Hundred			
34	16	14	4	78	38	7	0	112	55	1	4
35	17	4	2	79	38	16	10	Grofs			
36	17	14	0	80	39	6	8	144	70	16	0
37	18	3	10	81	39	16	6	Wey			
38	18	13	8	82	40	6	4	256	125	17	4
39	19	3	6	83	40	16	2	Days in a Year			
40	19	13	4	[84]	41	6	0	365	179	9	2
41	20	3	2	85	41	15	10	Feet in a Rod			
42	20	13	0	86	42	5	8	272	133	14	8
43	21	2	10	87	42	15	6				
44	21	12	8	88	43	5	4				

N.	l.	s.	d.	N.	l.	s.	d.	N.	l.	s.	d.
1	0	9	11	45	22	6	3	89	44	2	7
2	0	19	10	46	22	16	2	90	44	12	6
3	1	9	9	47	23	6	1	91	45	2	5
4	1	19	8	48	23	16	0	92	45	12	4
5	2	9	7	49	24	5	11	93	46	2	3
6	2	19	6	50	24	15	10	94	46	12	2
7	3	9	5	51	25	5	9	95	47	2	1
8	3	19	4	52	25	15	8	96	47	12	0
9	4	9	3	53	26	5	7	97	48	1	11
10	4	19	2	54	26	15	6	98	48	11	10
11	5	9	1	55	27	5	5	99	49	1	9
12	5	19	0	[56]	27	15	4	100	49	11	8
13	6	8	11	57	28	5	3	200	99	3	4
14	6	18	10	58	28	15	2	300	148	15	0
15	7	8	9	59	29	5	1	400	198	6	8
16	7	18	8	60	29	15	0	500	247	18	4
17	8	8	7	61	30	4	11	600	297	10	0
18	8	18	6	62	30	14	10	700	347	1	8
19	9	8	5	63	31	4	9	800	396	13	4
20	9	18	4	64	31	14	8	900	446	5	0
21	10	8	3	65	32	4	7	1000	495	16	8
22	10	18	2	66	32	14	6	2000	991	13	4
23	11	8	1	67	33	4	5	3000	1487	10	0
24	11	18	0	68	33	14	4	4000	1983	6	8
25	12	7	11	69	34	4	3	5000	2479	3	4
26	12	17	10	70	34	14	2	6000	2975	0	0
27	13	7	9	71	35	4	1	7000	3470	16	8
[28]	13	17	8	72	35	14	0	8000	3966	13	4
29	14	7	7	73	36	3	11	9000	4462	10	0
30	14	17	6	74	36	13	10	10000	4958	6	8
31	15	7	5	75	37	3	9				
32	15	17	4	76	37	13	8				
33	16	7	3	77	38	3	7	*Great Hundred*			
34	16	17	2	78	38	13	6	112	55	10	8
35	17	7	1	79	39	3	5	*Gross*			
36	17	17	0	80	39	13	4	144	71	8	0
37	18	6	11	81	40	3	3	*Wey*			
38	18	16	10	82	40	13	2	256	126	18	8
39	19	6	9	83	41	3	1	*Days in a Year*			
40	19	16	8	[84]	41	13	0	365	180	19	7
41	20	6	7	85	42	2	11	*Feet in a Rod*			
42	20	16	6	86	42	12	10	272	134	17	4
43	21	6	5	87	43	2	9				
44	21	16	4	88	43	12	8				

N.	l.	s.	d.	N.	l.	s.	d.	N.	l.	s.	d.
1	0	10	0	45	22	10	0	89	44	10	0
2	1	0	0	46	23	0	0	90	45	0	0
3	1	10	0	47	23	10	0	91	45	10	0
4	2	0	0	48	24	0	0	92	46	0	0
5	2	10	0	49	24	10	0	93	46	10	0
6	3	0	0	50	25	0	0	94	47	0	0
7	3	10	0	51	25	10	0	95	47	10	0
8	4	0	0	52	26	0	0	96	48	0	0
9	4	10	0	53	26	10	0	97	48	10	0
10	5	0	0	54	27	0	0	98	49	0	0
11	5	10	0	55	27	10	0	99	49	10	0
12	6	0	0	[56]	28	0	0	100	50	0	0
13	6	10	0	57	28	10	0	200	100	0	0
14	7	0	0	58	29	0	0	300	150	0	0
15	7	10	0	59	29	10	0	400	200	0	0
16	8	0	0	60	30	0	0	500	250	0	0
17	8	10	0	61	30	10	0	600	300	0	0
18	9	0	0	62	31	0	0	700	350	0	0
19	9	10	0	63	31	10	0	800	400	0	0
20	10	0	0	64	32	0	0	900	450	0	0
21	10	10	0	65	32	10	0	1000	500	0	0
22	11	0	0	66	33	0	0	2000	1000	0	0
23	11	10	0	67	33	10	0	3000	1500	0	0
24	12	0	0	68	34	0	0	4000	2000	0	0
25	12	10	0	69	34	10	0	5000	2500	0	0
26	13	0	0	70	35	0	0	6000	3000	0	0
27	13	10	0	71	35	10	0	7000	3500	0	0
[28]	14	0	0	72	36	0	0	8000	4000	0	0
29	14	10	0	73	36	10	0	9000	4500	0	0
30	15	0	0	74	37	0	0	10000	5000	0	0
31	15	10	0	75	37	10	0				
32	16	0	0	76	38	0	0				
33	16	10	0	77	38	10	0	Great Hundred			
34	17	0	0	78	39	0	0	112	56	0	0
35	17	10	0	79	39	10	0	Gross			
36	18	0	0	80	40	0	0	144	72	0	0
37	18	10	0	81	40	10	0	Wey			
38	19	0	0	82	41	0	0	256	128	0	0
39	19	10	0	83	41	10	0	Days in a Year			
40	20	0	0	[84]	42	0	0	365	182	10	0
41	20	10	0	85	42	10	0	Feet in a Rod			
42	21	0	0	86	43	0	0	272	136	0	0
43	21	10	0	87	43	10	0				
44	22	0	0	88	44	0	0				

N.	l.	s.	d.	N.	l.	s.	d.	N.	l.	s.	d.
1	0	10	6	45	23	12	6	89	46	14	6
2	1	1	0	46	24	3	0	90	47	5	0
3	1	11	6	47	24	13	6	91	47	15	6
4	2	2	0	48	25	4	0	92	48	6	0
5	2	12	6	49	25	14	6	93	48	16	6
6	3	3	0	50	26	5	0	94	49	7	0
7	3	13	6	51	26	15	6	95	49	17	6
8	4	4	0	52	27	6	0	96	50	8	0
9	4	14	6	53	27	16	6	97	50	18	6
10	5	5	0	54	28	7	0	98	51	9	0
11	5	15	6	55	28	17	6	99	51	19	6
12	6	6	0	[56]	29	8	0	100	52	10	0
13	6	16	6	57	29	18	6	200	105	0	0
14	7	7	0	58	30	9	0	300	157	10	0
15	7	17	6	59	30	19	6	400	210	0	0
16	8	8	0	60	31	10	0	500	262	10	0
17	8	18	6	61	32	0	6	600	315	0	0
18	9	9	0	62	32	11	0	700	367	10	0
19	9	19	6	63	33	1	6	800	420	0	0
20	10	10	0	64	33	12	0	900	472	10	0
21	11	0	6	65	34	2	6	1000	525	0	0
22	11	11	0	66	34	13	0	2000	1050	0	0
23	12	1	6	67	35	3	6	3000	1575	0	0
24	12	12	0	68	35	14	0	4000	2100	0	0
25	13	2	6	69	36	4	6	5000	2625	0	0
26	13	13	0	70	36	15	0	6000	3150	0	0
27	14	3	6	71	37	5	6	7000	3675	0	0
[28]	14	14	0	72	37	16	0	8000	4200	0	0
29	15	4	6	73	38	6	6	9000	4725	0	0
30	15	15	0	74	38	17	0	10000	5250	0	0
31	16	5	6	75	39	7	6				
32	16	16	0	76	39	18	0				
33	17	6	6	77	40	8	6				
34	17	17	0	78	40	19	0				
35	18	7	6	79	41	9	6				
36	18	18	0	80	42	0	0				
37	19	8	6	81	42	10	6				
38	19	19	0	82	43	1	0				
39	20	9	6	83	43	11	6				
40	21	0	0	[84]	44	2	0				
41	21	10	6	85	44	12	6				
42	22	1	0	86	45	3	0				
43	22	11	6	87	45	13	6				
44	23	2	0	88	46	4	0				

Great Hundred

112 | 58 16 0

Grofs

144 | 75 12 0

Wey

256 | 134 8 0

Days in a Year.

365 | 191 12 6

Feet in a Rod

272 | 142 16 0

T

N.	l.	s.	d.	N.	l.	s.	d.	N.	l.	s.	d.
1	0	11	0	45	24	15	0	89	48	19	0
2	1	2	0	46	25	6	0	90	49	10	0
3	1	13	0	47	25	17	0	91	50	1	0
4	2	4	0	48	26	8	0	92	50	12	0
5	2	15	0	49	26	19	0	93	51	3	0
6	3	6	0	50	27	10	0	94	51	14	0
7	3	17	0	51	28	1	0	95	52	5	0
8	4	8	0	52	28	12	0	96	52	16	0
9	4	19	0	53	29	3	0	97	53	7	0
10	5	10	0	54	29	14	0	98	53	18	0
11	6	1	0	55	30	5	0	99	54	9	0
12	6	12	0	[56]	30	16	0	100	55	0	0
13	7	3	0	57	31	7	0	200	110	0	0
14	7	14	0	58	31	18	0	300	165	0	0
15	8	5	0	59	32	9	0	400	220	0	0
16	8	16	0	60	33	0	0	500	275	0	0
17	9	7	0	61	33	11	0	600	330	0	0
18	9	18	0	62	34	2	0	700	385	0	0
19	10	9	0	63	34	13	0	800	440	0	0
20	11	0	0	64	35	4	0	900	495	0	0
21	11	11	0	65	35	15	0	1000	550	0	0
22	12	2	0	66	36	6	0	2000	1100	0	0
23	12	13	0	67	36	17	0	3000	1650	0	0
24	13	4	0	68	37	8	0	4000	2200	0	0
25	13	15	0	69	37	19	0	5000	2750	0	0
26	14	6	0	70	38	10	0	6000	3300	0	0
27	14	17	0	71	39	1	0	7000	3850	0	0
[28]	15	8	0	72	39	12	0	8000	4400	0	0
29	15	19	0	73	40	3	0	9000	4950	0	0
30	16	10	0	74	40	14	0	10000	5500	0	0
31	17	1	0	75	41	5	0				
32	17	12	0	76	41	16	0				
33	18	3	0	77	42	7	0		*Great Hundred*		
34	18	14	0	78	42	18	0	112	61	12	0
35	19	5	0	79	43	9	0		*Grofs*		
36	19	16	0	80	44	0	0	144	79	4	0
37	20	7	0	81	44	11	0		*Wey*		
38	20	18	0	82	45	2	0	256	140	16	0
39	21	9	0	83	45	13	0		*Days in a Year*		
40	22	0	0	[84]	46	4	0	365	200	15	0
41	22	11	0	85	46	15	0		*Feet in a Rod*		
42	23	2	0	86	47	6	0	272	149	12	0
43	23	13	0	87	47	17	0				
44	24	4	0	88	48	8	0				

N.	l.	s.	d.
1	0	11	6
2	1	3	0
3	1	14	6
4	2	6	0
5	2	17	6
6	3	9	0
7	4	0	6
8	4	12	0
9	5	3	6
10	5	15	0
11	6	6	6
12	6	18	0
13	7	9	6
14	8	1	0
15	8	12	6
16	9	4	0
17	9	15	6
18	10	7	0
19	10	18	6
20	11	10	0
21	12	1	6
22	12	13	0
23	13	4	6
24	13	16	0
25	14	7	6
26	14	19	0
27	15	10	6
[28]	16	2	0
29	16	13	6
30	17	5	0
31	17	16	6
32	18	8	0
33	18	19	6
34	19	11	0
35	20	2	6
36	20	14	0
37	21	5	6
38	21	17	0
39	22	8	6
40	23	0	0
41	23	11	6
42	24	3	0
43	24	14	6
44	25	6	0

N.	l.	s.	d.
45	25	17	6
46	26	9	0
47	27	0	6
48	27	12	0
49	28	3	6
50	28	15	0
51	29	6	6
52	29	18	0
53	30	9	6
54	31	1	0
55	31	12	6
[56]	32	4	0
57	32	15	6
58	33	7	0
59	33	18	6
60	34	10	0
61	35	1	6
62	35	13	0
63	36	4	6
64	36	16	0
65	37	7	6
66	37	19	0
67	38	10	6
68	39	2	0
69	39	13	6
70	40	5	0
71	40	16	6
72	41	8	0
73	41	19	6
74	42	11	0
75	43	2	6
76	43	14	0
77	44	5	6
78	44	17	0
79	45	8	6
80	46	0	0
81	46	11	6
82	47	3	0
83	47	14	6
[84]	48	6	0
85	48	17	6
86	49	9	0
87	50	0	6
88	50	12	0

N.	l.	s.	d.
89	51	3	6
90	51	15	0
91	52	6	6
92	52	18	0
93	53	9	6
94	54	1	0
95	54	12	6
96	55	4	0
97	55	15	6
98	56	7	0
99	56	18	6
100	57	10	0
200	115	0	0
300	172	10	0
400	230	0	0
500	287	10	0
600	345	0	0
700	402	10	0
800	460	0	0
900	517	10	0
1000	575	0	0
2000	1150	0	0
3000	1725	0	0
4000	2300	0	0
5000	2875	0	0
6000	3450	0	0
7000	4025	0	0
8000	4600	0	0
9000	5175	0	0
10000	5750	0	0

Great Hundred

112 | 64 8 0

Grofs

144 | 82 16 0

Wey

256 | 147 4 0

Days in a Year

365 | 209 17 6

Feet in a Rod

272 | 156 8 0

N.	l.	s.	d.	N.	l.	s.	d.	N	l.	s.	d.
1	0	12	0	45	27	0	0	89	53	8	0
2	1	4	0	46	27	12	0	90	54	0	0
3	1	16	0	47	28	4	0	91	54	12	0
4	2	8	0	48	28	16	0	92	55	4	0
5	3	0	0	49	29	8	0	93	55	16	0
6	3	12	0	50	30	0	0	94	56	8	0
7	4	4	0	51	30	12	0	95	57	0	0
8	4	16	0	52	31	4	0	96	57	12	0
9	5	8	0	53	31	16	0	97	58	4	0
10	6	0	0	54	32	8	0	98	58	16	0
11	6	12	0	55	33	0	0	99	59	8	0
12	7	4	0	[56]	33	12	0	100	60	0	0
13	7	16	0	57	34	4	0	200	120	0	0
14	8	8	0	58	34	16	0	300	180	0	0
15	9	0	0	59	35	8	0	400	240	0	0
16	9	12	0	60	36	0	0	500	300	0	0
17	10	4	0	61	36	12	0	600	360	0	0
18	10	16	0	62	37	4	0	700	420	0	0
19	11	8	0	63	37	16	0	800	480	0	0
20	12	0	0	64	38	8	0	900	540	0	0
21	12	12	0	65	39	0	0	1000	600	0	0
22	13	4	0	66	39	12	0	2000	1200	0	0
23	13	16	0	67	40	4	0	3000	1800	0	0
24	14	8	0	68	40	16	0	4000	2400	0	0
25	15	0	0	69	41	8	0	5000	3000	0	0
26	15	12	0	70	42	0	0	6000	3600	0	0
27	16	4	0	71	42	12	0	7000	4200	0	0
[28]	16	16	0	72	43	4	0	8000	4800	0	0
29	17	8	0	73	43	16	0	9000	5400	0	0
30	18	0	0	74	44	8	0	10000	6000	0	0
31	18	12	0	75	45	0	0				
32	19	4	0	76	45	12	0				
33	19	16	0	77	46	4	0	*Great Hundred*			
34	20	8	0	78	46	16	0	112	57	4	0
35	21	0	0	79	47	8	0	*Grofs*			
36	21	12	0	80	48	0	0	144	86	8	0
37	22	4	0	81	48	12	0	*Wey*			
38	22	16	0	82	49	4	0	256	153	12	0
39	23	8	0	83	49	16	0	*Days in a Year*			
40	24	0	0	[84]	50	8	0	365	219	0	0
41	24	12	0	85	51	0	0	*Feet in a Rod*			
42	25	4	0	86	51	12	0	272	163	4	0
43	25	16	0	87	52	4	0				
44	26	8	0	88	52	16	0				

N.	l.	s.	d.	N.	l.	s.	d.	N.	l.	s.	d.
1	0	12	6	45	28	2	6	89	55	12	6
2	1	5	0	46	28	15	0	90	56	5	0
3	1	17	6	47	29	7	6	91	56	17	6
4	2	10	0	48	30	0	0	92	57	10	0
5	3	2	6	49	30	12	6	93	58	2	6
6	3	15	0	50	31	5	0	94	58	15	0
7	4	7	6	51	31	17	6	95	59	7	6
8	5	0	0	52	32	10	0	96	60	0	0
9	5	12	6	53	33	2	6	97	60	12	6
10	6	5	0	54	33	15	0	98	61	5	0
11	6	17	6	55	34	7	6	99	61	17	6
12	7	10	0	[56]	35	0	0	100	62	10	0
13	8	2	6	57	35	12	6	200	125	0	0
14	8	15	0	58	36	5	0	300	187	10	0
15	9	7	6	59	36	17	6	400	250	0	0
16	10	0	0	60	37	10	0	500	312	10	0
17	10	12	6	61	38	2	6	600	375	0	0
18	11	5	0	62	38	15	0	700	437	10	0
19	11	17	6	63	39	7	6	800	500	0	0
20	12	10	0	64	40	0	0	900	562	10	0
21	13	2	6	65	40	12	6	1000	625	0	0
22	13	15	0	66	41	5	0	2000	1250	0	0
23	14	7	6	67	41	17	6	3000	1875	0	0
24	15	0	0	68	42	10	0	4000	2500	0	0
25	15	12	6	69	43	2	6	5000	3125	0	0
26	16	5	0	70	43	15	0	6000	3750	0	0
27	16	17	6	71	44	7	6	7000	4375	0	0
[28]	17	10	0	72	45	0	0	8000	5000	0	0
29	18	2	6	73	45	12	6	9000	5625	0	0
30	18	15	0	74	46	5	0	10000	6250	0	0
31	19	7	6	75	46	17	6				
32	20	0	0	76	47	10	0				
33	20	12	6	77	48	2	6				
34	21	5	0	78	48	15	0				
35	21	17	6	79	49	7	6				
36	22	10	0	80	50	0	0				
37	23	2	6	81	50	12	6				
38	23	15	0	82	51	5	0				
39	24	7	6	83	51	17	6				
40	25	0	0	[84]	52	10	0				
41	25	12	6	85	53	2	6				
42	26	5	0	86	53	15	0				
43	26	17	6	87	54	7	6				
44	27	10	0	88	55	0	0				

Great Hundred

112	70	0	0

Grofs

144	90	0	0

Wey

256	160	0	0

Days in a Year

365	228	2	6

Feet in a Rod

272	170	0	0

T 3

N.	l.	s.	d.	N.	l.	s.	d.	N.	l.	s.	d.
1	0	13	0	45	29	5	0	89	57	17	0
2	1	6	0	46	29	18	0	90	58	10	0
3	1	19	0	47	30	11	0	91	59	3	0
4	2	12	0	48	31	4	0	92	59	16	0
5	3	5	0	49	31	17	0	93	60	9	0
6	3	18	0	50	32	10	0	94	61	2	0
7	4	11	0	51	33	3	0	95	61	15	0
8	5	4	0	52	33	16	0	96	62	8	0
9	5	17	0	53	34	9	0	97	63	1	0
10	6	10	0	54	35	2	0	98	63	14	0
11	7	3	0	55	35	15	0	99	64	7	0
12	7	16	0	[56]	36	8	0	100	65	0	0
13	8	9	0	57	37	1	0	200	130	0	0
14	9	2	0	58	37	14	0	300	195	0	0
15	9	15	0	59	38	7	0	400	260	0	0
16	10	8	0	60	39	0	0	500	325	0	0
17	11	1	0	61	39	13	0	600	390	0	0
18	11	14	0	62	40	6	0	700	455	0	0
19	12	7	0	63	40	19	0	800	520	0	0
20	13	0	0	64	41	12	0	900	585	0	0
21	13	13	0	65	42	5	0	1000	650	0	0
22	14	6	0	66	42	18	0	2000	1300	0	0
23	14	19	0	67	43	11	0	3000	1950	0	0
24	15	12	0	68	44	4	0	4000	2600	0	0
25	16	5	0	69	44	17	0	5000	3250	0	0
26	16	18	0	70	45	10	0	6000	3900	0	0
27	17	11	0	71	46	3	0	7000	4550	0	0
[28]	18	4	0	72	46	16	0	8000	5200	0	0
29	18	17	0	73	47	9	0	9000	5850	0	0
30	19	10	0	74	48	2	0	10000	6500	0	0
31	20	3	0	75	48	15	0				
32	20	16	0	76	49	8	0				
33	21	9	0	77	50	1	0		*Great Hundred*		
34	22	2	0	78	50	14	0	112	72	16	0
35	22	15	0	79	51	7	0		*Gross*		
36	23	8	0	80	52	0	0	144	93	12	0
37	24	1	0	81	52	13	0		*Wey*		
38	24	14	0	82	53	6	0	256	166	8	0
39	25	7	0	83	53	19	0		*Days in a Year*		
40	26	0	0	[84]	54	12	0	365	237	5	0
41	26	13	0	85	55	5	0		*Feet in a Rod*		
42	27	6	0	86	55	18	0	272	176	16	0
43	27	19	0	87	56	11	0				
44	28	12	0	88	57	4	0				

N.	l.	s.	d.
1	0	13	6
2	1	7	0
3	2	0	6
4	2	14	0
5	3	7	6
6	4	1	0
7	4	14	6
8	5	8	0
9	6	1	6
10	6	15	0
11	7	8	6
12	8	2	0
13	8	15	6
14	9	9	0
15	10	2	6
16	10	16	0
17	11	9	6
18	12	3	0
19	12	16	6
20	13	10	0
21	14	3	6
22	14	17	0
23	15	10	6
24	16	4	0
25	16	17	6
26	17	11	0
27	18	4	6
[28]	18	18	0
29	19	11	6
30	20	5	0
31	20	18	6
32	21	12	0
33	22	5	6
34	22	19	0
35	23	12	6
36	24	6	0
37	24	19	6
38	25	13	0
39	26	6	6
40	27	0	0
41	27	13	6
42	28	7	0
43	29	0	6
44	29	14	0

N.	l.	s.	d.
45	30	7	6
46	31	1	0
47	31	14	6
48	32	8	0
49	33	1	6
50	33	15	0
51	34	8	6
52	35	2	0
53	35	15	6
54	36	9	0
55	37	2	6
[56]	37	16	0
57	38	9	6
58	39	3	0
59	39	16	6
60	40	10	0
61	41	3	6
62	41	17	0
63	42	10	6
64	43	4	0
65	43	17	6
66	44	11	0
67	45	4	6
68	45	18	0
69	46	11	6
70	47	5	0
71	47	18	6
72	48	12	0
73	49	5	6
74	49	19	0
75	50	12	6
76	51	6	0
77	51	19	6
78	52	13	0
79	53	6	6
80	54	0	0
81	54	13	6
82	55	7	0
83	56	0	6
[84]	56	14	0
85	57	7	6
86	58	1	0
87	58	14	6
88	59	8	0

N.	l.	s.	d.
89	60	1	6
90	60	15	0
91	61	8	6
92	62	2	0
93	62	15	6
94	63	9	0
95	64	2	6
96	64	16	0
97	65	9	6
98	66	3	0
99	66	16	6
100	67	10	0
200	135	0	0
300	202	10	0
400	270	0	0
500	337	10	0
600	405	0	0
700	472	10	0
800	540	0	0
900	607	10	0
1000	675	0	0
2000	1350	0	0
3000	2025	0	0
4000	2700	0	0
5000	3375	0	0
6000	4050	0	0
7000	4725	0	0
8000	5400	0	0
9000	6075	0	0
10000	6750	0	0

Great Hundred

112 | 75 12 0

Grofs

144 | 97 4 0

Wey

256 | 172 16 0

Days in a Year

365 | 246 7 6

Feet in a Rod

272 | 183 12 0

N.	l.	s.	d.	N.	l.	s.	d.	N.	l.	s.	d.
1	0	14	0	45	31	10	0	89	62	6	0
2	1	8	0	46	32	4	0	90	63	0	0
3	2	2	0	47	32	18	0	91	63	14	0
4	2	16	0	48	33	12	0	92	64	8	0
5	3	10	0	49	34	6	0	93	65	2	0
6	4	4	0	50	35	0	0	94	65	16	0
7	4	18	0	51	35	14	0	95	66	10	0
8	5	12	0	52	36	8	0	96	67	4	0
9	6	6	0	53	37	2	0	97	67	18	0
10	7	0	0	54	37	16	0	98	68	12	0
11	7	14	0	55	38	10	0	99	69	6	0
12	8	8	0	[56]	39	4	0	100	70	0	0
13	9	2	0	57	39	18	0	200	140	0	0
14	9	16	0	58	40	12	0	300	210	0	0
15	10	10	0	59	41	6	0	400	280	0	0
16	11	4	0	60	42	0	0	500	350	0	0
17	11	18	0	61	42	14	0	600	420	0	0
18	12	12	0	62	43	8	0	700	490	0	0
19	13	6	0	63	44	2	0	800	560	0	0
20	14	0	0	64	44	16	0	900	630	0	0
21	14	14	0	65	45	10	0	1000	700	0	0
22	15	8	0	66	46	4	0	2000	1400	0	0
23	16	2	0	67	46	18	0	3000	2100	0	0
24	16	16	0	68	47	12	0	4000	2800	0	0
25	17	10	0	69	48	6	0	5000	3500	0	0
26	18	4	0	70	49	0	0	6000	4200	0	0
27	18	18	0	71	49	14	0	7000	4900	0	0
[28]	19	12	0	72	50	8	0	8000	5600	0	0
29	20	6	0	73	51	2	0	9000	6300	0	0
30	21	0	0	74	51	16	0	10000	7000	0	0
31	21	14	0	75	52	10	0				
32	22	8	0	76	53	4	0				
33	23	2	0	77	53	18	0				
34	23	16	0	78	54	12	0				
35	24	10	0	79	55	6	0				
36	25	4	0	80	56	0	0				
37	25	18	0	81	56	14	0				
38	26	12	0	82	57	8	0				
39	27	6	0	83	58	2	0				
40	28	0	0	[84]	58	16	0				
41	28	14	0	85	59	10	0				
42	29	8	0	86	60	4	0				
43	30	2	0	87	60	18	0				
44	30	16	0	88	61	12	0				

Great Hundred

112	78	8	0

Gross

144	100	16	0

Wey

256	179	4	0

Days in a Year

365	255	10	0

Feet in a Rod

272	190	8	0

N.	l.	s.	d.	N.	l.	s.	d.	N.	l.	s.	d.
1	0	14	6	45	32	12	6	89	64	10	6
2	1	9	0	46	33	7	0	90	65	5	0
3	2	3	6	47	34	1	6	91	65	19	6
4	2	18	0	48	34	16	0	92	66	14	0
5	3	12	6	49	35	10	6	93	67	8	6
6	4	7	0	50	36	5	0	94	68	3	0
7	5	1	6	51	36	19	6	95	68	17	6
8	5	16	0	52	37	14	0	96	69	12	0
9	6	10	6	53	38	8	6	97	70	6	6
10	7	5	0	54	39	3	0	98	71	1	0
11	7	19	6	55	39	17	6	99	71	15	6
12	8	14	0	[56]	40	12	0	100	72	10	0
13	9	8	6	57	41	6	6	200	145	0	0
14	10	3	0	58	42	1	0	300	217	10	0
15	10	17	6	59	42	15	6	400	290	0	0
16	11	12	0	60	43	10	0	500	362	10	0
17	12	6	6	61	44	4	6	600	435	0	0
18	13	1	0	62	44	19	0	700	507	10	0
19	13	15	6	63	45	13	6	800	580	0	0
20	14	10	0	64	46	8	0	900	652	10	0
21	15	4	6	65	47	2	6	1000	725	0	0
22	15	19	0	66	47	17	0	2000	1450	0	0
23	16	13	6	67	48	11	6	3000	2175	0	0
24	17	8	0	68	49	6	0	4000	2900	0	0
25	18	2	6	69	50	0	6	5000	3625	0	0
26	18	17	0	70	50	15	0	6000	4350	0	0
27	19	11	6	71	51	9	6	7000	5075	0	0
[28]	20	6	0	72	52	4	0	8000	5800	0	0
29	21	0	6	73	52	18	6	9000	6525	0	0
30	21	15	0	74	53	13	0	10000	7250	0	0
31	22	9	6	75	54	7	6				
32	23	4	0	76	55	2	0				
33	23	18	6	77	55	16	6	*Great Hundred*			
34	24	13	0	78	56	11	0	112	81	4	0
35	25	7	6	79	57	5	6	*Grofs*			
36	26	2	0	80	58	0	0	144	104	8	0
37	26	16	6	81	58	14	6	*Wey*			
38	27	11	0	82	59	9	0	256	185	12	0
39	28	5	6	83	60	3	6	*Days in a Year*			
40	29	0	0	[84]	60	18	0	365	264	12	6
41	29	14	6	85	61	12	6	*Feet in a Rod*			
42	30	9	0	86	62	7	0	272	197	4	0
43	31	3	6	87	63	1	6				
44	31	18	0	88	63	16	0				

N.	l.	s.	d.	N.	l.	s.	d.	N.	l.	s.	d.
1	0	15	0	45	33	15	0	89	66	15	0
2	1	10	0	46	34	10	0	90	67	10	0
3	2	5	0	47	35	5	0	91	68	5	0
4	3	0	0	48	30	0	0	92	69	0	0
5	3	15	0	49	36	15	0	93	69	15	0
6	4	10	0	50	37	10	0	94	70	10	0
7	5	5	0	51	38	5	0	95	71	5	0
8	6	0	0	52	39	0	0	96	72	0	0
9	6	15	0	53	39	15	0	97	72	15	0
10	7	10	0	54	40	10	0	98	73	10	0
11	8	5	0	55	41	5	0	99	74	5	0
12	9	0	0	[56]	42	0	0	100	75	0	0
13	9	15	0	57	42	15	0	200	150	0	0
14	10	10	0	58	43	10	0	300	225	0	0
15	11	5	0	59	44	5	0	400	300	0	0
16	12	0	0	60	45	0	0	500	375	0	0
17	12	15	0	61	45	15	0	600	450	0	0
18	13	10	0	62	46	10	0	700	525	0	0
19	14	5	0	63	47	5	0	800	600	0	0
20	15	0	0	64	48	0	0	900	675	0	0
21	15	15	0	65	48	15	0	1000	750	0	0
22	16	10	0	66	49	10	0	2000	1500	0	0
23	17	5	0	67	50	5	0	3000	2250	0	0
24	18	0	0	68	51	0	0	4000	3000	0	0
25	18	15	0	69	51	15	0	5000	3750	0	0
26	19	10	0	70	52	10	0	6000	4500	0	0
27	20	5	0	71	53	5	0	7000	5250	0	0
[28]	21	0	0	72	54	0	0	8000	6000	0	0
29	21	15	0	73	54	15	0	9000	6750	0	0
30	22	10	0	74	55	10	0	10000	7500	0	0
31	23	5	0	75	56	5	0				
32	24	0	0	76	57	0	0				
33	24	15	0	77	57	15	0	*Great Hundred*			
34	25	10	0	78	58	10	0	112	84	0	0
35	26	5	0	79	59	5	0	*Grofs*			
36	27	0	0	80	60	0	0	144	108	0	0
37	27	15	0	81	60	15	0	*Wey*			
38	28	10	0	82	61	10	0	256	192	0	0
39	29	5	0	83	62	5	0	*Days in a Year*			
40	30	0	0	[84]	63	0	0	365	273	15	0
41	30	15	0	85	63	15	0	*Feet in a Rod*			
42	31	10	0	86	64	10	0	272	204	0	0
43	32	5	0	87	65	5	0				
44	33	0	0	88	66	0	0				

N.	l.	s.	d.
1	0	15	6
2	1	11	0
3	2	6	6
4	3	2	0
5	3	17	6
6	4	13	0
7	5	8	6
8	6	4	0
9	6	19	6
10	7	15	0
11	8	10	6
12	9	6	0
13	10	1	6
14	10	17	0
15	11	12	6
16	12	8	0
17	13	3	6
18	13	19	0
19	14	14	6
20	15	10	0
21	16	5	6
22	17	1	0
23	17	16	6
24	18	12	0
25	19	7	6
26	20	3	0
27	20	18	6
[28]	21	14	0
29	22	9	6
30	23	5	0
31	24	0	6
32	24	16	0
33	25	11	6
34	26	7	0
35	27	2	6
36	27	18	0
37	28	13	6
38	29	9	0
39	30	4	6
40	31	0	0
41	31	15	6
42	32	11	0
43	33	6	6
44	34	2	0

N.	l.	s.	d.
45	34	17	6
46	35	13	0
47	36	8	6
48	37	4	0
49	37	19	6
50	38	15	0
51	39	10	6
52	40	6	0
53	41	1	6
54	41	17	0
55	42	12	6
[56]	43	8	0
57	44	3	6
58	44	19	0
59	45	14	6
60	46	10	0
61	47	5	6
62	48	1	0
63	48	16	6
64	49	12	0
65	50	7	6
66	51	3	0
67	51	18	6
68	52	14	0
69	53	9	6
70	54	5	0
71	55	0	6
72	55	16	0
73	56	11	6
74	57	7	0
75	58	2	6
76	58	18	0
77	59	13	6
78	60	9	0
79	61	4	6
80	62	0	0
81	62	15	6
82	63	11	0
83	64	6	6
[84]	65	2	0
85	65	17	6
86	66	13	0
87	67	8	6
88	68	4	0

N.	l.	s.	d.
89	68	19	6
90	69	15	0
91	70	10	6
92	71	6	0
93	72	1	6
94	72	17	0
95	73	12	6
96	74	8	0
97	75	3	6
98	75	19	0
99	76	14	6
100	77	10	0
200	155	0	0
300	232	10	0
400	310	0	0
500	387	10	0
600	465	0	0
700	542	10	0
800	620	0	0
900	697	10	0
1000	775	0	0
2000	1550	0	0
3000	2325	0	0
4000	3100	0	0
5000	3875	0	0
6000	4650	0	0
7000	5425	0	0
8000	6200	0	0
9000	6975	0	0
10000	7750	0	0

Great Hundred

112	86	16	0

Gross

144	111	12	0

Wey

256	198	8	0

Days in a Year

365	282	17	6

Feet in a Rod

272	210	16	0

N.	l.	s.	d.	N.	l.	s.	d.	N.	l.	s.	d.
1	0	16	0	45	36	0	0	89	71	4	0
2	1	12	0	46	36	16	0	90	72	0	0
3	2	8	0	47	37	12	0	91	72	16	0
4	3	4	0	48	38	8	0	92	73	12	0
5	4	0	0	49	39	4	0	93	74	8	0
6	4	16	0	50	40	0	0	94	75	4	0
7	5	12	0	51	40	16	0	95	76	0	0
8	6	8	0	52	41	12	0	96	76	16	0
9	7	4	0	53	42	8	0	97	77	12	0
10	8	0	0	54	43	4	0	98	78	8	0
11	8	16	0	55	44	0	0	99	79	4	0
12	9	12	0	[56]	44	16	0	100	80	0	0
13	10	8	0	57	45	12	0	200	160	0	0
14	11	4	0	58	46	8	0	300	240	0	0
15	12	0	0	59	47	4	0	400	320	0	0
16	12	16	0	60	48	0	0	500	400	0	0
17	13	12	0	61	48	16	0	600	480	0	0
18	14	8	0	62	49	12	0	700	560	0	0
19	15	4	0	63	50	8	0	800	640	0	0
20	16	0	0	64	51	4	0	900	720	0	0
21	16	16	0	65	52	0	0	1000	800	0	0
22	17	12	0	66	52	16	0	2000	1600	0	0
23	18	8	0	67	53	12	0	3000	2400	0	0
24	19	4	0	68	54	8	0	4000	3200	0	0
25	20	0	0	69	55	4	0	5000	4000	0	0
26	20	16	0	70	56	0	0	6000	4800	0	0
27	21	12	0	71	56	16	0	7000	5600	0	0
[28]	22	8	0	72	57	12	0	8000	6400	0	0
29	23	4	0	73	58	8	0	9000	7200	0	0
30	24	0	0	74	59	4	0	10000	8000	0	0
31	24	16	0	75	60	0	0				
32	25	12	0	76	60	16	0				
33	26	8	0	77	61	12	0	Great Hundred			
34	27	4	0	78	62	8	0	112	89	12	0
35	28	0	0	79	63	4	0	Gross			
36	28	16	0	80	64	0	0	144	115	4	0
37	29	12	0	81	64	16	0	Wey			
38	30	8	0	82	65	12	0	256	204	16	0
39	31	4	0	83	66	8	0	Days in a Year			
40	32	0	0	[84]	67	4	0	365	292	0	0
41	32	16	0	85	68	0	0	Feet in a Rod			
42	33	12	0	86	68	16	0	272	217	17	0
43	34	8	0	87	69	12	0				
44	35	4	0	88	70	8	0				

N.	l.	s.	d.	N.	l.	s.	d.	N.	l.	s.	d.
1	0	16	6	45	37	2	6	89	73	8	6
2	1	13	0	46	37	19	0	90	74	5	0
3	2	9	6	47	38	15	6	91	75	1	6
4	3	6	0	48	39	12	0	92	75	18	0
5	4	2	6	49	40	8	6	93	76	14	6
6	4	19	0	50	41	5	0	94	77	11	0
7	5	15	6	51	42	1	6	95	78	7	6
8	6	12	0	52	42	18	0	96	79	4	0
9	7	8	6	53	43	14	6	97	80	0	6
10	8	5	0	54	44	11	0	98	80	17	0
11	9	1	6	55	45	7	6	99	81	13	6
12	9	18	0	[56]	46	4	0	100	82	10	0
13	10	14	6	57	47	0	6	200	165	0	0
14	11	11	0	58	47	17	0	300	247	10	0
15	12	7	6	59	48	13	6	400	330	0	0
16	13	4	0	60	49	10	0	500	412	10	0
17	14	0	6.	61	50	6	6	600	495	0	0
18	14	17	0	62	51	3	0	700	577	10	0
19	15	13	6	63	51	19	6	800	660	0	0
20	16	10	0	64	52	16	0	900	742	10	0
21	17	6	6	65	53	12	6	1000	825	0	0
22	18	3	0	66	54	9	0	2000	1650	0	0
23	18	19	6	67	55	5	6	3000	2475	0	0
24	19	16	0	68	56	2	0	4000	3300	0	0
25	20	12	6	69	56	18	6	5000	4125	0	0
26	21	9	0	70	57	15	0	6000	4950	0	0
27	22	5	6	71	58	11	6	7000	5775	0	0
[28]	23	2	0	72	59	8	0	8000	6600	0	0
29	23	18	6	73	60	4	6	9000	7425	0	0
30	24	15	0	74	61	1	0	10000	8250	0	0
31	25	11	6	75	61	17	6				
32	26	8	0	76	62	14	0				
33	27	4	6	77	63	10	6				
34	28	1	0	78	64	7	0				
35	28	17	6	79	65	3	6				
36	29	14	0	80	66	0	0				
37	30	10	6	81	66	16	6				
38	31	7	0	82	67	13	0				
39	32	3	6	83	68	9	6				
40	33	0	0	[84]	69	6	0				
41	33	16	6	85	70	2	6				
42	34	13	0	86	70	19	0				
43	35	9	6	87	71	15	6				
44	36	6	0	88	72	12	0				

Great Hundred

112 | 92 8 0

Gross

144 | 118 16 0

Wey

256 | 211 4 0

Days in a Year

365 | 301 2 6

Feet in a Rod

272 | 224 8 0

U

N.	l.	s.	d.	N.	l.	s.	d.	N.	l.	s.	d
1	0	17	0	45	38	5	0	89	75	13	0
2	1	14	0	46	39	2	0	90	76	10	0
3	2	11	0	47	39	19	0	91	77	7	0
4	3	8	0	48	40	16	0	92	78	4	0
5	4	5	0	49	41	13	0	93	79	1	0
6	5	2	0	50	42	10	0	94	79	18	0
7	5	19	0	51	43	7	0	95	80	15	0
8	6	16	0	52	44	4	0	96	81	12	0
9	7	13	0	53	45	1	0	97	82	9	0
10	8	10	0	54	45	18	0	98	83	6	0
11	9	7	0	55	46	15	0	99	84	3	0
12	10	4	0	[56]	47	12	0	100	85	0	0
13	11	1	0	57	48	9	0	200	170	0	0
14	11	18	0	58	49	6	0	300	255	0	0
15	12	15	0	59	50	3	0	400	340	0	0
16	13	12	0	60	51	0	0	500	425	0	0
17	14	9	0	61	51	17	0	600	510	0	0
18	15	6	0	62	52	14	0	700	595	0	0
19	16	3	0	63	53	11	0	800	680	0	0
20	17	0	0	64	54	8	0	900	765	0	0
21	17	17	0	65	55	5	0	1000	850	0	0
22	18	14	0	66	56	2	0	2000	1700	0	0
23	19	11	0	67	56	19	0	3000	2550	0	0
24	20	8	0	68	57	16	0	4000	3400	0	0
25	21	5	0	69	58	13	0	5000	4250	0	0
26	22	2	0	70	59	10	0	6000	5100	0	0
27	22	19	0	71	60	7	0	7000	5950	0	0
[28]	23	16	0	72	61	4	0	8000	6800	0	0
29	24	13	0	73	62	1	0	9000	7650	0	0
30	25	10	0	74	62	18	0	10000	8500	0	0
31	26	7	0	75	63	15	0				
32	27	4	0	76	64	12	0				
33	28	1	0	77	65	9	0		Great Hundred		
34	28	18	0	78	66	6	0	112	95	4	0
35	29	15	0	79	67	3	0		Gross		
36	30	12	0	80	68	0	0	144	122	8	0
37	31	9	0	81	68	17	0		Wey		
38	32	6	0	82	69	14	0	256	217	12	0
39	33	3	0	83	70	11	0		Days in a Year		
40	34	0	0	[84]	71	8	0	365	310	5	0
41	34	17	0	85	72	5	0		Feet in a Rod		
42	35	14	0	86	73	2	0	272	231	4	0
43	36	11	0	87	73	19	0				
44	37	8	0	88	74	16	0				

N.	l.	s.	d.	N.	l.	s.	d.	N.	l.	s.	d.
1	0	17	6	45	39	7	6	89	77	17	6
2	1	15	0	46	40	5	0	90	78	15	0
3	2	12	6	47	41	2	6	91	79	12	6
4	3	10	0	48	42	0	0	92	80	10	0
5	4	7	6	49	42	17	6	93	81	7	6
6	5	5	0	50	43	15	0	94	82	5	0
7	6	2	6	51	44	12	6	95	83	2	6
8	7	0	0	52	45	10	0	96	84	0	0
9	7	17	6	53	46	7	6	97	84	17	6
10	8	15	0	54	47	5	0	98	85	15	0
11	9	12	6	55	48	2	6	99	86	12	6
12	10	10	0	[56]	49	0	0	100	87	10	0
13	11	7	6	57	49	17	6	200	175	0	0
14	12	5	0	58	50	15	0	300	262	10	0
15	13	2	6	59	51	12	6	400	350	0	0
16	14	0	0	60	52	10	0	500	437	10	0
17	14	17	6	61	53	7	6	600	525	0	0
18	15	15	0	62	54	5	0	700	612	10	0
19	16	12	6	63	55	2	6	800	700	0	0
20	17	10	0	64	56	0	0	900	787	10	0
21	18	7	6	65	56	17	6	1000	875	0	0
22	19	5	0	66	57	15	0	2000	1750	0	0
23	20	2	6	67	58	12	6	3000	2625	0	0
24	21	0	0	68	59	10	0	4000	3500	0	0
25	21	17	6	69	60	7	6	5000	4375	0	0
26	22	15	0	70	61	5	0	6000	5250	0	0
27	23	12	6	71	62	2	6	7000	6125	0	0
[28]	24	10	0	72	63	0	0	8000	7000	0	0
29	25	7	6	73	63	17	6	9000	7875	0	0
30	26	5	0	74	64	15	0	10000	8750	0	0
31	27	2	6	75	65	12	6				
32	28	0	0	76	66	10	0				
33	28	17	6	77	67	7	6	Great Hundred			
34	29	15	0	78	68	5	0	112 | 98	0	0	
35	30	12	6	79	69	2	6	*Grofs*			
36	31	10	0	80	70	0	0	144 | 126	0	0	
37	32	7	6	81	70	17	6	*Wey*			
38	33	5	0	82	71	15	0	256 | 224	0	0	
39	34	2	6	83	72	12	6	*Days in a Year*			
40	35	0	0	[84]	73	10	0	365 | 319	7	6	
41	35	17	6	85	74	7	6	*Feet in a Rod*			
42	36	15	0	86	75	5	0	272 | 238	0	0	
43	37	12	6	87	76	2	6				
44	38	10	0	88	77	0	0				

N.	l.	s.	d.
1	0	18	0
2	1	16	0
3	2	14	0
4	3	12	0
5	4	10	0
6	5	8	0
7	6	6	0
8	7	4	0
9	8	2	0
10	9	0	0
11	9	18	0
12	10	16	0
13	11	14	0
14	12	12	0
15	13	10	0
16	14	8	0
17	15	6	0
18	16	4	0
19	17	2	0
20	18	0	0
21	18	18	0
22	19	16	0
23	20	14	0
24	21	12	0
25	22	10	0
26	23	8	0
27	24	6	0
[28]	25	4	0
29	26	2	0
30	27	0	0
31	27	18	0
32	28	16	0
33	29	14	0
34	30	12	0
35	31	10	0
36	32	8	0
37	33	6	0
38	34	4	0
39	35	2	0
40	36	0	0
41	36	18	0
42	37	16	0
43	38	14	0
44	39	12	0

N.	l.	s.	d.
45	40	10	0
46	41	8	0
47	42	6	0
48	43	4	0
49	44	2	0
50	45	0	0
51	45	18	0
52	46	16	0
53	47	14	0
54	48	12	0
55	49	10	0
[56]	50	8	0
57	51	6	0
58	52	4	0
59	53	2	0
60	54	0	0
61	54	18	0
62	55	16	0
63	56	14	0
64	57	12	0
65	58	10	0
66	59	8	0
67	60	6	0
68	61	4	0
69	62	2	0
70	63	0	0
71	63	18	0
72	64	16	0
73	65	14	0
74	66	12	0
75	67	10	0
76	68	8	0
77	69	6	0
78	70	4	0
79	71	2	0
80	72	0	0
81	72	18	0
82	73	16	0
83	74	14	0
[84]	75	12	0
85	76	10	0
86	77	8	0
87	78	6	0
88	79	4	0

N	l.	s.	d.
89	80	2	0
90	81	0	0
91	81	18	0
92	82	16	0
93	83	14	0
94	84	12	0
95	85	10	0
96	86	8	0
97	87	6	0
98	88	4	0
99	89	2	0
100	90	0	0
200	180	0	0
300	270	0	0
400	360	0	0
500	450	0	0
600	540	0	0
700	630	0	0
800	720	0	0
900	810	0	0
1000	900	0	0
2000	1800	0	0
3000	2700	0	0
4000	3600	0	0
5000	4500	0	0
6000	5400	0	0
7000	6300	0	0
8000	7200	0	0
9000	8100	0	0
10000	9000	0	0

Great Hundred

112 | 100 16 0

Grefs

144 | 129 12 0

Wey

256 | 230 8 0

Days in a Year

365 | 328 10 0

Feet in a Rod

272 | 244 16 0

N.	l.	s.	d.
1	0	18	6
2	1	17	0
3	2	15	6
4	3	14	0
5	4	12	6
6	5	11	0
7	6	9	6
8	7	8	0
9	8	6 -	6
10	9	5	0
11	10	3	6
12	11	2	0
13	12	0	6
14	12	19	0
15	13	17	6
16	14	16	0
17	15	14	6
18	16	13	0
19	17	11	6
20	18	10	0
21	19	8	6
22	20	7	0
23	21	5	6
24	22	4	0
25	23	2	6
26	24	1	0
27	24	19	6
[28]	25	18	0
29	26	16	6
30	27	15	0
31	28	13	6
32	29	12	0
33	30	10	6
34	31	9	0
35	32	7	6
36	33	6	0
37	34	4	6
38	35	3	0
39	36	1	6
40	37	0	0
41	37	18	6
42	38	17	0
43	39	15	6
44	40	14	0

N.	l.	s.	d.
45	41	12	6
46	42	11	0
47	43	9	6
48	44	8	0
49	45	6	6
50	46	5	0
51	47	3	6
52	48	2	0
53	49	0	6
54	49	19	0
55	50	17	6
[56]	51	16	0
57	52	14	6
58	53	13	0
59	54	11	6
60	55	10	0
61	56	8	6
62	57	7	0
63	58	5	6
64	59	4	0
65	60	2	6
66	61	1	0
67	61	19	6
68	62	18	0
69	63	16	6
70	64	15	0
71	65	13	6
72	66	12	0
73	67	10	6
74	68	9	0
75	69	7	6
76	70	6	0
77	71	4	6
78	72	3	0
79	73	1	6
80	74	0	0
81	74	18	6
82	75	17	0
83	76	15	6
[84]	77	14	0
85	78	12	6
86	79	11	0
87	80	9	6
88	81	8	0

N.	l.	s.	d.
89	82	6	6
90	83	5	0
91	84	3	6
92	85	2	0
93	86	0	6
94	86	19	0
95	87	17	6
96	88	16	0
97	89	14	6
98	90	13	0
99	91	11	6
100	92	10	0
200	185	0	0
300	277	10	0
400	370	0	0
500	462	10	0
600	555	0	0
700	647	10	0
800	740	0	0
900	832	10	0
1000	925	0	0
2000	1850	0	0
3000	2775	0	0
4000	3700	0	0
5000	4625	0	0
6000	5550	0	0
7000	6475	0	0
8000	7400	0	0
9000	8325	0	0
10000	9250	0	0

Great Hundred

112	103	12	0

Grofs

144	133	4	0

Wey

256	236	16	0

Days in a Year

365	337	12	6

Feet in a Rod

272	251	12	0

N.	l.	s.	d.	N.	l.	s.	d.	N.	l.	s.	d.
1	0	19	0	45	42	15	0	89	84	11	0
2	1	18	0	46	43	14	0	90	85	10	0
3	2	17	0	47	44	13	0	91	86	9	0
4	3	16	0	48	45	12	0	92	87	8	0
5	4	15	0	49	46	11	0	93	88	7	0
6	5	14	0	50	47	10	0	94	89	6	0
7	6	13	0	51	48	9	0	95	90	5	0
8	7	12	0	52	49	8	0	96	91	4	0
9	8	11	0	53	50	7	0	97	92	3	0
10	9	10	0	54	51	6	0	98	93	2	0
11	10	9	0	55	52	5	0	99	94	1	0
12	11	8	0	[56]	53	4	0	100	95	0	0
13	12	7	0	57	54	3	0	200	190	0	0
14	13	6	0	58	55	2	0	300	285	0	0
15	14	5	0	59	56	1	0	400	380	0	0
16	15	4	0	60	57	0	0	500	475	0	0
17	16	3	0	61	57	19	0	600	570	0	0
18	17	2	0	62	58	18	0	700	665	0	0
19	18	1	0	63	59	17	0	800	760	0	0
20	19	0	0	64	60	16	0	900	855	0	0
21	19	19	0	65	61	15	0	1000	950	0	0
22	20	18	0	66	62	14	0	2000	1900	0	0
23	21	17	0	67	63	13	0	3000	2850	0	0
24	22	16	0	68	64	12	0	4000	3800	0	0
25	23	15	0	69	65	11	0	5000	4750	0	0
26	24	14	0	70	66	10	0	6000	5700	0	0
27	25	13	0	71	67	9	0	7000	6650	0	0
[28]	26	12	0	72	68	8	0	8000	7600	0	0
29	27	11	0	73	69	7	0	9000	8550	0	0
30	28	10	0	74	70	6	0	10000	9500	0	0
31	29	9	0	75	71	5	0				
32	30	8	0	76	72	4	0				
33	31	7	0	77	73	3	0	Great Hundred			
34	32	6	0	78	74	2	0	112	106	8	0
35	33	5	0	79	75	1	0	Grofs			
36	34	4	0	80	76	0	0	144	136	16	0
37	35	3	0	81	76	19	0	Wey			
38	36	2	0	82	77	18	0	256	243	4	0
39	37	1	0	83	78	17	0	Days in a Year			
40	38	0	0	[84]	79	16	0	365	346	15	0
41	38	19	0	85	80	15	0	Feet in a Rod			
42	39	18	0	86	81	14	0	272	258	8	0
43	40	17	0	87	82	13	0				
44	41	16	0	88	83	12	0				

N.	l.	s.	d.	N.	l.	s.	d.	N.	l.	s.	d.
1	0	19	6	45	43	17	6	89	86	15	6
2	1	19	0	46	44	17	0	90	87	15	0
3	2	18	6	47	45	16	6	91	88	14	6
4	3	18	0	48	46	16	0	92	89	14	0
5	4	17	6	49	47	15	6	93	90	13	6
6	5	17	0	50	48	15	0	94	91	13	0
7	6	16	6	51	49	14	6	95	92	12	6
8	7	16	0	52	50	14	0	96	93	12	0
9	8	15	6	53	51	13	6	97	94	11	6
10	9	15	0	54	52	13	0	98	95	11	0
11	10	14	6	55	53	12	6	99	96	10	6
12	11	14	0	[56]	54	12	0	100	97	10	0
13	12	13	6	57	55	11	6	200	195	0	0
14	13	13	0	58	56	11	0	300	292	10	0
15	14	12	6	59	57	10	6	400	390	0	0
16	15	12	0	60	58	10	0	500	487	10	0
17	16	11	6	61	59	9	6	600	585	0	0
18	17	11	0	62	60	9	0	700	682	10	0
19	18	10	6	63	61	8	6	800	780	0	0
20	19	10	0	64	62	8	0	900	877	10	0
21	20	9	6	65	63	7	6	1000	975	0	0
22	21	9	0	66	64	7	0	2000	1950	0	0
23	22	8	6	67	65	6	6	3000	2925	0	0
24	23	8	0	68	66	6	0	4000	3900	0	0
25	24	7	6	69	67	5	6	5000	4875	0	0
26	25	7	0	70	68	5	0	6000	5850	0	0
27	26	6	6	71	69	4	6	7000	6825	0	0
[28]	27	6	0	72	70	4	0	8000	7800	0	0
29	28	5	6	73	71	3	6	9000	8775	0	0
30	29	5	0	74	72	3	0	10000	9750 .	0	0
31	30	4	6	75	73	2	6				
32	31	4	0	76	74	2	0				
33	32	3	6	77	75	1	6				
34	33	3	0	78	76	1	0				
35	34	2	6	79	77	0	6				
36	35	2	0	80	78	0	0				
37	36	1	6	81	78	19	6				
38	37	1	0	82	79	19	0				
39	38	0	6	83	80	18	6				
40	39	0	0	[84]	81	18	0				
41	39	19	6	85	82	17	6				
42	40	19	0	86	83	17	0				
43	41	18	6	87	84	16	6				
44	42	18	0	88	85	16	0				

Great Hundred
112 | 109 4 0

Grofs
144 | 140 8 0

Wey
256 | 249 12 0

Days in a Year
365 | 355 17 6

Feet in a Rod
272 | 265 4 0

TABLES

OF

INTEREST

At Five per Cent. per Annum.

To find the Number of Days from one Month to another, see the Table at the End.

l.	1 DAY.				2 DAYS.				3 DAYS.				4 DAYS.				5 DAYS.			
	l.	*s.*	*d.*	*q.*	*l.*	*s.*	*d.*	*q.*	*l.*	*s.*	*d.*	*q.*	*l.*	*s.*	*d.*	*q.*	*l.*	*s.*	*d.*	*q.*
1	0	0	0	0	0	0	0	0	0	0	0	0	0	0	0	0	0	0	0	0
2	0	0	0	0	0	0	0	0	0	0	0	0	0	0	0	1	0	0	0	1
3	0	0	0	0	0	0	0	0	0	0	0	1	0	0	0	1	0	0	0	1
4	0	0	0	0	0	0	0	0	0	0	0	1	0	0	0	2	0	0	0	2
5	—	—	—	1	—	—	—	1	—	—	—	1	—	—	—	2	—	—	—	3
6	0	0	0	0	0	0	0	1	0	0	0	2	0	0	0	3	0	0	0	3
7	0	0	0	0	0	0	0	1	0	0	0	2	0	0	0	3	0	0	1	0
8	0	0	0	1	0	0	0	2	0	0	0	3	0	0	1	0	0	0	1	1
9	0	0	0	1	0	0	0	2	0	0	0	3	0	0	1	0	0	0	1	1
10	—	—	1		—	—	—	2	—	—	—	3	—	—	1	—	—	1	—	2
20	0	0	0	2	0	0	1	1	0	0	1	3	0	0	2	2	0	0	3	1
30	0	0	0	3	0	0	1	3	0	0	2	3	0	0	3	3	0	0	4	3
40	0	0	1	1	0	0	2	2	0	0	3	3	0	0	5	1	0	0	6	2
50	—	—	1	2	—	—	3	1	—	—	4	3	—	—	6	2	—	—	8	—
60	0	0	1	3	0	0	3	3	0	0	5	3	0	0	7	3	0	0	9	3
70	0	0	2	1	0	0	4	2	0	0	6	3	0	0	9	0	0	0	11	2
80	0	0	2	2	0	0	5	1	0	0	7	3	0	0	10	2	0	1	1	0
90	0	0	2	3	0	0	5	3	0	0	8	3	0	0	11	3	0	1	2	3
100	—	—	3	1	—	—	6	2	—	—	9	3	—	1	1	—	—	1	4	1
200	0	0	6	2	0	1	1	0	0	1	7	2	0	2	2	1	0	2	8	3
300	0	0	9	3	0	1	7	2	0	2	5	2	0	3	3	1	0	4	1	1
400	0	1	1	0	0	2	2	1	0	3	3	1	0	4	4	2	0	5	5	2
500	0	1	4	1	0	2	8	3	0	4	1	1	0	5	5	3	0	6	10	0

l.	6. DAYS				7 DAYS				8 DAYS				9 DAYS				10 DAYS			
	l.	*s.*	*d.*	*q.*	*l.*	*s.*	*d.*	*q.*	*l.*	*s.*	*d.*	*q.*	*l.*	*s.*	*d.*	*q.*	*l.*	*s.*	*d.*	*q.*
1	0	0	0	0	0	0	0	0	0	0	0	0	0	0	0	1	0	0	0	1
2	0	0	0	1	0	0	0	1	0	0	0	0	0	0	0	2	0	0	0	2
3	0	0	0	2	0	0	0	2	0	0	0	3	0	0	0	2	0	0	0	3
4	0	0	0	3	0	0	0	3	0	0	1	0	0	0	1	0	0	0	1	1
5	—	—	—	3	—	—	1	—	—	—	1—1		—	—	1—1		—	—	1—2	
6	0	0	1	0	0	0	1	1	0	0	1	2	0	0	1	2	0	0	1	3
7	0	0	1	1	0	0	1	2	0	0	1	3	0	0	2	0	0	0	2	1
8	0	0	1	2	0	0	1	3	0	0	2	0	0	0	2	1	0	0	2	2
9	0	0	1	3	0	0	2	0	0	0	2	1	0	0	2	2	0	0	2	3
10	—	1—3			—	2—1			—	2—2			—,	2—3			—	3—1		
20	0	0	3	3	0	0	4	2	0	0	5	1	0	0	5	3	0	0	6	2
30	0	0	5	3	0	0	6	3	0	0	7	2	0	0	8	3	0	0	9	3
40	0	0	7	3	0	0	9	0	0	0	10	2	0	0	11	3	0	1	1	0
50	—	9—3			—11—2				—	1—1	—		—	1—2—3			—	1—4—1		
60	0	0	11	3	0	1	1	2	0	1	3	3	0	1	5	3	0	1	7	2
70	0	1	1	3	0	1	4	0	0	1	6	1	0	1	8	2	0	1	11	0
80	0	1	3	3	0	1	6	1	0	1	9	0	0	1	11	2	0	2	2	1
90	0	1	5	3	0	1	8	2	0	1	11	2	0	2	2	2	0	2	5	3
100	—	1—7—2			—	1 11	—		—,	2—2—1			—	2—5—2			2—8—3			
200	0	3	3	1	0	3	10	0	0	4	4	2	0	4	11	0	0	5	5	3
300	0	4	11	0	0	5	9	0	0	6	6	3	0	7	4	3	0	8	2	2
400	0	6	6	3	0	7	8	0	0	8	9	0	0	9	10	1	0	10	11	2
500	0	8	2	2	0	9	7	0	0	11	10	2	0	12	3	3	0	13	8	1

l.	11 DAYS				12 DAYS				13 DAYS				14 DAYS				15 DAYS			
	l.	*s.*	*d.*	*q.*	*l.*	*s.*	*d.*	*q.*	*l.*	*s.*	*d.*	*q.*	*l.*	*s.*	*d.*	*q.*	*l.*	*s.*	*d.*	*q.*
1	0	0	0	1	0	0	0	1	0	0	0	1	0	0	0	1	0	0	0	1
2	0	0	0	2	0	0	0	3	0	0	0	3	0	0	0	3	0	0	0	3
3	0	0	1	0	0	0	1	0	0	0	1	1	0	0	1	1	0	0	1	1
4	0	0	1	1	0	0	1	2	0	0	1	2	0	0	1	3	0	0	1	3
5	—	—	1—3		—	1—3			—	—	2—0		—	2—1			—	2—1		
6	0	0	2	0	0	0	2	1	0	0	2	2	0	0	2	3	0	0	2	3
7	0	0	2	2	0	0	2	3	0	0	2	3	0	0	3	0	0	0	3	1
8	0	0	2	3	0	0	3	0	0	0	3	1	0	0	3	2	0	0	3	3
9	0	0	3	1	0	0	3	2	0	0	3	3	0	0	4	0	0	0	4	1
10	—	3—2			—	3—3			—	4—1			—	4—2			—	4—3		
20	0	0	7	0	0	0	7	3	0	0	8	2	0	0	9	0	0	0	9	3
30	0	0	10	3	0	0	11	3	0	1	0	1	0	1	1	3	0	1	2	3
40	0	1	2	1	0	1	3	3	0	1	5	0	0	1	6	1	0	1	7	2
50	—	1—6	—		—	1—7—2			—	1—9—1			—	1 11	—		—	2	—	2
60	0	1	9	2	0	1	11	2	0	2	1	2	0	2	3	2	0	2	5	2
70	0	2	1	0	0	2	3	2	0	2	5	3	0	2	8	0	0	2	10	2
80	0	2	4	3	0	2	7	2	0	2	10	0	0	3	0	2	0	3	3	1
90	0	2	8	2	0	2	11	2	0	3	2	1	0	3	5	1	0	3	8	1
100	—	3	—	—	—	3—3—1			—	3—6—2			—	3 10	—		—	4—1—1		
200	0	6	0	1	0	6	6	3	0	7	1	1	0	7	8	0	0	8	2	2
300	0	9	0	1	0	9	10	1	0	10	8	0	0	11	6	0	0	12	3	3
400	0	12	0	2	0	13	1	3	0	14	2	3	0	15	4	0	0	16	5	1
500	0	15	0	3	0	16	5	1	0	17	9	2	0	19	2	0	1	0	6	2

l.	16 DAYS.				17 DAYS.				18 DAYS.				19 DAYS.				20 DAYS.			
	s.	d.	q.		s.	d.	q.		s.	d.	q.		s.	d.	q.		s.	d.	q.
1	0	0	2		0	0	2		0	0	2		0	0	2		0	0	2
2	0	1	0		0	1	0		0	1	0		0	1	0		0	1	1
3	0	1	2		0	1	2		0	1	3		0	1	3		0	1	3
4	0	2	0		0	2	0		0	2	1		0	2	1		0	2	2
5	—	2	2		—	2	3		—	2	3		—	3	—		—	3	1
6	0	3	0		0	3	1		0	3	2		0	3	2		0	3	3
7	0	3	2		0	3	3		0	4	0		0	4	1		0	4	2
8	0	4	0		0	4	1		0	4	2		0	4	3		0	5	1
9	0	4	2		0	5	0		0	5	1		0	5	2		0	5	3
10	—	5	1		—	5	—		—	5	3		—	6	—		—	6	2
20	0	10	2		0	11	0		0	11	3		1	0	1		1	1	0
30	1	3	3		1	4	3		1	5	3		1	6	2		1	7	2
40	1	9	0		1	10	1		1	11	2		2	0	3		2	2	1
50	—	2 2	1		—	2 3	3		—	2 5	2		—	2 7	—		—	2 8	3
60	2	7	2		2	9	2		2	11	2		3	1	1		3	3	1
70	3	0	3		3	3	0		3	5	1		3	7	2		3	10	0
80	3	6	0		3	8	2		3	11	1		4	1	3		4	4	2
90	3	11	1		4	2	1		4	5	1		4	8	0		4	11	0
100	—	4 4	2		—	4 7	3		—	4 11	—		—	5 2	1		—	5 5	3
200	0	8	9		0	9	3		0	9	10		0	10	4		0	10	11
300	0	13	1		0	13	11		0	14	9		0	15	7		0	16	5
400	0	17	6		0	18	7		0	19	8		1	0	9		1	1	11
500	1	1	11		1	3	3		1	4	7		1	6	0		1	7	4

l.	21 DAYS.				22 DAYS.				23 DAYS.				24 DAYS.				25 DAYS.			
	s.	d.	q.		s.	d.	q.		s.	d.	q.		s.	d.	q.		s.	d.	q.
1	0	0	2		0	0	2		0	0	3		0	0	3		0	0	3
2	0	1	0		0	1	1		0	1	2		0	1	2		0	1	2
3	0	2	0		0	2	0		0	2	1		0	2	1		0	2	1
4	0	2	3		0	2	2		0	3	0		0	3	0		0	3	1
5	—	3	1		—	3	2		—	3	3		—	3	3		—	4	—
6	0	4	0		0	4	1		0	4	2		0	4	2		0	4	3
7	0	4	3		0	5	0		0	5	1		0	5	2		0	5	3
8	0	5	2		0	5	3		0	6	0		0	6	1		0	6	2
9	0	6	0		0	6	2		0	6	3		0	7	0		0	7	1
10	—	6	3		—	7	—		—	7	2		—	7	3		—	8	—
20	0	1 1	3		0	1 2	1		0	1 3	0		0	1 3	3		0	1 4	1
30	0	1 8	2		0	1 9	2		0	1 10	2		0	1 11	2		0	2 0	2
40	0	2 3	2		0	2 4	3		0	2 6	0		0	2 7	2		0	2 8	3
50	—	2 10	2		—	3 —	—		—	3 1	3		—	3 3	1		—	3 5	—
60	0	3 5	1		0	3 7	1		0	3 9	1		0	3 11	1		0	4 1	1
70	0	4 0	1		0	4 2	2		0	4 4	3		0	4 7	0		0	4 9	2
80	0	4 7	0		0	4 9	3		0	5 0	1		0	5 3	0		0	5 5	3
90	0	5 2	0		0	5 5	0		0	5 8	0		0	5 11	0		0	6 1	3
100	—	5 9	—		—	6 —	1		—	6 3	2		—	6 6	3		—	6 10	—
200	0	11	6		0	12	0		0	12	7		0	13	1		0	13	8
300	0	17	3		0	18	0		0	18	10		0	19	8		1	0	6
400	1	3	0		1	4	1		1	5	2		1	6	3		1	7	4
500	1	8	9		1	10	1		1	11	6		1	12	10		1	14	2

	26 DAYS				27 DAYS				28 DAYS				29 DAYS				30 DAYS			
l.	*l.*	*s.*	*d.*	*q.*	*l.*	*s.*	*d.*	*q.*	*l.*	*s.*	*d.*	*q.*	*l.*	*s.*	*d.*	*q.*	*l.*	*s.*	*d.*	*q.*
1	0	0	0	3	0	0	0	3	0	0	0	3	0	0	0	3	0	0	0	3
2	0	0	1	2	0	0	1	3	0	0	1	3	0	0	1	3	0	0	1	3
3	0	0	2	2	0	0	2	2	0	0	2	3	0	0	2	3	0	0	2	3
4	0	0	3	1	0	0	3	2	0	0	3	2	0	0	3	3	0	0	3	3
5	—	—	4—1		—	—	4—1		—	—	4—2		—	—	4—3		—	—	4—3	
6	0	0	5	0	0	0	5	1	0	0	5	2	0	0	5	2	0	0	5	3
7	0	0	5	3	0	0	6	0	0	0	6	1	0	0	6	2	0	0	6	3
8	0	0	6	3	0	0	7	0	0	0	7	1	0	0	7	2	0	0	7	3
9	0	0	7	2	0	0	7	3	0	0	8	1	0	0	8	2	0	0	8	3
10	—	—	8—2		—	—	8—3		—	—	9	—	—	—	9—2		—	—	9—3	
20	0	1	5	0	0	1	5	3	0	1	6	1	0	1	7	0	0	1	7	2
30	0	2	1	2	0	2	2	2	0	2	3	2	0	2	4	2	0	2	5	2
40	0	2	10	0	0	2	11	2	0	3	0	2	0	3	2	0	0	3	3	1
50	—	3—6—2			—	3—8—1			—	3 10	—		—	3 11—2			—	4—1—1		
60	0	4	3	1	0	4	5	1	0	4	7	0	0	4	9	0	0	4	11	0
70	0	4	11	3	0	5	2	0	0	5	4	1	0	5	6	2	0	5	9	0
80	0	5	8	1	0	5	11	0	0	6	1	2	0	6	4	1	0	6	6	3
90	0	6	4	3	0	6	7	3	0	6	10	3	0	7	1	3	0	7	4	3
100	—	7—1—1			—	7—4—3			—	7—8	—		—	7 11—1			—	8—2—2		
200	0	14	2	3	0	14	9	2	0	15	4	0	0	15	10	2	0	16	5	1
300	1	1	4	1	1	2	2	1	1	3	0	0	1	3	10	4	1	4	7	3
400	1	8	5	3	1	9	7	0	1	10	8	0	1	11	9	1	1	12	10	2
500	1	15	7	1	1	16	11	3	1	18	4	1	1	19	8	2	2	1	1	0

	31 DAYS				32 DAYS				33 DAYS				34 DAYS				35 DAYS			
l.	*l.*	*s.*	*d.*	*q.*	*l.*	*s.*	*d.*	*q.*	*l.*	*s.*	*d.*	*q.*	*l.*	*s.*	*d.*	*q.*	*l.*	*s.*	*d.*	*q.*
1	0	0	1	0	0	0	1	0	0	0	1	0	0	0	1	0	0	0	1	0
2	0	0	2	0	0	0	2	0	0	0	2	0	0	0	2	0	0	0	2	1
3	0	0	3	0	0	0	3	0	0	0	3	1	0	0	3	1	0	0	3	1
4	0	0	4	0	0	0	4	0	0	0	4	1	0	0	4	1	0	0	4	2
5	—	—	5	—	—	—	5—1		—	—	5—1		—	—	5—2		—	—	5—3	
6	0	0	6	0	0	0	6	1	0	0	6	2	0	0	6	2	0	0	6	3
7	0	0	7	0	0	0	7	1	0	0	7	2	0	0	7	3	0	0	8	0
8	0	0	8	0	0	0	8	1	0	0	8	2	0	0	8	3	0	0	9	0
9	0	0	9	1	0	0	9	1	0	0	9	3	0	0	10	0	0	0	10	1
10	—	—	10	—	—	—	10—2		—	—	10—3		—	—	11	—	—	—	11—2	
20	0	1	8	1	0	1	9	0	0	1	9	2	0	1	10	1	0	1	11	0
30	0	2	6	2	0	2	7	2	0	2	8	2	0	2	9	2	0	2	10	2
40	0	3	4	3	0	3	6	0	0	3	7	1	0	3	8	2	0	3	10	0
50	—	4—2—3			—	4—4—2			—	4—6	—		—	4—7—3			—	4—9—2		
60	0	5	1	0	0	5	3	0	0	5	5	0	0	5	7	0	0	5	9	0
70	0	5	11	1	0	6	1	2	0	6	3	3	0	6	6	0	0	6	8	2
80	0	6	9	2	0	7	0	0	0	7	2	3	0	7	5	1	0	7	8	0
90	0	7	7	2	0	7	10	2	0	8	1	2	0	8	4	2	0	8	7	2
100	—	8—5—3			—	8—9			—	9	—		1	9—3—3			—	9—7	—	
200	0	16	11	3	0	17	6	1	0	18	0		0	18	7	2	0	19	2	0
300	1	5	5	1	1	6	3	2	1	7	1	1	1	7	11	1	1	8	9	0
400	1	13	11	2	1	15	0	3	1	16	1	3	1	17	3	0	1	18	4	1
500	2	2	5	2	2	3	10	0	2	5	2	1	2	6	6	3	2	7	11	1

l.	36 Days				37 Days				38 Days				39 Days				40 Days			
	l.	s.	d.	q.	l.	s.	d.	q.	l.	s.	d.	q.	l.	s.	d.	q.	l.	s.	d.	q.
1	0	0	0	½	0	0	1	0	0	0	1	0	0	0	1		0	0	1	1
2	0	0	2	1	0	0	2	1	0	0	2	1	0	0	2	2	0	0	2	2
3	0	0	3	2	0	0	3	2	0	0	3	2	0	0	3	3	0	0	3	3
4	0	0	4	2	0	0	4	3	0	0	4	3	0	0	5	0	0	0	5	1
5			5	3			6	—			6	—			6	1			6	2
6	0	0	7	0	0	0	7	1	0	0	7	1	0	0	7	2	0	0	7	3
7	0	0	8	1	0	0	8	2	0	0	8	2	0	0	8	3	0	0	9	0
8	0	0	9	1	0	0	9	2	0	0	9	2	0	0	10	1	0	0	10	2
9	0	0	10	2	0	0	10	3	0	0	11	0	0	0	11	2	0	0	11	3
10			11	3		1	—			1	—			1	—			1	1	—
20	0	1	11		0	2	0	·	0	2	0	3	0	2	1	2	0	2	2	2
30	0	2	11	2	0	3	0	1	0	3	1	1	0	3	2	1	0	3	3	1
40	0	3	11	1	0	4	0	2	0	4	1	3	0	4	3	1	0	4	4	2
50		4	11	—		5	—	3		5	2	1		5	4	—		5	5	3
60	0	5	11	0	0	6	0	3	0	6	2	3	0	6	4	3	0	6	6	3
70	0	6	10	3	0	7	1	0	0	7	3	1	0	7	5	2	0	7	8	0
80	0	7	10	2	0	8	1	0	0	8	3	3	0	8	6	2	0	9		●
90	0	8	10	2	0	9	1	1	0	9	4	1	0	9	7	1	0	9	10	1
100		9	10	1		10	1	2		10	4	3		10	8	—		10	11	2
200	0	19	8	2	1	0	3	1	1	0	9	3	1	1	4	1	1	1	11	0
300	1	9	7	0	1	10	4	3	1	11	2	3	1	12	0	2	1	12	10	2
400	1	19	5	1	2	0	6	2	2	1	7	2	2	2	8	3	2	3	10	0
500	2	9	3	3	2	10	8	0	2	12	0	.	2	13	5	0	2	14	9	2

l.	41 Days				42 Days				43 Days				44 Days				45 Days			
	l.	s.	d.	q.	l.	s.	d.	q.	l.	s.	d.	q.	l.	s.	d.	q.	l.	s.	d.	q.
1	0	0	1	1	0	0	1	1	0	0	1	1	0	0	1	1	0	0	1	1
2	0	0	2	2	0	0	2	3	0	0	2	3	0	0	2	3	0	0	2	3
3	0	0	4	0	0	0	4	0	0	0	4	0	0	0	4	1	0	0	4	1
4	0	0	5	1	0	0	5	2	0	0	5	2	0	0	5	2	0	0	5	3
5			6	2			6	3			7	—			7	—			7	1
6	0	0	8	0	0	0	8	1	0	0	8	1	0	0	8	2	0	0	8	3
7	0	0	9	1	0	0	9	2	0	0	9	3	0	0	10	0	0	0	10	1
8	0	0	10	3	0	0	11	0	0	0	11	1	0	0	11	2	0	0	11	3
9	0	1	0	0	0	1	0	1	0	1	0	2	0	1	1	0	0	1	1	1
10		1	—	1		1	—	1		1	2	—		1	2	—		1	2	3
20	0	2	2	2	0	2	3	3	0	2	4	1	0	2	4	3	0	2	5	2
30	0	3	4	1	0	3	5	1	0	3	6	1	0	3	7	1	0	3	8	1
40	0	4	5	3	0	4	7	0	0	4	8	2	0	4	9	3	0	4	11	0
50		5	7	1		5	9	—		5	10	2		6	—	—		6	1	3
60	0	6	8	3	0	6	10	3	0	7	0	3	0	7	2	3	0	7	4	3
70	0	7	10	1	0	8	0	2	0	8	2	3	0	8	5	1	0	8	7	1
80	0	8	11	3	0	9	2	1	0	9	5	0	0	9	7	2	0	9	10	1
90	0	10	1	1	0	10	4	1	0	10	7	0	0	10	10	0	0	11	1	0
100		11	2	3		11	6	—		11	9	1		12	—	—		12	3	3
200	1	2	5	2	1	3	0	0	1	3	6	2	1	4	1	1	1	4	7	3
300	1	13	8	1	1	14	6	0	1	15	4	0	1	16	1	3	1	16	11	3
400	2	4	11	0	2	6	0	1	2	7	1	1	2	8	2	2	2	9	3	3
500	2	16	1	3	2	17	6	1	2	18	10	●	3	0	3	1	3	1	7	2

l.	46 Days.				47 Days.				48 Days.				49 Days.				50 Days.			
	l.	s.	d.	q.	l.	s.	d.	q.	l.	s.	d.	q.	l.	s.	d.	q.	l.	s.	d.	q.
1	0	0	1	2	0	0	1	2	0	0	1	2	0	0	1	2	0	0	1	2
2	0	0	3	0	0	0	3	0	0	0	3	0	0	0	3	0	0	0	3	1
3	0	0	4	2	0	0	4	2	0	0	4	2	0	0	4	3	0	0	4	3
4	0	0	6	0	0	0	6	0	0	0	6	1	0	0	6	1	0	0	6	2
5	—	7	—2		—	7	—2		—	7	—3		—	8	—		—	8	—	
6	0	0	9	0	0	0	9	1	0	0	9	1	0	0	9	2	0	0	9	3
7	0	0	10	2	0	0	10	3	0	0	11	0	0	0	11	1	0	0	11	2
8	0	1	0	0	0	1	0	1	0	1	0	2	0	1	0	3	0	1	1	0
9	0	1	1	2	0	1	1	3	0	1	2	0	0	1	2	1	0	1	2	3
10	—	1	—3	—	—	1	—3	—1	—	1	—3	—3	—	1	—4	—	—	1	—4	—1
20	0	2	6	0	0	2	6	3	0	2	7	2	0	2	8	0	0	2	8	3
30	0	3	9	1	0	3	10	1	0	3	11	1	0	4	0	1	0	4	1	1
40	0	5	0	1	0	5	1	3	0	5	3	0	0	5	4	1	0	5	5	3
50	—	6	—3	—2	—	6	—5	—1	—	6	—6	—3	—	6	—8	—2	—	6	10	—
60	0	7	6	2	0	7	8	2	0	7	10	2	0	8	0	2	0	8	2	2
70	0	8	9	3	0	9	0	0	0	9	2	1	0	9	4	3	0	9	7	0
80	0	10	0	3	0	10	3	0	0	10	6	0	0	10	8	3	0	10	11	2
90	0	11	4	0	0	11	7	0	0	11	10	0	0	12	0	3	0	12	3	3
100	—	12	—7	—	—	12	10	—2	—	13	—1	—3	—	13	—5	—	—	13	—8	—1
200	1	5	2	1	1	5	9	0	1	6	3	2	1	6	10	0	1	7	4	3
300	1	17	9	2	1	18	7	2	1	19	5	1	2	0	3	1	2	1	1	0
400	2	10	4	3	2	11	6	0	2	12	7	0	2	13	8	1	2	14	9	2
500	3	3	0	0	3	4	4	2	3	5	9	0	3	7	1	1	3	8	5	3

l.	60 Days.				100 Days.				200 Days.				300 Days.				365 Days		
	l.	s.	d.	q.	l.	s.	d.	q.	l.	s.	d.	q.	l.	s.	d.	q.	l.	s.	d.
1	0	0	1	3	0	0	3	1	0	0	6	2	0	0	9	3	0	1	0
2	0	0	3	3	0	0	6	2	0	1	1	0	0	1	7	2	0	2	0
3	0	0	5	3	0	0	9	3	0	1	7	2	0	2	5	2	0	3	0
4	0	0	7	3	0	1	1	0	0	2	2	1	0	3	3	1	0	4	0
5	—	9	—3		—	1	—4	—1	—	2	—8	—3	—	4	—1	—1	—	5	—
6	0	0	11	3	0	1	7	2	0	3	3	1	0	4	11	0	0	6	0
7	0	1	1	3	0	1	11	0	0	3	10	0	0	5	9	0	0	7	0
8	0	1	3	3	0	2	2	1	0	4	4	2	0	6	6	3	0	8	0
9	0	1	5	3	0	2	5	2	0	4	11	0	0	7	4	2	0	9	0
10	—	1	—7	—2	—	2	—8	—3	—	5	—5	—3	—	8	—2	—2	—	10	—
20	0	3	3	1	0	5	5	3	0	10	11	2	0	16	5	1	1	0	0
30	0	4	11	0	0	8	2	2	0	16	5	1	1	4	7	3	1	10	0
40	0	6	6	3	0	10	11	2	1	1	11	0	1	12	10	2	2	0	0
50	—	8	—2	—2	—	13	—8	—1	1	—7	—4	—3	2	—1	—1	—	2	10	—
60	0	9	10	1	0	16	5	1	1	12	10	2	2	9	3	3	3	0	0
70	0	11	6	0	0	19	2	0	1	18	4	1	2	17	6	1	3	10	0
80	0	13	1	3	1	1	11	0	2	3	10	0	3	5	9	0	4	0	0
90	0	14	9	2	1	4	7	3	2	9	3	3	3	13	11	2	4	10	0
100	—	16	—5	—1	1	—7	—4	—3	2	14	—9	—2	4	—2	—2	—1	5	—	—
200	1	12	10	2	2	14	9	2	5	9	7	0	8	4	4	2	10	0	0
300	2	9	3	3	4	2	2	1	8	4	4	2	12	6	6	3	15	0	0
400	3	5	9	0	5	9	7	0	10	19	2	0	16	8	9	0	20	0	0
500	4	2	2	1	6	16	11	3	13	13	11	2	20	10	11	2	25	0	0

X   Commission,

Goods or Stock ſold	At ⅛ per Cent.			At ¼ per Cent.			At ⅜ per Cent.			At ½ per Cent.		
Pounds.	l.	s.	d.q.	l.	s.	d.q.	l.	s.	d.q.	l.	s.	d.q.
10000	12	10	0 0	25	0	0 0	37	10	0 0	50	0	0 0
9000	11	5	0 0	22	10	0 0	33	15	0 0	45	0	0 0
8000	10	0	0 0	20	0	0 0	30	0	0 0	40	0	0 0
7000	8	15	0 0	17	10	0 0	26	5	0 0	35	0	0 0
6000	7	10	0 0	15	0	0 0	22	10	0 0	30	0	0 0
5000	6	5	0 0	12	10	0 0	18	15	0 0	25	0	0 0
4000	5	0	0 0	10	0	0 0	15	0	0 0	20	0	0 0
3000	3	15	0 0	7	10	0 0	11	5	0 0	15	0	0 0
2000	2	10	0 0	5	0	0 0	7	10	0 0	10	0	0 0
1000	1	5	0 0	2	10	0 0	3	15	0 0	5	0	0 0
900	1	2	6 0	2	5	0 0	3	7	6 0	4	10	0 0
800	1	0	0 0	2	0	0 0	3	0	0 0	4	0	0 0
700	0	17	6 0	1	15	0 0	2	12	6 0	3	10	0 0
600	0	15	0 0	1	10	0 0	2	5	0 0	3	0	0 0
500	0	12	6 0	1	5	0 0	1	17	6 0	2	10	0 0
400	0	10	0 0	1	0	0 0	1	10	0 0	2	0	0 0
300	0	7	6 0	0	15	0 0	1	2	6 0	1	10	0 0
200	0	5	0 0	0	10	0 0	0	15	0 0	1	0	0 0
100	0	2	6 0	0	5	0 0	0	7	6 0	0	10	0 0
90	0	2	3 0	0	4	6 0	0	6	9 0	0	9	0 0
80	0	2	0 0	0	4	0 0	0	6	0 0	0	8	0 0
70	0	1	9 0	0	3	6 0	0	5	3 0	0	7	0 0
60	0	1	6 0	0	3	0 0	0	4	6 0	0	6	0 0
50	0	1	3 0	0	2	6 0	0	3	9 0	0	5	0 0
40	0	1	0 0	0	2	0 0	0	3	0 0	0	4	0 0
30	0	0	9 0	0	1	6 0	0	2	3 0	0	3	0 0
20	0	0	6 0	0	1	0 0	0	1	6 0	0	2	0 0
10	0	0	3 0	0	0	6 0	0	0	9 0	0	1	0 0
9	0	0	2 2	0	0	5 1	0	0	8 0	0	0	10 3
8	0	0	2 1	0	0	4 3	0	0	7 0	0	0	9 2
7	0	0	2 0	0	0	4 0	0	0	6 1	0	0	8 1
6	0	0	1 3	0	0	3 2	0	0	5 1	0	0	7 0
5	0	0	1 2	0	0	3 0	0	0	4 2	0	0	6 0
4	0	0	1 0	0	0	2 1	0	0	3 2	0	0	4 3
3	0	0	0 3	0	0	1 3	0	0	2 2	0	0	3 2
2	0	0	0 2	0	0	1 0	0	0	1 3	0	0	2 1
1	0	0	0 1	0	0	0 2	0	0	0 3	0	0	1 0
Shill. 10	—			0	0	0 1	0	0	0 2	0	0	0 2
9	—			0	0	0 1	0	0	0 2	0	0	0 2
8	—			0	0	0 1	0	0	0 1	0	0	0 2
7	—			0	0	0 1	0	0	0 1	0	0	0 2
6	—			0	0	0 1	0	0	0 1	0	0	0 1
5	—			0	0	0 1	0	0	0 1	0	0	0 1
4	—			—			0	0	0 1	0	0	0 1
3	—			—			0	0	0 1	0	0	0 1
2												
1												

Goods or Stock fold	At ⅝ per Cent.				At ¾ per Cent.				At ⅞ per Cent.				At 1 per Cent.			
Pounds.	*l.*	*s.*	*d.*	*q.*	*l.*	*s.*	*d.*	*q.*	*l.*	*s.*	*d.*	*q.*	*l.*	*s.*	*d*	*q.*
10000	62	10	0	0	75	0	0	0	87	10	0	0	100	0	0	0
9000	56	5	0	0	67	10	0	0	78	15	0	0	90	0	0	0
8000	50	0	0	0	60	0	0	0	70	0	0	0	80	0	0	0
7000	43	15	0	0	52	10	0	0	61	5	0	0	70	0	0	0
6000	37	10	0	0	45	0	0	0	52	10	0	0	60	0	0	0
5000	31	5	0	0	37	10	0	0	43	15	0	0	50	0	0	0
4000	25	0	0	0	30	0	0	0	35	0	0	0	40	0	0	0
3000	18	15	0	0	22	10	0	0	26	5	0	0	30	0	0	0
2000	12	10	0	0	15	0	0	0	17	10	0	0	20	0	0	0
1000	6	5	0	0	7	10	0	0	8	15	0	0	10	0	0	0
900	5	12	6	0	6	15	0	0	7	17	6	0	9	0	0	0
800	5	0	0	0	6	0	0	0	7	0	0	0	8	0	0	0
700	4	7	6	0	5	5	0	0	6	2	6	0	7	0	0	0
600	3	15	0	0	4	10	0	0	5	5	0	0	6	0	0	0
500	3	2	6	0	3	15	0	0	4	7	6	0	5	0	0	0
400	2	10	0	0	3	0	0	0	3	10	0	0	4	0	0	0
300	1	17	6	0	2	5	0	0	2	12	6	0	3	0	0	0
200	1	5	0	0	1	10	0	0	1	15	0	0	2	0	0	0
100	0	12	6	0	0	15	0	0	0	17	6	0	1	0	0	0
90	0	11	3	0	0	13	6	0	0	15	9	0	0	18	0	0
80	0	10	0	0	0	12	0	0	0	14	0	0	0	16	0	0
70	0	8	9	0	0	10	6	0	0	12	3	0	0	14	0	0
60	0	7	6	0	0	9	0	0	0	10	6	0	0	12	0	0
50	0	6	3	0	0	7	6	0	0	8	9	0	0	10	0	0
40	0	5	0	0	0	6	0	0	0	7	0	0	0	8	0	0
30	0	3	9	0	0	4	6	0	0	5	3	0	0	6	0	0
20	0	2	6	0	0	3	0	0	0	3	6	0	0	4	0	0
10	0	1	3	0	0	1	6	0	0	1	9	0	0	2	0	0
9	0	1	1	2	0	1	4	0	0	1	6	3	0	1	9	2
8	0	1	0	0	0	1	2	1	0	1	4	3	0	1	7	0
7	0	0	10	2	0	1	0	2	0	1	2	2	0	1	4	3
6	0	0	9	0	0	0	10	3	0	1	0	2	0	1	2	1
5	0	0	7	2	0	0	9	0	0	0	10	2	0	1	0	0
4	0	0	6	0	0	0	7	0	0	0	8	1	0	0	9	2
3	0	0	4	2	0	0	5	1	0	0	6	1	0	0	7	0
2	0	0	3	0	0	0	3	2	0	0	4	0	0	0	4	3
1	0	0	1	2	0	0	1	3	0	0	2	0	0	0	2	1
Shill. 10	0	0	0	3	0	0	0	3	0	0	1	0	0	0	1	0
9	0	0	0	3	0	0	0	3	0	0	1	0	0	0	1	0
8	0	0	0	2	0	0	0	3	0	0	0	3	0	0	1	0
7	0	0	0	2	0	0	0	3	0	0	0	3	0	0	0	3
6	0	0	0	2	0	0	0	2	0	0	0	3	0	0	0	3
5	0	0	0	1	0	0	0	1	0	0	0	2	0	0	0	2
4	0	0	0	1	0	0	0	1	0	0	0	2	0	0	0	2
3	0	0	0	1	0	0	0	1	0	0	0	1	0	0	0	1
2	0	0	0	1	0	0	0	1	0	0	0	1	0	0	0	1
1													0	0	0	1

A TABLE

A TABLE,

Shewing the Number of Days, from any Day in one Month, to the same Day in any other.

To	Jan.	Feb.	Mar.	Apr.	May	June	July	Aug.	Sept.	Oct.	Nov.	Dec.
January	365	31	59	90	120	151	181	212	243	273	304	334
February	334	365	28	59	89	120	150	181	212	242	273	303
March	306	337	365	31	61	92	122	153	184	214	245	275
April	275	306	334	365	30	61	91	122	153	183	214	244
May	245	276	304	335	365	31	61	92	123	153	184	214
June	214	245	273	304	334	365	30	61	92	122	153	183
July	184	215	243	274	304	335	365	31	62	92	123	153
Auguſt	153	184	212	243	273	304	334	365	31	61	92	122
September	122	153	181	212	242	273	304	334	365	30	61	91
October	92	123	151	182	212	242	273	304	335	365	31	61
November	61	92	120	151	181	212	242	273	304	334	365	30
December	31	62	90	121	151	182	212	243	274	304	335	365

THE ABOVE TABLE EXPLAINED.

How many days are there from November 1 to July 1? Find November in the firſt column, and July at the head of the table, and in the angle of meeting is 242, the number of days required. But if the given days be different, 'tis only adding or fubtracting the difference: for inſtance, had the above example been from November 1 to July 10, you muſt have added 9 days to the number found in the table; and on the other hand, had it been from November 10 to July 1, you muſt have fubtracted 9 days; and ſo in every other inſtance, when the day of one month is different from that of the other. In leap year, if February 29 is included between the days propoſed, you muſt add one day to the number found as above.

FINIS.